FIFTY YEARS
IN THE
CHURCH OF ROME
(ABRIDGED EDITION)

The life story of Pastor
Chiniquy, who was for
twenty-five years a priest in
the Roman Catholic Church

by
Charles Chiniquy

*Abridged from the 1886 edition originally printed in London
by the Protestant Literature Depository*

Printed in the United States of America

Published by Chick Publications
P.O. Box 3500, Ontario, CA 91761-1019 USA

Call for a free Chick Publications catalog
Tel: (909) 987-0771 • Fax: (909) 941-8128

Outside the U.S. call for a distributor nearest you or see our entire listing
on the Internet at: **www.chick.com/distrib.asp**

HOW TO REACH US:
Complete list of Chick titles on World Wide Web: www.chick.com
E-Mail: postmaster@chick.com

DEDICATION

Faithful ministers of the gospel! I present you this book that you may know that the monster Church of Rome, who shed the blood of your forefathers, is still at work today, at your very door, to enchain your people to the feet of her idols. You will see the inside life of popery from the supreme art with which the mind of the young and timid child is fettered, to the unspeakable degradation of the priest under the iron heel of the bishop.

The superstitions, the ridiculous and humiliating practices, the secret and mental agonies of the monks, the nuns and the priests, will be shown to you. The errors of Romanism are discussed and refuted with clearness and simplicity.

To the bishops, priests, and people of Romanism this book is also dedicated for the sake of your immortal souls. By the mercy of God, you will find, in its pages, how you are cruelly deceived by your vain and lying traditions.

You will see that you are not saved through your ceremonies, masses, confessions, purgatory, indulgences, fastings, etc. Salvation is a gift! Eternal life is a gift! Forgiveness of sin is a gift! Christ is a gift! You have nothing to do but to believe, repent, and love.

CONTENTS

CHAPTER XIII

CHAPTER XLII   Page

CHAPTER LVIII

CHAPTER LIX

CHAPTER LX

CHAPTER LXI

CHAPTER LXII

PASTOR CHARLES CHINIQUY.

FIFTY YEARS

IN THE

CHURCH OF ROME.

CHAPTER I

My father, Charles Chiniquy, born in Quebec, had studied there for the priesthood. But a few days before making his vows he witnessed a great iniquity in the high quarters of the church. He changed his mind, studied law, and married Reine Perrault. In 1803 he settled in Kamoraska, where I was born on the 30th July, 1809.

Four or five years later we emigrated to Murray Bay, which had no school. My mother became my first teacher.

Before leaving the seminary, my father had received from one of the Superiors, as a token of his esteem, a beautiful French and Latin Bible. That Bible was the first book, after the A B C, in which I was taught to read. My mother selected interesting chapters which I read every day till I knew many of them by heart.

How many delicious hours I have spent by my mother's side reading to her from the sublime pages of the divine book. Sometimes she interrupted me to see if I understood what I read. When my answers made her sure that I understood it, she used to kiss me and press me on her bosom as an expression of her joy.

We were some distance from the Church and on rainy days the roads were very bad. On the Sabbath days the neighboring farmers were accustomed to gather at our house in the evening. Then my parents used to put me up on a large table in the midst of the assembly, and I delivered to those good people the most beautiful parts of the Old and New Testaments. When I tired, my mother, who had a fine voice, sang some of the beautiful French hymns with which her memory was filled.

When the weather allowed us to go to church, the farmers would take me into their buggies at the door of the temple, and request of me some chapter of the Gospel. With perfect attention they listened to the voice of the child, whom the Good Master had chosen to give them the bread which comes from heaven. More than once, I remember, when the bell called us to the church, they regretted that they could not hear more.

One beautiful day in 1818 my father was writing in his office, my mother was working with her needle, and I was at the door playing. Suddenly I saw a priest coming near the gate and felt a chill of uneasiness. It was his first visit to our home.

The priest was of short stature with an unpleasant appearance. His shoulders were large and he was very corpulent. His hair was long and uncombed, and his double chin seemed to groan under the weight of his flabby cheeks.

I hastily ran and whispered to my parents, "Mr. Curate is coming." The sound was hardly out of my lips when the Rev. Courtois was at the door. My father shook hands with him in welcome.

The priest was born in France, where he had a narrow escape, having been condemned to death under the bloody administration of Robespierre. He had taken refuge with many other French priests in England, then came to Quebec. Here the bishop had given him charge of the parish at Murray Bay.

His conversation was animated and interesting for the first quarter of an hour. It was a real pleasure to hear him. But all of a sudden, his countenance changed as if a dark cloud had come over his mind, and he stopped talking. My parents had been respectfully reserved as they listened. The silence which followed was exceedingly unpleasant for all the parties, like the heavy hour before a storm.

At length the priest, addressing my father, said, "Mr. Chiniquy, is it true that you and your child read the Bible?"

"Yes, sir," was the quick reply, "my little boy and I read the Bible, and what is still better, he has learned by heart a great number of its most interesting chapters. If you will allow it, Mr. Curate, he will give you some of them."

"I did not come for that purpose," abruptly replied the priest. "But do you not know that you are forbidden by the Council of Trent to read the Bible in French?"

"It makes very little difference to me whether I read the Bible in French, Greek, or Latin," answered my father, "for I understand these languages equally well."

"But are you ignorant of the fact that you cannot allow your child to read the Bible?" replied the priest.

"My wife directs her own child in the reading of the Bible, and I cannot see that we commit any sin."

"Mr. Chiniquy," rejoined the priest, "you have gone through a whole course of theology. You know the duties of a curate. You know it is my painful duty to come here, get the Bible from you and burn it."

My grandfather was a fearless Spanish sailor (our original name was Etchiniquia), and there was too much Spanish blood and pride in my father to hear such a sentence with patience in his own house. Quick as lightening he was on his feet. I pressed myself, trembling, near my mother, who trembled also.

At first I feared lest some unfortunate and violent scene should occur, for my father's anger in that moment was really terrible.

But I feared more lest the priest should lay his hands on my dear Bible, which was just before him on the table. It was mine, given me the last year as a Christmas gift. Fortunately my father had subdued himself but was pacing the room with his lips pale and trembling, and he was muttering between his teeth.

The priest was closely watching my father, his hands convulsively pressing his heavy cane, and his face evidencing a too well-grounded terror.

It was clear that the ambassador of Rome did not find himself infallibly sure of his position. Since his last words he had remained as silent as a tomb.

At last my father suddenly stopped before the priest. "Sir, is that all you have to say here?"

"Yes, sir," said the trembling priest.

"Well, sir," added my father, "you know the door by which you entered my house; please take the same door and go away quickly."

The priest went out immediately. I felt inexpressible joy that my Bible was safe. I ran to my father's neck, kissed and thanked him for his victory. And to pay him, in my childish way, I jumped upon the large table and recited, in my best style, the fight between David and Goliath. Of course, in my mind, my father was David and the priest of Rome was the giant whom the little stone from the brook had stricken down.

Thou knowest, O God, that to that Bible, read on my mother's knees, I owe, by Thy infinite mercy, the knowledge of the truth today; that the Bible had sent, to my young heart and intelligence, rays of light which all the sophisms and dark errors of Rome could never completely extinguish.

CHAPTER II

In June, 1818, my parents sent me to an excellent school at St. Thomas. There one of my mother's sisters was the wife of an industrious miller, Stephen Eschenbach. They had no children, and they received me as their own son.

The beautiful village of St. Thomas had already, at that time, a considerable population. Two fine rivers uniting there before flowing into the St. Lawrence, supplied the water power for several mills and factories.

The school of Mr. Allen Jones was worthy of its wide-spread reputation. As a teacher he deserved and enjoyed the highest respect and confidence of his pupils and their parents. But being a Protestant, the priest was much opposed to him, and every effort was made to induce my relatives to send me to the school under his care.

Dr. Tache was the leading man of St. Thomas. He had no need of the influence of the priests, and he frequently gave vent to his supreme contempt for them. Once a week there was a meeting in his house of the principal citizens of St. Thomas, where the highest questions of history and religion were freely and warmly discussed; but the premises as well as the conclusions were invariably adverse to the priests and religion of Rome, and too often to every form of Christianity.

Though these meetings were not entirely secret societies, they were secret to a great extent. My friend Cazeault was Dr. Tache's nephew and boarded at his house. He was punctual in telling me the days and hours of the meetings, and I used to go with him to an adjoining room, where we could hear everything without being suspected. From what I heard and saw in these meetings I most certainly would have been ruined, had not the Word of God, with which my mother had filled my young mind and heart, been my shield and strength.

There was also in St. Thomas one of the former monks of Canada, known under the name of Capuchin or Recollets, whom the conquest of Canada by Great Britain had forced to leave their monastery. He was a clockmaker and lived honorably by his trade.

Brother Mark, as he was called, was a remarkably well-built man with the most beautiful hands I ever saw. His life was a solitary one, always alone with his sister, who kept his house. Brother Mark spent a couple of hours a day in fishing and I used to meet him often along the banks of the beautiful rivers of St. Thomas. As soon as he found a place where the fish were abundant, he would call me, that I might share in his good luck. I appreciated his attention and repaid him with sincere gratitude.

He often invited me to his solitary but neat little home. His good sister would overwhelm me with attention and love. There was a mixture of timidity and dignity in Brother Mark which I have found in no one else. He was fond of children and gracefully smiled when I showed appreciation for his kindness. But that smile, and any other expression of joy, was very transient. Suddenly it would change, as if some mysterious cloud passed over his heart.

He and the other monks of the monastery had been released by the pope from their vows of poverty and obedience. They could become independent and even rise to a respectable position in the world by their honorable efforts. But the pope had been inflexible about their vows of celibacy. The honest desires of the good monk to live according to the laws of God, with a wife whom heaven might have given him, had become an impossibility — the pope vetoed it.

Brother Mark was endowed with such a loving heart! He must have suffered much trying in vain to annihilate the instincts and affections which God Himself had implanted in him.

One day I was with a few other young friends near the house of Brother Mark. Suddenly we saw something covered with blood thrown from the window and falling a short distance from us. At the same instant we heard loud cries coming from the monk's house: "O my God! Have mercy upon me! Save me! I am lost!"

Brother Mark's sister rushed out and cried to some men who were passing by: "Come to our help! My poor brother is dying! For God's sake make haste, he is losing all his blood!"

I ran to the door, but the lady shut it abruptly saying, "We do not want children here."

I had a sincere affection for the good brother. He had been so kind to me! But I had to go back among the crowd which was fast gathering. The singular mystery in which they were trying to wrap the poor monk, filled me with trouble and anxiety.

But that trouble was soon changed into an unspeakable confusion when I heard the convulsive laughing and shameful jokes of the crowd, after the doctor had told the nature of the wound. I was struck with such horror that I fled away; I did not want to know any more of that tragedy. I had already known too much!

Poor Brother Mark had ceased to be a man — he had become an eunuch!

O cruel and godless church of Rome! How many hearts hast thou broken with that celibacy which Satan alone could invent! This unfortunate victim did not, however, die from his rash action.

He soon recovered his usual health.

Having, meanwhile, ceased to visit him, some months later I was fishing in a very solitary place. I was completely absorbed when I felt on my shoulder the gentle pressure of a hand. It was Brother Mark's.

I thought I would faint through the opposite sentiments of surprise, of pain and joy, which at the same time crossed my mind. With an affectionate and trembling voice he said, "My dear child, why do you not any more come to see me?"

I did not dare to look at him. I liked him for his acts of kindness, but the fatal hour when, in the street before the door, I had suffered so much on his account, was on my heart as a mountain. I could not answer him.

He then asked me again with the tone of a criminal who sues for mercy: "Why is it, my dear child, that you do not come any longer to see me? You know that I love you."

"Dear Brother Mark," I answered, "I will never forget your kindness to me. I will forever be grateful to you! I wish that it would be in my power to continue, as formerly, to go and see you. But I cannot, and you ought to know the reason why I cannot."

I had pronounced these words with the timidity and ignorance of a child. But the action of that unfortunate man had struck me with such a horror that I could not entertain the idea of visiting him any more.

He spent two or three minutes without saying a word, and without moving. But I heard his sobs and his cries of despair and anguish, like I have never heard since.

I could not contain myself any longer; I was suffocating with suppressed emotion. The tears did me good — they did him good also — they told him that I was still his friend.

He took me in his arms and pressed me to his bosom — his tears were mixed with mine. But I could not speak — the emotions of my heart were too much for my age. I sat on a damp, cold stone in order not to faint. He fell on his knees by my side. His eyes, swollen and red with weeping, were raised to heaven, his hand lifted in supplication; he was crying out with an accent which seemed as though it would break my heart — "My God! My God! what a wretched man am I!"

The twenty-five years that I have been a priest of Rome, have revealed to me that the cries of desolation I heard that day were but the echo of the cries of desolation which go out from almost every nunnery, every parsonage and every house where human beings are bound by Romish celibacy.

CHAPTER III

No words can express the consternation, anxiety and shame of a poor Romish child, when he hears, for the first time, his priest saying from the pulpit, in a grave and solemn tone, "This week you will send your children to confession. Make them understand that this action is one of the most important of their lives. It will decide their eternal happiness or misery. Fathers and mothers, if your child conceals his sins and commences lying to the priest, who holds the place of God Himself, this sin is often irreparable. The devil will take possession of his heart. His life will be a series of sacrileges; his death and eternity those of the reprobate."

I was in the church of St. Thomas when these words fell upon me like a thunderbolt.

I had often heard my mother say that upon the first confession depended my eternal happiness or misery. That week was, therefore, to decide about my eternity.

Pale and dismayed, I left the church and returned to the house of my relatives. I took my place at the table, but could not eat. I went to my room to examine my conscience and recall all my sinful actions, words and thoughts. Although I was scarcely over ten years of age, this task was really overwhelming. When I commenced counting my sins, my memory became confused, my head grew dizzy, my heart beat rapidly, and by brow was covered with perspiration. I felt despair. It was impossible for me to remember everything.

The night was almost sleepless. In a frightful dream, I felt as if I had been cast into hell for not having confessed all my sins to the priest. I awoke, fatigued by the phantoms of that terrible night. In similar troubles of mind were passed the three days which preceded my first confession. I had constantly before me the countenance of that stern priest who had never smiled upon me. He was present in my thoughts during the day, and in my dreams during the night, as the minister of an angry God, justly irritated against me on account of my sins. Forgiveness had indeed been promised on condition of a good confession; but my place had also been shown to me in hell, if my confession was not as near perfection as possible. Now, my troubled conscience told me that there were ninety-nine chances against one that my confession would be bad, whether by forgetting some sins, or by lack of contrition of which I had heard so much, but the nature and effects of which were a perfect chaos in my mind.

Thus the cruel Church of Rome took from my young heart the good and merciful Jesus, whose love and compassion had caused me to shed tears of joy when I was beside my mother. The Saviour, whom that church made me to worship, through fear, was not the Saviour who called little children unto Him, to bless them and take them in His arms. Her impious hands were soon to place me at the feet of a pale and severe man — worthy representative of a pitiless God. I trembled at the footstool of an implacable divinity, while the gospel asked only tears of love and joy, shed at the feet of the Friend of sinners.

At length came the day of confession; or rather of judgment and condemnation. I presented myself to the priest.

Mr. Beaubien was a new priest, who did not favor our school any more than his predecessor. He had even taken upon himself to preach a sermon against the heretical school. His want of love for us was fully reciprocated.

Mr. Beaubien also lisped and stammered. One of my favorite amusements was to imitate him, which brought bursts of laughter from us all. I had to examine myself upon the number of times I had mocked him. This circumstance was not calculated to make my confession more agreeable.

At last I knelt at the side of my confessor. My whole frame trembled. I repeated the prayer preparatory to confession, scarcely knowing what I said.

By the instructions given us before confession, we believed that the priest was almost the personification of Jesus Christ. Consequently I believed my greatest sin had been that of mocking the priest. Having been told it was best to confess the greatest sin first, I commenced thus: "Father, I accuse myself of having mocked a priest!"

Scarcely had I uttered these words, when this pretended representative of the humble Saviour asked abruptly, "What priest did you mock, my boy?" I would rather have cut out my tongue than tell him to his face who it was. I was therefore silent for awhile, my silence made him very nervous and almost angry. With a haughty tone of voice he said, "What priest did you take the liberty of thus mocking?"

I saw that I had to answer. Happily his haughtiness had made me firmer and bolder. I said "Sir, you are the priest whom I mocked."

"But how many times did you take upon you to mock me, my boy?"

"I tried to find out," I answered, "but I never could."

"You must tell me how many times; for to mock one's own priest is a great sin."

"It is impossible for me to give you the number of times," I answered.

"Well, my child, I will help your memory by asking you questions. Tell me the truth. Do you think you have mocked me ten times?"

"A great many times more, sir."

"Fifty times?"

"Many more still."

"A hundred times?"

"Say five hundred times, and perhaps more," I answered.

"Why, my boy, do you spend all your time in mocking me?"

"Not all, but unfortunately I do it very often."

"Well may you say *unfortunately,* for to mock your priest, who holds the place of our Lord Jesus Christ, is a great sin for you. But tell me, my little boy, what reason have you for mocking me thus?"

In my examinations of conscience I had not foreseen that I should be obliged to give the reasons for mocking the priest and I was really thunderstruck by his questions. I dared not answer, dumb with the shame that overpowered me. But with a harassing perseverance the priest insisted upon my telling why I had mocked him, telling me that I should be damned if I did not tell the whole truth. So I said, "I mocked you for several things."

"What made you first mock me?" continued the priest.

"I laughed at you because you lisped. Among the pupils of our school, it often happens that we imitate your preaching to excite laughter."

"Have you often done that?"

"Almost every day, especially since you preached against us."

"For what other reasons did you laugh at me, my little boy?"

For a long time I was silent. Every time I opened my mouth to speak, courage failed me. He continued to urge me. I said at last, "It is rumored in town that you love girls; that you visit the Misses Richards every evening, and this often makes us laugh."

The poor priest was evidently overwhelmed by my answer, and ceased questioning me on this subject. Changing the conversation, he said, "What are your other sins?"

I began to confess them in the order in which they came to my memory. But the feeling of shame which overpowered me in repeating all my sins to this man was a thousand times greater than that of having offended God. It left no room for any religious feeling at all.

When I had confessed all the sins I could remember, the priest began to ask me the strangest questions on matters about which my pen must be silent. I replied, "Father, I do not understand what you ask me."

"I question you on the sixth commandment (seventh in the

Bible). Confess all. You will go to hell, if through your fault you omit anything."

Thereupon he dragged my thoughts to regions which, thank God, had hitherto been unknown to me.

I answered him, "I do not understand you," or "I have never done these things."

Then, skillfully shifting to some secondary matter, he would soon cunningly come back to his favorite subject, sins of licentiousness.

His questions were so unclean that I blushed, sick with disgust and shame. More than once I had been, to my regret, in the company of bad boys, but not one of them had offended my moral nature so much as this priest. In vain did I tell him that I was not guilty of such things, that I did not even understand what he asked me; he would not let me off. Like a vulture, that cruel priest seemed determined to defile and ruin my heart.

At last he asked me a question in a form of expression so bad that a feeling of horror made me shudder. I was so filled with indignation that I told him, "Sir, I am very wicked; I have seen, heard and done many things which I regret, but I never was guilty of what you mention to me. My ears have never heard anything so wicked as what they have heard from your lips. Please do not ask me any more of those questions; do not teach me any more evil than I already know."

The remainder of my confession was short. The firmness of my voice had evidently frightened the priest, and made him blush. He stopped short and began to give me some good advice, which might have been useful if the deep wounds of his questions had not so absorbed my thoughts.

He gave me a short penance and dismissed me.

I left the confessional irritated and confused. I went into a retired corner of the church to do my penance; that is, to recite the prayers he had indicated to me. I remained a long time in church. I needed calm after the terrible trial. But vainly sought I for rest. The shameful questions which had been asked me, the new world of iniquity into which I had been introduced, the impure phantoms by which my childish heart had been defiled, confused and troubled my mind so strangely that I began to weep bitterly.

Why those tears? Why that desolation? Wept I over my sins? Alas! My sins did not call forth these tears. I was thinking of my mother, who had taken such good care of me, and who had so well succeeded in keeping away from my thoughts those impure forms of sin, the thoughts of which had just now defiled my heart. I said to myself, "Ah! if my mother had heard those questions; if she

could see the evil thoughts which overwhelm me at this moment
— if she knew to what school she sent me when she advised me in
her last letter to go to confession, how her tears would mingle with
mine!" It seemed to me that my mother would love me no more —
that she would see the pollution with which that priest had pro-
faned my soul.

I felt so disappointed at being removed farther from the Saviour
by that confessional which had promised to bring me nearer to
Him. I left the church only when forced by nightfall, and came to
my uncle's house with that feeling of having done a bad action and
the fear of discovery.

This uncle, like most of the principal citizens of St. Thomas,
was Roman Catholic by name, yet did not believe a word of its
doctrines. He laughed at the priests, their masses, their purgatory,
and especially their confession. He did not conceal that, when
young, he had been scandalized by the words and actions of a
priest in the confessional. He spoke to me jestingly, increasing my
trouble and grief. "Now," he said,"you will be a good boy. But if you
have heard as many new things as I did the first time I went to
confess, you are a very learned boy." And he burst into laughter.

I blushed and remained silent. My aunt, who was a devoted
Roman Catholic, said to me, "Your heart is relieved, is it not, since
you confessed all your sins?" I gave her an evasive answer, but I
could not conceal my sadness.

I thought I was the only one whom the priest had asked those
polluting questions. But great was my surprise, when I learned
that my fellow pupils had fared no better. But instead of being
grieved, they laughed at it.

"Did the priest ask you such and such questions?" they would
demand, laughing boisterously.

I refused to reply, and said, "Are you not ashamed to speak of
these things?"

"Ah! ah! how very scrupulous you are," continued they. "If it is
not a sin for the priest to speak to us on these matters, how can it
be a sin for us?"

I stopped, confounded, not knowing what to say.

I soon perceived that even the young schoolgirls had been polluted and scandalized by the questions of the priest. Although
keeping at a distance, to prevent us from hearing, I could understand that they had been asked about the same questions. Some
were indignant, while others laughed heartily.

I do not mean to convey the idea that this priest was more to
blame than others, or that he did more than fulfill the duties of his
ministry. Such was my opinion at the time and I detested that

man with all my heart until I knew better. This priest had only done his duty. He was only obeying the pope 'and his theologians.

The misfortune of Mr. Beaubien, like all the priests of Rome, was that of having bound himself by terrible oaths not to think for himself, or to use the light of his own reason.

Had Mr. Beaubien been left to himself, he was naturally too much of a gentleman to ask such questions. But no doubt he had read Liguori, Dens, Debreyne, authors approved by the pope, and he was obliged to take darkness for light, and vice for virtue.

CHAPTER IV

Shortly after the trial of auricular confession, my young friend, Louis Cazeault, accosted me and said, "Do you know what happened last night?"

"No," I answered.

"You know that our priest spends almost all his evenings at Mr. Richards' house. Everybody thinks that he goes there for the sake of the two daughters. Well, in order to cure him, my uncle, Dr. Tache, and six others, masked and whipped him without mercy as he was coming back at eleven o'clock at night. It is already known by everyone in the village, and they split their sides laughing."

My first feeling was one of joy. His questions had so wounded me that I could not forgive him. However, I concealed my pleasure and answered.

"You are telling me a wicked story; I can't believe a word of it."

"Well," said young Cazeault, "come at eight o'clock this evening to my uncle's. A secret meeting is to take place then. No doubt they will speak of the pill given to the priest last night. We shall place ourselves as usual and hear everything. You may be sure that it will be interesting."

"I will go," I answered, "but I do not believe a word of that story."

At school, most of the pupils were grouped in lively conversation and convulsive laughter. Something uncommon had taken place in the village.

I approached several of these groups, and all received me with the question:

"Do you know that the priest was whipped last night as he was coming from the Misses Richards'?"

"That is a story invented for fun," said I. "If anybody had whipped the priest he would not surely boast of it."

"But we heard his screams," answered many voices.

"But you were surely mistaken about the voice," said I.

"But," said several, "we ran to his help and we recognized the priest's voice. He is the only one who lisps in the village."

"And we saw him with our own eyes," said several.

The school bell put an end to this conversation. As soon as school was out I returned home and found my uncle and aunt engaged in a very warm debate. My uncle wished to conceal the fact that he was among those who had whipped the priest. But he gave the details so precisely, he was so merry over the adventure, that it was easy to see that he had a hand in the plot. My aunt was indignant.

That bitter debate annoyed me so that I withdrew to my study. I changed my resolution many times about going to the secret meeting in the evening. I had refused to go to the two last meetings, and a silent voice told me I had done well. Then I was tormented by the desire to know precisely what had taken place.

A quarter hour before the meeting my friend came and said, "Make haste, the members of the association are coming."

All my good resolutions vanished and a few minutes later I was placed in an angle of that little room where I learned so many strange and scandalous things about the lives of the priests of Canada.

Dr. Tache presided. He was naturally eloquent and he spoke with the deepest conviction. His short and cutting sentences penetrated even the secret folds of the soul. He spoke in substance as follows:

"Gentlemen, I am happy to see you here more numerously than ever. The grave events of last night have, no doubt, decided many of you to attend debates which some began to forsake, but the importance of which, it seems, increases day by day.

"The question debated in our last meeting — 'The Priest' — is one of life and death, not only for our young and beautiful Canada, but morally for our families and for every one of us.

"There is, I know, only one opinion among us on the subject of priests. I am glad that this opinion is held by all educated men in Canada and France — nay, of the whole world. The reign of the priest is the reign of ignorance, corruption, and the most barefaced immorality, under the mask of the most refined hypocrisy. The reign of the priest is the death of our schools; it is the degradation of our wives, the prostitution of our daughters; it is the reign of tyranny — the loss of liberty.

"We have only one good school in all our county and it is a great honor to our village. Now see how energetically all the priests who come here work for the closing of that school. They use every means to destroy that focus of light which we support by so many sacrifices.

"With the priest of Rome our children do not belong to us: he is their master. Let me explain. The priest honors us with the belief that the bodies, the flesh and bones of our children, are ours, and that our duty in consequence is to clothe and feed them. But the nobler and more sacred part, the intellect, the heart, the soul, the priest claims as his property. The priest has the audacity to tell us that to him alone it belongs to enlighten those intelligences, to form those hearts, to fashion those souls as it may best suit him. He has the impudence to tell us that we are too silly or perverse to know our duties in this respect. We have not the right of choosing our school teachers. We have not the right to give to those souls who hunger and thirst after truth a single crumb of that food prepared with so much wisdom and success by enlightened men of all ages.

"By the confessional the priests poison the springs of life in our children. They initiate them into such mysteries of iniquity as would terrify old galley slaves. Before I was fifteen years old I had learned more real blackguardism from the mouth of my confessor than I have learned since in my studies and in my life as a physician for twenty years.

"A few days ago I questioned my little nephew, Louis Cazeault, what he had learned in his confession. He repeated things which I would be ashamed to utter in your presence, and which you, fathers of families, could not listen to without blushing. Not only of little boys are those questions asked, but also of our dear little girls. Are we not the most degraded of men if we do not break the iron yoke under which the priest keeps our dear country, and by means of which he keeps us, with our wives and children, at his feet like vile slaves.

"Shall I forget its effects upon our wives and upon ourselves? Need I tell you that, for most women, the confessional is a rendezvous of coquetry and of love? Do you not feel as I do, that by means of the confessional the priest is more the master of the hearts of our wives than ourselves? Do not our wives go invariably to the feet of the priest, opening to him the most sacred and intimate secrets of our lives as husbands and fathers? The husband is no more his wife's guide through the dark and difficult paths of life: it is the priest! We are no more their friends and natural advisers. Their anxieties and cares they do not confide to us. They do not expect from us the remedies for the miseries of this life. Towards the priest they turn their thoughts and desires. He has their entire and exclusive confidence. In a word, it is the priest who is the real husband of our wives! It is he who possesses their respect and their hearts to a degree which no one of us need ever aspire!

"Were the priest an angel, were he not flesh and bones just as we are, then might we be indifferent to what might take place between him and our wives, whom he has at his feet, in his hands — even more, in his heart. But what does my experience tell me, not only as a physician, but also as a citizen of St. Thomas? What does yours tell you?

"Our experience tells us that the priest, instead of being stronger, is weaker than we generally are with respect to women. His sham vows of perfect chastity, far from rendering him more invulnerable to the arrows of Cupid, make him more easily the victim.

"In fact, of the last four priests who came to St. Thomas, have not three seduced many of the wives and daughters of our most respectable families? Is not the whole parish filled with indignation at the long nightly visits made by our present priest to two girls whose dissolute morals are a secret to nobody?

"At our last meeting many thought it would be well to speak to the bishop about the scandal caused by those nightly visits. But the majority judged that the bishop would either pay no attention to our complaint, or replace him with one no better. That majority became unanimous that we take justice into our own hands. The priest is our servant. We pay him a large tithe. We have therefore claims upon him. He has abused us by his public neglect of the most elementary laws of morality. His nightly visits give our youth an example of perversity the effects of which no one can estimate.

"It was unanimously decided that he should be whipped. Without my telling you by whom it was done, you may be assured that Mr. Beaubien's flagellation of last night will never be forgotten by him!

"Heaven grant that this brotherly correction will teach all the priests of Canada that their golden reign is over, that the eyes of the people are opened, and that their domination is drawing to an end!"

This discourse was listened to with deep silence, and Dr. Tache saw by the applause that his speech had been the expression of everyone.

Next followed a gentleman named Dubord, who in substance spoke as follows:

"Mr. President, — I was not among those who gave the priest this expression of public feeling with the energetic tongue of the whip. I wish I had been, however; I would heartily have cooperated in giving that lesson to the priests of Canada. Let me give my reason.

"My daughter who is twelve years old, went to confession with the others a few weeks ago. It was against my will. I know by my own experience that, of all actions, confession is the most degrading in a person's life.

"Why are Roman Catholic nations inferior to Protestant ones? The oftener the individuals in those nations go to confession, the more rapidly they sink in intelligence and morality. A terrible example of this I had in my own house.

"As I said, I was against my daughter going to confession; but her poor mother, who is under the control of the priest, earnestly wanted her to go. Not to have a disagreeable scene, I had to yield to the tears of my wife.

"On the day following they believed I was absent; but I was in my office, with the door sufficiently open to hear what was said. My wife and daughter had the following conversation:

"'What makes you so thoughtful and sad, my dear Lucy, since you went to confession? It seems to me you should feel happier since confessing your sins.'

"Lucy made no answer.

"After a silence of two or three minutes her mother said, 'Why do you weep, dear child? Are you ill?'

"Still no answer from the child.

"Of course I was all attention. I had my suspicions about the dreadful ordeal which had taken place. My heart throbbed with uneasiness and anger.

"After a short time my wife spoke with sufficient firmness to force her to answer. In a trembling voice and half suppressed with sobs my dear little daughter answered, "'Ah! mama, if you knew what the priest asked me, and what he said to me in the confessional, you would be as sad as I am.'

"'But what did he say to you? He is a holy man. You surely did not understand him if you think he said anything to pain you.'

"'Dear mother,' as she threw herself into her mother's arms, 'do not ask me to confess what the priest said! He told me things so shameful that I cannot repeat them. But that which pains me most is the impossibility of banishing from my thoughts the hateful things which he has taught me. His impure words are like the leeches put upon the chest of my friend Louise — they could not be removed without tearing the flesh. What must have been his opinion of me to ask such questions!'

"My child said no more, and began to sob again.

"After a short silence my wife rejoined, 'I'll go to the priest. I'll tell him to beware how he speaks in the confessional. I have noticed myself that he goes too far with his questions. I, however, thought that he was more prudent with children. I ask of you, however, never to speak of this to anybody, especially your poor father, for he has little enough religion already, and this would leave him without any at all.'

"I could contain myself no longer. I abruptly entered the parlor. My daughter threw herself, weeping, into my arms. My wife screamed with terror, and almost fell into a swoon.

"I said to my child, 'If you love me, put your hand on my heart and promise me that you'll never go to confession again. Fear God, my child; walk in His presence, for His eye seeth you everywhere. Day and night He is ready to forgive us. Never place yourself again at the feet of a priest to be defiled and degraded by him!'

"This my daughter promised me.

"When my wife had recovered from her surprise I said to her, 'Madam, for a long time the priest has been everything, and your husband nothing to you. There is a hidden and terrible power that governs your thoughts, affections and deeds — it is the power of the priest. This you have often denied; but providence has decided today that this power should be forever broken for you and me. I want to be the ruler in my own house; and from this moment the power of the priest over you must cease, unless you prefer to leave my house forever. The priest has reigned here too long! But now that I know he has stained and defiled the soul of my daughter, his empire must fall! If you again go and take your heart and secrets to the feet of the priest, be so kind as not to come back to the same house with me.'"

Three other discourses followed, all pregnant with details and facts to prove that the confessional was the principal cause of the deplorable demoralization of St. Thomas.

CHAPTER V

The following day I wrote to my mother: "For God's sake, come for me; I can stay here no longer. If you knew what my eyes have seen and my ears have heard, you would not delay."

Indeed, had it not been for crossing the St. Lawrence, I would have started for Murray Bay the day after the secret meeting. I remembered the happy and peaceful days spent with my mother in reading the beautiful chapters of the Bible, so well chosen by her to instruct and interest me! What a difference there was between our conversations after these readings, and the conversations I heard at St. Thomas!

Happily my parents' desire to see me again was as great as mine. In a few weeks, my mother came for me. She pressed me to her heart, and brought me back to the arms of my father.

I arrived home July 17, 1821 and spent the afternoon and evening by my father's side. With pleasure he examined me in grammar, algebra, and even in geometry. More than once I noticed tears of joy in his eyes when he saw that my answers were correct. "What an admirable teacher this Mr. Jones must be," he would say, "to have advanced a child so much in the short space of fourteen months!"

How sweet but short, were those hours! We had family worship. I read from Luke the return of the prodigal son. My mother then sang a hymn of joy and gratitude, and I went to bed with my heart full of happiness to take the sweetest sleep of my life. But, O God! what an awful awakening Thou hadst prepared for me!

About four o'clock in the morning my mother's heartrending screams fell upon my ear.

"What is the matter, dear mother?"

"Oh, my dear child, you have no more a father! He is dead!"

In saying these words she lost consciousness and fell on the floor!

While a friend who had passed the night with us gave her proper care, I hastened to my father's bed. I pressed him to my heart, I kissed him, I covered him with my tears, I moved his head, I pressed his hands, I tried to lift him up on his pillow. I could not believe that he was dead! It seemed to me that even if dead he would come back to life, that God could not thus take my father away from me at the very moment when I had come back to him after so long an absence! I knelt to pray. But my tears and cries were useless. He was dead! He was already cold as ice!

Two days later he was buried. My mother was so overwhelmed with grief that she could not follow the funeral procession. I remained with her as her only earthly support. Poor mother! How many tears she shed in those days of supreme grief! Though I was young, I could understand the greatness of our loss, and I mingled my tears with hers.

How painful the sleepless nights of a woman when God takes suddenly her husband away in the prime of his life, and leaves her alone, plunged in misery, with three small children, two even too young to know their loss! Every object in the house and every step she takes reminds her of her loss. How bitter are the tears when her youngest child throws himself into her arms and says:

"Mamma, where is papa? Why does he not come back? I am lonely!"

I heard her sobs during the long hours of the days and nights. Many times on her knees she implored God to be merciful to her and her three unhappy orphans. I could do nothing then to comfort her but love her, pray and weep with her!

Only a few days after the burial, I saw Mr. Courtois coming to our house. He was the parish priest who had tried to take away our Bible. He was reputed to be rich so my first thought was that he had come to comfort and to help us. I could see that my mother had the same hopes. She welcomed him as an angel from heaven.

From his very first words, however, I could see we were wrong. He tried to be sympathetic and spoke of the confidence we should have in God in times of trial, but his words were cold and dry.

Turning to me, he said: "Do you continue to read the Bible, my little boy?"

"Yes, sir," answered I, my voice trembling with fear that he would try again to take away that treasure now that I had no longer a father to defend it.

Then he said: "Madam, I told you that it was not right for you or your child to read that book."

My mother cast down her eyes, and answered only by the tears which ran down her cheeks.

After a long silence, the priest continued: "Madam, there is something due for the prayers which have been sung, and the services which you requested to be offered for the repose of your husband's soul. I will be very much obliged to you if you pay me that little debt."

"Mr. Courtois," answered my mother, "my husband left me nothing but debts. I have only my own hands to procure a living. For these orphans' sake, if not for mine, do not take the little that is left."

"But, madam, your husband died suddenly without any preparation; he is therefore in the flames of purgatory. To deliver him you must unite your personal sacrifices to the prayers and masses of the Church."

"As I said, my husband has left me absolutely without means, and it is impossible for me to give you any money," replied my mother.

"But, madam, the masses offered for the rest of your husband's soul must be paid for," answered the priest.

My mother covered her face with her handkerchief and wept.

My feelings were not those of grief, but of anger and unspeakable horror. My eyes were fixed on the face of that man who tortured my mother's heart. My hands were clenched, as if ready to strike. I felt inclined to say to him: "Are you not ashamed, you who are so rich, to come and take away the last piece of bread from our mouths?" But my physical and moral strength were not sufficient and I was filled with regret and disappointment.

After a long silence, my mother raised her eyes, reddened with tears, and said:

"Sir, you see that cow in the meadow? Her milk and butter form the principal part of my children's food. I hope you will not take her away from us. If, however, such a sacrifice must be made to deliver my poor husband's soul from purgatory, take her as payment of the masses to be offered to extinguish those devouring flames."

The priest instantly arose, saying, "Very well, madam," and went out.

Our eyes anxiously followed him as he directed his steps towards the meadow, and drove the cow in the direction of his home.

I screamed with despair: "Oh, mother! he is taking our cow! What will become of us?"

My mother also cried out with grief as she saw the priest taking away the only means which heaven had left her to feed her children.

Throwing myself into her arms, I asked her: "Why have you given away our cow? What will become of us? We shall surely die of hunger!"

"Dear child," she answered. "I did not think the priest would be so cruel as to take away the last resource which God had left us. Ah! if I had believed him to be so unmerciful I would never have spoken to him as I did. As you say, my dear child, what will become of us? But have you not often read to me in your Bible that God is the Father of the widow and the orphan? He will listen to our prayers and see our tears. Let us kneel and ask Him to be merciful to us."

We both knelt down. She took my right hand in her left, and, lifting the other hand towards heaven, she offered a prayer for her poor children such as I have never since heard. When her words were choked by sobs she would speak with her burning eyes raised to heaven, and with her hand uplifted. I also prayed to God with her, and repeated her words, which were broken by my sobs.

When her prayer was ended she remained for a long time pale and trembling. Then drawing me to her bosom, she said: "Dear child, if ever you become a priest, *I ask of you never to be so hard-hearted towards poor widows as are the priests of today.*" When she said these words, I felt her burning tears falling upon my cheek.

The memory of these tears has never left me. I felt them constantly during the twenty-five years I spent in preaching the inconceivable superstitions of Rome.

I was not better than many of the other priests. I believed the impious fables of purgatory. I accepted the money which the rich gave me for the masses I said to extinguish the flames. But the remembrance of my mother's words and tears kept me from being so cruel and unmerciful towards the poor widows.

The Lord, I believe, had put into my mother's mouth those words, so simple but so full of eloquence and beauty, as one of His great mercies towards me. Those tears the hand of Rome has never been able to wipe off.

How long, O Lord, shall that insolent enemy of the gospel, the Church of Rome, fatten herself upon the tears of the widow and the orphan with that cruel, pagan invention, purgatory? Oh, remove the veil from the eyes of the priests and people of Rome, as Thou hast removed it from mine! Make them to understand that their hopes of purification must not rest on these fires, but only on the blood of the Lamb shed on Calvary to save the world.

CHAPTER VI

God had heard the poor widow's prayer. A few days after the priest had taken our cow she received a letter from each of her two sisters, Genevieve and Catherine.

The former, married to Etienne Eschenbach of St. Thomas, told her to sell all she had and come, with her children, to live with her.

"We have no family," she said, "and God has given us abundance. We shall be happy to share it with you."

The latter, married in Kamouraska to the Hon. Amable Dionne wrote, "We have learned the sad news of your husband's death. We have lately lost our only son. We wish to fill the emptiness with Charles, your eldest. We shall bring him up as our own, and soon he will be your support. Meanwhile, sell by auction all you have, and go to St. Thomas with your two younger."

In a few days all our furniture was sold. Unfortunately, though I had carefully concealed my cherished Bible, it disappeared. I never discovered what became of it. Had mother, frightened by the priest, relinquished that treasure? Or had some of our relatives, believing it their duty, destroyed it? I do not know. I deeply felt the loss.

On the following day, with bitter tears and sobs, I bade farewell to my poor mother and young brothers. They went to St. Thomas and I to Kamouraska.

My uncle and aunt welcomed me with sincere affection. When they learned that I wished to become a priest, it was arranged for me to study Latin under Rev. Mr. Morin, vicar of Kamouraska.

He was a learned man, about forty or fifty years old, and had been a priest in Montreal. But, as with the majority of priests, his vow of celibacy was not sufficient guarantee against the charms of one of his beautiful parishioners. The scandal had cost him his position, and the bishop sent him to Kamouraska where he was not known. He was good to me, and I responded with sincere affection.

One day early in 1822, he called me aside and said, "Mr. Varin (the parish priest) is in the habit of giving a great festival on his birthday. Now, the principal citizens of the village wish to present him with a bouquet. I am appointed to write an address, and to choose someone to deliver it before the priest. You are the one I have chosen . What do you think?"

"But I am very young," I replied.

"Your youth will only give more interest," said the priest.

"Well, I have no objection, provided the piece is short and that I have time to learn it."

All was prepared and the time arrived. The best society of Kamouraska, about fifteen gentlemen and as many ladies, were assembled in the beautiful parlors of the parsonage. Mr. Varin was there when Squire Paschall Tache and his lady entered with me. I was placed in the midst of the guests. My head was crowned with flowers, for I was to represent the angel of the parish chosen to give to their pastor the expression of public admiration and gratitude. When the address was finished, I presented to the priest the beautiful bouquet.

Mr. Varin was small but well built. Intelligence and goodness beamed from his expressive black eyes and gracious smile. He was a charming host and passionately fond of these little fetes.

He was moved to tears upon hearing the address and expressed his joy and gratitude at being so highly appreciated by his parishioners.

After the happy pastor had expressed his thanks, the ladies sang two or three beautiful songs. The door of the dining room was then opened. Before us stood a long table laden with the most delicious meats and wines that Canada could offer.

I had never before been present at a priest's dinner. Besides Mr. Varin and his vicar, three other priests were artistically placed among the most beautiful ladies of the company. The ladies, after honoring us with their presence for an hour or so retired to the drawing room.

Mr. Varin rose and said, "Gentlemen, let us drink to the health of these amiable ladies, whose presence has thrown so many charms over the first part of our little fete."

Following Mr. Varin, each guest filled and emptied his wine glass. Squire Tache then proposed, "The health of the most venerable and beloved priest of Canada, The Rev. Mr. Varin." Again the glasses were filled and emptied, except for mine, for I was seated next to my uncle Dionne, who with a stern look said, "If you drink another I will send you from the table."

It would have been difficult to count the healths which were drank, for after each health a song or a story was called for, several of which produced applause, shouts of joy, and convulsive laughter.

When my turn to propose a health came, I wished to be excused, but they refused to exempt me. Arising from my chair, I turned to Mr. Varin and said, "Let us drink to the health of our Holy Father, the Pope."

Nobody had yet thought of the pope, so the mention of his name under such circumstances by a child, appeared so droll to the priests and their merry guests that they burst into laughter, stamped their feet, and shouted "Bravo! bravo! To the health of the pope!"

So many healths could not be drunk without having their natural effect — intoxication. The first to succumb was Father Noel. I had noticed that instead of using his wine glass he frequently drank from a large tumbler. The symptoms of his intoxication began to show when he endeavored to fill his glass, but his hand shook so that the bottle fell to the floor and broke. Wishing to keep up the merriment he began to sing a Bacchic song, but could not finish; his head dropped on to the table. While attempting to rise, he fell heavily upon his chair.

The other priests and their guests just looked at him, laughing loudly. In a desperate effort, he rose, but after taking two or three steps, fell headlong on the floor. His two neighbors came to his aid, but they were not much better. The trio rolled under the table. At length another, less affected by the wine, took him by the feet and dragged him into an adjoining room, where they left him.

This first scene seemed strange enough to me, for I had never before seen a priest intoxicated. But what astonished me most was the laughter of the other priests over that spectacle.

When the priests and their friends had sung, laughed, and drank for more than an hour, Mr. Varin rose and said, "The ladies must not be left alone all the evening. Will not our joy and happiness be doubled if they are pleased to share them with us?"

This proposition was applauded and we passed into the drawing-room, where the ladies awaited us.

Several pieces of music, well executed, gave new life to this part of the entertainment. This resource, however, was soon exhausted. Besides, some of the ladies could well see that their husbands were half drunk, and they felt ashamed. Mr. Varin feared nothing more than an interruption in the festivities, which frequently took place in his parsonage.

"Well, well, ladies and gentlemen, let us entertain no dark thoughts on this evening, the happiest of my life. Let us play blind man's buff."

"Let us play blind man's buff!" was repeated by everybody.

"But whose eyes shall be covered first?" asked the priest.

"Yours, Mr. Varin," cried all the ladies. "We look to you for the good example, and we shall follow it."

Mr. Varin consented and immediately one of the ladies placed her nicely-perfumed handkerchief over the eyes of her priest and led him to the center of the room, giving him a gentle push. She said, "Mr. Blindman! Let everyone flee! Woe to him who is caught!"

There is nothing more curious and comical than watching a man walk when he is intoxicated, especially if he wishes nobody to notice it. Such was the position of priest Varin.

He would take one forward and two backward steps, and would then stagger to the right and to the left. Everybody laughed to tears. One after another they would all either pinch him or touch him gently on his hand, arm, or shoulder, and, passing rapidly off, would exclaim, "Run away!" Suddenly he caught the arm of a lady who had come too near. She struggled in vain to escape, but the priest's hand held her firmly.

Using his other hand he tried to touch her head so he might know the name of his pretty captive. But at that moment his legs gave way, dragging his beautiful parishioner to the floor. She turned upon him in order to escape, but he soon turned on her in order to hold her better.

Although the affair lasted only a moment, it was long enough to cause the ladies to blush and cover their faces. This ended the game. Never in my life had I seen anything so shameful!

Only the women felt ashamed because the men were too intoxicated to blush. The priests were either too drunk or too much accustomed to such scenes to be ashamed.

On the following day every one of those priests celebrated mass, and ate what they called the body and blood, the soul and divinity of Jesus Christ, just as if they had spent the previous evening in prayer and meditation on the laws of God!

Thus, O perfidious Church of Rome, thou deceivest the nations who follow thee, and ruinest even the priests whom thou makest thy slaves.

CHAPTER VII

Roman Catholic priests devote two or three months every year to preparing ten to twelve year old children for their first communion. They are obliged to attend Church almost every day, memorize the catechism, and must thoroughly understand its teachings. Through this preparation the Church of Rome lays the very foundation of the idolatries and superstitions which she claims is the religion of Jesus Christ.

Besides corrupting the most sacred truths of the Gospel through this catechism, she secures for the pope and his representatives that adoration which is the secret of Rome's power. It is during this religious instruction that Jesus is removed from the hearts for which He paid so great a price, and Mary is put in His place. This great iniquity is so skillfully executed that it is almost impossible for a poor child to escape. This is how Mary took the place of my precious Saviour during my own childhood.

The priest who instructed us was the Rev. Mr. Morin. He was exceedingly kind and we respected and loved him sincerely. One day he said to me, "Stand up, my child, and answer the many important questions which I have to ask you."

I stood up.

"My child," he said, "when you were guilty of wrong doing at home, who punished you most severely, your father or your mother?"

After a few moments of hesitation I answered, "My father."

"Correct, my child," said the priest. "As a matter of fact, the father is almost always more impatient and ready to punish than the mother."

"Now, my child, tell us which parent punished you more severely?"

"My father," I said again, without hesitation.

"Still true, my child. The superior goodness of a kind mother is perceived even in correction where her blows are lighter. Further, when you deserved to be chastised, did not someone often come between you and your father's rod, taking it away from him and pacifying him?"

"Yes," I said. "More than once my mother did that and saved me from severe punishment."

"Now my children, have not your good mothers often saved you from your father's corrections even when you deserved it?"

"Yes, sir," we all answered.

"One question more. When your father was coming to whip you, did you not throw yourself into the arms of someone to escape?"

"Yes, sir. More than once, I threw myself into my mother's arms. She pleaded so well for me that I often escaped punishment."

Turning to the children, he continued, "You have a Father and a Mother in heaven. Your Father is Jesus, and your Mother is Mary. Never forget that a mother's heart is always more tender and merciful."

"Often your sins make your Father angry against you. Your Father takes His rod to punish you. He threatens to crush you with His roaring thunder; He opens the gates of hell to cast you in. You would have been damned long ago had not your heavenly Mother disarmed your angry and irritated Father. When Jesus would punish you, the good Virgin Mary places herself between Him and you. She obtains your pardon."

"Thus, my children, when your conscience says you are guilty, and Jesus is angry, hasten to Mary! Throw yourselves into the arms of that good mother; have recourse to her sovereign power over Jesus, and be assured that you will be saved through her!"

Thus in the Church of Rome, not Jesus, but Mary, represents the infinite love and mercy of God for the sinner. His hope is directed to Mary for his escape from deserved chastisement! It is not Jesus, but Mary, who saves the sinner!

The Church of Rome constantly invites sinners to turn their thoughts, their hopes, their affections, not to Jesus, but to Mary!

By that impious doctrine Rome deceives the intellects, seduces the hearts, and destroys the souls of the young forever. Under the pretext of honoring the Virgin Mary, she insults her by outrageously misrepresenting her adorable Son.

Old pagan idolatry is brought back under a new name.

CHAPTER VIII

For the Roman Catholic child, how beautiful yet sad is his first communion! With joy and anxiety he is about to eat for the first time what he has been taught to believe to be his God! Not in a symbolical or commemorative way but to eat His flesh, His bones,

His hands, His feet, His head, His whole body! I had to believe this or be cast forever into hell. Yet all the time, my eyes, my hands, my mouth, my tongue, my reason told me that I was eating only bread!

Shall I say that I believed this? I believed like all good Roman Catholics believe. I believed as a corpse believes. My reason and senses had been sacrificed at the feet of that terrible modern god, the pope! Foolishly I had said to my intellectual faculties and my senses, "Hush, you are liars! Till now I had believed you were given by God to help me walk in the dark paths of life, but, behold! the holy pope teaches me that you are only instruments of the devil to deceive me!"

Such was my own condition on the day of my first communion. Two feelings were at war in my mind. I rejoiced that I would soon have full possession of Jesus Christ. At the same time I was humbled by the absurdity of it. Though scarcely twelve I had been in the habit of trusting my eyes. I thought that I could easily distinguish between a small piece of bread and a full grown man!

Besides, I extremely abhorred the idea of eating human flesh and drinking human blood, even when assured that they were the flesh and blood of Jesus Christ Himself. But what troubled me most was the idea that God, so great, so glorious, so holy, could be eaten by me like common bread! Terrible then was the struggle in my young heart, where joy and dread, trust and fear, faith and unbelief by turns had the upper hand.

While in the cold perspiration of that secret struggle, known only to God and to myself, I prayed to God and the Holy Virgin for mercy, strength and light during these hours of anguish.

The Church of Rome is the most skillful human machine the world has ever seen. Those who guide her dark paths are often men of deep thought. They understand the struggle in the minds of children at the supreme moment when they would have to sacrifice their reason on the altar of Rome. To prevent those struggles, always so dangerous to the Church, nothing has been neglected to distract the mind to other subjects.

First, the parish priest, helped by the vanity of the parents themselves, sees that the children are clothed in every way best calculated to flatter their vanity. The church building is pompously decorated and the service charmed with choice vocal and instrumental music. Incense ascends from the altar in a sweet smelling cloud. People come from every direction to enjoy the beautiful spectacle. Priests from neighboring churches add to the solemnity. The officiating priest is dressed in the most costly attire. Silver and gold altar cloths are displayed before the wondering spectators. Often a lighted candle is placed in the hand of each young communicant. This itself would draw his whole attention, for a single false motion would set fire to the clothes of his neighbor, or his own, a misfortune which has happened more than once in my presence.

Now, in the midst of that wonderful spectacle, busy holding the lighted taper to keep from being burned alive, the moment of communion arrives without time for him to think of what he is about to do!

He opens his mouth, and the priest puts upon his tongue a flat, thin cake of unleavened bread, which either firmly sticks to his palate or melts in his mouth, soon to go down into his stomach just like the food he takes three times a day!

The first feeling of the child, then, is surprise at the thought that the Creator of heaven and earth, the upholder of the universe, the Saviour of the world, could so easily pass down his throat!

Now, follow those children to their homes after that great and monstrous comedy. Listen to their conversation and their bursts of laughter! Study their manners, their glances of satisfaction on their fine clothes, and the vanity which they manifest in return for the congratulations. Notice the lightness of their actions and conversation immediately after their communion and tell me if you think they believed in the terrible dogma they have been taught.

No, and they will never believe it with the firmness of faith accompanied by intelligence. The poor child thinks he believes, and he sincerely tries to do so. He believes as Roman Catholics believe. He believes as an idiot believes!!

The first communion has made of him, for the rest of his life, a real machine in the hands of the pope. It is the first most powerful link of that long chain of slavery which the priest and the Church pass around his neck. The pope holds the end of that chain, and with it will make his victim go right or left at his pleasure, just as we govern the lower animals. As Loyola said, "If those children have made a good first communion they will be submissive to the pope. Like the stick in the hands of the traveler, they will have no will, no thought of their own!"

My soul has known the weight of those chains, the ignominy of that slavery! But the great Conqueror of souls cast a merciful eye upon me and broke my chains. With His holy Word He has made me free.

May His name be forever blessed.

CHAPTER IX

I finished college at Nicolet August, 1829. I could easily have learned in three or four years what had taken seven. Our teachers cared more to pass our time than enlarge our understanding. As soon as the intelligence, guided by the Jesuit, has ascended to the feet of the pope, it must remain there, prostrate itself and fall asleep.

Though my intelligence often revolted I forced myself to accept these fables as gospel truths. These were times of terrible struggle in my soul. I remember the day I expressed my doubts to my professor of philosophy.

"When my superior abuses his authority over me to deceive me by false doctrines, or commands me to do things I consider wrong and dishonest, shall I not be lost if I obey him?"

He answered, "You will never have to give an account to God for what you are ordered to do by your legitimate superiors. If they deceive you, being themselves deceived, *they alone* would be responsible. You do not sin if you follow the basic golden rule of all Christian philosophy and perfection: humility and obedience!"

Little satisfied, I expressed my reluctance to several of my fellow-students including Joseph Turcot, who later became Minister of Public Works in Canada. He answered, "The more I study what they call their principles of Christian philosophy and logic, the more I think that they intend to make *asses of every one of us!*"

The next day I opened my heart to our principal, Mr. Leprohon, whom I venerated as a saint and loved as a father. I wrote down his answer:

"My dear Chiniquy, how did Adam and Eve bring upon us all the deluge of evils? Is it not because they raised their miserable reason above that of God? They had the promise of eternal life if they had submitted their reason to their Supreme Master. They were lost by rebelling against the authority of God. So it is today. All the evils, the errors, the crimes by which the world is overflooded come from the same revolt of the human will and reason against the will and reason of God. God reigns yet over a part of the world, the world of the elect, through the pope, who controls the teachings of our infallible and holy Church. In submitting ourselves to God, who speaks to us through the pope, we are saved. We walk in the paths of truth and holiness. But we would err and perish as soon as we put our reason above that of our superior, the pope, speaking to us in person, or through some of our superiors who have received from him the authority to guide us."

"But," said I, "if my reason tells me that the pope, or other supe-

riors put by him over me are mistaken and command me something wrong, would I not be guilty before God if I obey them?"

"Impossible," answered Mr. Leprohon, "for the pope and the
bishops who are united to him have the promise of never failing in
the faith. They cannot lead you into any errors, nor command you
anything against the law of God. But suppose they do commit any
error, or compel you to believe or do something contrary to the
Gospel, God would not hold you accountable when you are obeying
your legitimate superior."

I had to content myself with that answer, but in spite of my respectful silence, he saw that I was yet uneasy and sad. To convince
me he put into my hands the two works of De Maistre, — "Le
Pape" and "Les Soirees de St. Petersburgh," where I found the
same doctrines supported. He was honest in is convictions for he
had found them in these books approved by the "infallible popes."

I know Rome can show a certain number of intelligent men in
every branch of science who have studied in their colleges. But
these remarkable men had from the beginning secretly broken for
themselves the chains with which their superiors had tried to bind
them. Nine-tenths of them have been persecuted,
excommunicated, tortured, some even put to death for having
dared to think for themselves.

Galileo was a Roman Catholic, one of the greatest men whom
science claims. But was he not sent to a dungeon and publicly
flogged? Had he not to ask pardon from God and man for thinking
differently from the pope about the motion of the earth around the
sun!

Copernicus was surely one of the greatest lights of his time, but
was censured and excommunicated for his admirable scientific
discoveries?

France does not know any greater genius among her most
gifted sons than Pascal. He was a Catholic. But he lived and died
excommunicated.

Those pupils of Roman Catholic colleges of whom sometimes
the priests so imprudently boast, have gone out from the hands of
their Jesuit teachers to proclaim their supreme contempt for the
priesthood and Papacy. They have seen with their own eyes that
the priest of Rome is the most dangerous, the most implacable
enemy of intelligence, progress and liberty.

Voltaire studied in a Roman Catholic college, and it was probably there that he nerved himself for his terrible battle against
Rome. Catholicism will never recover from the blow which Voltaire has struck at her in France.

When you see Roman Catholic colleges and nunneries raising

their haughty steeples over some commanding hills or in the midst of some beautiful valleys, you may confidently expect that the self-respect and the manly virtues of the people will soon disappear — intelligence, progress, prosperity will soon be replaced by superstition, idleness, drunkenness, Sabbath-breaking, ignorance, poverty and degradation of every kind. The colleges and nunneries are the high citadels from which the pope darts his surest missiles against the rights and liberties of nations.

It is in the colleges and nunneries of Rome that men learn that they are created to obey the pope in everything, that the Bible must be burnt, and that liberty must be destroyed at any cost.

CHAPTER X

To understand moral education of students in Roman Catholic colleges, one must only understand that from the beginning to the end they are surrounded by an atmosphere in which nothing but paganism is breathed.

For instance, our superiors convinced us that scapulars, medals, holy water, etc., would be of great service in battling with the most dangerous temptations, as well as in avoiding the most common dangers of life. Consequently, we kept them with the greatest respect, kissing them morning and evening with affection, as if they were powerful instruments of the mercy of God. Then we discovered in the Greek and Latin historians that they were nothing but a remnant of paganism.

The modern Pontifex Maximus (the Pope of Rome), supposed successor of St. Peter, the Vicar of Jesus Christ, resembled the "Pontifex Maximus" of the great republic of Rome like two drops of water. Our pope preserved the name, the attributes, the pageantry, the pride, and even the garb of that high pagan priest. Was not the worship of the saints absolutely the same as the worship of the demigods of olden time? Was not our purgatory minutely described by Virgil? Were not our prayers to the Virgin and to the saints repeated, almost in the same words, by the worshipers before the images of their gods, just as we repeated them every day before the images in our churches? Was not our holy water in use among the idolaters, and for the same purpose?

We knew by history the year in which the magnificent temple consecrated *to all the gods,* bearing the name of Pantheon, had been built at Rome. Words cannot express the shame we felt on learning that the Roman Catholics of our day, under the very eyes and with the sanction of the pope, still prostrated themselves before the SAME IDOLS, in the SAME TEMPLE, and to obtain the SAME FAVORS!

When we asked, "What is the difference between the religion of heathen Rome and that of the Rome of today?" more than one student would answer: "The only difference is in the name. Instead of calling this statue Jupiter, we call it Peter; and instead of calling that one Minerva or Venus, it is called St. Mary. It is the old idolatry coming to us under Christian names."

I earnestly desired to be an honest and sincere Roman Catholic. These impressions and thoughts distracted me greatly. Unfortunately many of the books placed in our hands by our superiors to confirm our faith, form our moral character, and sustain our piety and our confidence in the dogmas of the Church of Rome, had a frightful resemblance to the histories I had read of the gods and goddesses. The miracles attributed to the Virgin Mary often appeared to be only a reproduction of the tricks and deceits of the priests of Jupiter, Venus, Minerva, etc. Some of those miracles of the Virgin Mary equaled or surpassed in absurdity the most hideous accounts of the heathen gods and goddesses.

After reading the monstrous metamorphoses of the gods of Olympus, the student feels a burning desire to nourish himself with the Words of Life. But the priest of the college places himself between the student and Christ, and instead of allowing him to be nourished with the Bread of Life he offers him fables, husks with which to appease his hunger.

God alone knows what I have suffered during my studies to find myself absolutely deprived of the privilege of eating this bread of life, His Holy Word!

During the last years of my studies my superiors often confided to me the charge of the library. One holiday, I remained alone in the college. Shutting myself in the library I began to examine all the books. I discovered that the books which were the most proper to instruct us were marked forbidden. I felt an inexpressible shame on seeing with my own eyes that only the most indifferent books were placed in our hands. Several students more advanced than myself, had already made that observation to me, but I did not believe them. Until then I had spurned the idea that, with the rest of the students, I was the victim of an incredible system of moral and intellectual blindness.

Among the forbidden books I found a splendid Bible. I seized it like a miser finding a lost treasure. I lifted it to my lips, and kissed it respectfully. I pressed it against my heart, as one embraces a friend from whom he has long been separated. This Bible brought back to my memory the most delightful hours of my life. I read in its divine pages till the scholars returned.

The next day Rev. Mr. Leprohon, our director, called me to his room and said: "You seem to be troubled today. Have you any cause of grief or are you sick?"

I could not sufficiently express my love and respect for this venerable man. He was at the same time my friend and benefactor. For four years he and Rev. Mr. Brassard had been paying my board. By reading the Bible the previous day I had disobeyed my benefactor, for when he entrusted me with the care of the library he made me promise not to read the books in the forbidden catalog.

It was painful to me to sadden him by acknowledging that I had broken my word of honor, but it pained me far more to deceive him by concealing the truth. I therefore answered him: "You are right that I am uneasy and sad. I confess there is one thing which perplexes me greatly. I never dared to speak to you about it: but as you wish to know the cause of my sadness, I will tell you. You have placed in our hands, not only to read, but to learn by heart, books which are, as you know, partly inspired by hell, and you forbid us to read the only book whose every word is sent from heaven! This disturbs and scandalizes me! Your dread of the Bible shakes my faith, and causes me to fear that we are going astray in our church."

Mr. Leprohon answered, "I have been the director of this college for more than twenty years, and I have never heard from the lips of any of the students such remarks and complaints. Have you no fear of being the victim of a deception of the devil, in meddling with a question so strange and so new for a scholar whose only aim should be to obey his superiors?"

"It may be," said I, "that I am the first to speak to you in this manner, for it is very probable that I am the only student in this college who has read the Holy Bible in his youthful days. I can assure you that the perusal of that admirable book has done me a good that is still felt. I know by personal experience that there is no book in the world so good and proper to read, that I am extremely grieved, and even scandalized, by the dread you have of it. I acknowledge to you I spent the afternoon of yesterday in the library reading the Bible. I found things in it which made me weep for joy and happiness; things that did more good to my soul and heart than all you have given me to read for six years. And I am so sad today because you approve of me when I read the words of the devil, and condemn me when I read the Word of God."

My superior answered, "Since you have read the Bible, you must know that there are things in it on matters of such a delicate nature that it is improper for a young man, and more so for a young lady, to read them."

"I understand," answered I; "but you know very well that Satan speaks to us about them day and night in order that we may like it and be lost. But when the God of purity speaks to us of evil things (of which it is pretty much impossible for men to be ignorant), He does it that we may hate and abhor them, and He gives us grace to avoid them. Since you cannot prevent the devil from whispering to seduce us, how dare you hinder God from speaking of the same things to shield us from their allurements? Besides, when my God desires to speak to me Himself on any question whatever, where is your right to obstruct His word on its way to my heart?"

Though Mr. Leprohon's intelligence was wrapped in the darkness of Rome, his heart had remained honest and true; and while I respected and loved him as my father, though differing from him in opinion, I knew he loved me as if I had been his own child. He was thunderstruck by my answer. He turned pale, and I saw tears about to flow from his eyes. He sighed deeply, and looked at me some time reflectingly, without answering.

At last he said: "My dear Chiniquy, your answer and your arguments have a force that frightens me, and if I had no other but my own personal ideas to disprove them, I acknowledge I do not know how I would do it. But I have something better than my own weak thoughts. I have the thoughts of the Church, and of our Holy Father the Pope. *They forbid us to put the Bible in the hands of our students.* This should put an end to your troubles. To obey his legitimate superiors in all things is the rule a Christian scholar like you should follow; and if you have broken it yesterday, I hope it will be the last time that the child whom I love better than myself will cause me such pain."

On saying this he threw his arms around me, clasped me to his heart, and bathed my face with tears. I wept also. Yes, I wept abundantly.

But God knoweth, that though the regret of having grieved my benefactor and father caused me to shed tears at that moment, yet I wept much more on perceiving that I would no more be permitted to read His Holy Word.

The gods of the heathen spoke to us daily by their apostles and disciples, Homer, Virgil, Pindar, Horace! — and the God of the Christians had not permission to say a single word to us!

I must say, though with a sad heart, that moral and religious education in Roman Catholic colleges is worse than void. From them has been excluded the only true standard of morals and religion, — THE WORD OF GOD!

CHAPTER XI

In the history of paganism parents often slew their children upon the altars of their gods to appease their wrath or obtain their favors. But we now see a stranger thing. It is Christian parents forcing their children into the temples and to the very feet of the idols of Rome, under the fallacious notion of having them educated! While the pagan parent destroyed only the temporal life of his child, the Christian parent, for the most part, destroys his eternal life. The pagan was consistent. He believed in the almighty power and holiness of his gods; he sincerely THOUGHT that they ruled the world, and that they blessed both the victims and those who offered them.

But where is the consistency of the Protestant who sacrifices his child on the altars of the pope! Does he believe in his holiness or in his supreme and infallible power? Then why does he not go and throw himself at his feet? The Protestants say, as an excuse, that the superiors of colleges and convents have assured them that their religious convictions would be respected, and that nothing should be said or done to take away or even shake the religion of their children.

Our first parents were no more cruelly deceived by the seductive words of the serpent than the Protestants are by the deceitful promises of the priests and nuns of Rome.

I myself witnessed this promise given by our superior to a father who was a judge in New York. Then a few days later that same superior said to me, "You know some English, and this young man knows French enough to understand each other. Try to become his friend and bring him over to our holy religion. His father is a most influential man in the United States and this only son is the heir of an immense fortune. Great results for the future of the Church in the U.S. might follow his conversion."

I replied, "Have you forgotten the promise you have made to his father, never to say or do anything to shake or take away the religion of that young man?"

My superior smiled at my simplicity, and said, "When you shall have studied theology you will know that Protestantism is not a religion, but that it is the negation of religion. Protesting cannot be the basis of any doctrine. Thus, when I promised Judge Pike that the religious convictions of his child should be respected, and that I would not do anything to change his faith, I promised the easiest thing in the world, since I promised not to meddle with a thing *which has no existence.*"

Blinded by the reasoning of my superior, I set myself to work to make a good Roman Catholic of that young friend. I would probably have succeeded had not a serious illness forced him to return home.

Protestants who read this may be indignant against such deceit but your contempt should be upon your own selves. The superior, Mr. Leprohon was honest. He acted upon principle which he thought good and legitimate and would cheerfully have given his last drop of blood for them. The priest of Rome is not the traitor here. It is the Protestant who wishes to have his children educated by a Jesuit who is a man of no religion. Nothing is more ridiculous than to hear such a man begging respect for his religious principles! It was not the priest of Rome who was contemptible, dishonest and a traitor to his principles, but it was the Protestant who was false to his Gospel and to his own conscience by having his child educated by the servants of the pope.

When I was in the Church of Rome, we often spoke of the necessity of making superhuman efforts to attract young Protestants into our colleges and nunneries, as the shortest and only means of ruling the world before long. The priests of Rome themselves boast that more than half of the pupils of the nuns are the children of Protestants, and that seven-tenths of those Protestant children, sooner or later, become the firmest disciples and the true pillars of popery in the United States.

"But," say many Protestants, "where can we get safer securities that the morals of our girls will be sheltered than in those convents? The faces of those good nuns, their angelic smiles, even their lips, from which seems to flow a perfume from heaven — are not these the unfailing signs that nothing will taint the hearts of our dear children when they are under the care of those holy nuns?"

Angelic smiles! Lips from which flow a perfume from heaven! Expressions of peace and holiness of the good nuns! Delusive allurements! Cruel deceptions! Mockery of comedy! Yes, *all* these angelic smiles, all these expressions of joy and happiness, are but allurements to deceive honest but too trusting men!

For a long time I believed that there was something true in all the display of peace and happiness which I saw in the faces of a good number of nuns. But how soon my delusions passed away when I read with my own eyes, in a book of the *secret rules* of the convent, that one of their rules is *always,* especially in the presence of strangers, to have an appearance of joy and happiness, even when the soul is overwhelmed with grief and sorrow! The motives given for thus wearing a continual mask, is to secure the esteem and respect of the people, and to win more securely the young ladies to the convent!

The poor nun's heart is often full of sorrow, and her soul is drowned in a sea of desolation; but she is obliged, under oath, always to appear joyful!

Ah! if the Protestants could know, as I do, how much the hearts of those nuns bleed, how much those poor victims of the pope feel themselves wounded to death, how almost every one of them die at an early age, broken-hearted, they would weep at their profound misery. Instead of helping Satan to maintain those sad dungeons by giving their gold and their children, they would let them crumble into dust, and thus check the torrents of silent, bitter tears which those cells hide.

"But," says one, "the education is so cheap in the nunnery." I answer, "If it were half the price it would still cost twice more than it is worth. Cheap things are always too highly paid for."

Intellectually, the education in the nunnery is completely null. The great object of the pope and the nuns is to captivate and destroy the intelligence.

And what kind of moral education can a young girl receive from a nun who believes that she can live as she pleases, that nothing evil can come of her, neither in this life nor in the next, if only she is devout to the Virgin Mary?

Let Protestants read the "Glories of Mary," by St. Liguori, a book found in the hands of every nun and priest, and they will understand what kind of morality is practised and taught inside the walls of the Church of Rome.

CHAPTER XII

The word EDUCATION is a beautiful word. It comes from the Latin *educare,* which means to raise up, to take from the lowest degrees to the highest spheres of knowledge. The object of education is, then, to feed, expand, raise, enlighten, and strengthen the intelligence.

When a Protestant speaks of education, that word is used and understood in its true sense. When he sends his little boy to a Protestant school, he honestly desires that he should be reared up in the spheres of knowledge as much as his intelligence will allow. When the son of a Protestant has acquired a little knowledge, he wants to acquire more. Like the young eagle, he trims his wings for a higher flight. A noble and mysterious ambition has suddenly seized his young soul. Then he begins to feel something of that unquenchable thirst for knowledge which God Himself has put in the breast of every child of Adam.

It ought then to be a duty with both Roman Catholics and Protestants to assist the pupil in his flight. But is it so? No.

When you Protestants send your children to school, you put no fetters to their intelligence. The Protestant scholar goes on from timid flutter to the bold confident flight, from one region of knowledge to another still higher, till he loses himself in that ocean of light and truth and life which is God.

Thus only the truly *great,* truly *powerful,* and the truly *free* nations in the world are Protestants! Everywhere they are the advanced guard in the ranks of progress, science and liberty, leaving far behind the unfortunate nations whose hands are tied by the ignominious iron chains of popery.

That young Roman Catholic scholar is born with the same bright intelligence as the Protestant one; he is endowed by his Creator with the same powers of mind as his Protestant neighbor. He has the same noble aspirations implanted by God. He is sent to school, like the Protestant boy, to receive what is called "education." He at first understands that word in its true sense; he goes to school in the hope of being *raised,* elevated as high as his intelligence and his personal efforts will allow.

But here begin the disappointments and tribulations of the Roman Catholic student. He is allowed to raise himself only high enough to be on a level with the big toes of the pope. Remember that the pope is the only source of science, knowledge, and truth. The knowledge of the pope is the ultimate limit of learning and light to which humanity can attain. You are not allowed to know and believe what his Holiness does not know and believe. On the 22nd of June, 1663, Galileo was obliged to fall on his knees to escape the cruel death ordered by the pope. He signed with his own hand the following retraction: "I abjure, curse, and detest the error and heresy of the motion of the earth," etc., etc.

That learned man had to degrade himself by swearing a lie, that the earth does not move around the sun. Thus the wings of that giant eagle of Rome were clipped by the scissors of the pope. But God would not allow that giant intellect to be entirely strangled by the bloody hands of that implacable enemy of light and truth, the pope. Sufficient strength and life had remained in Galileo to enable him to say, when rising up, "This will not prevent the earth from moving!"

The infallible decree of the infallible pope, Urban VIII, against the motion of the earth is signed by the Cardinals Felia, Guido, Desiderio, Antonio, Bellingero, and Fabriccio. It says: "In the name and by the authority of Jesus Christ, the plenitude of which resides in His Vicar, the pope, that the proposition that the earth is not the center of the world, and that it moves with a diurnal motion is absurd, philosophically false, and erroneous in faith."

What a glorious thing for the pope of Rome to be infallible! He infallibly knows that the earth does not move around the sun! And what a blessed thing for the Roman Catholics to be governed and taught by such an *infallible* being. In consequence of that infallible decree, you will admire the following act of humble submission of two celebrated Jesuit astronomers, Lesueur and Jacquier: "Newton assumes in his third book the hypothesis of the earth moving around the sun. The propositions of that author could not be explained, except through the same hypothesis: we have, therefore, been forced to act a character not our own. *But we declare our entire submission to the decrees of the Supreme Pontiffs of Rome against the motion of the earth.*" (Newton's "Principia," vol. iii., p. 450.)

Here you see two other learned Jesuits, who have written a very able work to prove that the earth moves around the sun, trembling at Vatican threats to kill them, submit to the decrees of the popes of Rome against the motion of the earth. These two learned Jesuits tell a most contemptible and ridiculous lie to save themselves from the wrath of that great light-extinguisher whose throne is in the city of the seven hills.

Had the Newtons, the Franklins, the Fultons, the Morses been Romanists, their names would have been lost in the obscurity which is the natural heritage of the abject slaves of the popes. Being told from their infancy that no one had any right to make use of his "private judgment," intelligence and conscience in the research of truth, they would have remained mute and motionless at the feet of the modern and terrible god of Rome, the pope.

But they were Protestants! In that great and glorious word "Protestant" is the secret of the marvelous discoveries with which they have changed the face of the world. They were Protestants! Yes, they had passed their young years in Protestant schools, where they had read a Book which told them that they were created in the image of God, and that that great God had sent His eternal Son Jesus to make them free from the bondage of man. They had read in that Protestant book (for the Bible is the most Protestant book in the world) that man had not only a conscience, but an intelligence to guide him; they had learned that that intelligence and conscience had no other master but God, no other guide but God, no other light but God. On the walls of their Protestant schools the Son of God had written the marvelous words: "Come unto Me; I am the Light, the Way, the Life."

Why is it that Roman Catholic nations not only remain stationary, but decay? Go to their schools and look at the principles which are sown in the young intelligences of their unfortunate slaves, and you will have the key to that sad mystery.

What is the first and daily school lesson taught to the Roman Catholic? Is it not that one of the greatest crimes which a man can commit is to follow his "private judgment?" This means that he has eyes, ears, and intelligence, but he cannot make use of them without danger of being eternally damned. His superiors, the priest and the pope, must see for him, hear for him, and think for him.

If this appears to be an exaggeration, allow me to force the Church of Rome to come here and speak for herself. Here are the very words of the so-called "Saint" Ignatius Loyola, the founder of the Jesuit Society: "As for holy obedience, this virtue must be perfect in every point, in execution, in will, in intellect; doing which is enjoined with all celerity, spiritual joy and perseverance; persuading ourselves that everything is just, suppressing every repugnant thought and judgment of one's own in a certain obedience; and let every one persuade himself, that he who lives under obedience should be moved and directed, under Divine Providence, by his superior, JUST AS IF HE WERE A CORPSE (perinde acsi cadaver esset) which allows itself to be moved and led in every direction."

You ask me what can be the use of hundreds of millions of moral corpses? Why not let them live? The answer is easy. The great, the only object of the thoughts and workings of the pope and the priests is to raise themselves above the rest of the world. They want to be high above the heads not only of the common people, but of the kings and emperors of the world. They want to be even higher than God. Speaking of the pope the Holy Ghost says: "He opposeth and exalteth himself above all that is called God, or that is worshiped; so that he, as God, sitteth in the temple of God, shewing himself that he is God." (II Thess. 2:4)

To attain their object, the priests have persuaded their millions and millions of slaves that they were mere corpses; that they must have no will, no conscience, no intelligence of their own. When they have made a pyramid of all those motionless, inert corpses so high that its top goes to into the very abode of the old divinities of the pagan world, they put themselves and their popes at the top and say to the rest of the world: "Who among you are as high as we are? Where are the kings and the emperors whose thrones are as elevated as ours? Are we not at the very top of humanity?"

Yes! yes! I answer to the priests of Rome. You are high, very high indeed! Your throne is higher than anything we know. But it is a throne of corpses!!!

Let me put before your eyes another extract of the Jesuit teachings from the "Spiritual Exercises," by their founder, Ignatius Loyola: " . . . We ought ever to hold as a fixed principle that what I see white I believe to be black, if the superior authorities of the Church define it to be so."

You all know that it is the avowed desire of Rome to have public education in the hands of the Jesuits. She says everywhere that they are the best, the model teachers. Why so? Because they more boldly and more successfully than any other of her teachers aim at the destruction of the intelligence and conscience of their pupils. When a man has been trained a sufficient time by them, he most perfectly becomes a moral corpse. His superiors can do what they please with him. Listen to the words of that "infallible" Pope Gregory XVI, in his celebrated Encyclical of the 15th of August, 1832: "If the holy Church so requires, let us sacrifice our own opinions, our knowledge, *our intelligence,* the splendid dreams of our imagination, and the most sublime attainments of the human understanding."

It is when considering those anti-social principles of Rome that Mr. Gladstone wrote, not long ago: "No more cunning plot was ever devised against the freedom, the happiness and the virtue of mankind than Romanism." ("Letter to Earl Aberdeen.")

Now, Protestants, do you begin to understand the great distance between the word "education" among you, and the meaning of the same word in the Church of Rome? By education you mean to raise man to the highest sphere of manhood. Rome means to lower him below the most stupid brutes. By education you mean to teach man that he is a free agent, that liberty within the limits of the laws of God and of his country is a gift to every one; that it is better to die a free man than to live a slave. Rome wants to teach that there is only one man who is free, the pope, and that all the rest are born to be his abject slaves in thought, will and action.

I ask of you, American Protestants, what would become of your fair country if you allow the Church of Rome to teach the children of the United States? What future of shame, degradation, and slavery you prepare for your country if Rome succeeds in forcing you to support such schools? What kind of women would come out from the schools of nuns who would teach them that the highest pitch of perfection in a woman is when she obeys her superior, the priest, *in everything he commands her!* that your daughter will never be called to give an account to God for the actions she will have done to please and obey her superior, the priest, the bishop, the pope? Again, what kind of men and citizens will come out from the schools of those Jesuits who believe and teach that a man has attained the perfection of manhood only when he is a perfect spiritual corpse before his superior?

CHAPTER XIII

Theology is the study of the knowledge of the laws of God. Nothing, then, is more noble. How solemn were my thoughts and elevated my aspirations in 1829 when I commenced my theological course of study at Nicolet. I supposed that my books of theology were to bring me more perfect knowledge of God's holy will and sacred laws.

The principal theologians studied were Bailly, Dens, St. Thomas, and above all Liguori, who has since been canonized. Never did I open one without offering up a fervent prayer to God and to the Virgin Mary for light for myself and for the people whose pastor I was to become.

But how surprised I was to discover that, in order to accept the principles of the theologians I had to put away all truth, of justice, of honor and holiness! What long and painful efforts it cost me to extinguish, one by one, the lights of truth and of reason kindled by the hand of my merciful God in my intelligence. For to study theology in the Church of Rome is to learn to speak falsely, to deceive, to commit robbery, to perjure one's self!

I know that Roman Catholics and even Protestants will bravely and squarely deny what I now say. Nevertheless, it is true. My witnesses cannot be contradicted by anyone. My witnesses are even infallible. They are none other than the Roman Catholic theologians themselves, approved by infallible popes! These very men who corrupted my heart, perverted my intelligence and poisoned my soul, as they have done with each and every priest of their Church, will be my witnesses, my only witnesses to testify against themselves!

Liguori states that one may lie when under oath. In his treatise on oaths he says: "It is a certain and a common opinion amongst all divines that for a just cause it is lawful to use equivocation (deception) . . . and to confirm it (equivocation) with an oath . . .

Now a just cause is any honest end in order to preserve good things for the spirit, or useful things for the body." (Mor. Theol. t. ii. cap. ii. de jur p. 316, n. 151. Mech. 1845).

Liguori says that a woman guilty of adultery may deny it under oath if she has confessed it to a priest. He says: "If sacramentally she confessed adultery, she can answer, 'I am innocent of this crime,' because by confession it was taken away."

Liguori maintains that one may commit a minor crime in order to avoid a greater crime. He says: "Hence Sanchez teaches, etc., that it is lawful to persuade a man, determined to slay someone, that he should commit theft or fornication." (Mor. Theol. t. ii. lib. iii. cap. ii. n. 57, p. 157.)

Liguori also justifies a servant who helps his master commit fornication by bringing a ladder. The Salmanticenses say that a servant can steal from his master when he feels he is not adequately paid.

Ligouri, in Dubium II., considers what may be the quantity of stolen property necessary to constitute mortal sin. He says: "If any one on an occasion should steal only a moderate sum . . . not intending to acquire any notable sum, neither to injure his neighbor to a great extent by several thefts, he does not sin grievously, nor do these, taken together, constitute a mortal sin; however, after it may have amounted to a notable sum, by detaining it, he can commit mortal sin. But even this mortal sin may be avoided, if either then he be unable to restore, or have the intention of making restitution immediately . . ." (Mor. Theol. t. iii. p. 257, n. 533. Mech. 1845.)

The theologians of Rome assure us that we may, and even that we must, conceal and disguise our faith: "When you are asked concerning the faith, not only is it lawful, but often more conducive to the glory of God and the utility of your neighbor to cover the faith than to confess it; for example, if concealed among heretics (Protestants) you may accomplish a greater amount of good; or if, from the confession of the faith more of evil would follow, for example, great trouble, death, the hostility of a tyrant, . . . torture. Whence it is often rash to offer one's self willingly." (Mor. Theol. t. ii. p. 817, n. 14. Mech 1845.)

The pope has the right to release from all oaths: "As for an oath made for a good and legitimate object, it seems that there should be no power capable of annulling it. However, when it is for the good of the public, a matter which comes under the immediate jurisdiction of the pope, who has the supreme power over the Church, the pope has full power to release from that oath." (St. Thomas, Quest. 89, art. 9, vol. iv.)

The Roman Catholics have not only the right, but it is their duty to kill heretics: "Any man excommunicated is deprived of all civil communication with the faithful, in such a way that if he is not tolerated they can have no communication with him, as it is in the following verse, 'It is forbidden to kiss him, pray with him, salute him, to eat or to do any business with him,'"(St. Liguori, vol. ix., page 62.)

"Though heretics must not be tolerated . . . , we must bear with them till, by a second admonition, they may be brought back to the faith of the Church. But those who, after a second admonition, remain obstinate in their errors must not only be excommunicated, but they must be delivered to the secular powers to be exterminated."

"Though the heretics who repent must always be accepted to penance, as often as they have fallen, they must not in consequence of that always be permitted to enjoy the benefits of this life. When they fall again they are admitted to repent. But the sentence of death must not be removed." (St. Thomas, vol. iv., Page 91.)

A king does not need to be obeyed if he is excommunicated: "When a man is excommunicated for his apostasy, . . . all those who are his subjects are released from the oath of allegiance by which they were bound to obey him." (St. Thomas, vol. iv., page 91.)

Every heretic and Protestant is condemned to death, and every oath of allegiance to a government which is Protestant or heretic is voided by the Council of Lateran, held in A.D. 1215: "We excommunicate and anathematize every heresy that exalts itself against the holy, orthodox and Catholic faith, condemning all heretics, by whatever name they may be known; for though their faces differ, they are tied together by their tails. Such as are condemned are to be delivered over to the existing secular powers, to receive due punishment. If laymen, their goods must be confiscated. If priests, they shall be first degraded from their respective orders, and their property applied to the church in which they have officiated. Secular powers of all ranks and degrees are to be warned, induced, and, if necessary, compelled by ecclesiastical censure, to swear that they will exert themselves to the utmost in the defense of the faith, and extirpate (kill) all heretics denounced by the Church who shall be found in their territories. And whenever any person shall assume government, whether it be spiritual or temporal, he shall be bound to abide by this decree.

"If any temporal lord, after being admonished and required by the Church, shall neglect to clear his territory of heretical depravity, the metropolitan and the bishops of the province shall unite in excommunicating him. Should he remain contumacious (rebellious) for a whole year, the fact shall be signified to the Supreme Pontiff, who will declare his vassals released from their allegiance from that time, and will bestow the territory on Catholics to be occupied by them, on the condition of exterminating the heretics and preserving the said territory in the faith . . .

"We decree, further, that all who may have dealings with heretics, and especially such as receive, defend, or encourage them, shall be excommunicated. He shall not be eligible to any public office. He shall not be admitted as a witness. He shall neither have the power to bequeath his property by will, nor to succeed to any inheritance. He shall not bring an action against any person, but anyone can bring an action against him. Should he be a judge, his decision shall have no force, nor shall any cause be brought before him. Should he be an advocate, he shall not be allowed to plead. Should he be a lawyer, no instruments made by him shall be held valid, but shall be condemned with their author."

I should have to write several large volumes were I to quote all the Roman Catholic doctors and theologians who approve of lying, of perjury, of adultery, theft and murder, for the greatest glory of God and the good of the Roman Church! But I have quoted enough for those who have eyes to see and ears to hear.

With such principles, is it a wonder that all the Roman Catholic nations, without a single exception, have declined so rapidly? The great Legislator of the World, the only Saviour of nations, has said: "Man shall not live by bread alone, but by every word that proceedeth out of the mouth of God."

A nation can be great and strong only according to the truths which form the basis of her faith and life. "Truth" is the only bread which God gives to the nations that they may prosper and live. Deceitfulness, duplicity, perjury, adultery, theft, murder, are the deadly poisons which kill nations.

Then, the more the priests of Rome, with their theology, are venerated and believed by a people, the sooner that people will decay and fall. "The more priests the more crimes," a profound thinker has said; for then the more hands will be at work to pull down the only sure foundations of society.

How can any man be sure of the honesty of his wife as long as a hundred thousand priests tell her that she may commit any sin with her neighbor in order to prevent him from doing something worse? or when she is assured that, though guilty of adultery, she can swear that she is pure as an angel!

What will it avail to teach the best principles of honor, decency and holiness to a young girl, when she is bound to go many times a year to a bachelor priest, who is bound in conscience to give her the most infamous lessons of depravity under the pretext of helping her to confess all her sins?

How will the rights of justice be secured, and how can the judges and the juries protect the innocent and punish the guilty, so long as the witnesses are told by one hundred thousand priests that they can conceal the truth, give equivocal answers, and even perjure themselves under a thousand pretexts?

What government can make people walk with a firm step in the ways of light, progress, and liberty, as long as there is a dark power over them which has the right, at every hour of the day or night, to break and dissolve all the most sacred oaths of allegiance?

Armed with his theology, the priest of Rome has become the most dangerous and determined enemy of truth, justice, and liberty. He is the most formidable obstacle to every good government, and often without being aware of it the greatest enemy of God and man.

CHAPTER XIV

If I write all the ingenious tricks, pious lies, perversions of the Word of God made to entice poor victims into the trap of perpetual celibacy, I would need ten large volumes, instead of a short chapter.

The pope takes his victim to the top of a high mountain, and there shows him all the honors, praise, wealth, peace and joys of this world, plus the most glorious throne of heaven, and then tells him: "I will give you all those things if you fall at my feet, promise me absolute submission, and swear never to marry in order to serve me better."

Who can refuse such glorious things? But the unfortunate victims sometimes have forebodings of the terrible miseries in store for them. Approaching the fatal hour of the impious vow, the young victims often feel their hearts fainting with terror. With pale cheeks, trembling lips and cold-dropping sweat they ask their superiors, "Is it possible that our merciful God requires of us such a sacrifice?"

Oh! how the merciless priest of Rome then becomes eloquent in depicting celibacy as the only way to heaven, or in showing the eternal fires of hell ready to receive cowards and traitors who, after having put their hand to the plow of celibacy, look back! He overwhelms them with a thousand pious lies about the miracles wrought by Christ in favor of his virgins and priests. He bewitches them by numerous texts of Scripture, though they have not the slightest reference to such vows.

The strangest of these abuses is made using Matthew 19:12: "For there are eunuchs which were born from their mother's womb; and there are some eunuchs which were made eunuchs of men; and there are eunuchs which have made themselves eunuchs for the kingdom of heaven's sake. He that is able to receive it, let him receive it."

Upon one occasion our superior made a very pressing appeal to our religious feelings from this text. But the address, though zealous, seemed deficient in logic. At the next conference, after respectfully asking and obtaining permission to express our objections I spoke about as follows:

"Dear and venerable sir: You told us that the following words of Christ, '*There be eunuchs which have made themselves eunuchs for the kingdom of heaven's sake*' show us that we must make the vow of celibacy and make ourselves eunuchs if we want to become priests. It seems to us that that text does not in any way show that an eunuch is nearer the kingdom of God than he who obeys the laws of God. If it was not good for man to be without his wife when he was so holy and strong in the Garden of Eden, how can it be good now that he is so weak and sinful?

"Our Saviour clearly shows that He finds no sanctifying power in the state of an eunuch. When the young man asked Him, 'Good Master, what must I do that I may have eternal life?' (Matt. 19:16), did the good Master answer him in the language we heard from you two days ago? No; but He said, 'Keep the commandments!' Would He not say to me, 'Keep the commandments!' Where is the commandment, in the Old or New Testament, to make the vow of celibacy? The promise of a place in heaven is not attached in any way to the vow of celibacy. Christ has not a word about that doctrine.

"How can we understand the reasons or the importance of such a strict and unnatural obligation in our day, when we know very well that the holy apostles themselves were living with their wives, and that the Saviour had not a word of rebuke for them?"

This free expression took our superior by surprise. He answered me with "Is that all you have to say?"

"It is not quite all we have to say," I answered; "but before we go further we would be much gratified to receive from you the light we want on the difficulties which I have just stated."

"You have spoken as a true heretic," replied Mr. Leprohon, with unusual vivacity; "and if I did not hope that you have said these things to receive the light, I would at once denounce you to the bishop. You speak of the Holy Scriptures just as a Protestant would. You appeal to them as the only source of Christian truth and knowledge. Have you forgotten the holy traditions, the authority of which is equal to the Scriptures?

"You are correct that the Bible does not enforce the vows of celibacy. But we find it in the holy traditions. The vow of celibacy is ordered by Jesus Christ, through His Church. The ordinances of the Church bind our consciences just as the commandments of God upon Mount Sinai. There is no salvation to those who do not submit their reason to the teachings of the Church.

"You are not required to understand all the reasons for the vow of celibacy; but you are bound to believe in its *necessity* and *holiness*, as the Church has pronounced her verdict upon that question. It is not your business to argue; but your duty is to obey the Church, as dutiful children obey a kind mother.

"But who can doubt when we remember that Christ ordered His apostles to separate themselves from their wives? St. Peter said to our Saviour, 'Behold, we have forsaken all and followed Thee; what shall we have, therefore?' (Matt. 19:27) Is not the priest the true representative of Christ on earth? In his ordination, is not the priest made the equal and in a sense the superior of Christ? For when he celebrates Mass he commands Christ, and that very Son of God is bound to obey. He must come down from heaven every time the priest orders Him. The priest shuts Him up in the holy tabernacles or takes Him out of them, according to his own will.

"By becoming priests you will be raised to a dignity much above angels. The priest must raise himself to a degree of holiness much above the level of the common people, a holiness equal to that of the angels. Has not our Saviour, when speaking of the angels, said, 'They marry not, nor are given in marriage?' Surely, since the priests are the messengers and angels of God, on earth they must be clad with angelic holiness and purity.

"Does not Paul say that virginity is superior to marriage? Does not that saying of the apostle show that the priest, whose hands every day touch the divine body and blood of Christ, must be chaste and pure, not defiled by the duties of married life? Jesus Christ, through His holy Church, commands that vow to His priests as the most efficacious remedy against our corrupt nature.

"I will be happy to answer your other objections, if you have any more," said Mr. Leprohon.

"We are much obliged to you for your answers," I replied, "and we will avail ourselves of your kindness to present you with some other observations.

"But first, thank you for having told us that the Word of God does not support the vows of celibacy, that only the traditions of the Church prove their necessity and holiness. It appeared that you desired us to believe it was founded on the Holy Scriptures. If you permit, we will discuss the traditions another time, and will confine ourselves today to the different texts to which you referred in favor of celibacy.

"When Peter says, 'We have given up everything,' it seems to us that he had no intention of saying that he had forever given up his wife by a vow. For St. Paul positively says, many years after, that Peter had his wife; that he was not only living with her in his own house, but was traveling with her when preaching the gospel. The words of Scripture can neither be obscured by any shrewd explanation nor by any tradition.

"Though you know the words of Paul on that subject, you will allow us to read them: 'Have we not power to eat and drink? have we not power to lead about a sister, a wife, as well as other apostles and as the brethren of the Lord, and Cephas?' (I Cor. 9:4-5) St. Peter saying 'We have forsaken everything' could not then mean that he would never live with his wife as a married man. Evidently the words of Peter mean only that Jesus had the first place in his heart, that everything else, even the dearest objects of his love, as father, mother, wife, were only secondary in his affections and thoughts.

"Your other text about the angels does not seem to bear on that subject. When our Saviour speaks of men who are like angels, and who do not marry, He speaks of the state of men *after the resurrection.* If the church had the same rule for us we would not have the slightest objection.

"You tell us that the vow of celibacy is the best remedy against the inclinations of our corrupt nature. Is it not strange that God does tell us that the best remedy he had prepared against the inclinations of our corrupt nature is in the blessings of a holy marriage? But now our Church has found another remedy, which is more accordant to the dignity of man and the holiness of God, and that remedy is the vow of celibacy!"

Our venerable superior, unable any longer to conceal his indignation, abruptly interrupted me, saying: "I do exceedingly regret to have allowed you to go so far. This is not a Christian and humble discussion between young Levites and their superior, to receive from him the light they want. It is the exposition and defense of the most heretical doctrines I have ever heard. Are you not ashamed, when you try to make us prefer your interpretation of the Holy Scriptures to that of the Church? Is it to you, or to His holy Church, that Christ promised the light of the Holy Ghost? Is it you who teach the Church, or the Church who must teach you? Is it you who will govern and guide the Church, or the Church who will govern and guide you?

"My dear Chiniquy, if there is not a great and prompt change in you and in those whom you pretend to represent, I fear much for you all. You show a spirit of infidelity and revolt which frightens me. Just like Lucifer, you rebel against the Lord! Do you not fear the eternal pains of his rebellion?

"You are supporting a Protestant error when you say that the apostles were living with their wives in the usual way. It is true that Paul says that the apostles had women with them, and that they were even traveling with them. But the holy traditions of the Church tell us that those women were holy virgins, traveling with the apostles, ministering to their different wants, washing their underclothes, preparing their meals, just like the housekeeper whom the priests have today. It is a Protestant impiety to think and speak otherwise.

"But only a word more, and I am done. If you accept the teaching of the Church, and submit yourselves as dutiful children to that most holy Mother, she will raise you to the dignity of the priesthood, a dignity much above kings and emperors in this world. If you serve her with fidelity, she will secure to you the respect and veneration of the whole world while you live, and procure you a crown of glory in heaven.

"But if you reject her doctrines, and persist in your rebellious views and listen to your own deceitful reason rather than the Church, in interpreting the Holy Scriptures, you become heretics, apostates and Protestants. You will lead a dishonored life in this world, and you will be lost for all eternity."

Our superior left us immediately after these fulminating words. Some of the theological students, after his exit, laughed heartily, and thanked me for having so bravely fought and gained so glorious a victory. Two of them, disgusted by the logical absurdities of our superior, left the seminary a few days later.

Had I listened to my conscience I would have left the seminary that day. I had confounded my superior and pulverized all his arguments. Reason told me that the vow of celibacy was a sin against logic, morality and God. But I was a most sincere Roman Catholic. More than ever I determined to have no knowledge, no thought, no will, no light, no desires, no science but that which my Church would give me through my superior. I was fallible, she was infallible! I was a sinner, she was the immaculate spouse of Jesus Christ! I was weak, she had more power than the great waters of the ocean! I was but an atom, she was covering the world with her glory! What, therefore, could I have to fear in humbling myself at her feet, to live of her life, to be strong of her strength, wise of her wisdom, holy with her holiness? Had not my superior repeatedly told me that no error, no sin would be imputed to me as long as I obeyed my Church and walked in her ways?

With these sentiments of a most profound and perfect respect for my Church, I irrevocably consecrated myself to her service on the 4th of May, 1832, by making the vow of celibacy and accepting the office of subdeacon.

CHAPTER XV

"The mother of harlots and abominations" — Rev. xvii.5.

Before the day on which the theology of Rome was inspired by Satan, the world had certainly witnessed many dark deeds; but vice had never been clothed with the mantle of theology: the most shameful forms of iniquity had never been the objects of the most minute study, under the pretext of saving the world and glorifying God.

Let those who would understand read "The Priest, the Woman, and the Confessional," and decide whether they are not enough to shock the feelings of the most depraved.

Has the world ever witnessed such sacrilege? A young man about twenty years of age has been enticed to make a vow of perpetual celibacy, and the very next day the Church of Rome fills his memory with the most disgusting images! Rome does not even try to conceal the overwhelming power of this kind of teaching; but BRAVELY TELLS them that the study of those questions will act with an irresistible power upon their organs, and without a blush says that "pollution must follow!!!"

But in order that she may more certainly destroy her victims, she tells them, "There is no sin for you in those pollutions!" (Dens, vol. i. p. 315.)

How can the Roman Catholic nations hope to raise themselves in the scale of Christian dignity and morality as long as there remain priests in their midst, bound in conscience every day to pollute the minds and the hearts of their mothers, their wives and their daughters!

And let me say, once for all, that I do not speak from contempt or unchristian feeling against the professors who initiated me into those mysteries of iniquity. They were crushed, like us, under a yoke which bound their understanding and polluted their hearts without measure. Every time they gave us our lessons, it was evident that they blushed in the inmost part of their souls. Their consciences as honest men were forbidding them to open their mouths on such matters, while, on the other hand, as slaves and priests of the pope, they were compelled to speak without reserve.

After our lessons we students were filled with such shame that sometimes we hardly dared to look at each other. More than one of my fellow students told me, with tears of shame and rage, that they regretted to have bound themselves by perpetual oaths to minister at the altars of the Church.

One day one of the students, Desaulnier, who was sick in the same room with me, asked: "Chiniquy, what do you think of our present theological studies? Is it not a burning shame that we must allow our minds to be so polluted?"

"I cannot sufficiently tell you my feelings of disgust," I answered.

"Do you know," said Desaulnier, "that I am determined never to consent to be ordained as a priest; for when I think of the fact that the priest is bound to confer with the women on all these polluting matters, I feel an insurmountable disgust and shame."

"I am not less troubled," I replied. "My head aches and my heart sinks when I hear our theologians telling us that we will be in conscience bound to speak to strange women on matters so defiling!"

"But we are near the hour at which the good Mr. Leprohon is in the habit of visiting us. Will you," I said, "promise to stand by me in what I will ask him on this subject? I am sure our pure and holy superior has never said a word to females on those degrading matters. In spite of all the theologians, surely he will allow us to keep our tongues and our hearts, as well as our bodies, pure in the confessional."

"I have had the desire to speak to him for some time," rejoined Desaulnier, "but my courage always failed me. I will certainly support you. If we are at liberty never to speak to women on these horrors, I will consent to serve the Church as a priest; but if not, I WILL NEVER BE A PRIEST."

A few minutes later our superior entered to see how we were. I thanked him and opened the volumes of Dens and Liguori to one of the infamous chapters and said to him with a blush, "After God, you have the first place in my heart since my mother's death, and you know it. Therefore I trust you will tell me all I want to know in these hours of anxiety. I have taken the vow of perpetual celibacy, but I had not a clear understanding of what I was doing. Dens,

Liguori and St. Thomas have directed our minds into regions which were quite new and unexplored by us. For God's sake, please tell us if we will be bound in conscience to speak in the confessional to the married and unmarried women, on such impure and defiling questions?"

"Most undoubtedly," replied Rev. Mr. Leprohon, "because the learned and holy theologians are positive on that question. It is absolutely necessary for, as a general thing, girls and married women are too timid to confess those sins, therefore they must be helped by questioning them."

"But," I rejoined, "we have made an oath that we should always remain pure and undefiled? Would it not be better to experience those things in the holy bonds of marriage, according to the laws of God, than in company and conversation with strange women?"

Here Desaulnier interrupted me: "My dear Mr. Leprohon, I concur in everything Chiniquy has just been telling you. I ask you, my dear sir, what will become of my vow of perfect and perpetual chastity, when the seducing presence of my neighbor's wife, or the enchanting words of his daughter, will have defiled me through the confessional. After all, I may be looked upon by the people as a chaste man; but what will I be in the eyes of God? Men will think that I am an angel of purity; but my own conscience will tell me that I am nothing but a skillful hypocrite. For according to all the theologians, the confessional is the tomb of the chastity of priests!"

Desaulnier's fearless and energetic words had evidently made a very painful impression upon our superior. It was not a usual thing for his disciples to speak with such freedom. He did not conceal his pain at what he called our unbecoming and unchristian attack upon some of the most holy ordinances of the Church. After he had refuted Desaulnier as best he could, he turned to me: "My dear Chiniquy, I have repeatedly warned you against the habit you have of listening to your own frail reasoning. Were we to believe you, we would immediately set to work to reform the Church and abolish the confession of women to priests; we would throw all our theological books into the fire and have new ones written, better adapted to your fancy. The devil of pride is tempting you as he has tempted all the so-called Reformers. If you do not take care, you will become another Luther!

"The theological books of St. Thomas, Liguori and Dens have been approved by the Church. On one side, then, I see all our holy popes and Catholic bishops, all our learned theologians and priests and on the other side what do I see? Nothing but my small, though very dear Chiniquy!

"Is it not just as absurd for you to reform the Church by your small reason, as it is for the grain of sand at the foot of the great mountain to try to turn that mighty mountain out of its place?

"Take my friendly advice," continued our superior, "before it is too late. Let the small grain of sand remain still at the foot of the majestic mountain. All the good priests before us have had their souls saved, even when their bodies were polluted; for those carnal pollutions are nothing but human miseries, which cannot defile a soul which desires to remain united to God. So the heart of a good priest, as I hope my dear Chiniquy will be, will remain pure and holy in spite of the accidental and unavoidable defilement of the flesh.

"Apart from those things, in your ordination you will receive a special grace which will change you into another man; and the Virgin Mary, to whom you will constantly address yourself, will obtain for you a perfect purity from her Son.

"The defilement of the flesh spoken of by the theologians, and which, I confess, is unavoidable when hearing the confessions of women, must not trouble you; for they are not sinful, as Dens and Liguori assure us. (Dens. vol. i., pages 299, 300.)

"But enough. I forbid you to speak to me any more on those idle questions, and, as much as my authority is anything to you both, I forbid you to say a word more to each other on that matter!!"

I had hoped for some good and reasonable arguments; but he, to my surprise, silenced the voice of our conscience by *un coup d'etat.* Desaulnier, just as he had foretold me, refused to be a priest. He remained all his life in the orders of sub-deaconate, in the College of Nicolet, as a Professor of Philosophy.

He was a good logician and a profound mathematician; and although affable to everyone, he was not communicative. I was probably the only one to whom he opened his mind concerning the great questions of Christianity: faith, history, the Church and her discipline. He repeatedly said to me: "I wish I had never opened a book of theology. Our theologians are without heart, soul or logic. Many of them approve of theft, lies and perjury; others drag us without a blush into the most filthy pits of iniquity. Every one of them would like to make an assassin of every Catholic. According to their doctrine, Christ is nothing but a Corsican brigand, whose bloodthirsty disciples are bound to destroy all the heretics with fire and sword. Were we acting according to the principles of those theologians, we would slaughter all Protestants with the same coolness as we would shoot the wolf. With their hand still reddened with the blood of St. Bartholomew, they speak to us of charity, religion and God."

For me, the idea of that miserable grain of sand which so ridiculously attempted to remove the stately mountain, singularly struck and humbled me. I remained silent and confused, though not convinced. Almost every month which I had passed in the seminary of Nicolet, priests of the district of Three Rivers and elsewhere were sent by the bishops to spend two to three weeks in doing penances for having bastards by their nieces, their housekeepers, or their fair penitents. These public and undeniable facts were not much in harmony with those beautiful theories of our venerable director. But my respect for Mr. Leprohon sealed my lips.

In my room I fell on my knees to ask God to pardon me for having, for a moment, thought otherwise than the popes and theologians of Rome. But, alas! I was not yet aware that when Jesus in His mercy sends into a perishing soul a single ray of His grace, that there is more light and wisdom in that soul than in all the popes and their theologians!

God alone knows what a dark and terrible night I passed after this meeting! I had again to smother my conscience, dismantle my reason, and bring them all under the turpitudes of the theologies of Rome, which are so well calculated to keep the world fettered in ignorance and superstition.

CHAPTER XVI

There are several imposing ceremonies at the ordination of a priest; and I will never forget the joy I felt when the Roman Pontiff, presenting to me the Bible, ordered me, with a solemn voice, to study and preach it. That order passed through my soul as a beam of light. When holding the sacred volume, I accepted the command with unspeakable joy but I felt as if a thunderbolt had fallen upon me when I pronounced the awful oath which is required from every priest: *"I will never interpret the Holy Scriptures except according to the unanimous consent of the Holy Fathers."*

Many times the other students and I had discussed that strange oath. Alone in the presence of God, my conscience had shrunk in terror from its consequences. But I was not the only one who contemplated its evidently blasphemous nature.

About six months before, Stephen Baillargeon, one of my fellow theological students, had said to our superior, the Rev. Mr. Raimbault: "One of the things which my conscience cannot reconcile is the solemn oath we will have to take never to interpret the Scriptures except according to the *unanimous* consent of the

Holy Fathers! We have not given a single hour yet to the serious study of the Holy Fathers. I know many priests and none of them has ever studied the Holy Fathers!

"In the name of common sense, how can we swear that we will follow the sentiments of men of whom we know absolutely nothing, and about whom, it is more probable, we will never know anything, except by mere vague hearsay?"

Our superior gave a weak answer, but his embarrassment grew when I said: "If you will allow me, Mr. Superior, I have some more formidable objections. Would to God that I could say, with Baillargeon, I know nothing of the Holy Fathers. But my regret is that we know already too much of the Holy Fathers to be exempt from perjuring ourselves, when we swear that we will not interpret the Holy Scriptures except according to their *unanimous* consent.

"Please, Mr. Superior, tell us what are the texts of Scripture on which the Holy Fathers are *unanimous*. You respect yourself too much to answer. And if you, one of the most learned men of France, cannot put your finger on the texts of the Holy Bible and say, 'The Holy Fathers are perfectly unanimous on these texts!' how can we dare to swear before God and men to interpret *every text of the Scriptures* only according to the unanimous consent of those Holy Fathers?

"The consequences of that oath are *legion*, and every one of them seems to me the death of our ministry, the damnation of our souls! Henrion, Berrault, Bell, Costel, and Fleury all testify that the Church has constantly been filled with the noise of the controversies of Holy Fathers with Holy Fathers. Some say, with our best modern theologians, St. Thomas, Bellarmine and Liquori, that we must kill heretics as we kill wild beasts; while many others say that we must tolerate them! You all know the name of the Holy Father who sends to hell all the widows who marry a second time, while other Holy Fathers disagree.

"Some had very different notions about purgatory. Others in Africa and Asia refused to accept the supreme jurisdiction of the pope over all churches. Several have laughed at the excommunications of the popes, and gladly died without doing anything to reconcile themselves to him! And have you not concluded that St. Jerome and St. Augustine agreed on only one thing, which was to disagree on every subject they treated? St. Augustine, at the end of his life, even agreed with the Protestants of our day, that 'upon that rock' means only Christ, and not Peter.

"And now we are gravely asked, in the name of the God of Truth, to swear that we will interpret the Holy Scriptures only according to the *unanimous consent* of those Holy Fathers, who have been unanimous but in one thing, which was never to agree with each other, and sometimes not even with themselves.

"If you require from us an oath, why put into our hands the history of the Church, which has stuffed our memory with the endless fierce divisions of the Holy Fathers on almost every question which the Scriptures present to our faith?

"If I am too ignorant or stupid to understand St. Mark, St. Luke and St. Paul, how can I be intelligent enough to understand Jerome, Augustine and Tertullian? And if St. Matthew, St. John and St. Peter have not got from God the grace of writing with a sufficient degree of light and clearness to be understood by men of goodwill, how is it that Justin, Clemens and Cyprian have received from our God a favor which He denied to His apostles and evangelists? If I cannot rely upon my private judgment when studying, with the help of God, the Holy Scriptures, how can I rely on my private judgment when studying the Holy Fathers?

"This dogma, or article of our religion, by which we must go to the Holy Fathers in order to know what 'The Lord saith,' and not to the Holy Scriptures, is to my soul what a handful of sand would be to my eyes. It makes me perfectly blind.

"What a frightful alternative we have! We must either perjure ourselves, by swearing to follow a unanimity which is a fable, in order to remain Roman Catholics, or we must plunge into the abyss of impiety and atheism by refusing to swear that we will adhere to a unanimity which never existed."

It was visible during the class that we had spoken the sentiments of every one of the students in theology. But our Superior did not dare to face or answer a single one of our arguments. His embarrassment was only surpassed by his joy when the bell announced the end of the class.

He promised to answer us but the next day he did nothing but throw dust into our eyes and abuse us to his heart's content. He began by forbidding me to read any more of the controversial books I had bought and I had to give back other books which I had been given liberty, as a privilege, to read. It was decided that my intelligence was not clear enough, and that my faith was not sufficiently strong to read those books. I had nothing to do but to bow my head under the yoke and obey, without a word. The darkest night was made around our understandings, and we had to believe that that awful darkness was the shining light of God! We did the most degrading action a man can do, we silenced the voice of our conscience, and we consented to follow our superior's views, as a brute follows the order of his master.

During the months before my ordination, I did all I could to annihilate my thoughts on that subject. But, to my dismay, when the time came to perjure myself, a chill of horror and shame ran through my frame in spite of myself. In my inmost soul my wounded conscience cried, "You annihilate the Word of God! You rebel against the Holy Ghost! You deny the Holy Scriptures to follow the steps of sinful men! You reject the pure waters of eternal life, to drink the waters of death."

In order to choke again the voice of my conscience, I did what my Church advised me to do — I cried to my wafer god and to the blessed Virgin Mary that they might come to my help, and silence the voices which were troubling my peace by shaking my faith.

With the utmost sincerity, the day of my ordination, I renewed the promise that I had already so often made, and said in the presence of God and His angels, "I promise that I will never believe anything except according to the teachings of my Holy and Apostolic Church of Rome."

And on that pillow of folly, ignorance, and fanaticism I laid my head to sleep the sleep of spiritual death, with the millions of slaves whom the pope sees at his feet.

And I slept that sleep till the God of our salvation, in His great mercy, awoke me, by giving my soul the light, the truth, and the life which are in Jesus Christ.

CHAPTER XVII

I was ordained in the Cathedral of Quebec, September, 1833, by the Right Reverend Signaie, first Archbishop of Canada. This delegate of the pope, by imposing his hands on my head, gave me the power of converting a real wafer into the real substantial body, blood, soul and divinity of Jesus Christ! The bright illusion of Eve, when the deceiver told her "Ye shall be as gods," was child's play compared with what I felt. My infallible Church placed me, not only on equal terms with my Saviour and God, but in reality above Him! Hereafter I would not only command, but *create* Him, not in a spiritual and mystical, but in a real, personal and most irresistible way.

The dignity which I had just received was above all the dignities and thrones of this world. I was to be a priest of my God for ever and ever. Christ now so perfectly associated me with Himself as the great and eternal Sacrificer, that I was to renew, every day of my life, His atoning SACRIFICE! At my bidding, the only and eternally begotten Son of my God was now to come into my hands in

Person! The same Christ who sits at the right hand of the Father was to come down every day to unite His flesh to my flesh, His blood to my blood, His divine soul to my poor sinful soul, in order to walk, work and live in me and with me in the most perfect unity and intimacy!

I passed that whole day and the greater part of the night in contemplating these superhuman honors and dignities. Many times I fell on my knees to thank God for His mercies towards me. In the presence of God and His angels, I said to my lips and my tongue, "Be holy now; for you will not only speak to your God: you will give Him a new birth every day!" I said to my heart, "Be holy and pure now; for you will bear every day the Holy of Holies!" To my soul I said, "Be holy now; for you will henceforth be most intimately and personally united to Christ Jesus. You will be fed with the body, blood, soul and divinity of Him before whom the angels do not find themselves pure enough!"

Looking on my table, where my pipe, filled with tobacco, and my snuff-box were lying, I said: "Impure and noxious weeds, you will no more defile me! I am the priest of the Almighty. It is beneath my dignity to touch you any more!" and opening the window I threw them into the street, never to make use of them again.

The next day I was to say my first Mass, and work that incomparable miracle which the Church of Rome calls TRANSUBSTANTIATION. Long before dawn I was dressed and on my knees. This was to be the most holy and glorious day of my life! Raised the day before to great dignity, I was now, for the first time, to work a miracle at the altar which no angel or seraph could do.

It is not an easy thing to go through all the ceremonies of a Mass. There are more than *one hundred different ceremonies and positions* of the body which must be observed with the utmost perfection. To omit *one* of them willingly, or through a culpable neglect or ignorance, is eternal damnation. But thanks to a dozen exercises the previous week, and to the kind friends who guided me, I went through the performances much more easily than I expected. It lasted about an hour. But when it was over, I was really exhausted by the effort made to keep my mind and heart in unison with the infinite greatness of the mysteries accomplished by me.

To make one's self believe that he can convert a piece of bread into God requires such a supreme effort of the will, and complete annihilation of intelligence, that the state of the soul, after the effort is over, is more like death than life.

I had really persuaded myself that I had done the most holy and sublime action of my life, when, in fact I had been guilty of the most outrageous act of idolatry! My eyes, my hands and lips, my mouth and tongue, and all my senses and intelligence, were telling me that what I had seen, touched, eaten, was nothing but a wafer; but the voices of the pope and his Church were telling me that it was the real body, blood, soul and divinity of Jesus Christ. I had persuaded myself that the voices of my senses and intelligence were the voices of Satan, and that the deceitful voice of the pope was the voice of the God of Truth! Every priest of Rome must come to that strange folly and perversity, every day of his life, to remain a priest of Rome.

"I must carry the 'good God' tomorrow to a sick man," says the priest to his servant girl. "But there are no more particles in the tabernacle. Make some small cakes that I may consecrate them tomorrow." And the obedient domestic takes some wheat flour, for no other kind of flour is fit to make the god of the pope. A mixture of any other kind would make the miracle of "transubstantiation" a great failure. The servant girl accordingly takes the dough and bakes it between two heated irons. When the whole is well baked, she takes her scissors and cuts those wafers, which are about four or five inches large, into smaller ones of the size of an inch, and respectfully hands them over to the priest.

The next morning the priest takes the newly-baked wafers to the altar, and changes them into the body, blood, soul, and divinity of Jesus Christ. It was one of those wafers that I had taken to the altar in that solemn hour of my first Mass, and which I had turned into my Saviour by the five magical words — HOC EST ENIM CORPUS MEUM!

Where, I ask, is the difference between the adoration of the calf-god of Aaron and the wafer-god which I had made on September 22, 1833? The only difference was, that the idolatry of Aaron lasted but one day, while the idolatry in which I lived lasted a quarter of a century, and has been perpetuated in the Church of Rome for more than a thousand years.

What has the Church of Rome done by giving up the words of Christ, "Do this in remembrance of Me," and substituting her dogma of Transubstantiation? She has brought the world back to the old heathenism. The priest of Rome worships a Saviour called Christ. Yes; but that Christ is not the Christ of the gospel. It is a false Christ smuggled from the Pantheon of Rome, and sacrilegiously called by the adorable name of our Saviour, Jesus Christ.

I have often been asked: "Was it possible that you sincerely believed that the wafer could be changed into God by you?" And, "Have you really worshiped that wafer as your Saviour?"

To my shame, and to the shame of poor humanity, I must say "Yes."

I was saying to the people, as I presented it to them, "This is the lamb of God, who takes away the sins of the world; let us adore Him;" and prostrating myself on my knees I was adoring the god made by myself, with the help of my servant; and all the people prostrated themselves to adore the newly-made god!

I must confess, further, that though I was bound to believe in the existence of Christ in heaven, and was invited by my Church to worship Him as my Saviour and my God, I had, as every Roman Catholic has, more confidence, faith, and love towards the Christ which I had created with a few words of my lips than towards the Christ of heaven.

My Church told me that though the Christ of heaven was angry against me on account of my sins; that He was constantly disposed to punish me, according to His terrible justice; that He was armed with lightning and thunder to crush me; and that, were it not for His mother, who day and night was interceding for me, I should be cast into hell for my sins. Not only had I to believe this doctrine, but I had to preach it to the people.

Besides this, I had to believe that the Christ of heaven was a mighty monarch, a most glorious king, surrounded by innumerable hosts of servants, officers and friends, and that it would not do for a poor rebel to present himself before his irritated King to get his pardon but he must address himself to some of His most influential courtiers, or to His beloved mother, to whom nothing can be refused, that they might plead his cause.

But there were no such terrors or fears in my heart when I approached the Saviour whom I had created myself! Such an humble and defenseless Saviour, surely had no thunder in His hands to punish His enemies. He could have no angry looks for me. He was my friend, as well as the work of my hands. Had I not brought Him down from heaven? And had He not come into my hands that He might hear, bless, and forgive me? that He might be nearer to me, and I nearer to Him?

No words can give any idea of the pleasure I used to feel when alone, prostrated before the Christ whom I had made at the morning Mass, I poured out my heart at His feet. It is impossible for those who have not lived under those terrible illusions to understand with what confidence I spoke to the Christ who was then before me, bound by the ties of His love for me! How many times, in the colder days of winter, in churches which had never seen any fire, with an atmosphere 15 degrees below zero, had I passed whole hours alone, in adoration of the Saviour whom I had made only a few hours before!

How often have I looked with silent admiration to the Divine

Person who was there alone, passing the long hours of the day and night, rebuked and forsaken, that I might have an opportunity of approaching Him, and of speaking to Him as a friend to his friend, as a repenting sinner to his merciful Saviour. My faith, I should rather say my awful delusion, was then so complete that I scarcely felt the biting of the cold! I may say with truth, that the happiest hours I ever had, during the long years of darkness into which the Church of Rome had plunged me, were the hours which I passed in adoring the Christ whom I had made with my own lips. And every priest of Rome would make the same declaration were they questioned on the subject.

It is a similar principle of monstrous faith that leads widows in India to leap with cries of joy into the fire which will burn them into ashes with the bodies of their deceased husbands. Their priests have assured them that such a sacrifice will secure eternal happiness to themselves and their departed husbands.

In fact, the Roman Catholics have no other Saviour to whom they can betake themselves than the one made by the consecration of the wafer. He is the only Saviour who is not angry with them, and who does not require the mediation of virgins and saints to appease His wrath. This is the reason why Roman Catholic churches are so well filled by the poor blind Roman Catholics. See how they rush to the foot of their altars at almost every hour of the day, sometimes long before the dawn! Even on a stormy morning, you will see crowds of worshipers walking through the mud to pass an hour at the foot of their tabernacles!

Every soul yearns for a God to whom it can speak, and who will hear its supplications with a merciful heart, and who will wipe away the penitential tears.

The children of light, the disciples of the gospel, who protest against the errors of Rome, know that their Heavenly Father is *everywhere* ready to hear, forgive, and help them. They find Jesus in their most secret closets when they enter them to pray; they meet Him when in the fields, behind the counter, and while traveling. Everywhere they meet with Him, and speak to Him as friend to friend.

It is not so with the followers of the pope. They are told contrary to the gospel (Matt. 24:23), that Christ is in this Church, in that secret chamber or tabernacle! Cruelly deceived by their priests, they run, they brave the storms to go as near as possible to that place where their merciful Christ lives. They go to the Christ who will give them a hearty welcome, who will listen to their humble prayers, and be compassionate to their tears of repentance.

Let Protestants cease to admire poor deluded Roman Catholics who dare the storm and go to church even before the dawn of day. This devotion, which so dazzles them, should excite compassion, and not admiration; for it is the logical result of the most awful spiritual darkness. It is the natural consequence of the belief that the priest of Rome can create Christ and God by the consecration of a wafer, and keep Him in a secret chamber.

The Egyptians worshiped God under the form of crocodiles and calves. The Greeks made their gods of marble or of gold. The Persian made the sun his god. The Hottentots make their gods with whalebone, and go far through the storms to adore them. The Church of Rome makes her god out of a piece of bread! Is this not idolatry?

From the year 1833 to the day that God in His mercy opened my eyes, my servant had used more than a bushel of wheat flour to make the little cakes which I had to convert into the Christ of the Mass. Some of these I ate; others I carried about with me for the sick, and others I placed in the tabernacle for the adoration of the people.

I am often asked, "How is it that you could be guilty of such a gross act of idolatry?" My only answer is the answer of the blind man of the gospel: "I know not; one thing I know, that, whereas I was blind, now I see." (John 9:25)

CHAPTER XVIII

In the month of January, 1834, I heard the following account from the Rev. Mr. Paquette, curate of St. Gervais, at a grand dinner which he had given to the neighboring priests:

"When young, I was the vicar of a curate who could eat as much as two of us, and drink as much as *four*. He was tall and strong, and he has left the dark marks of his hard fists on the nose of more than one of his beloved sheep; for his anger was really terrible after he had drunk a bottle of wine.

"One day, after a sumptuous dinner, he was called to carry the 'good god' (Le Bon Dieu), to a dying man. It was in midwinter. The cold was intense. The wind was blowing hard. There were at least five or six feet of snow, and the roads were almost impassable. It was really a serious matter to travel nine miles on such a day, but there was no help. The messenger was one of the first elders and the dying man was one of the first citizens of the place. The curate, after a few grumblings, drank a tumbler of good Jamaica with his driver, as a preventive against the cold; went to church, took the 'good god' (Le Bon Dieu), and threw himself into the sleigh, wrapped as well as possible in his large buffalo robes.

"Though there were two horses, one before the other, to drag the sleigh, the journey was a long and tedious one, which was made still worse by an unlucky circumstance. They were met half way by another traveler coming from the opposite direction. The road was too narrow to allow the two sleighs and horses to remain easily on firm ground when passing. When once horses are sunk into five or six feet of snow, the more they struggle the deeper they sink.

"The driver, who was carrying the 'good god,' with the curate, naturally hoped to have the privilege of keeping the middle of the road, and escaping the danger of getting his horses wounded and his sleigh broken. He cried to the other traveler in a high tone of authority, 'Traveler! let me have the road. Turn your horses into the snow. Make haste, I am in a hurry. I carry the 'good god!'

"Unfortunately that traveler was a heretic, who cared much more for his horses than for the 'good god.' He answered: 'The devil take your "good god" before I break the neck of my horse. If your god has not taught you the rules of law and of common sense, I will give you a free lecture on that matter,' and jumping out of his sleigh he took the reins of the front horse of the curate to help him to walk on the side of the road, and keep the half of it for himself.

"But the driver, who was naturally a very impatient and fearless man, had drunk too much with my curate before he left the parsonage, to keep cool, as he ought to have done. He also jumped out of his sleigh, ran to the stranger, took his collar in his left hand and raised his right to strike him in the face.

"Unfortunately for him, the heretic seemed to have foreseen all this. He had left his overcoat in the sleigh, and was more ready for the conflict than his assailant. He was also a real giant in size and strength. As quick as lightning his right and left fists fell like iron masses on the face of the poor driver, who was thrown upon his back in the soft snow, where he almost disappeared.

"Till then the curate had been a silent spectator; but the sight and cries of his friend, whom the stranger was pommelling without mercy, made him lose his patience. Taking the little silk bag which contained the 'good god' from about his neck, he put it on the seat of the sleigh, and said, 'Dear good god! Please remain neutral; I must help my driver. Take no part in this conflict, and I will punish that infamous Protestant as he deserves.'

"But the unfortunate driver was entirely put out of combat before the curate could go to his help. His face was horribly cut, three teeth were broken, the lower jaw dislocated, and the eyes were so terribly damaged that it took several days before he could see anything.

"When the heretic saw the priest coming to renew the battle, he threw down his other coat, to be freer in his movements. The curate had not been so wise. Relying too much on his herculean strength, covered with his heavy overcoat, he threw himself on the stranger.

"Both of these combatants were real giants, and the first blows must have been terrible on both sides. But the 'infamous heretic' probably had not drunk so much as my curate before leaving home, or perhaps he was more expert in the exchange of these savage blows. The battle was long, and the blood flowed pretty freely on both sides. The cries of the combatants might have been heard at a long distance, were it not for the roaring noise of the wind which at that instant was blowing a hurricane.

"The storm, the cries, the blows, the blood, the surplice, and the torn clothing reddened with gore, made such a terrible spectacle, that the horses of the curate took fright and threw themselves into the snow, turned their backs to the storm and made for home. They dragged the fragments of the upset sleigh a pretty long distance, and arrived at the door of their stable with only some diminutive parts of the harness.

"The 'good god' had evidently heard the prayer of my curate, and he had remained neutral; at all events, he had not taken the part of his priest, for he lost and the infamous Protestant remained master of the battlefield. The curate had to help his driver out of the snow where he had lain buried like a slaughtered ox. Both had to crawl nearly half a mile in snow before they could reach the nearest farmhouse, where they arrived when it was dark.

"But the worst is not told. The horses had dragged the sleigh a certain distance, upset and smashed it. The little silk bag, with the silver box and its precious contents, was lost in the snow, and though several hundred people had looked for it, it could not be found. It was only late in the month of June, that a little boy, seeing some rags in the mud of the ditch along the highway lifted them and a little silver box fell out. Suspecting that it was what the people had looked for so many days during the last winter, he took it to the parsonage.

"I was there when it was opened; we had the hope that the 'good god' would be found pretty intact, but we were doomed to be disappointed. *The 'good god' was entirely melted away. Le Bon Dieu etait fondu!*"

"During the recital of that spicy story, which was told in the most amusing and comical way, the priests had drunk freely and laughed heartily. But when the conclusion came: "Le Bon Dieu etait fondu!" there was a burst of laughter such as I never heard, the priests striking the floor with their feet, and the table with their hands, filled the house with the cries, "Le Bon Dieu est fondu!" "Le Bon Dieu est fondu!" Yes, the god of Rome, dragged away by a drunken priest, had really melted away in the muddy ditch. This glorious fact was proclaimed by his own priests in the midst of convulsive laughter, and at tables covered with scores of bottles just emptied by them!"

About the middle of March, 1839, I had one of the most unfortunate days of my priestly life. At about two o'clock in the afternoon, a poor Irishman had come in haste from beyond the high mountains to ask me to go and anoint a dying woman. It took me ten minutes to run to the church, put the "good god" in the little silver box, shut the whole in my vest pocket and jump into the Irishman's rough sleigh. The roads were exceedingly bad, and we had to go very slowly. At 7 p.m. we were yet more than three miles from the sick woman's house. It was very dark, and the horse was so exhausted that it was impossible to go any further through the gloomy forest. I determined to pass the night at a poor Irish cabin which was near the road. I knocked at the door, asked hospitality, and was welcomed with that warm hearted demonstration of respect which the Roman Catholic Irishman knows, better than any other man, how to pay to his priests.

The shanty, twenty-four feet long by sixteen wide, was built with round logs, between which was a liberal supply of clay to prevent the wind and cold from entering. Six fat, though not absolutely well-washed, healthy boys and girls, halfnaked, presented themselves around their good parents, as the living witnesses that this cabin, in spite of its ugly appearance, was really a happy home for its dwellers.

Besides the eight human beings sheltered beneath that hospitable roof, I saw, at one end, a magnificent cow, with her newborn calf, and two fine pigs. These last two boarders were separated from the rest of the family only by a branch partition two or three feet high.

"Please your reverence," said the good woman, after she had prepared her supper, "excuse our poverty, but be sure that we feel happy and much honored to have you in our humble dwelling for the night. My only regret is that we have only potatoes, milk and butter to give you for your supper. In these backwoods, tea, sugar, and wheat flour are unknown luxuries."

I thanked that good woman for her hospitality, assuring her that good potatoes, fresh butter and milk, were the best delicacies which could be offered to me in any place. I sat at the table, and ate one of the most delicious suppers of my life. The potatoes were exceedingly well-cooked, the butter, cream and milk of the best quality, and my appetite was not a little sharpened by the long journey over the steep mountains.

I had not told these good people, nor even my driver, that I had "Le Bon Dieu," the "good god," with me in my vest pocket. It would have made them too uneasy, and would have added too much to my other difficulties. When the time of sleeping arrived I went to bed with all my clothing, and I slept well; for I was very tired by the tedious and broken roads from Beauport to these distant mountains.

Next morning, before breakfast and the dawn of day, I was up, and as soon as we had a glimpse of light to see our way, I left for the house of the sick woman after offering a silent prayer.

I had not traveled a quarter of a mile when I put my hand into my vest pocket, and to my indescribable dismay I found that the little silver box, containing the "good god," was missing. A cold sweat ran through my frame. I told my driver to stop and turn back immediately, that I had lost something which might be found in the bed where I had slept. It did not take five minutes to retrace our way.

On opening the door I found the poor woman and her husband almost beside themselves. They were pale and trembling as criminals who expected to be condemned.

"Did you not find a little silver box after I left?" I said.

"O my God!" answered the desolate woman; "yes, I have found it, but would to God I had never seen it. There it is."

"But why do you regret finding it, when I am so happy to find it here, safe in your hands?" I replied.

"Ah, your reverence, you do not know what a terrible misfortune has happened to me, not more than half a minute before knocked at the door."

"What misfortune can have fallen upon you in so short a time?" I asked.

"Well, please your reverence, open the little box and you will understand me."

I opened it, but the "good god" was not in it!! Looking in the face of the poor distressed woman, I asked her, "What does this mean? It is empty!"

"It means," answered she, "that I am the most unfortunate of women! Not more than five minutes after you had left the house, I went to your bed and found that little box. Not knowing what it was I showed it to my children and to my husband. I asked him to open it, but he refused to do it. I then turned it on every side, trying to guess what it could contain, till the devil tempted me so much that I determined to open it. I came to this corner, where this pale lamp is and I opened it. But, oh my God! I do not dare to tell the rest."

At these words she fell on the floor in a fit of hysteria, her cries were piercing, her mouth was foaming. She was cruelly tearing her hair with her own hands. The shrieks and lamentations of the children were so distressing that I could hardly prevent myself from crying also.

After a few moments of the greatest agony, seeing that the poor woman was becoming calm, I addressed myself to the husband, and said: "Please give me the explanation of these strange things."

He could hardly speak at first, but as I was very pressing he told me with a trembling voice: "Please your reverence; look into that vessel which the children use, and you will perhaps understand our desolation! When my wife opened the little silver box she did not observe the vessel was there, just beneath her hands. In the opening, what was in the silver box fell into that vessel and sank! We were all filled with consternation when you knocked at the door and entered."

I felt struck with such unspeakable horror at the thought that the body, blood, soul and divinity of my Saviour, Jesus Christ, was there, sunk into that vessel that I remained speechless, and for a long time did not know what to do. At first it came into my mind to plunge my hands into the vessel and try to get my Saviour out of that sepulchre of ignominy. But I could not muster courage to do so.

At last I requested the poor desolated family to dig a hole three feet deep in the ground, and deposit it, with its contents, and I left the house, after I had forbidden them from ever saying a word about that awful calamity.

In one of the most sacred books of the laws and regulations of the Church of Rome (Missale Romanum), we read, page 58, "If the priest vomit the Eucharist, if the species appear entire, let them be reverently swallowed, unless sickness arise; for then let the consecrated species be cautiously separated and laid up in some sacred place till they are corrupted; and afterwards let them be cast into the sacrarium. But if the species do not appear, let the vomit be burned, and the ashes cast into the sacrarium."

When a priest of Rome, I was bound, with all the Roman Catholics, to believe that Christ had taken His own body, with His own hands, to His mouth; and that He had eaten Himself, not in a spiritual, but in a substantial material way! After eating Himself,

He had given it to each of His apostles, who then ate Him also!!

Has the world, in its darkest ages of paganism, ever witnessed such a system of idolatry so debasing, impious, ridiculous and diabolical in its consequences as the Church of Rome teaches in the dogma of transubstantiation!

When, with the light of the gospel in hand, the Christian goes into those horrible recesses of superstition, folly, and impiety, he can hardly believe his eyes and his ears. It seems impossible that men can consent to worship a god whom the rats can eat! A god who can be dragged away and lost in a muddy ditch by a drunken priest! A god who can be eaten, vomited, and eaten again by those who are courageous enough to eat again what they have vomited!!

The religion of Rome is not a religion; it is the mockery, the destruction, the ignominious caricature of religion. The Church of Rome, as a public fact, is nothing but the accomplishment of the awful prophecy: "Because they received not the love of the truth that they might be saved. And for this cause God shall send them strong delusion, that they should believe a lie." (II Thess. 2:10,11)

CHAPTER XIX

On the 24th September, 1833, the Rev. Mr. Casault, secretary of the Bishop of Quebec, presented to me the official letters which named me the vicar of the Rev. Mr. Perras, arch-priest and curate of St. Charles. I was soon on my way with a cheerful heart, to fill the post assigned to me by my superior.

The parish of St. Charles is beautifully situated about twenty miles southwest of Quebec, on the banks of a river. Its large farm houses and barns, neatly whitewashed with lime, were the symbols of peace and comfort.

I had often heard of the Rev. Mr. Perras as one of the most learned, pious, and venerable priests of Canada. When I arrived, he was absent on a sick call, but his sister received me with every mark of refined politeness. Under the burden of her fifty five years she had kept all the freshness and amiability of youth. After a few words of welcome, she showed me my study and sleeping room. The two rooms were the perfection of neatness and comfort. I shut the doors and fell on my knees to thank God and the blessed Virgin for having given me such a home. Ten minutes later I came back to the large parlor where I found Miss Perras waiting to offer me a glass of wine. She then told me how her brother, the curate, and herself were happy when they heard that I was to come and live with them. She had known my mother before her marriage, and she told me how she had passed several happy days in her company.

She could not speak to me of any subject more interesting than my mother; for, though she had died a few years before, she had never ceased to be present in my mind, and near and dear to my heart.

Soon curate arrived and I rose to meet him, but it is impossible to adequately express what I felt at that moment. Rev. Mr. Perras was then about sixty-five years old. He was a tall man, almost a giant. No king ever bore his head with more dignity. But his beautiful blue eyes were the embodiment of kindness. There was on his face an expression of peace, calm, piety and kindness, which entirely won my heart and my respect. When with a smile on his lips, he extended his hands towards me, I fell on my knees and said: "Mr. Perras, God sends me to you that you may be my teacher and my father. You will have to guide my first and inexperienced steps in the holy ministry. Do bless me, and pray that I may be a good priest as you are yourself."

That unpremeditated and earnest act of mine so touched the good old priest, that he could hardly speak. Leaning towards me he raised me up and pressed me to his bosom. With a voice trembling with emotion he said: "May God bless you, my dear sir, and may He also be blessed for having chosen you to help me to carry the burden of the ministry in my old age." After half an hour of the most interesting conversation, he showed me his library which was very large and composed of the best books which a priest of Rome is allowed to read; and he very kindly put it at my service.

During the eight months which it was my privilege to remain with the venerable Mr. Perras, the conversation was exceedingly interesting and I never heard from him any idle, frivolous talking, as is so much the habit among the priests. He was well versed in the literature, philosophy, history and theology of Rome. He had personally known almost all the bishops and priests of the last fifty years, and his memory was well stored with anecdotes and facts concerning the clergy, from almost the days of the conquest of Canada. I could write many interesting things, were I to publish what I heard from him, concerning the doings of the clergy. I will only give two or three of the facts of that interesting period of the church in Canada.

A couple of months before my arrival at St. Charles, the vicar who preceded me, called Lajus, had publicly eloped with one of his beautiful penitents. After three months of public scandal, she had repented and come back to her heartbroken parents. About the same time a neighboring curate, in whom I had great confidence, compromised himself also with one of his fair parishioners, in a most shameful, though less public way. These two scandals distressed me exceedingly and for nearly a week I felt so overwhelmed with shame that I dreaded to show my face in public, and I almost regretted that I ever became a priest. My nights were sleepless; I could hardly eat anything. My conversations with Mr. Perras had lost their charms.

"Are you sick, my young friend?" said he to me one day.

"No, sir, I am not sick, but I am sad."

He replied, "Can I know the cause of your sadness? You used to be cheerful and happy since you came here. Please tell me what is the matter with you? I am an old man, and I know many remedies for the soul as well as the body."

"The two last awful scandals by the priests," I answered, "are the cause of my sadness. The news has fallen upon me like a thunderbolt. Though I had heard something of that nature when I was a simple ecclesiastic in the college, the human frailty of so many, is really distressing. How can one hope to stand up on one's feet when one sees such strong men fall by one's side? What will become of our holy church in Canada, and all over the world, if her most devoted priests are so weak and have so little self respect, and so little fear of God?"

"My dear young friend," answered Mr. Perras. "Our holy church is infallible. The gates of hell cannot prevail against her; but the assurance of her perpetuity and infallibility does not rest on any human foundation. It does not rest on the personal holiness of her priests; but it rests on the promises of Jesus Christ. Her perpetuity and infallibility are a perpetual miracle. It requires the constant working of Jesus Christ to keep her pure and holy, in spite of the sins and scandals of her priests. Even the clearest proof that our holy church has a promise of perpetuity and infallibility is drawn from the very sins and scandals of her priests; for those sins and scandals would have destroyed her long ago, if Christ was not in the midst to save and sustain her.

"Just as the ark of Noah was miraculously saved by the mighty hand of God, when the waters of the deluge would otherwise have wrecked it, so our holy church is miraculously prevented from perishing in the flood of iniquities by which too many priests have deluged the world. Let, therefore, your faith and confidence in our holy church, and your respect for her, remain firm and unshaken in the midst of all these scandals. Just as the valiant soldier makes superhuman efforts to save the flag when he sees those who carried it fall on the battlefield. Oh! you will see more of our flag bearers slaughtered before you reach my age. I am near the end of my course, and, thanks be to God, my faith in our holy church is stronger than ever, though I have seen and heard many things, compared with which, the facts which just now distress you are mere trifles.

"In order the better to prepare you to the conflict, I think it is my duty to tell you a fact which I got from the late Lord Bishop Plessis. I have never revealed it to anybody, but my interest in you is so great that I will tell it to you, and my confidence in your wisdom is so absolute, that I am sure you will never abuse it. We must never let it be known to the people, for it would diminish, if not destroy their respect and confidence in us, without which, it would become almost impossible to lead them.

"I have already told you that the late venerable Bishop Plessis was my personal friend. Every summer, when he had reached the end of the three months of episcopal visitation of his diocese, he used to come and spend eight or ten days of absolute rest and enjoyment of private and solitary life with me in this parsonage. The two rooms you occupy were his, and he told me many times that the happiest days of his episcopal life were those passed in this solitude.

"One summer he came, more worn out than ever, and I was almost frightened by the air of distress which covered his face. I supposed that this was due to his extreme fatigue, and I hoped that the next morning, he would again be the most amiable and interesting of men.

"I was also completely worn out and slept soundly till three o'clock in the morning. I was then suddenly awakened by sobs and half-suppressed lamentations and prayers which were coming from the bishop's room. Without losing a moment, I went and knocked at the door, inquiring about the cause of these sobs. Evidently the poor bishop had not suspected that I could hear him.

"'Sobs! sobs!' he answered, 'What do you mean by that. Please go back to your room and sleep. Do not trouble yourself about me, I am well,' and he absolutely refused to open the door of his room. The remaining hours of the night, of course, were sleepless ones for me. The sobs of the bishop were more suppressed, but he could not prevent me from hearing them.

"The next morning his eyes were red and his face showed that he had suffered intensely. After breakfast I said to him: 'My lord, last night has been one of desolation to your lordship; for God's sake, and in the name of the sacred ties of friendship, please tell me the cause of your sorrow. It will become less the very moment you share it with your friend.'

"The bishop answered me: 'You are right when you think that I am under the burden of a great desolation; but its cause is of such a nature, that I cannot reveal it even to you, my dear friend.'

"In vain, the rest of the day, I did all that I could to persuade Monseigneur Plessis to reveal the cause of his grief. His lordship, that evening, withdrew to his sleeping room sooner than usual, but sleep was out of the question for me that night, for his desolation seemed to be so great, I feared finding my dear friend dead in his bed the next morning. I watched him from the adjoining room, from ten o'clock till the next morning. I could see that his sorrow was still more intense that night.

"I formed an extreme resolution, which I put into effect the very moment that he came out of his room the next morning. 'My Lord,' said I, 'I thought till the night before last, that you honored me with your friendship, but I see today that I was mistaken. You do not consider me as your friend, for if I were a friend worthy of your confidence, you would unburden your heart into mine. What is the use of friendship if it be not to help each other to carry the burdens of life! I found myself honored by your presence in my house, so long as I considered myself as your own friend. Besides, it seems to me very probable that the terrible burden which you want to carry alone, will kill you, and that very soon. I do not at all like the idea of finding you suddenly dead in my parsonage, and having the coroner making painful inquiries. Then, my lord, be not offended if I respectfully request your lordship to find another lodging as soon as possible.'

"My words fell upon the bishop like a thunderbolt. With a deep sigh he looked in my face with his eyes rolling in tears, and said: 'You are right, Perras, I ought never to have concealed my sorrow from such a friend as you have always been. But you are the only one to whom I can reveal it. No doubt your priestly and Christian heart will not be less broken than mine; but you will help me with your prayers and wise counsels to carry it. However, before I initiate you into such an awful mystery, we must pray.' We then knelt down and said together a chaplet to invoke the power of the Virgin Mary, after which we recited a Psalm.

"Then the bishop said: 'You know that I have just finished the visit of my immense diocese of Quebec. I will not speak to you of the people. They are in general, truly religious and faithful to the church. But the priests. O Great God! will I tell you what they are? My dear Perras, I would almost die with joy, if God would tell me that I am mistaken. But, alas! I am not mistaken. The sad, the terrible truth is this: The priests, with the exception of you and three others, are infidels and atheists! O my God! my God! what will become of the church in the hands of such wicked men!' and covering his face with his hands, the bishop burst into tears and for one hour could not say a word. I myself remained mute.

"At first I regretted having pressed the bishop to reveal such an unexpected 'mystery of iniquity.' But, after an hour of silence, almost unable to look each other in the face, I said: 'My lord, what you have told me is surely the saddest thing that I ever heard; but allow me to tell you that your sorrow is out of limits.'

"I led him to the library, and opened the pages of the history of the church, and showed him the names of more than fifty popes who had been atheists and infidels. I read to him the lives of Borgia, Alexander VI, and a dozen others, who would surely and justly be hanged today by the executioner of Quebec, were they, in that city, committing one-half of the public crimes of adultery, murder, debauchery of every kind, which they committed in Rome, Avignon, Naples, etc. I clearly proved to him that his priests, though infidels and atheists, were angels of pity, modesty, purity, and religion, when compared with a Borgia, who publicly lived as a married man with his own daughter, and had a child by her. He agreed with me that several of the Alexanders, the Johns, the Piuses, and the Leos were sunk much deeper in the abyss of iniquity than his priests.

"My conclusion was, that if our holy church had been able to resist the deadly influence of such scandals during so many centuries in Europe, she would not be destroyed in Canada, even by the legion of atheists by whom she is served today.

"The bishop acknowledged my conclusion. He thanked me for preventing him from despairing of the future of our holy church in Canada. The rest of the days which he spent with me, he was almost as cheerful and amiable as before.

"Now, my dear young friend," added Mr. Perras, "I hope you will be as reasonable and logical in your religion as Bishop Plessis, who was probably the greatest man Canada has ever had. When Satan tries to shake your faith by the scandals you see, remember that pope, who through revenge against his predecessor, had him exhumed, brought his dead body before judges, then charged him with the most horrible crimes, which he proved by the testimony of scores of eyewitnesses, got the dead pope condemned to be beheaded and dragged with ropes through the muddy streets of Rome, and thrown into the river Tiber. Yes, when your mind is oppressed by the secret crimes of the priests, which you will know, either through the confessional or by public rumor, remember that more than twelve popes have been raised to that high and holy dignity by the rich and influential prostitutes of Rome, with whom they were publicly living in the most scandalous way.

Remember young John XI, the son of Pope Sergius, who was consecrated pope when only twelve years old by the influence of his prostitute mother, Marosia, but who was so horribly profligate that he was deposed by the people and the clergy of Rome.

"Well, if our holy church has been able to pass through such storms without perishing, is it not a living proof that Christ is her pilot, that she is imperishable and infallible because St. Peter is her foundation?"

Oh, my God! Shall I confess what my thoughts were during that lecture of my curate, which lasted more than an hour! Yes, I must say the truth. When the priest was exhibiting to me the unmentionable crimes of so many of our popes, a mysterious voice was repeating to the ears of my soul the dear Saviour's words: "A good tree cannot bring forth evil fruit, neither can a corrupt tree bring forth good fruit. Every tree that bringeth not good fruit is hewn down and cast into the fire. Wherefore by their fruits ye shall know them." (Matt. 7:18-20) In spite of myself the voice of my conscience cried in thundering tones that a church, whose head and members were so horribly corrupt, could not, by any means, be the Church of Christ.

CHAPTER XX

As a general thing, the priests lived in cordial and fraternal unity, and, were, in turn, in the habit of giving a grand dinner every Thursday.

Several days in advance, preparations were made to collect everything that could please the taste of the guests. The best wines were purchased. The fattest turkeys, chickens, lambs, or sucking pigs were hunted up. The most delicate pastries were brought from the city, or made at home, at any cost. The rarest and most costly fruits and desserts were ordered. There was a strange competition among those curates, who would surpass his neighbors. Several extra hands were engaged, some days before, to help the ordinary servants to prepare the "GRAND DINNER."

The second Thursday of May, 1834, was Mr. Perras' turn, and at twelve o'clock noon, we were fifteen priests seated around the table.

I must here render homage to the sobriety and perfect moral habits of the Rev. Mr. Perras. Though he took his social glass of wine, I never saw him drink more than a couple of glasses at the same meal. I wish I could say the same thing of all those who were at his table that day.

Never did I see, before nor after, a table covered with so many tempting and delicate viands. The good curate had surpassed himself. One of the most remarkable features of these dinners was the levity, the absolute want of seriousness and gravity. Not a word was said in my presence, there, which could indicate that these men had anything else to do in this world but to eat and drink, tell and hear merry stories, laugh and lead a jolly life!

Though, at first, I was pleased with all I saw, heard and tasted; though I heartily laughed with the rest of the guests at their spicy stories about their fair penitents, or at the funny caricatures they drew of each other, I felt, by turns, uneasy. Now and then the lessons of priestly life, received from the lips of my venerable and dear Mr. Leprohon, were knocking hard at the door of my conscience. Some words of the Holy Scriptures were also making a strange noise in my soul. My own common sense was telling me that this was not quite the way Christ taught His disciples to live.

I made a great effort to stifle those troublesome voices. Sometimes I succeeded, and then I became cheerful: but a moment after I was overpowered by them, and I felt chilled, as if I had perceived on the walls of the festive room, the finger of my angry God, writing "MENE, MENE, TEKEL, UPHARSIN." Then all my cheerfulness vanished, and in spite of all my efforts to look happy, the Rev. Mr. Paquette, curate of St. Gervais, observed it on my face. That priest was probably the one who most enjoyed everything of that feast. Under the snowy mantle of sixty-five years, he had kept the warm heart and the joviality of youth. He was loved by all, particularly by the young priests, who were the objects of his constant attentions. He had always been exceedingly kind to me, and I dare say that my most pleasant hours were those passed in his parsonage.

Looking at me the very moment when my whole intellectual being was, in spite of myself, under the darkest cloud, he said: "My dear little Father Chiniquy, are you falling into the hands of some blue devils, when we are all so happy? You were so cheerful half an hour ago! Are you sick? You look as grave and anxious as Jonah, when in the big whale's stomach! Has any of your fair penitents left you to go to confess to another?"

At these funny questions, the dining-room was shaken with convulsive laughter. I wished I could join in but there was no help for it. A moment before I had seen the servant girls blush. They had been scandalized by a very improper word from a young priest about one of his young female penitents; a word which he would surely never have uttered, had he not drunk too much wine. I answered: "I am much obliged to you for your kind interest, I find myself much honored to be here in your midst; but as the brightest days are not without clouds, so it is with us all sometimes. I am young, and without experience; I have not yet learned to look at certain things in their proper light. When older, I hope I shall be wiser, and not make an ass of myself as I do today."

"Tah! tah! tah!" said old Mr. Paquette, "this is not the hour of dark clouds and blue devils. Be cheerful, as it behooves your age. There will be hours enough in the rest of your life for sadness and somber thoughts." And appealing to all, he asked, "Is not this correct, gentlemen?"

"Yes, yes," unanimously rejoined all the guests.

"Now," said the old priest, "you see that the verdict of the jury is unanimously in my favor and against you. Tell me the reason for your grief, and I pledge myself to console you, and make you happy as you were at the beginning of the dinner."

"I would rather that you continued to enjoy this pleasant hour without noticing me," I answered. "Please excuse me if I do not trouble you with the causes of my personal folly."

"Well, well," said Mr. Paquette, "I see it, the cause of your trouble is that we have not yet drank together a single glass of sherry. Fill your glass with that wine, and it will surely drown the blue devil which I see at its bottom."

"With pleasure," I said. "I feel much honored to drink with you," and I put some drops of wine into my glass.

"Oh! oh! what do I see you doing there? Only a few drops in your glass! This will not even wet the cloven feet of the blue devil which is tormenting you. It requires a full glass, an over-flowing glass to drown and finish him. Fill, then, your glass with that precious wine, the best I ever tasted in my whole life."

"But I cannot drink more than those few drops," I said.

"Why not?" he replied.

"Because, eight days before her death, my mother wrote me a letter, requesting me to promise her that I would never drink more than two glasses of wine at the same meal. I gave her that promise in my answer, and the very day she got my pledge, she left this world to convey it, written on her heart, into heaven, to the feet of her God!"

"Keep that sacred pledge," answered the old curate; "but tell me why you are so sad when we are so happy?"

"Yes, yes," said all the priests. "You know that we deeply feel for you. Please tell us the reason of this sadness."

I then answered, "It would be better for me to keep my own secret, for I know I will make a fool of myself here, but as you are unanimous in your request, you will have them.

"You well know that I have been prevented till this day from attending any of your grand dinners. Twice I had to go to Quebec. Sometimes I was not well enough to be present. Several times I was called to visit some dying person, and at other times the weather, or the roads were too bad to travel. This, then is the first grand dinner, attended by you all, which I have the honor of attending.

"But before going any further, I must tell you that during the eight months it has been my privilege to sit at Rev. Mr. Perras' table, I have never seen such things in this parsonage as have just taken place. Sobriety, moderation, truly evangelical temperance in drink and food were the invariable rule. Never a word was said which could make our poor servant girls, or the angels of God blush. Would to God that I had not been here today! For, I tell you, honestly, that I am scandalized by the epicurean table which is before us and the incredible number of bottles of most costly wines emptied at this dinner.

"However, I hope I am mistaken in my appreciation of what I have seen and heard. I hope you are all right and I am wrong. I am the youngest of you all. It is not my business to teach you, but it is my duty to be taught by you."

"Oh! oh! my dear Chiniquy," replied the old curate, "you hold the stick by the wrong end. Are we not the children of God?"

"Yes, sir," I answered, "we are the children of God."

"Now, does not a loving father give what he considers the best part of his goods to his beloved children?"

"Yes, sir," I replied.

"Is not that loving father pleased when he sees his beloved children eat and drink the good things he has prepared for them?"

"Yes, sir," was my answer.

"Then," rejoined the logical priest, "the more we, the beloved children of God, eat of these delicate viands and drink of those precious wines which our heavenly Father puts into our hands, the more He is pleased with us. The more we, the most beloved ones of God, are merry and cheerful, the more He is Himself pleased and rejoiced in His heavenly kingdom. But if God our Father is so pleased with us, why are you so sad?"

This masterpiece of argumentation was received by all (except Mr. Perras), with convulsive cries of approbation, and repeated "Bravo! bravo!"

I was too cowardly to say what I felt. I tried to conceal my increased sadness under the forced smiles of my lips. It was then half past one p.m. At two o'clock, the whole party went to the church, where, after kneeling for a quarter of an hour before their wafer God, they fell on their knees to the feet of each other, to confess their sins, and get their pardon, in the absolution of their confessors!

At three p.m. they were all gone, and I remained alone with my venerable old curate Perras. After a few moments of silence, I said to him: "My dear Mr. Perras, I have no words to express to you my regret for what I have said at your table. I beg your pardon for every word of that unfortunate and unbecoming conversation, into which I was dragged in spite of myself. When I requested Mr. Paquette to tell me in what I might be wrong, I had not the least idea that we would hear, from the lips of one of our veterans in the priesthood, the name of God connected with such deplorable and awful impieties."

Mr. Perras answered me: "Far from being displeased with what I have heard from you at this dinner, I must tell you that you have gained much in my esteem by it. I am, myself, ashamed of that dinner. We priests are the victims, like the rest of the world, of the fashions, vanities, pride and lust of that world against which we are sent to preach. The expenditure we make at those dinners is surely a crime in the face of the misery of the people by whom we are surrounded. This is the last dinner I give with such foolish extravagance. The brave words you have uttered have done me good. They will do them good also; they were not so intoxicated as not to remember what you have said."

Then, pressing my hand in his, he said, "I thank you, my good little Father Chiniquy, for the short but excellent sermon. It will not be lost. You have drawn my tears when you have shown us your saintly mother going to the feet of God in heaven, with your sacred promise written in her heart. Oh! you must have had a good mother! I knew her when she was very young. She was then, already, a very remarkable girl for her wisdom and the dignity of her manners."

Then he left me alone in the parlor and went to visit a sick man in one of the neighboring houses.

When alone I fell on my knees, to pray and weep. My soul was filled with emotions impossible to express. I could not contain myself. I wept over my own sins, for I did not find myself much better than the rest, though I had not eaten or drunk quite so much as several of them. I wept over my friends whom I had seen so weak; for they were my friends. I loved them, and I knew they loved me. I wept over my church, which was served by such poor, sinful priests. Yes! I wept there, when on my knees, to my heart's content, and it did me good. But my God had another trial in store for his poor unfaithful servant.

After my prayer, I had not been ten minutes alone sitting in my study, when I heard strange cries, and a noise as if a murderer were at work. A door had evidently been broken open upstairs and someone was running down stairs. The cries of "Murder, Murder!" reached my ears, and the cries of "Oh! my God! my God! where is Mr. Perras?" filled the air.

I quickly ran to the parlor to see what was the matter, and there I found myself face to face with a woman absolutely naked! Her long black hair was flowing on her shoulders; her face was pale as death — her dark eyes fixed in their sockets. She stretched her hands towards me with a horrible shriek, and before I could move a step, she seized my two arms with her hands. My bones were cracking under her grasp, and my flesh was torn by her nails. I tried to escape, but it was impossible. I cried for help but the living specter cried still louder: "You have nothing to fear. Be quiet. I am sent by God Almighty and the Blessed Virgin Mary to give you a message. The priests whom I have known, without a single exception, are a band of vipers; they destroy their female penitents through auricular confession. They have destroyed me, and killed my female child! Do not follow their example!" Then she began to sing with a beautiful voice, to a most touching tune, a kind of poem she had composed, which I secretly got afterwards from one of her servant maids, the translation of which is as follows:

> "Satan's priests have defiled my heart!
> Damned my soul! murdered my child!
> O my child! my darling child!
> From thy place in heaven, dost thou see
> Thy guilty mother's tears?
> Canst thou come and press me in thine arms?
> My child! my darling child!
> Will never thy smiling face console me?"

When she was singing these words, big tears were rolling down her pale cheeks, and her sad voice could have melted a heart of stone. I was petrified in the presence of that living phantom! I could not dare to touch her in any way with my hands. I felt horrified and paralyzed at the sight of that pale, cadaverous, naked specter. When the poor servant girl tried in vain to drag her away from me, she struck her with terror by crying, "If you touch me, I will instantly strangle you!"

"Where is Mr. Perras? Where is Miss Perras and the other servants? For God's sake call them," I cried out to the servant girl, who was trembling and beside herself.

"Miss Perras is running to the church after the curate," she answered, "and I do not know where the other girl is gone."

In that instant Mr. Perras entered, rushed towards his sister and said, "Are you not ashamed to present yourself naked before such a gentleman?" and with his strong arms he tried to force her to give me up.

Turning her face towards him, with tigress eyes, she cried out "Wretched brother! what have you done with my child? I see her blood on your hands!"

When she was struggling with her brother, I made a sudden and extreme effort to get out of her grasp; and this time I succeeded: but seeing that she wanted to throw herself again upon me, I jumped through a window which was opened. Quick as lightning she passed out of the hands of her brother and jumped also through the window to run after me. I promptly fell headlong, with my feet entangled in my long, black priestly robe.

Providentially, two strong men, attracted by my cries, came to my rescue. They wrapped her in a blanket and brought her back into her upper chambers, where she remained safely locked, under the guard of two strong servant maids.

The history of that woman is sad indeed. When in her priest-brother's house, when young and of great beauty, she was seduced by her father confessor, and became mother of a female child, which she loved with a real mother's heart. She determined to keep it and bring it up.

But this did not meet the views of the curate. One night, when the mother was sleeping, the child had been taken away from her. The awakening of the unfortunate mother was terrible. When she understood that she could never see her child any more, she filled the parsonage with her cries and lamentations, and, at first, refused to take any food, in order that she might die. But she soon became a maniac.

Mr. Perras, too much attached to his sister to send her to a lunatic asylum, resolved to keep her in his own parsonage, which was very large. A room in its upper part had been fixed in such a way that her cries could not be heard, and where she would have all the comfort possible in her sad circumstances. Two servant maids were engaged to take care of her. All this was so well arranged, that I had been eight months in that parsonage, without even suspecting that there was such an unfortunate being under the same roof with me.

It appears that occasionally, for many days, her mind was perfectly lucid. Then she passed her time in praying and singing the poem which she had composed herself, and which she sang while holding me in her grasp. In her best moments she had fostered an invincible hatred of the priests whom she had known. Hearing her attendants often speak of me, she had, several times, expressed the desire to see me, which, of course, had been denied her. Before she had broken her door, and escaped from the hands of her keeper, she had passed several days in saying that she had received from God a message for me which she would deliver, even if she had to pass on the dead bodies of all in the house.

Unfortunate victim of auricular confession! How many others could sing the sad words of thy song: "Satan's priests have defiled my heart. Damned my soul! murdered my child!"

CHAPTER XXI

Charlesbourgh, May 25th, 1834.

Rev. Mr. C. Chiniquy:

My Dear Sir: My Lord Panet has again chosen me, this year, to accompany him in his episcopal visit. I have consented, with the condition that you should take my place at the head of my dear parish during my absence. For I will have no anxiety when I know that my people are in the hands of a priest who, though so young, has raised himself so high in the esteem of all those who know him.

Please come as soon as possible to meet me here, that I may tell you many things which will make your ministry more easy and blessed in Charlesbourgh.

His Lordship has promised me that when you pass through Quebec, he will give you all the powers you want to administer my parish, as if you were its curate during my absence.

Your devoted brother priest, and friend in the love and
heart of Jesus and Mary,
ANTOINE BEDARD

I felt absolutely confounded by that letter. It seemed evident to me that my friends and my superiors had strangely exaggerated my feeble capacity. In my answer I respectfully remonstrated against such a choice . But a letter received from the bishop himself ordered me to go to Charlesbourgh without delay.

The Rev. Mr. Bedard welcomed me with words of such kindness that my heart was melted. He was about sixty-five years of age, short in stature, large shoulders, indomitable energy, and bright eyes coupled with an expression of unsurpassed kindness.

He was one of the few priests in whom I have found a true, honest faith in the Church of Rome. He believed with a child's faith, all the absurdities which the Church of Rome teaches, and he lived according to his honest and sincere faith.

In Mr. Perras' religion there was real calmness and serenity, while the religion of Mr. Bedard had more of the flash of lightning and the noise of thunder. Who could hear his sermons without feeling his heart moved and his soul filled with terror? I never heard anything more thrilling than his words when speaking of the judgments of God and the punishment of the wicked. Mr. Perras never fasted, except on the days appointed by the church: Mr. Bedard condemned himself to fast besides twice every week.

Mr. Perras slept the whole night as a guiltless child. Mr. Bedard, almost every night I was with him, rose up, and lashed himself in the most merciless manner with leather thongs, at the end of which were small pieces of lead. When inflicting upon himself those terrible punishments, he used to recite, by heart, the fifty-first Psalm in Latin, "Have mercy upon me, O Lord, according to Thy lovingkindness." Though he seemed to be unconscious of it, he prayed with such a loud voice, that I heard every word he uttered; he also struck his flesh with such violence that I could count all the blows.

One day I respectfully remonstrated against such a cruel self-infliction as ruining his health and breaking his constitution. "Cher petit Frere" (dear little brother), he answered "our health and constitution cannot be impaired by such penances, but they are easily and commonly ruined by our sins. I am one of the healthiest men of my parish, though I have inflicted upon myself those salutary and too well-merited chastisements for many years. Though I am old, I am still a great sinner. I have an implacable and indomitable enemy in my depraved heart, which I cannot subdue except by punishing my flesh. If I do not do those penances for my numberless transgressions, who will do penance for me? If I do not pay the debts I owe to the justice of God, who will pay them for me?"

"But," I answered, "has not our Saviour, Jesus Christ, paid our debts on Calvary? Has He not saved and redeemed us all by His death on the cross? Why, then, should you or I pay again to the justice of God that which has been so perfectly and absolutely paid by our Saviour?"

"Ah! my dear young friend," quickly replied Mr. Bedard, "that doctrine you hold is Protestant, which has been condemned by the Holy Council of Trent. Christ has paid our debts certainly; but not in such an absolute way that there is nothing more to be paid by us. St. Paul says in his Epistle to the Colossians, 'I fill up that which is behind of the sufferings of Christ in my flesh for His body's sake, which is the Church.' Though Christ could have entirely and absolutely paid our debts, if it had been His will, it is evident that such was not His holy will. He left something behind which Paul, you, I, and every one of His disciples, should take and suffer in our flesh for His Church. By the mercy of God, the penances which I impose upon myself, and the pains I suffer from these flagellations, purify my guilty soul, and raising me up from this polluting world, they bring me nearer and nearer to my God every day. The more we do penance and inflict pains on our bodies by our fastings and floggings, the more we feel happy in the assurance of thus raising ourselves more and more above the dust of this sinful world, of approaching more and more to that state of holiness of which our Saviour spoke when He said, 'Be holy as I am holy Myself.'"

When Mr. Bedard was feeding my soul with these husks, he was speaking with great animation and sincerity. Like myself, he was far away from the good Father's house. He had never tasted of the bread of the children. Neither of us knew anything of the sweetness of that bread. We had to accept those husks as our only food, though it did not remove our hunger.

I answered him: "What you tell me here is what I find in all our ascetic books and theological treatises, and in the lives of all our saints. But I read this morning in the 2nd chapter of Ephesians: 'But God who is rich in mercy, for His great love wherewith He loved us, even when we were dead in sins, hath quickened us together with Christ. For by grace are ye saved, through faith, and that not of ourselves, it is the gift of God; not of works, lest any man should boast.'

"Now, my dear and venerable Mr. Bedard, allow me respectfully to ask, how is it possible that your salvation is only by grace, if you have to purchase it every day by tearing your flesh and lashing your body in such a fearful manner? Is it not a strange form of grace which reddens your skin with your blood, and bruises your flesh every night?"

"Dear little brother," answered Mr. Bedard, "when Mr. Perras spoke to me of your piety, he did not conceal that you had a very dangerous defect, which was to spend too much time in reading the Bible in preference to every other of our holy books. He said that you had a fatal tendency to interpret the Holy Scriptures too much according to your own mind, and in a way which is more Protestant than Catholic. I am sorry to see that the curate of St. Charles was but too correct.

"But, as he added that, though your reading too much the Holy Scriptures brought some clouds in your mind, you always ended by yielding to the sense given by our holy Church. This did not prevent me from desiring to have you in my place during my absence, and I hope I will not regret it, for we are sure that our dear young

Chiniquy will never be a traitor to our holy Church."

These words, which were given with a great solemnity, mixed with the most sincere kindness, went through my soul like a two-edged sword. I felt an inexpressible confusion and regret, and, biting my lips, I said: "I have sworn never to interpret the Holy Scriptures except according to the unanimous consent of the Holy Fathers, and with the help of God, I will fulfill my promise. I regret exceedingly to have differed for a moment from you. You are my superior by your age, your learning and your piety. Please pardon me that momentary deviation from my duty, and pray that I may be as you are: a faithful and a fearless soldier of our holy Church to the end."

At that moment the niece of the curate came to tell us that dinner was ready. We went to the modest, though exceedingly well-spread table, and to my great pleasure that painful conversation was dropped. We had not sat at the table five minutes, when a poor man knocked at the door and asked a piece of bread for the sake of Jesus and Mary. Mr. Bedard rose from the table, went to the poor stranger, and said: "Come, my friend, sit between me and our dear little Father Chiniquy. Our Saviour was the friend of the poor: He was the father of the widow and the orphan, and we, His priests, must walk after Him. Be not troubled; make yourself at home. Though I am the curate of Charlesbourgh, I am your brother. It may be that in heaven you will sit on a higher throne than mine, if you love our Saviour Jesus Christ and His holy mother Mary more than I do."

With these words, the best things that were on the table were put in the plate of the poor stranger, who with some hesitation finished by doing honor to the excellent viands.

After this, I need not say that Mr. Bedard was charitable to the poor: he always treated them as his best friends. So also was my former curate of St. Charles; and, though his charity was not so demonstrative and fraternal as that of Mr. Bedard, I had yet never seen a poor man go out of the parsonage of St. Charles whose breast ought not to have been filled with gratitude and joy.

Mr. Bedard was as exact as Mr. Perras in confessing once, and sometimes twice, every week; and, rather than fail in that humiliating act, they both, in the absence of their common confessors, and much against my feelings, several times humbly knelt at my youthful feet to confess to me.

Those two remarkable men had the same views about the immorality and the want of religion of the greater part of the priests. Both have told me things about the secret lives of the clergy which would not be believed were I to publish them. Both repeatedly said that auricular confession was the daily source of unspeakable depravities between the confessors and their female as well as male penitents; but neither of them had sufficient light to conclude from those deeds that auricular confession was a diabolical institution. They both sincerely believed as I did then, that the institution was good, necessary and divine, and that it was a source of perdition to so many priests only on account of their want of faith and piety; and principally from their neglect of prayers to the Virgin Mary.

They did not give me those terrible details with a spirit of criticism against our weak brethren. Their intention was to warn me against the dangers, which were as great for me as for others. They both invariably finished those confidences by inviting me more and more to pray constantly to the mother of God, the blessed Virgin Mary, and to watch over myself, and avoid remaining alone with a female penitent; advising me also to treat my own body as my most dangerous enemy, by reducing it into subjection to the law, and crucifying it day and night.

The revelations which I received from those worthy priests did not in any way shake my faith in my Church. She even became dearer to me; just as a dear mother gains in the affection and devotedness of a dutiful son as her trials and afflictions increase. It seemed to me that after this knowledge it was my duty to do more than I had ever done to show my unreserved devotedness, respect and love to my holy and dear mother, the Church of Rome, out of which (I sincerely believed then) there was no salvation.

Though these two priests professed to have a most profound love and respect for the Holy Scriptures, they gave very little time to their study. Both several times rebuked me for passing too many hours in their perusal, and repeatedly warned me against the habit of constantly appealing to them against certain practices and teachings of our theologians. As good Roman Catholic priests they had no right to go to the Holy Scriptures alone to know what "the Lord saith!" The traditions of the Church were their fountain of science and light! Both of them often distressed me with the facility with which they buried out of view, under the dark clouds of their traditions, the clearest texts of Holy Scriptures which I used to quote in defense of my positions in our conversations and debates.

They both, with an equal zeal, and unfortunately with too much success, persuaded me that it was right for the Church to ask me to swear that I would never interpret the Holy Scriptures, except according to the unanimous consent of the Holy Fathers. But when I showed them that the Holy Fathers had never been unanimous in anything except in differing from one another on almost every subject they had treated; when I demonstrated by our Church historians that some Holy Fathers had very different views from ours on many subjects, they never answered my questions except by silencing me by the text: "If he does not hear the Church let him be as a heathen or a publican," and by giving me long lectures on the danger of pride and self-confidence.

They both taught me that the inferior must blindly obey his superior, just as the stick must obey the hand that holds it; assuring me at the same time that the inferior was not responsible for the errors he commits when obeying his legitimate superior.

Mr. Bedard and Mr. Perras had a great love for their Saviour, Jesus; but the Jesus Christ whom they loved and respected and adored was not the Christ of the Gospel, but the Christ of the Church of Rome.

Mr. Perras and Mr. Bedard had a great fear, as well as a sincere love for their God, while yet they professed to make Him every morning by the act of consecration. They also most sincerely believed and preached that idolatry was one of the greatest crimes a man could commit, but they themselves were every day worshiping an idol of their own creating. They were forced by their Church to renew the awful iniquity of Aaron, with this difference only, that while Aaron made his gods of melted gold, they made theirs with flour, baked between two heated and well polished irons, and in the form of a crucified man.

When Aaron spoke of his golden calf to the people, he said: "These are thy gods, O Israel, which brought thee out of the land of Egypt." So likewise Mr. Bedard and Mr. Perras, showing the wafer to the deluded people, said: "Ecce agnus Dei qui tollit peccata mundi!" ("Behold the Lamb of God which taketh away the sins of the world!")

These two sincere and honest priests placed the utmost confidence also in relics and scapulars. I have heard both say that no fatal accident could happen to one who had a scapular on his breast — no sudden death would overtake a man who was faithful in keeping those blessed scapulars about his person. Both of them, nevertheless, died suddenly, the saddest of deaths. Mr. Bedard dropped dead on the 19th of May, 1837, at a great dinner given to his friends. He was in the act of swallowing a glass of that drink of which God says: "Look not upon the wine when it is red, when it giveth its color in a cup, when it moveth itself aright. At the last it biteth like a serpent and stingeth like an adder."

The Rev. Mr. Perras, sad to say, became a lunatic in 1845, and died on the 29th of July, 1847, in a fit of delirium.

CHAPTER XXII

In the beginning of September, 1834, the Bishop Synaie gave me the enviable position of one of the vicars of St. Roch, Quebec, where the Rev. Mr. Tetu had been curate for about a year. He was one of the seventeen children of Mr. Francis Tetu, one of the most respectable and wealthy farmers of St. Thomas. So amiable was my new curate, that I never saw him in bad humor a single time during the four years I was there. Although I sometimes unintentionally sorely tried his patience, I never heard an unkind word proceed from his lips.

In one of the pleasant hours which we used to pass after dinner, one of the vicars, Mr. Louis Parent, said to the Rev. Mr. Tetu, "I have handed this morning more than one hundred dollars to the bishop, as the price of the masses which my pious penitents have requested me to celebrate, the greatest part of them for souls in purgatory. Every week I have to do the same thing, just as you, and every one of the hundreds of priests in Canada have to do. Now I would like to know how the bishops can dispose of all these masses, and what they do with the large sums of money which go into their hands from every part of the country."

The good curate answered in a joking manner, as usual: "If they are all celebrated, purgatory must be emptied twice a day. For I have calculated that the sums given for those masses in Canada cannot be less than 4,000 dollars every day. There are three times as many Catholics in the United States as here, so there is no exaggeration in saying that 16,000 dollars at least are given every day in these two countries to throw cold water on the burning flames of that fiery prison. Now multiplied by the 365 days of the year, make the handsome sum of 5,840,000 dollars every year. But, as we all know more than twice as much is paid for high masses than for the low, it is evident that more than 10,000,000 dollars are expended to help the souls of the purgatory end their tortures every twelve months, in North America alone.

There is not a sufficient number of priests in the world to say all the masses which are paid for by the people. I do not know any more than you do what the bishops do with those millions of dollars. But, if you want to know my mind on that delicate subject, I will tell you that the least we think and speak of it the better it is for us. I reject those thoughts as much as possible, and I advise you to do the same thing."

The other vicars seemed inclined, with Mr. Parent, to accept that conclusion; but, as I had not said a single word, they requested me to give them my views which I did: "There are many things in our holy church which look like dark spots; but I hope that this is due only to our ignorance. So long as we do not know what the bishops do with those numberless masses paid into their hands, I prefer to believe that they act as honest men." I had hardly said these few words, when I was called to visit a sick parishioner, and the conversation was ended.

Eight days later, I was alone in my room, reading the "L'Ami de la Religion et du Roi," a paper which I received from Paris, edited by Picot. My curiosity was not a little excited, when I read, at the head of a page, in large letters: "Admirable Piety of the French Canadian People." The reading of that page made me shed tears of shame, and shook my faith to its foundation.

I ran to the curate and the vicars and said to them: "A few days ago we tried, but in vain, to find what becomes of the large sums of money paid by our people to the bishops, to say masses. Here is the answer." We then read together the article, the substance of which was that the venerable bishops of Quebec had sent not less than one hundred thousand francs, at different times, to the priests of Paris, that they might say four hundred thousand masses at five cents each! Here we had the sad evidence that our bishops had taken for themselves four hundred thousand francs from our poor people, under the pretext of saving the souls from purgatory! That article fell upon us as a thunderbolt. Our tongues were paralyzed by shame.

At last, Baillargeon, addressing the curate, said: "Is it possible that our bishops are swindlers and we their tools to defraud our people? What would that people say if they knew that not only we do not say the masses for which they constantly fill our hands with their hard-earned money, but that we send those masses to be said in Paris for five cents! What will our good people think of us all when they know that our bishop pockets twenty cents out of each mass they ask us to celebrate according to their wishes."

The curate answered: "It is very lucky that the people do not know, for they would surely throw us all into the river. Let us keep that shameful trade as secret as possible. For what is the crime of simony if this be not an instance of it?"

I replied: "How can you hope to keep that traffic of the body and blood of Christ a secret, when not less than 40,000 copies of this paper are circulated in France, and more than 100 copies come to the United States and Canada! The danger is greater than you suspect; Is it not because of such public and undeniable crimes and vile tricks of the clergy of France, that the French people in general, half a century ago, condemned all the bishops and priests of France to death?

"But that sharp operation of our bishops takes a still darker color, when we consider that those 'five-cent masses' which are said in Paris are not worth a cent. For who among us is ignorant of the fact that the greatest part of the priests of Paris are infidels, and that many of them live publicly with concubines? Would our people put their money in our hands if we were honest enough to tell them that their masses would be said for five cents in Paris by such priests? Do we not deceive them when we accept their money, under the well understood condition that we shall offer the holy sacrifice according to their wishes? But, if you allow me to speak a little more, I have another strange fact to consider with you."

"Yes! speak, speak!" answered all four priests.

I then resumed: "Do you remember how you were enticed into the 'Three Masses Society?' Who among us had the idea that the greatest part of the year would be spent in saying masses for the priests, and thus become impossible to satisfy the pious demands of the people who support us? We already belonged to the societies of the Blessed Virgin Mary and of St. Michael, which raised to five the number of masses we had to celebrate for the dead priests. Dazzled by the idea that we would have two thousand masses said for us at our death, we bit at the bait presented to us by the bishop. We have had to say 165 masses for the 33 priests who died during the past year which means that each of us has to pay forty-one dollars to the bishop for masses which he has had said in Paris for eight dollars. Being forced the greatest part of the year to celebrate the holy sacrifice for the benefit of the dead priests, we cannot celebrate the masses for which we are daily paid by the people, and are therefore forced to transfer them into the hands of the bishop, who sends them to Paris, after spiriting away twenty cents each. Then the more priests he enrolls in his society of 'Three Masses,' the more twenty cents he pockets from us and from our pious people. That explains his admirable zeal to enroll every one of us. It is not the value of the money but I feel desolate when I see that we become the accomplices of his simoniacal trade. However, why should we lament over the past? There is no remedy for it. Let us learn from the past how to be wise in the future."

Mr. Tetu answered: "You have shown us our error. Now, can you indicate any remedy?"

"That remedy is to abolish the society of 'Three Masses,' and to establish another of 'One Mass,' which will be said at the death of every priest. In that way it is true that instead of 2,000 masses, we shall have only 1,200 at our death. But if 1,200 masses do not open to us the gates of heaven, it is because we shall be in hell. We shall be enabled to say more masses at the request of our people, and shall diminish the number of five cent masses said by the priests in Paris at the request of our bishop. If you take my advice, we will immediately name the Rev. Mr. Tetu president of the new society, Mr. Parent will be its treasurer, and I consent to act as your secretary. When our society is organized, we will send our resignations to the president of the other society. We shall immediately address a circular to all the priests, to give them the reason for the change, and respectfully ask them to unite with us in this new society, in order to diminish the number of masses which are celebrated by the five cent priests of Paris."

Within two hours the new society was fully organized, the reasons of its formation written in a book, and our names were sent to the bishop, with a respectful letter informing him that we were no more members of the 'Three Masses Society.' That letter was signed, C. Chiniquy, Secretary. Three hours later, I received the following note from the bishop's palace:

"My Lord Bishop of Quebec wants to see you immediately upon important affairs. Do not fail to come without delay.

Truly yours,
CHARLES F. CAZEAULT, Secy."

I showed the missive to the curate and the vicars, and told them: "A big storm is raging on the mountain; this is the first peal of thunder — the atmosphere looks dark and heavy. Pray for me that I may speak and act as an honest and fearless priest."

In the first parlor of the bishop I met my personal friend, Secretary Cazeault. He said to me: "My dear Chiniquy, you are sailing on a rough sea — you must be a lucky mariner if you escape the wreck. The bishop is very angry at you; but be not discouraged, for the right is on your side." He then kindly opened the door of the bishop's parlor, and said: "My lord, Mr. Chiniquy is here, waiting for your orders."

"Let him come, sir," answered the bishop.

I entered and threw myself at his feet. But, stepping backward, he told me in a most excited manner: "I have no benediction for you till you give me a satisfactory explanation of your strange conduct."

I arose to my feet and said: "My lord, what do you want from me?"

"I want you, sir, to explain to me the meaning of this letter signed by you as secretary of a new-born society called, 'One Mass Society.'"

I answered him: "My lord, the letter is in good French. Your lordship must have understood it well. I cannot see how any explanation on my part could make it clearer."

"I want to know your object in leaving the old and respectable 'Three Masses Society'? Is it not composed of your bishops and of all the priests of Canada? Did you not find yourself in sufficiently good company? Do you object to the prayers said for the souls of purgatory?"

I replied: "My lord, I will answer by revealing to your lordship a fact which has not sufficiently attracted your attention. The great number of masses which we say for the souls of the dead priests makes it impossible for us to say the masses for which the people pay into our hands; we are forced to transfer this money into your hands; and then instead of having these holy sacrifices offered by the good priests of Canada, your lordship has recourse to the priests of France, where you get them said for five cents. We see two great evils in this: First, our masses are said by priests in whom we have not the least confidence; for between you and me, the masses said by the priests of France, particularly of Paris, are not worth one cent. The second evil is still greater, one of the greatest crimes which our holy church has always condemned, the crime of simony."

"Do you mean to say," indignantly replied the bishop, "that I am guilty of the crime of simony?"

"Yes! my lord; it is just what I mean to say. I do not see how your lordship does not understand that the trade in masses by which you gain 400,000 francs on a spiritual merchandise, which you get for 100,000, is not simony."

"You insult me! You are the most impudent man I ever saw. If you do not retract what you have said, I will suspend and excommunicate you!"

"My suspension and my excommunication will not make the position of your lordship much better. For the people will know that you have excommunicated me because I protested against your trade in masses. They will know that you pocket twenty cents on every mass, and that you get them said for five cents in Paris by priests, the greater part of whom live with concubines, and you will see that they will in one voice bless me for my protest and condemn you for your simoniacal trade."

I uttered these words with such perfect calmness that the bishop saw that I had not the least fear of his thunders.

"It is evident to me," said he, "that you aim to be a reformer, a Luther, in Canada. But you will never be anything else than a monkey!"

I saw that my bishop was beside himself, and that my perfect calmness added to his irritation. I answered him: "If Luther had never done anything worse than I do today, he ought to be blessed by God and man. I respectfully request your lordship to be calm. The subject on which I speak to you is more serious than you think. You are digging under your own feet, and under the feet of your priests the same abyss in which the Church of France nearly perished, not half a century ago. I am your best friend when I fearlessly tell you this truth before it is too late. God knows, it is because I love and respect you, as my own father, that I profoundly deplore the terrible consequences that will follow. Woe to your lordship! Woe to me, woe to our holy church, the day that our people know that in our holy religion the blood of Christ is turned into merchandise to fill the treasury of the bishops and popes!"

It was evident that these last words, said with the most perfect self-possession, had not all been lost. The bishop had become calmer. He answered me: "I could punish you for this freedom with which you have dared to speak to your bishop, but I prefer to warn you to be more respectful and obedient in the future. You have requested me to take away your name from the 'Three Mass Society' — you and the four simpletons who have committed the same act of folly, are the only losers in the matter. Instead of two thousand masses said for the deliverance of your souls from the flames of purgatory, you will have only twelve hundred. But, be sure of it, there is too much wisdom and true piety in my clergy to follow your example. You will be left alone, and, I fear, covered with ridicule. For they will call you the 'little reformer.'"

I answered the bishop: "I am young, it is true, but the truths I have said to your lordship are as old as the Gospel. I have such confidence in the infinite merits of the holy sacrifice of the mass that I sincerely believe that twelve hundred masses said by good priests are enough to cleanse my soul and extinguish the flames of purgatory. But, besides, I prefer twelve hundred masses said by one hundred sincere Canadian priests, to a million said by the five cent priests of Paris."

These last words, spoken half serious, half jest, brought a change on the face of my bishop. I thought it was a good moment to get my benediction and take leave of him. I took my hat, knelt at his feet, obtained his blessing, and left.

CHAPTER XXIII

The hour of my absence had been one of anxiety for the curate and the vicars. But my prompt return filled them with joy.

"What news?" they all exclaimed.

"Good news," I answered; "the battle has been fierce but short. We have gained the day; and if we move quickly another great victory is in store for us. The bishop is so sure that no one will follow us that he will not move a finger to stop them. This will insure our success. But we must not lose a moment. Let us address our circular to every priest in Canada."

Within twenty-four hours more than three hundred letters were carried to all the priests, giving them the reasons why we should try, by all fair means, to put an end to the shameful simoniacal trade in masses which was going on between Canada and France.

The week was scarcely ended, when letters came from almost all curates and vicars to the bishop, respectfully requesting to withdraw from "The Society of the Three Masses." Only fifty refused to comply with our request.

Our victory was more complete than we had expected. But the Bishop of Quebec, hoping to regain his lost ground, immediately wrote to the Bishop of Montreal, my Lord Telemesse, to come to his help and show us the enormity of the crime in rebelling against the will of our ecclesiastical superiors.

A few days later, to my great dismay, I received a short, very cold note from the secretary, telling me that the Bishops of Montreal and Quebec, wanted to see me at the palace without delay. I had never seen the Bishop of Montreal, and expected a man of gigantic proportions. To my surprise he was very small. His eyes were piercing as the eagle's; but when fixed on me, I saw in them the marks of a noble and honest heart.

The motions of his head were rapid, his sentences short, and he seemed to know only one line, the straight one, when approaching a subject or dealing with a man. He had the merited reputation of being one of the most learned and eloquent men of Canada. The Bishop of Quebec had remained on his sofa, and left the Bishop of Montreal to receive me. I fell at his feet and asked his blessing, which he gave me in the most cordial way. Then putting his hand upon my shoulder, he said, in a Quaker style: "Is it possible that *thou* art Chiniquy — that young priest who makes so much noise?

How can such a small man make so much noise?"

There being a smile on his countenance as he uttered these words, I saw at once that there was no anger or bad feeling in his heart; I replied: "My lord; do you not know that the most precious pearls and perfumes are put up in the smallest vases?"

The bishop saw that this was a compliment to his address; he smilingly replied: "Well, well, if thou art a noisy priest, thou art not a fool. But, tell me, why dost thou want to destroy our 'Three Masses Society' and establish that new one on its ruins, in spite of thy superiors?"

"My lord, my answer will be as respectful, short, and plain as possible. I have left the 'Three Masses Society' because it was my right to do it, without anybody's permission. I hope our venerable Canadian bishops do not wish to be served by slaves!"

"I do not say," replied the bishop, "that thou wert bound in conscience to remain, but can I know why thou hast left such a respectable association, at the head of which thou seest thy bishops and the most venerable priests in Canada?"

"I will again be plain in my answer, my lord. If your lordship wants to go to hell with your venerable priests by spiriting away twenty cents from every one of our honest and pious penitents for masses which you get said for five by bad priests in Paris, I will not follow you. Moreover, if your lordship wants to be thrown into the river by the furious people when they know how long and how cunningly we have cheated them with our simoniacal trade, I do not want to follow you into the cold stream."

"Well! well," answered the bishop, "let us drop that matter for ever."

He uttered this short sentence with such sincerity and honesty, that I saw he really meant it. He had, at a glance, seen that his ground was untenable. My joy was great indeed at such a prompt and complete victory. I fell again at the bishop's feet, and asked his benediction before taking leave of him to go and tell the curates and vicars the happy news.

From that time till now, at the death of every priest, the Clerical Press never failed mentioning whether the deceased priest, belonged to the "Three" or "One Mass Society."

We had, to some extent, diminished the simoniacal and infamous trade in masses; but unfortunately we had not destroyed it; and I know that today it has revived. Since I left the Church of Rome, the Bishops of Quebec have raised the "Three Masses Society" from its grave. It is a public fact that the trade in masses is still conducted on a large scale with France. There are in Paris and other large cities in that country, public agencies to carry on that shameful traffic.

In 1874, the house of Mesme was doing an immense business with its stock of masses, but the government became suspicious and the books were examined. It was then found that an incredible number of masses never reached their destination, but only filled the purse of the Parisian mass merchant; and so the unlucky Mesme was unceremoniously sent to the penitentiary to meditate on the infinite merits of the Holy Sacrifice of the Mass.

But these facts are not known by the poor Roman Catholics of Canada, who are fleeced more and more by their priests, under the pretext of saving souls from purgatory.

CHAPTER XXIV

One of the first things done by the curate Tetu, after his new vicars had been chosen, was to divide, by casting lots, his large parish into four parts. My lot gave me the northeast of the parish, which contained the Quebec Marine Hospital.

The number of sick sailors I had to visit almost every day in that noble institution, was between twenty-five and a hundred. Having no place there to celebrate mass and keep the Holy Sacrament, I soon found myself in what, at first, seemed to me a grave difficulty Frequently I had to administer the viaticum (holy communion) to a dying sailor.

Till then I had never carried the good God to the dying without being accompanied by several people walking or riding on horseback. I would wear a white surplice over my long black robe to strike the people with awe. A man ringing a bell would go before me to announce to the people that the great God was passing by; that they had to fall on their knees in their houses, or along the public roads, or in their fields, and adore Him.

This went well in St. Charles or Charlesbourgh, but could I do that in Quebec, where so many miserable heretics were more disposed to laugh at my god than to adore him? In my zeal and sincere faith, I was, however, determined to dare the heretics of the whole world and to expose myself to their insults rather than give up the supreme respect and adoration which were due to my god everywhere. Twice I carried him to the hospital with the usual solemnity.

In vain my curate tried to persuade me to change my mind. He then kindly invited me to go with him to confer with the bishop. How can I express my dismay when the bishop told me, with a levity which I had not yet observed in him, "that on account of the Protestants whom we had to meet everywhere, it was better to make our 'god' travel *incognito* in the streets of Quebec."

He added in a high and joking tone: "Put him in your vest pocket, as do the rest of the city priests. Never aim at being a reformer and doing better than your venerable brethren in the priesthood. We must not forget that we are a conquered people. If we were masters, we would carry him to the dying with the public honors we used to give him before the conquest; but the Protestants are the stronger. Our governor is a Protestant, as well as our queen. The garrison, which is inside the walls of their impregnable citadel, is composed chiefly of Protestants. According to the laws of our holy church, we have the right to punish, even by death, the miserable people who ridicule the mysteries of our holy religion. But though we have that right, we are not strong enough to enforce it. We must, then, bear the yoke in silence. After all, it is our god himself, who in his inscrutable judgment, has deprived us of the power of honoring him as he deserves. If, in his good providence, we could break our fetters, and become free to pass again the laws to prevent the heretics from settling among us, then we would carry him as we used to do in those happy days."

"But," said I, "when I walk in the streets with my good god in my vest pocket, what will I do if I meet any friend who wants to shake hands and have a joke with me?"

The bishop laughed and answered: "Tell your friend you are in a hurry, and go your way as quickly as possible; but if there is no help, have your talk and your joke with him, without any scruple of conscience. The important point in this delicate matter is that the people should not know we are carrying our god through the streets *incognito,* for this knowledge would surely shake and weaken their faith. The common people are, more than we think, kept in our holy church, by the impressing ceremonies of our processions and public marks of respect we give to Jesus Christ, when we carry Him to the sick; for the people are more easily persuaded by what they see with their eyes and touch with their hands, than by what they hear with their ears."

I submitted to the order of my ecclesiastical superior; but the jocose way in which he had spoken of the most awful and adorable mystery of the church, left the impression that he did not believe one iota of the dogma of transubstantiation.

It took several years before I could accustom myself to carry my god in my vest pocket as the other priests did, without any more ceremony than with a piece of tobacco. So long as I was walking alone I felt happy. I could then silently converse with my Saviour, and give Him all the expression of my love and adoration. But no words can express my sadness when, as was often the case, I met some friends forcing me to shake hands with them, and began one of those idle talks, so common everywhere. With the utmost efforts I then put on a smiling mask to conceal the expressions of adoration, and earnestly cursed the day when my country had fallen under the yoke of Protestants.

How many times I would pray to my wafer god, whom I was personally pressing to my heart, to grant us an opportunity to break those fetters and destroy for ever the power of Protestant England over us! Then we should be free again to give our Saviour all the public honors which were due to His Majesty. Then we should put in force the laws by which no heretic had any right to settle and live in Canada.

CHAPTER XXV

When by the casting of the lots I became the first chaplain of the Quebec Marine Hospital, I was sure that God had directed this for my good and His own glory, and I was right. In the beginning of November, 1834, Mr. Glackmayer, the superintendent came to tell me that there was an unusually large number of sick left by the Fall fleets. In danger of death, they were day and night calling for me. He added, secretly, that several had already died of smallpox of the worst type, and that many were also dying from the terrible cholera morbus which was still raging among the sailors.

This sad news came to me as an order from heaven to run to the rescue of my dear sick seamen. The first man I met was Dr. Douglas who confirmed the number of sick and added that the prevailing diseases were of the most dangerous kind.

Dr. Douglas, who was one of the founders and governors of the hospital was one of the ablest surgeons of Quebec. Though a staunch Protestant he honored me with his confidence and friendship from the first day we met. I may say I have never known a nobler heart, a larger mind and a truer philanthropist.

After thanking him for the useful though sad news, I requested Mr. Glackmayer to give me a glass of brandy, which I immediately swallowed.

"What are you doing?" said Dr. Douglas.

"You see," I answered; "I have drunk a glass of excellent brandy."

"But please tell me why."

"Because it a good preservative against the pestilential atmosphere I will breathe all day," I replied. "I will have to hear the confessions of all those people dying from smallpox or cholera, and breathe the putrid air which is around their pillows. Does not common sense warn me to take some precautions against the contagion?"

"Is it possible," rejoined he, "that a man for whom I have such a sincere esteem is so ignorant of the deadly workings of alcohol in the human frame? What you have just drank is nothing but poison; and far from protecting yourself against the danger, you are now much more exposed to it than before you drank that beverage."

"You poor Protestants," I answered in a joking way, "are a band of fanatics, with your extreme doctrines on temperance. You will never convert me to your views on that subject. Is it for the use of the dogs that God has created wine and brandy? No; it is for the use of men who drink them with moderation and intelligence."

"My dear Mr. Chiniquy, you are joking; but I am in earnest when I tell you that you have poisoned yourself with that glass of brandy," replied Dr. Douglas.

"If good wine and brandy were poisons," I answered, "you would be long ago the only physician in Quebec, for you are the only one of the medical body whom I know to be an abstainer. But, though I am much pleased with your conversation, excuse me if I leave you to visit my dear sick sailors, whose cries for spiritual help ring in my ears."

"One word more," said Dr. Douglas. "Tomorrow morning we will make the autopsy of a sailor who has just died suddenly here. Have you any objection to come and see in the body of that man, what your glass of brandy has done in your own body."

"No, sir; I have no objection," I replied. "I have been anxious for a long time to make a special study of anatomy. It will be my first lesson; I cannot get it from a better teacher."

I then shook hands with him and went to my patients, with whom I passed the remainder of the day and the greater part of the night. Fifty of them wanted to make general confessions of all the sins of their whole lives; and I had to give the last sacraments to twenty-five who were dying from smallpox or cholera morbus. The next morning I was, at the appointed hour, by the corpse of the dead man when Dr. Douglas kindly gave me a very powerful microscope.

"I have not the least doubt," said he, "that this man has been instantly killed by a glass of rum. That rum has caused the rupture of the aorta."

While talking thus the knife was doing its work so quickly that the horrible spectacle of the broken artery was before our eyes almost as the last word fell from his lips.

"Look here," said the doctor. "All along the artery you will see thousands, perhaps millions, of reddish spots, which are as many holes perforated through it by alcohol. Just as the musk rats of the Mississippi River dig little holes through the dams and cause the waters to break through and carry desolation and death along its shores, so alcohol every day causes the sudden death of thousands of victims by perforating the veins of the lungs and the whole body. Look at the lungs and count, if you can, the thousands and thousands of reddish, dark and yellow spots, and little ulcers. Every one of them is the work of alcohol causing corruption and death all over these marvelous organs. Alcohol is one of the most dangerous poisons. It has killed more men than all the other poisons together.

"Alcohol cannot go to any part of the human frame without bringing disorder and death to it. For it cannot in any possible way unite with any part of our body. The water we drink and the wholesome food we eat is sent to the lungs, to the brain, the nerves, the muscles, the bones — wherever it goes it receives, so to speak, letters of citizenship; it is allowed to remain there in peace and work for the public good. But not so with alcohol. The very moment it enters the stomach it brings disorder, ruin and death, according to the quantity taken.

"Look here with your microscope and you will see every place where King Alcohol has put his foot has been turned into a battlefield, spread with ruin and death. By a most extraordinary working of nature, or rather by the order of God, every vein and artery through which alcohol has to pass suddenly contracts, as if to prevent its passage or choke it as a deadly foe. Every vein and artery has evidently heard the voice of God: 'Wine is a mocker; it bites like a serpent and stings as an adder!' Every nerve and muscle which alcohol touched, trembled and shook as if in the presence of an implacable and unconquerable enemy. Yes, at the presence of alcohol every nerve and muscle loses its strength, just as the bravest man, in the presence of a horrible monster or demon, suddenly loses his natural strength, and shakes from head to foot."

I cannot repeat all I heard that day from the lips of Dr. Douglas, and what I saw with my own eyes of the horrible workings of alcohol through every part of that body. It would be too long. Suffice to say that I was struck with horror at my own folly, and at the folly of so many people who make use of intoxicating drinks.

During the four years I was chaplain of the Marine Hospital, more than one hundred corpses were opened before me. It is my conviction that the first thing a temperance orator ought to do is to study anatomy; get the bodies of drunkards, as well those of so called temperate drinkers, opened before him, and study there the working of alcohol in the different organs of man. These bodies were books written by the hand of God Himself, and they spoke to me as no man could speak. But here is the time to tell how God forced me, almost in spite of myself, to give up the use of intoxicating drinks.

Among my penitents was a young lady belonging to one of the most respectable families of Quebec. She had a beautiful child, a girl, almost a year old. Of course that young mother idolized her. Unfortunately that lady, as is too often the case, even among the most refined, had learned in her father's house, and by the example of her own mother, to drink wine at table, and when visiting friends. Little by little she began to drink, when alone, a few drops of wine, at first by the advice of her physician, but soon only to satisfy the craving appetite, which grew stronger day by day. I was the only one, excepting her husband, who knew this fact. He was my intimate friend, and several times, with tears trickling down his cheeks, he had requested me, in the name of God, to persuade her to abstain from drinking. That young man was so happy with his accomplished wife and his incomparably beautiful child! He was rich, had a high position in the world, numberless friends, and a palace for his home! Every time I had spoken to that young lady, either when alone or in the presence of her husband, she had shed tears of regret; she had promised to reform, and take only the few glasses prescribed by her doctor. But, alas! that fatal prescription of the doctor was kindling a fire which nothing could quench.

One day, which I will never forget, a messenger came in haste and said: "Mr. A. wants you to come to his home immediately. A terrible misfortune has just happened — his beautiful child has just been killed. His wife is half crazy; he fears she will kill herself."

I leaped into the elegant carriage drawn by two fine horses, and in a few minutes I was in the presence of the most distressing spectacle I ever saw. The young lady, tearing her robes into fragments, tearing her hair with her hands, and cutting her face with the nails of her fingers, was crying, "Oh! for God's sake, give me a knife that I may cut my throat! I have killed my child! My darling is dead! I am the murderess of my own dear Lucy! My hands are reddened with her blood. Oh! may I die with her!"

I was thunderstruck, and at first remained mute and motionless. The young husband, with two other gentlemen, Mr. Blanchet and Coroner Panet, were trying to hold the hands of his unfortunate wife. He did not dare to speak. At last the young wife, casting her eyes upon me, said: "Oh, dear Father Chiniquy, for God's sake give me a knife that I may cut my throat! When drunk, I took my precious darling in my arms to kiss her; but I fell — her head struck the sharp corner of the stove. Her brain and blood are there spread on the floor! My child! My own child is dead! I have killed her! Cursed liquor! Cursed wine! My child is dead! I am damned! Cursed drink!"

I could not speak, but I could weep and cry. I wept, and mingled my tears with those of that unfortunate mother. Then, with an expression of desolation which pierced my soul as with a sword, she said: "Go and see." I went to the next room, and there I saw that once beautiful child, dead, her face covered with her blood and brains! There was a large gap made in the right temple. The drunken mother, by falling with her child in her arms, had caused the head to strike with such a terrible force on the stove that it upset on the floor.

The burned coals were spread on every side, and the house had been very nearly on fire. But that blow, with the awful death of her child, had suddenly brought her to her senses, and put an end to her intoxication. At a glance she saw the whole extent of her misfortune. Her first thought had been to run to the sideboard, seize a large, sharp knife, and cut her own throat. Providentially, her husband was on the spot. With great difficulty, and after a terrible struggle, he took the knife out of her hands, and threw it into the street through the window.

It was then about five o'clock in the afternoon. After an hour passed in indescribable agony of mind and heart, I attempted to leave and go back to the parsonage. But my unfortunate young friend requested me, in the name of God, to spend the night with him. "You are the only one," he said, "who can help us in this awful night. My misfortune is great enough, without destroying our good name by spreading it in public. I want to keep it as secret as possible. With our physician and coroner, you are the only man on earth whom I trust to help me. Please pass the night with us."

I remained, but tried in vain to calm the unfortunate mother. She was constantly breaking our hearts with her lamentations — her convulsive efforts to take her own life. Every minute she was crying, "My child! my darling Lucy! Just when thy little arms were so gently caressing me, and thy angelic kisses were so sweet on my lips, I have slaughtered thee! When thou wert pressing me on thy loving heart and kissing me, I, thy drunken mother, gave thee the deathblow! My hands are reddened with thy blood! My breast is covered with thy brains! Oh! for God's sake, my dear husband, take my life. I cannot consent to live a day longer! Dear Father Chiniquy, give me a knife that I may mingle my blood of my child! Oh that I could be buried in the same grave with her!"

In vain I tried to speak to her of the mercies of God towards sinners; she would not listen to anything I could say; she was absolutely deaf to my voice. At about ten o'clock she had a most terrible fit of anguish and terror. Though we were four men to keep her quiet, she was stronger than we all. She was strong as a giant. She slipped from our hands and ran to the room where the dead child was lying in her cradle. Grasping the cold body in her hands, she tore the bands of white linen which had been put round the head to cover the horrible wound, and with cries of desolation she pressed her lips, her cheeks, her very eyes on the horrible gap from which the brain and blood were oozing, as if wanting to heal it and recall the poor dear one to life.

"My darling, my beloved, my own dear Lucy," she cried, "open thy eyes — look again at your mother! Give me a kiss! Press me again to thy bosom! But thine eyes are shut! Thy lips are cold! Thou dost not smile on me any longer! Thou art dead, and I, thy mother, have slaughtered thee! Canst thou forgive me thy death? Canst thou ask Jesus Christ, our Saviour, to forgive me! Canst thou ask the blessed Virgin Mary to pray for me? Will I never see thee again? Ah, no! I am lost — I am damned! I am a drunken mother who has murdered her own darling Lucy! There is no mercy for the drunken mother, the murderess of her own child."

And when speaking thus to her child she was sometimes kneeling down, then running around the room as if flying before a phantom. But even then she was constantly pressing the motionless body to her bosom or convulsively passing her lips and cheeks over the horrible wound, so that her lips, her whole face, her breast and hands were literally besmeared with blood flowing from the wound. I will not say that we were all weeping and crying, for the words "weeping and crying" cannot express the desolation — the horror we felt. At about eleven o'clock, when on her knees, clasping her child to her bosom, she lifted her eyes towards me, and said:

"Dear Father Chiniquy, why is it that I have not followed your charitable advice when, more with your tears than with words, you tried so often to persuade me to give up those cursed intoxicating wines? How many times you have given me the very words which come from heaven: 'Wine is a mocker; it bites as a serpent, and stings as an adder!' How many times, in the name of my dear child, in the name of my dear husband, in the name of God, you have asked me to give up the use of those cursed drinks! But listen now to my prayer. Go all over Canada; tell all the fathers never to put any intoxicating drink before the eyes of their children. It was at my father's table that I first learned to drink that wine which I will curse during all eternity! Tell all the mothers never to taste these abominable drinks. It was my mother who first taught me to drink that wine which I will curse as long as God is!

"Take the blood of my child, and go redden the top of the doors of every house in Canada, and say to all those who dwell in those houses that that blood was shed by the hand of a murderess mother when drunk. With that blood write on the walls of every house in Canada that 'wine is a mocker.' Tell the French Canadians how, on the dead body of my child, I have cursed that wine which has made me wretchedly miserable and guilty."

She then stopped, as if to breathe a little for a few minutes. She added: "In the name of God, tell me, can my child forgive me her death? Can she ask God to look upon me with mercy? Can she cause the blessed Virgin Mary to pray for me and obtain my pardon?"

But before I could answer, she horrified us by the cries, "I am lost! When drunk I killed my child! Cursed wine!"

And she fell a corpse on the floor. Torrents of blood were flowing from her mouth on her dead child, which she was pressing to her bosom even after her death!

That terrible drama was never revealed to the people of Quebec. The coroner's verdict was that the child's death was accidental, and that the distressed mother died from a broken heart six hours after. Two days later the unfortunate mother was buried with the body of her child clasped in her arms.

After such a terrible storm I was in need of solitude and rest, but above everything I was in need of praying. I shut myself in my little room for two days, and there, alone in the presence of God, I meditated on the terrible justice and retribution which He had called me to witness. That unfortunate woman had not only been my penitent: she had been, with her husband, among my dearest and most devoted friends. It was only lately that she had become a slave to drunkenness. Before that, her piety and sense of honor were of the most exalted kind known in the Church of Rome.

Her last words were not the commonplace expressions which ordinary sinners proffer at the approach of death; her words had a solemnity for me which almost transformed them into oracles of God in my mind.

In the middle of that memorable night, when the darkness was most profound and the stillness fearful, was I awake, was I sleeping? I do not know. But I saw the calm, beautiful, and cherished form of my dear mother standing by me, holding by the hand the late murderess, still covered with the blood of her child. Yes! my beloved mother was standing before me; and she said, with power and authority which engraved every one of her words on my soul, as if written with letters of tears, blood, and fire: "Go all over Canada; tell every father of a family never to put any intoxicating drink before his children. Tell all the mothers never to take a drop of those cursed drinks. Tell the whole people of Canada never to touch nor look at the poisoned cup. And thou, my beloved son, give up for ever the use of those detestable beverages, which are cursed in hell, in heaven, and on earth. It bites like a serpent; it stings like an adder."

When the sound of that voice, so sweet and powerful, was hushed, and my soul had ceased seeing that strange vision, I remained for some time exceedingly agitated and troubled. I said to myself, "Is it possible that the terrible things I have seen and heard these last few days will destroy my mind, and send me to the lunatic asylum?" I then threw myself on my knees to weep and pray. This did me good. I soon felt myself stronger and calmer.

Raising again my mind to God, I said: "O my God, let me know Thy holy will, and grant me the grace to do it. Do the voices I have just heard come from Thee or is all this nothing but the vain dreams of my distressed mind?

"Is it Thy will, O my God, that I should go and tell my country what Thou hast so providentially taught me of the horrible and unsuspected injuries which wine and strong drink cause to the bodies as well as the souls of men? Or is it Thy will that I should conceal from the eyes of the world the wonderful things Thou has made known to me, and that I might bury them with me in my grave?"

As quick as lightning the answer was suggested to me. "What I have taught thee in secret, go and tell it on the housetops!" Overwhelmed with an unspeakable emotion, and my heart filled with a power which was not mine, I raised my hands toward heaven and said to my God:

"For my dear Saviour Jesus' sake, and for the good of my country, O my God, I promise that I will never make any use of intoxicating drinks; I will, moreover, do all in my power to persuade the other priests and the people to make the same sacrifice!"

Fifty years have passed since I took that pledge, and, thanks be to God, I have kept it.

For the next two years I was the only priest in Canada who abstained from the use of wine and other intoxicating drinks; and God only knows what sneers, and rebukes and insults of every kind I had silently to bear! How many times the epithets of *fanatic, hypocrite, reformer, half-heretic,* have been whispered into my ear, not only by the priest, but also by the bishops.

But I was sure that my God knew the motives of my actions, and by His grace I remained calm and patient. In His infinite mercy *He* has looked down upon His unprofitable servant and He chose the day when my humiliations were to be turned into great joy. The day came when I saw those same priests and bishops, at the head of their people, receiving the pledge and blessing of temperance from my hands. Those very bishops who had unanimously, at first, condemned me, soon invited the first citizens of their cities to present me with a golden medal, as a token of their esteem, after giving me, officially, the title of "Apostle of Temperance of Canada."

It was the will of my God that I should see with my own eyes my dear Canada taking the pledge of temperance and giving up the use of intoxicating drinks. How many tears were dried in those days! Thousands and thousands of broken hearts were consoled and filled with joy. Happiness and abundance reigned in many once desolate homes, and the name of our merciful God was blessed everywhere in my beloved country. Surely this was not the work of poor Chiniquy!

It was the Lord's work, for the Lord, who is wonderful in all His doings, had once more chosen the weakest instrument to show His mercy towards the children of men. He had called the most unprofitable of His servants to do the greatest work of reform Canada has ever seen, that the praise and glory might be given to Him, and Him alone!

CHAPTER XXVI

"Out of the Church of Rome there is no salvation," is one of the doctrines which the priests of Rome have to believe and teach to the people. That dogma, once accepted, caused me to devote all my energies to the conversion of Protestants. To prevent one of those immortal and precious souls from going into hell seemed to me more important and glorious than the conquest of a kingdom. In view of showing them their errors, I filled my library with the best controversial books which could be got in Quebec, and I studied the Holy Scriptures with the utmost attention. In the Marine

Hospital, as well as with the people of the city, I had several occasions of meeting Protestants and talking to them; but I found at once that, with very few exceptions, they avoided speaking with me on religion. This distressed me. Learning one day that the Rev. Mr. Anthony Parent, superior of the Seminary of Quebec, had converted several hundred Protestants during his long ministry, I went to ask him if this were true. For answer he showed me the list of his converts, which numbered more than two hundred, among whom were some of the most respectable English and Scotch families of the city.

After reviewing that long list of converts, I said to Mr. Parent: "Please tell me how you have been able to persuade these Protestant converts to consent to speak with you on the errors of their religion. Many times I have tried to show the Protestants that they would be lost if they do not submit to our holy church, but, with few exceptions, they laughed at me as politely as possible, and turned the conversation to other matters. Would you not be kind enough to give me your secret, that I may be able also to prevent some of those precious souls from perishing?"

"You are right when you think that I have a secret," answered Mr. Parent. "The majority of Protestants in Quebec have Irish Roman Catholic servant girls. These came to confess to me and I ask them if their masters and mistresses were truly devoted and pious Protestants, or if they were indifferent and cold in performing their duties. Then I wanted to know if they were on good terms with their ministers? From the answers of the girls I knew both the moral and religious habits of their masters as if I belonged to their households.

"Thus I learned that many Protestants have no more religion and faith than our dogs. They awake in the morning and go to bed at night without praying to God any more than the horses in their stables. Many of them go to church on the Sabbath day more to laugh at their ministers and criticize their sermons than for anything else. Through the confessions of these honest girls I learned that many Protestants liked the fine ceremonies of our Church; that they often favorably contrasted them with the cold performances of their own, and expressed their views in glowing terms about the superiority of our educational institutions, nunneries, etc., over their own high schools or colleges. Besides, you know that a great number of our most respectable and wealthy Protestants trust their daughters to our good nuns for their education.

"I took notes of all these things, and formed my plans of battle. The glorious result you have under your eyes. My first step with the Protestants whom I knew to be without any religion, or even already well disposed towards us, was to go to them with some-times £5, or even £25, which I presented to them as being theirs. They, at first, looked at me in amazement. The following conversation then almost invariably took place.

"'Are you positive, sir, that this money is mine?'

"'Yes, sir,' I answered, 'I am certain that this money is yours.'

"'But,' they replied, 'please tell me how you know that it belongs to me? It is the first time I have the honor of talking with you, and we are perfect strangers to each other.'

"I answered: 'I cannot say, sir, how I know that this money is yours, except by telling you that the person who deposited it in my hands for you has given me your name and your address so correctly that there is no possibility of any mistake.'

"'But can I not know the name of the one who has put that money into your hands for me?' rejoined the Protestant.

"'No, sir; the secret of confession is inviolable,' I replied. 'We have no example that it has ever been broken; and I, with every priest of our Church, would prefer to die rather than betray our penitents and reveal their confession. We cannot even act from what we have learned through their confession, except at their own request.'

"'But this auricular confession must then be a most admirable thing,' added the Protestant; 'I had no idea of it before this day.'

"'Yes, sir, auricular confession is a most admirable thing,' I used to reply, 'because it is a divine institution. But, sir, please excuse me; my ministry calls me to another place. I must take leave of you, to go where my duty calls me.'

"'I am very sorry that you go so quickly,' generally answered the Protestant. 'Can I have another visit from you? Please do me the honor of coming again. I would be so happy to present you to my wife; and I know she would be happy also, and much honored to make your acquaintance.'

"'Yes, sir, I accept with gratitude your invitation. I will feel much pleased and honored to make the acquaintance of the family of a gentleman whose praises are in the mouth of everyone, and whose industry and honesty are an honor to our city. If you allow me, next week, at the same hour, I will have the honor of presenting my respectful homage to your lady.'

"The very next day all the papers reported that Mr. So-and-So had received £5, or £10, or even £25 as a restitution, through auricular confession, and even the staunch Protestant editors of those papers could not find words sufficiently eloquent to praise me and our sacrament of penance.

"Three or four days later the faithful servant girls were in the confessional box, glowing with joy to tell me that now their masters and mistresses could not speak of anything else than the amiability and honesty of the priests of Rome. They raised them a thousand miles over the heads of their own ministers. From those pious girls we invariably learned that to every friend they eulogized auricular confession, and even expressed regret that the reformers had swept away such a useful institution.

"Now, my dear young friend, you see how, by the blessing of God, the little sacrifice of a few pounds destroyed all the prejudices of those poor heretics against auricular confession and our holy church in general. At the appointed hour I never failed from paying the requested visit, and I was invariably received like a Messiah. The only topic on which we could speak, of course, was the great good done by auricular confession. I easily showed them how it works as a check to all the evil passions of the heart; how it is admirably adapted to all the wants of the poor sinners who find a friend, a counselor, a guide, a father, a real savior in their confessor.

"It is very seldom that I do not succeed in bringing that family to our holy church before one or two years; and if I fail from gaining the father or mother, I am nearly sure to persuade them to send their daughters to our good nuns and their boys to our colleges, where they sooner or later become our most devoted Catholics. So you see that the few dollars I spend every year for that holy cause are the best investments ever made."

I thanked him for these interesting details. But I told him, "Though I cannot but admire your perfect skill and shrewdness, allow me to ask if you do not fear to be guilty when you make them believe that the money has come to you through auricular confession?"

"I have not the least fear of that," promptly answered the old priest. "If you had paid attention to what I have told you, you must acknowledge that I have not said positively that the money was coming from auricular confession. If those Protestants have been deceived, it is only due to their own want of a more perfect attention to what I said. I know that there were things that I kept in my mind which would have made them understand the matter in a very different way if I had said them. But Liguori and all our theologians among the most approved of our holy church tell us that these reservations of the mind are allowed, when they are for the good of souls and the glory of God."

"Yes," answered I, "I know that such is the doctrine of Liguori, and it is approved by the popes. I must confess that this seems to me entirely opposed to what we read in the sublime gospel. The simple and sublime 'Yea, yea' and 'Nay, nay' of our Saviour seems to me in contradiction with the art of deceiving, even when not saying absolute and direct falsehoods."

In an angry manner, Mr. Parent replied: "Now, my dear young friend, I understand the truth of what the Rev. Messrs. Perras and Bedard told me lately about you. Though these remarkable priests are full of esteem for you, they see a dark cloud on your horizon; they say that you spend too much time in reading the Bible, and not enough in studying the doctrines and holy traditions of the Church. You are too much inclined also to interpret the Word of God according to your own fallible intelligence, instead of going to the Church *alone* for that interpretation. This is the dangerous rock on which Luther and Calvin were wrecked. Take my advice. Do not try to be wiser than the Church. Obey her voice when she speaks to you through her holy theologians. This is your only safeguard. The bishop would suspend you at once were he aware of your want of faith in the Church."

These last words were said more like a sentence of condemnation than anything else. I felt that the only way of preventing him from denouncing me to the bishop as a heretic and a Protestant was to make an apology, and withdraw from the dangerous ground on which I had put myself. He accepted my explanation, but I saw that he bitterly regretted having trusted me with his secret. I withdrew from his presence, much humiliated by my want of prudence and wisdom. However, though I could not approve of all the methods of the Superior of Quebec, I could not but admire then the glorious results of his efforts in converting Protestants; and I took the resolution of devoting myself more than ever to show them their errors and make them good Catholics. In this I was too successful; for during my twenty-five years of priesthood I have persuaded ninety-three Protestants to give up their gospel light and truth in order to follow the dark and lying traditions of Rome. I cannot enter into details of their conversions, or rather perversions; suffice to say that I soon found that my only chance of proselytizing work was among the Ritualists (e.g. Episcopalian and Anglican). I saw immediately that Calvin and Knox had dug a really impassable abyss between the Presbyterians, Methodists, Baptists, and the Church of Rome. If these Ritualists remain Protestants, and do not make the very short step back to Rome, I will be astonished. Some people are surprised that so many eminent and learned men in Great Britain and America give up their Protestantism to submit to the Church of Rome; but my wonder is that there are so few of them who fall into that bottomless abyss of idolatry and folly, when they spend their whole life on the very brink of the chasm.

CHAPTER XXVII

The three years which followed the cholera epidemic will be long remembered in Quebec for the number of audacious thefts and the murders which kept the whole population in constant terror. At last five: Chambers, Mathieu, Gagnon, Waterworth, and Lemoine, were caught in 1836, tried, found guilty, and condemned to death in March, 1837.

One night, during the trial, I was called to visit a sick man. I asked the name of the sick from the messenger. He answered that it was Francis Oregon. I said that that sick man was a perfect stranger to me. When I was near the carriage, the messenger left abruptly and disappeared. Looking at the faces of the two men who had come for me in the carriage, it seemed that they both wore masks.

"What does this mean?" I said; "each of you wear a mask. Do you mean to murder me?"

"Dear Father Chiniquy," answered one of them, in a low, trembling voice, and in a supplicating tone, "fear not. We swear before God that no evil will be done to you. We have in our hands a great part of the silver articles stolen these last three years. The police are on our track, and we are in great danger of being caught. For God's sake come with us. We will put all those stolen things in your hands, that you may give them back to those who have lost them. We will then immediately leave the country, and lead a better life. We are Protestants, and the Bible tells us that we cannot be saved if we keep in our hands what is not ours. You do not know us, but we know you well. You are the only man in Quebec to whom we can so trust our lives and this terrible secret. We have worn these masks that you may not know us, and that you may not be compromised if you are ever called before a court of justice."

My first thought was to leave them and run back to the door of the parsonage; but such an act of cowardice seemed to me, after a moment's reflection, unworthy of a man. They are Protestants, and they trust me. Well, well, they will not regret to have put their trust in a Catholic priest.

I then answered them: "What you ask from me is of a very delicate, and even dangerous nature. Before I do it, I want to take the advice of one whom I consider the wisest man of Quebec — the Rev. Mr. Demars, ex-president of the seminary of Quebec. I cannot promise to grant you your request if he tells me not to go."

"All right," they both said, and in a very short time I was alone in the room of Mr. Demars.

"Sir, I need advice on a very strange matter." I explained the situation to him under the seal of confession, so neither of us could be compromised.

Before answering me the venerable priest said: "I am very old, but I have never before heard of such a strange thing in my life. Are you not afraid to go alone with these two thieves?"

"No, sir," I answered; "I do not see any reason to fear."

"Well! well," rejoined Mr. Demars, "If you are not afraid, your mother has given you a brain of diamond and nerves of steel."

"Now, my dear sir. Please, in the shortest possible way, tell me your mind? Do you advise me to go with them?"

He replied, "There are so many considerations to make, that it is impossible to weigh them all. The only thing we have to do is to pray God and His Holy Mother for wisdom. Let us pray."

After the prayer Mr. Demars replied, "Yes! go! go! If you are not afraid," answered the old priest, with a voice full of emotion and tears in his eyes.

I fell on my knees and said: "Before I start, please give me your blessing, and pray for me."

I left the seminary and took my seat at the right hand of one of my unknown companions, while the other was on the front seat driving the horse. Not a word was said on the way. But I perceived that the stranger who was at my left, was praying to God; though in such a low voice that I understood only these words twice repeated: "O Lord! have mercy upon me — such a sinner!"

These words touched me to the heart, and brought to my mind the dear Saviour's words: "The publicans and harlots shall go into the kingdom of God before you," and I also prayed for that poor repenting sinner and for myself by repeating the sublime 50th Psalm: "Have mercy upon me, O Lord!"

It took about half an hour to reach the house. The carriage was enclosed and the night exceedingly dark so that it was impossible for me to understand where I was. The only person I saw, when in the house, was a tall woman covered with a long black veil, whom I took to be a disguised man, on account of her size and strength; for she was carrying very heavy bags with as much ease as a handful of straw. A small candle behind a screen cast phantom-like shadows around us.

Not a word was said, except by one of my companions, who whispered in a very low voice, "Please, look at the tickets which are on every bundle; they will indicate to whom these things belong."

As soon as these bundles were put into the carriage we left for the parsonage, where we arrived a little before dawn of day. Not a word was exchanged between us on the way, and my impression was that my penitent companions were joining their silent prayers with mine to the feet of that merciful God who has said to all sinners, "Come unto Me, all ye who are heavy laden, and I will give you rest."

They carried the bundles into my trunk, which I locked with great attention. When all was over I accompanied them to the door. Then, each seizing one of my hands, by a spontaneous movement of gratitude and joy, they pressed them on their lips, shedding tears, and saying in a low voice: "God bless you a thousand times for the good work you have just performed. After Christ, you are our savior."

As these two men were speaking, it pleased God to send forth into my soul one of those rays of happiness which He gives us only at great intervals. These two men had ceased to be robbers in my eyes. They were dear brethren, precious friends, such as are seldom to be seen. The narrow and shameful prejudices of my religion were silent before the fervent prayers that I had heard from their lips; they disappeared in those tears of repentance, gratitude and love, which fell from their eyes on my hands. I pressed their hands in mine, saying to them:

"I thank and bless you for choosing me as the confidant of your misfortunes and repentance. To you I owe three of the most precious hours of my life. Adieu! We shall see one another no more on this earth; but we shall meet in heaven. Adieu!"

It was impossible to sleep the remainder of that memorable night. Besides, I had in my possession more stolen articles than would have caused fifty men to be hanged. At ten o'clock in the morning, I was at Mr. Amiot's, the wealthiest goldsmith of Quebec, with my heavy satchel of melted silver. After obtaining from him the promise of secrecy, I handed it over to him, giving him at the same time its history. I asked him to weigh it, keep its contents, and let me have its value, which I was to distribute according to its label.

He told me there was a thousand dollars worth of melted silver, which amount he immediately gave me. I went down directly to give about half of it to Rev. Mr. Cazeault, chaplain of the congregation which had been robbed, and I distributed the remainder to the parties indicated on the labels attached to this enormous ingot.

The good Lady Montgomery could scarcely believe her eyes when, after obtaining from her the promise of the most inviolable secrecy on what I was going to show her, I displayed on her table the magnificent dishes of silver, fruit baskets, tea and coffee pots, sugar bowls, cream jugs, and a great quantity of spoons and forks of the finest silver, which had been taken from her in 1835. It seemed to her a dream which brought before her eyes these precious family relics. She then related in a most touching manner what a terrible moment she had passed when the thieves, having seized her with her maid and a young man, rolled them in carpets to stifle their cries.

This excellent lady was a Protestant, and it was the first time in my life that I met a Protestant whose piety seemed so enlightened and sincere. I could not help admiring her. When she had most sincerely thanked and blessed me, she asked if I would pray with her to aid her in thanking God for the favor He had just shown her. I told her I should be happy in uniting with her to bless the Lord for His mercies. Upon this she gave me a Bible, magnificently bound, and we read each in turn a verse, slowly and on our knees the sublime Psalm 103: "Bless the Lord, O my soul," etc.

As I was about to leave, she offered me a purse containing one hundred dollars in gold, which I refused, telling her that I would rather lose my two hands than receive a cent for what I had done.

"You are," said she, "surrounded with poor people. Give them this that I offer to the Lord as a feeble testimony of my gratitude, and be assured that as long as I live I will pray God to pour His most abounding favors upon you."

In leaving I could not hide from myself that my soul had been embalmed with the true perfume of a piety that I had never seen in my own church.

Before the day closed I had given back to their rightful owners the effects whose value amounted to more than 7,000 dollars, and had my receipts in good form.

I thought it my duty to give my venerable friend, the Grand Vicar Demars, a detailed account. He heard me with the deepest interest, and could not retain his tears when I related the touching scene of my separation from my two new friends that dark night, yet it has remained one of the brightest of my life.

When my story ended, he said: "I am, indeed, very old, but I must confess that never did I hear anything so strange and so beautiful as this story."

After the incidents of the last twenty-four hours, I was in great need of rest, but it was impossible for me to sleep. For the first time I stood face to face with that Protestantism which my Church had taught me to hate and fight but when that faith was placed in the scale against my own religion, it appeared a heap of pure gold opposite a pile of rotten rags. In spite of myself, I could hear incessantly the cries of that penitent thief: "Lord, have mercy on me, so great a sinner!"

Then, the sublime piety of Lady Montgomery, the blessings she had asked God to pour on me, His unprofitable servant, seemed, as so many coals of fire heaped upon my head by God, to punish me for having said so much evil of Protestants, and so often decried their religion.

A secret voice arose within me: "Seest thou not how these Protestants, whom thou wishest to crush with thy disdain, know how to pray, repent, and make amends for their faults much more nobly than the unfortunate wretches whom thou holdest as so many slaves at thy feet by means of the confessional? Has ever auricular confession worked as efficiently on sinners as the Bible on these thieves to change their hearts? Judge this day, by their fruits, which of the two religions is led by the spirit of darkness, or the Holy Ghost?"

Not wishing to condemn my religion, nor allow my heart to be attracted by Protestantism during the long hours of that restless night, I remained anxious, humiliated, and uneasy.

CHAPTER XXVIII

A few days after the strange and providential night spent with the repentant thieves, I received the following letter signed by Chambers and his unfortunate criminal friends who had been arrested during the series of robberies and murders:

"Dear Father Chiniquy: — We are condemned to death. Please come and help us to meet our sentence as Christians."

I will not attempt to say what I felt when I entered the damp and dark cells where the culprits were enchained. No human words can express those things. Their tears and their sobs were going through my heart as a two-edged sword.

After the others had requested me to hear the confession of their sins, and prepare them for death, Chambers said: "You know that I am a Protestant. But I am married to a Roman Catholic, who is your penitent. You have persuaded my two dear sisters to convert to Catholicism. I have many times desired to follow them. My criminal life alone has prevented me from doing so. But now I am determined to do what I consider to be the will of God in this important matter. Please tell me what I must do to become a Catholic."

I was a sincere Roman Catholic priest, believing that out of the Church of Rome there was no salvation. The conversion of that great sinner seemed to me a miracle of God; it was for me a happy distraction in the desolation I felt in that dungeon.

I spent the next eight days in hearing their confessions and I instructed Chambers in the faith of the Church of Rome. I asked them to tell me some of the details of the murders and thefts they had committed, which might be to me a lesson of human depravity. The facts I then heard convinced me of the need we have. When absolutely left to his own without any religion to stop his uncontrollable passions, man is more cruel than the wild beasts. The existence of society would be impossible without a religion and a God to protect it.

Though I am in favor of liberty of conscience in its higher sense, I think that the atheist ought to be punished like the murderer and the thief — for his doctrines tend to make a murderer and a thief of every man. No law, no society is possible if there is no God.

As that fatal day approached, when I would go to the scaffold with those unfortunate men and see them launched into eternity, the more horrified I felt. They were dearer to me than my own life — not only was I happy to mix my tears with theirs, and unite my ardent prayers to God for mercy with them, but I would have felt happy to shed my blood in order to save their lives.

The governor, Lord Gosford was my friend and since several of the men belonged to the most reputable families of Quebec, I organized a petition to have their sentence changed to permanent exile on the distant penal colony of Botany Bay, Australia. It was signed by the bishop, the Catholic priests, ministers of various Protestant denominations and hundreds of the principal citizens of Quebec. I presented the petition myself, accompanied by the secretary of the Archbishop. But to my great distress the governor answered me that those men had committed so many murders, and kept the country in terror for so many years, that it was absolutely necessary they should be punished.

Who can tell the desolation of those unfortunate men, when, with a voice choked by sobs and my tears, I told them the governor had refused. They were to be hanged the next day. They filled their cells with cries which would have broken the hardest heart.

There was a fear which was haunting me as a phantom from hell the last three days. It seemed that, in spite of all my efforts, prayers, confessions, absolutions, and sacraments, these men were not converted, and that they were to be launched into eternity with all their sins. When I compared the calm and true repentance of the two thieves with whom I spent the night a few weeks before in the carriage, with the noisy expressions of sorrow of those newly converted sinners, I could not help finding an immeasurable distance between the two.

I was saying to myself with anxiety: "Would it be possible that those Protestants, who were with me in the carriage, had the true ways of repentance, pardon, peace, and life eternal and that we Roman Catholics with our signs of the cross and holy waters, our crucifixes and prayers to the saints, our scapulars and medals, our so humiliating auricular confession, were only distracting the mind, the soul, and the heart of the sinner from the true and only source of salvation, Christ?" In the midst of those distressing thoughts I almost regretted having helped Chambers give up his Protestantism for my Romanism.

At about 4 p.m. I made a supreme effort to shake off my desolation, and nerve myself for the solemn duties God had entrusted to me. I put a few questions to those desolated men, to see if they were really repentant and converted. Their answers added to my fear. It is true I had spoken of Christ and His death to them, but this had been so much mixed up with exhortation to trust in Mary, put their confidence in their medals, scapulars, confessions, etc., that it seemed in our religion that Christ was like a precious pearl lost in a mountain of sand. This fear soon caused my distress to be unbearable.

I then went to the private little room which the jailer had kindly allotted to me, and I fell on my knees to pray to God for myself and for my poor convicts. Though this prayer brought some calm, my distress was still very great. It was then that the thought came again to my mind to go to the governor and make another supreme effort to have the sentence of death changed into that of perpetual exile. Without a moment of delay I went to his palace.

It was about 7 p.m. when he reluctantly admitted me to his presence, telling me, when shaking hands, "I hope, Mr. Chiniquy, you are not coming to renew your request of the morning, for I cannot grant it."

Without a word to answer I fell on my knees, and for more than ten minutes I spoke as I had never spoken before. I spoke as we speak when we are the ambassadors of God on a mission of mercy. For some time the governor was mute and as if stunned. He was not only a noble-minded man, but he had a most tender, affectionate, and kind heart. His tears soon began to flow with mine, and his sobs mixed with my sobs; with a voice half-suffocated by his emotion, he extended his friendly hand and said:

"Father Chiniquy, you ask me a favor which I ought not to give, but I cannot resist your arguments, when your tears, your sobs, and your cries are like arrows which pierce and break my heart. I will give you the favor you ask."

It was nearly 10 p.m. when I knocked at the door of the jailer asking his permission to see my dear friends in their cells, to tell them that I had obtained their pardon. He could hardly believe me.

Looking at the parchment, he said: "Have you noticed that it is covered and almost spoiled by the spots made with the tears of the governor. You must be a sorcerer to melt the heart of such a man. I know he was absolutely unwilling to grant the pardon." I convinced him I was not and that it was the work of our Saviour Jesus Christ.

"Please, make haste and open the cells of those unfortunate men that I may tell what our merciful God has done for them." When entering I was unable to contain myself; I cried out: "Rejoice and bless the Lord, my dear friends! You will not die tomorrow! I have your pardon with me!" Two of them fainted, and the others were crying and weeping for joy. They threw their arms around me and covered me with their tears of joy. I knelt with them and thanked God.

The next day I was with them before 7 a.m. The crowds were beginning to gather at that early hour to witness the death of those great culprits. But when they heard the news that the sentence had been changed, the crowd became furious. For a time it was feared that the mob would break the doors of the jail and lynch the culprits. The chief of police advised me not to show myself for a few days in the streets.

Upon their departure a month later for Botany Bay, I gave each a Roman Catholic New Testament, translated by De Sacy, to read and meditate on during their long and tedious journey. I bade them adieu, recommending them to the mercy of God, and the protection of the Virgin Mary and all the Saints. Some months later I heard, that on the sea Chambers had broken his chains and those of some of his companions with the intention of taking possession of the ship and escaping on some distant shore. But he had been betrayed and was hanged on his arrival at Liverpool.

I had almost lost sight of those emotional days of my young priesthood, when, in 1878, I was called by the providence of God to lecture on Romanism in Australia. Some time after my arrival, a venerable gentleman knocked at the door. In saluting me, the stranger said: "Is Father Chiniquy here?"

"Yes, sir, I am Father Chiniquy," I answered.

"Oh, dear Father Chiniquy," quickly replied the stranger, "is it possible that it is you? Can I be absolutely alone with you for half an hour?"

"Certainly," I said; "Please, sir, come and follow me."

When alone with me the stranger said: "Do you not know me?"

"How can I know you, sir?" I answered. "I do not even remember ever having seen you?"

"Do you remember Chambers, who was condemned to death in Quebec in 1837 with his accomplices?" asked the stranger.

"Yes, sir; I remember well," I replied.

"Well, dear Father Chiniquy, I am one of the criminals who filled Canada with terror for several years, and was caught and rightly condemned to death. You obtained our pardon; the sentence of death was commuted into a life of exile to Botany Bay. My name in Canada was A_____, but here they call me B_____. God has blessed me since in many ways; but it is to you I owe my life, and all the privileges of my present existence. After God, you are my saviour. I come to thank and bless you for what you have done for me."

But his joy did not exceed mine. I asked him to relate to me the details of his strange and marvelous story. Here is a short *resume* of his answer: "After your last benediction on board the ship, the first thing I did was to open the New Testament you had given me. It was the first time in my life I had that book in my hand. To tell you the truth, the first reading of the Gospel went far to demolish my Roman Catholic faith, and to make a wreck of the religion taught me by my parents and at the college, and even by you. The only good that first reading did me was to give me more serious thoughts, and prevent me from uniting myself to Chambers and his conspirators in their foolish plot.

"But if my first reading of the Gospel did not do me much good, I cannot say the same thing of the second. I remember that you had told us never to read it except after a fervent prayer to God for help and light to understand it. I was really tired of my former life. In giving up the fear and the love of God I had fallen into the deepest abyss of human depravity and misery, till I had come very near ending my life on the scaffold. I felt the need of a change. You had often repeated to us the words of our Saviour, 'Come unto Me, all ye who are weary and heavy laden, and I will give you rest;' but, with all the other priests, you had always mixed those admirable and saving words with the invocation to Mary, the confidence in our medals, scapulars, signs of the cross, etc. The sublime appeal of Christ had always been drowned in the Church of Rome by those absurd and impious superstitions and practices.

"One morning, after I had spent a sleepless night and feeling pressed down under the weight of my sins, I opened my Gospel book, after an ardent prayer for light and guidance, and my eyes fell on these words of John, 'Behold, the Lamb of God, who taketh away the sin of the world!' (John 1:29). These words fell upon my poor guilty soul with a divine, irresistible power. With tears of unspeakable desolation I spent the day crying, 'O Lamb of God, who taketh away the sins of the world, have mercy upon me! Take away my sins!"

The day was not over when I felt and knew that the Lamb of God had taken away my sins! He had changed my heart and made quite a new man of me. From that day the reading of the Gospel was like bread to the hungry man, and pure, refreshing waters are to the thirsty traveler. My joy, my unspeakable joy, was to read the holy book and speak with my companions in chains of the dear Saviour's love for the poor sinners. Thanks be to God, a good number of them have found Him altogether precious, having been sincerely converted in the dark holes of that ship.

When working hard at Sydney with the other culprits, I felt my chains to be as light as feathers when I was sure that the heavy chains of my sins were gone; and though working hard under a burning sun from morning till night, I felt happy, and my heart was full of joy when I was sure that my Saviour had prepared a throne for me in His kingdom, and that He had bought a crown of eternal glory for me by dying on the cross to redeem my guilty soul.

"I had hardly spent a year in Australia in the midst of the convicts, when a minister of the Gospel, accompanied by another gentleman, came to me and said: 'Your perfectly good behavior and your Christian life have attracted the attention and admiration of the authorities, and the governor sends us to hand you this document, which says that you are no more a criminal before the law, but that you have your pardon, and you can live the life of an honorable citizen, by continuing to walk in the ways of God.' After speaking so, the gentleman put one hundred dollars in my hands, and added: 'Go and be a faithful follower of the Lord Jesus, and God Almighty will bless you and make you prosper in all your ways.' I spent several days and nights in joy and blessing the God of my salvation, Jesus the Redeemer of my soul and my body.

"Some years after that we heard of the discoveries of the rich gold mines in several parts of Australia. After having prayed to God to guide me, I started for the mines in search of gold. After a long march, I was very tired. I sat on a flat stone to take my dinner, and quenched my thirst from the brook. I was eating and blessing my God, when suddenly my eyes fell on a stone by the brook which was about the size of a goose egg. I went and picked it up. The stone was almost all gold of the purest kind!

"I knelt to thank and bless God for this new token of His mercy toward me, and I began to look around. You may imagine my joy when I found that the ground was literally covered with pieces of gold. When I had about £80,000 deposited in the banks, a gentleman offered me £80,000 more for my claim, and I sold it. I invested in a piece of land which soon became the site of an important city, and I became one of the wealthy men of Australia. I then began to study hard and improve the little education I had received in Canada. I married, and my God has made me father of several children. The people where I settled with my fortune and wife, not knowing my past, have raised me to the first dignities of the place. Please, dear Mr. Chiniquy, come and take dinner with me tomorrow, that I may show you my properties, and introduce you to my wife and children."

When telling me his marvelous adventures, his voice was many times choked by his emotion. "Now, I understood why my God gave me such a marvelous power over the governor of Canada when I wrenched your pardon from his hands almost in spite of himself," I said. "That merciful God willed to save you, and you are saved! May His name be for ever blessed."

The next day, it was my privilege to be with his family at dinner. And never in my life have I seen a more happy mother and a more interesting family. After dinner he showed me his beautiful garden and his rich palace after which, throwing himself into my arms, he said: "Dear Father Chiniquy, all those things belong to you. It is to you after God that I owe my life, all the blessings of a large and Christian family, and the honor of the high position I have in this country. May the God of heaven for ever bless you for what you have done for me."

I answered him: "Dear friend, you owe me nothing, I have been nothing but a feeble instrument of the mercies of God towards you. To that great merciful God alone be the praise and the glory. Please ask your family to come here and join with us in singing to the praise of God, the 103rd Psalm." After singing, I bade him adieu for the second time, never to meet him again except in that Promised Land where we shall sing the eternal Hallelujah around the throne of the Lamb, who was slain for us, and who redeemed us in His blood.

CHAPTER XXIX

The merchant fleet of the Fall of 1836 had filled the Marine Hospital of Quebec with the victims of a typhoid fever of the worst kind. In the epidemic doctors and the majority of the servants were swept away during the winter months. In the spring of 1837 I was almost the only one spared. To prevent panic the situation at the hospital was kept secret but by the end of May I caught the disease forcing me to reveal the situation to the bishop, so another chaplain could be appointed. The young Mons. D. Estimanville was chosen. It took me more than an hour to show him all the rooms, and introduce him to the poor, sick, and dying mariners.

I felt then so exhausted that two friends had to support me on my return to the parsonage of St. Roche. My physicians were immediately called. My case was so dangerous that three other physicians were called in. For nine days I suffered the most horrible tortures in my brain and the very marrow of my bones. My only nourishment was a few drops of water. The physicians told the bishop there was no hope. The last sacraments were administered to me and I prepared myself to die. The tenth day I was absolutely motionless.

Though all my physical faculties seemed dead, my memory, intelligence, and soul were acting with more power than ever. During the course of the fever I had awful visions. Once I was surrounded by merciless enemies, whose daggers and swords were plunged through my body. There were many others which I still remember in minute detail. Death had, at first, no terror for me. I had done, to the best of my ability, all that my Church had told me to do, to be saved.

"He is dead, or if not, he has only a few minutes to live. He is already cold and breathless, and we cannot feel his pulse." Though these words had been said in a very low tone, they fell upon my ears as thunder. "He is dead!" was ringing in my ears. I suddenly saw that I was in danger of being buried alive. Words can't express my horror. An icy wave began to move slowly from my extremities towards my heart. At that moment I made a great effort to be saved by invoking the help of the blessed Virgin Mary. Like lightning a terrible vision struck: I saw all my good works and penances in which my Church had told me to trust for salvation, on one side of the balances of the justice of God. My sins were on the other side. My good works seemed only as a grain of sand compared with the weight of my sins.

This awful vision entirely destroyed my false and pharisaical security and filled my soul with an unspeakable terror. I could not cry to Jesus Christ, nor to God, His Father, for mercy; for I sincerely believed that they were both angry with me because of my sins. With much anxiety I turned my hopes towards St. Anne and St. Philomene. My confidence in St. Anne came from the numberless crutches, etc., which covered the church of "La Bonne St. Anne du Nord." St. Philomene's body had lately been miraculously discovered, and the world was filled with the noise of the miracles wrought through her intercession. Her medals were everywhere.

With entire confidence in the will and power of these two saints to obtain any favor for me, I invoked them to pray God to grant me a few years more of life; and with the utmost honesty of purpose, I promised to add to my penances, live a more holy life in the service of the poor and the sick. Also I promised to have a painting of the two saints put in St. Anne's Church, to proclaim to the world their great power in heaven, if they would obtain my cure and restore my health.

Strange to say! The last words of my prayer were scarcely uttered, when I saw above my head St. Anne and St. Philomene sitting in the midst of a great light, on a beautiful golden cloud. Both were looking at me with great kindness.

However, the kindness of St. Anne was mixed with such an air of awe and gravity that I did not like her looks; while St. Philomene had such an expression of superhuman love and kindness that I felt myself drawn to her by a magnetic power, when she said, distinctly: "You will be cured," and the vision disappeared.

But I was cured, perfectly cured! At the disappearance of the two saints, I felt as though an electric shock went through my whole frame; the pains were gone, the tongue was untied, the nerves were restored to their natural and usual power; my eyes were opened, the cold and icy waves which were fast going from the extremities to the regions of my heart became a most pleasant warm bath, restoring life and strength to every part of my body. I raised my head, stretched out my hands which I had not moved for three days, and looking around I saw the four priests. I said to them: "I am cured, please give me something to eat."

Astonished beyond measure, two of them threw their arms around my shoulders to help me to sit a moment, and change my pillow; while two others ran to get me some food "What does this mean?" they all said. "The doctors told us last evening that you were dead; and we have passed the night not only weeping over your death, but praying for your soul, to rescue it from the flames of purgatory. Now you look so hungry, so cheerful and well."

I answered: "It means that when I felt that I was to die, I prayed to St. Anne and St. Philomene to come to my help and cure me; and they have come. I have seen them both, there above my head. It is St. Philomene who spoke to me as the messenger of the mercies of God. I have promised to have their portraits painted and put into the church of The Good St. Anne du Nord."

The physicians, having heard of my sudden cure, hastened to come and see what it meant. At first they could scarcely believe their eyes. The night before they had given me up for dead. And, there I was, the very next morning, perfectly cured! They minutely asked me all the circumstances connected with that strange, unexpected cure; and I told them simply but plainly what had occurred at the very moment I expected to die. Two of my physicians were Roman Catholics, and three Protestants. While the Roman Catholic doctors seemed to believe in my miraculous cure, the Protestants energetically protested against that view in the name of science and common sense.

Dr. Douglas put me the following questions, and received the following answers.

He said: "Dear Father Chiniquy, you know you have not a more devoted friend in Quebec than I, and you know me too well to suspect that I want to hurt your religious feelings when I tell you that there is not the least appearance of a miracle in your so happy and sudden cure. If you will be kind enough to answer my questions, you will see that you are mistaken in attributing to a miracle a thing which is most common and natural. Though you are perfectly cured, you are very weak; please answer only 'yes' or 'no' to my questions, in order not to exhaust yourself. Please tell us if this is the first vision you have had during the period of that terrible fever?"

ANS. "I have had many other visions, but I took them as being the effect of the fever."

DOCTOR. "Please make your answers shorter, or else I will not ask you another question. Tell us simply, if you have not seen in those visions, at times, very frightful and terrible, and at others, very beautiful things."

ANS. "Yes, sir."

DOCTOR. "Have not those visions stamped themselves on your mind with such a power and vividness that you never forget them, and that you deem them more realities than mere visions of a sickly brain?"

ANS. "Yes, sir."

DOCTOR. "Did you not feel sometimes much worse, and sometimes much better after those visions, according to their nature?"

ANS. "Yes, sir."

DOCTOR. "When at ease in your mind during that disease, were you not used to pray to the saints, particularly to St. Anne and St. Philomene?"

ANS. "Yes, sir."

DOCTOR. "When you considered that death was very near (and it was indeed) when you had heard my imprudent sentence that you had only a few minutes to live, were you not taken suddenly, by such a fear of death as you never felt before?"

ANS. "Yes, sir."

DOCTOR. "Did you not then make a great effort to repel death from you?"

ANS. "Yes, sir."

DOCTOR. "Do you know that you are a man of an exceedingly strong will, and that very few men can resist you when you want to do something? Do you not know that your will is such an exceptional power that mountains of difficulties have disappeared before you here in Quebec? Have you not seen even me, with many others, yielding to your will almost in spite of ourselves?"

With a smile I answered, "Yes, sir."

DOCTOR. "Do you not remember seeing, many times, people suffering dreadfully from a toothache coming to us to have their teeth extracted, who were suddenly cured at the sight of the knives and other surgical instruments we put upon the table for use?"

I answered with a laugh, "Yes, sir. I have seen that very often, and it has occurred to me once."

DOCTOR. "Do you think that there was a supernatural power, then, in the surgical implements, and that those sudden cures of toothache were miraculous?"

ANS. "No, sir!"

DOCTOR. "Have you not read the volume of the 'Medical Directory' I lent you on typhoid fever, where several cures exactly like yours are reported?"

ANS. "Yes, sir."

Then addressing the physicians, Doctor Douglas said to them:

"We must not exhaust our dear Father Chiniquy, but from his answers you understand that there is no miracle here. His sudden cure is a very natural thing. The vision was what we call the turning-point of the disease, when the mind is powerfully bent on some very exciting object, when that mysterious thing of which we know so little as yet, called the will, the spirit, the soul, fights as a giant against death, in which battle, pains, diseases, and even death are put to flight and conquered.

"My dear Father Chiniquy, from your own lips, we have it; you have fought, last night, the fever and approaching death, as a giant. No wonder that you won the victory, and I confess, it is a great victory. I know it is not the first victory you have gained, and I am sure it will not be the last. God has given you an irresistible will. In that sense only does your cure come from Him."

An old proverb says: "There is nothing so difficult as to persuade a man who does not want to be persuaded." Though the reasoning and kind words of the doctor ought to have been gladly listened to they had only bothered me. It seemed more agreeable to God, and more according to my faith, to believe that I had been miraculously cured. Of course, the bishop, my confessor and numberless priests and Roman Catholics who visited me during my convalescence, confirmed me in my views.

The skillful painter, Mr. Plamonon was called to paint the tableau I had promised to put in the church of St. Anne du Nord. It was one of the most beautiful and remarkable paintings of that artist. Three months after my recovery, I was at the parsonage of the curate of St. Anne, the Rev. Mr. Ranvoize, a relative of mine. He was about sixty-five years of age, very rich, and had a magnificent library. When young, he had enjoyed the reputation of being one of the best preachers in Canada. It was evening when I arrived with my tableau.

As soon as we were left alone, the old curate said: "Is it possible, my dear young cousin, that you will make such a fool of yourself tomorrow? Your so-called miraculous cure was a dream of your sickly brain as it generally occurs in the moment of the supreme crisis of the fever. It is what is called 'the turning-point' of the disease, when a desperate effort of nature kills or cures the patient. As for the vision of that beautiful girl, whom you call St. Philomene, who has done you so much good, she is not the first girl, surely, who has come to you in your dreams, and done you good!" At these words he laughed so heartily that I feared he would split his sides. Twice he repeated this unbecoming joke.

I was, at first, so shocked at this unexpected rebuke, which I considered to border on blasphemy, that I came very near leaving without a word. But after a moment's reflection, I said to him: "How can you speak with such levity on so solemn a thing? Do you not believe in the power of the saints, who being more holy and pure than we are, see God face to face, speak to Him and obtain favors which He would refuse us rebels? Are you not the daily witness of the miraculous cures wrought in your own church, under your own eyes? Thousands of crutches literally cover the walls of your church!"

My earnest appeal to the daily miracles, the mere mention of the crutches produced such a Homeric laugh, that I was disconcerted and saddened beyond measure. I remained absolutely mute; I wished I had never come. When he had laughed at me to his heart's content, he said: "My dear cousin, you are the first one to whom I speak in this way. I do it because, first: I consider you a man of intelligence, and hope you will understand me. Secondly: because you are my cousin. Were you one of those idiotic priests, real blockheads, who form the clergy today; or a stranger, I would let you go your way believing those ridiculous, degrading superstitions of our poor, ignorant people.

"I've known you from your infancy, and I knew your father. He was one of my dearest friends. You are very young and I very old. It is a duty of honor and conscience to reveal to you a thing which I have kept secret between God and myself. I have been here more than thirty years, and though our country is constantly filled with the noise of the great and small miracles wrought in my church every day, I am ready to swear before God, and to prove to any man of common sense that not a single miracle has been wrought in my church since I came here. Every one of these miraculous cures are sheer deceptions, the work of either fools, or skillful imposters and hypocrites.

"Believe me, my dear cousin, I have studied carefully the history of all those crutches. Ninety-nine out of a hundred have been left by poor, lazy beggars, who, at first, thought with good reason that by walking from door to door with one or two crutches, they would create more sympathy and bring more into their purses. Those crutches are their keys to open both hearts and purses. But the day comes when that beggar has bought a pretty good farm with his stolen alms; or when he is really tired, disgusted with his crutches and wants to get rid of them! How can he do this without compromising himself? By a miracle!

"Then he will sometimes travel hundreds of miles from door to door, begging as usual, but this time he asks the prayers of the whole family, saying: 'I am going to the "good St. Anne du Nord" to ask her to cure my leg (or legs). I hope she will cure me, as she has cured so many others. I have great confidence in her power!' Each one gives twice, nay, ten times as much as before to the poor cripple, making him promise that if he is cured, he will return, so they may bless the good St. Anne with him. When he arrives here, he gives me sometimes one, sometimes five dollars, to say mass for him.

"I take the money, for I would be a fool to refuse it when I know that his purse has been so well filled. During the celebration of the mass, when he receives the communion, I hear generally, a great noise, cries of joy! A miracle! A miracle!! The crutches are thrown on the floor, and the cripple walks as well as you or I! And the last act of that religious comedy is the most lucrative one, for he fulfills his promise, stopping at every house he had ever been to with his crutches. He gives a detailed account of his miraculous cure. Tears of joy flow from every eye. The last cent of that family is generally given to the imposter.

"This is the case in ninety-nine out of every hundred cures wrought in my church. The hundredth is upon people as honest, but, pardon the expression, as blind and superstitious as you are; they are really cured, for they were really sick. But their cures are the natural effects of the great effort of the will. It is the result of a happy combination of natural causes which work together on the frame, and kill the pain, expel the disease and restore the health, just as I was cured of a most horrible toothache some years ago. In pain I went to the dentist. Hardly had his knife and other surgical instruments come before my eyes than the pain disappeared. I quietly took my hat and left, bidding a hearty 'good-bye' to the dentist, who laughed at me to his heart's content every time we met.

"One of the weakest points of our religion is in the ridiculous, I venture to say, diabolical miracles, performed and believed every day among us, with the so-called relics and bones of the saints. But, don't you know that, for the most part, these relics are nothing but chicken's or sheep's bones? And what could I not say, were I to tell you what I know of the daily miraculous impostures of the scapulars, holy water, chaplets and medals of every kind. Were I a pope, I would throw all these mummeries, which come from paganism, into the sea, and would present to the eyes of the sinners, nothing but Christ and Him crucified as the object of their faith and hope just as the Apostles Paul, Peter and James do in their Epistles."

I cannot repeat here, all that I heard that night from that old relative, against the ridiculous practices of the Church of Rome. It would take too long, for he spoke three hours as a real Protestant. Sometimes what he said seemed to me according to common sense, but as it was against the practices of my church, and against my personal practices, I was exceedingly scandalized and pained, and not at all convinced. I pitied him for having lost his former faith and piety.

I told him at the end, without ceremony: "I heard, long ago, that the bishops did not like you, but I knew not why. However, if they could hear what you think and say here about the miracles of St. Anne, they would surely interdict you."

"Will you betray me?" he added, "and will you report our conversation to the bishop?"

"No, my cousin," I replied, "I would prefer to be burnt to ashes. I will not sell your kind hospitality for the traitor's money."

It was two o'clock in the morning when we parted to go to our sleeping rooms. But that night was again a sleepless one. It was sad and strange for me to see that that old and learned priest was secretly a Protestant!

The next morning the crowds arrived to hear the history of my miraculous cure and see with their own eyes the picture of the two saints who had appeared to me. At ten a.m., more than 10,000 people were crowded in and around the church.

After describing the miracle, I disclosed the picture and presented it to their admiration and worship. There were tears rolling on every cheek and cries of admiration and joy from every lip. The picture represented me dying in my bed of sufferings, with the two saints a distance above me stretching their hands as if to say: "You will be cured." It was hung on the wall in a conspicuous place where thousands and thousands have come to worship it from that day to the year 1858, when the curate was ordered by the bishop to burn it, for that was the very year God took the scales away from my eyes.

The apparition of the two saints had left such a deep impression on my mind that during the first week after my conversion I very often said to myself: "How is it that I now believe that the Church of Rome is false, when such a miracle has been wrought on me as one of her priests?"

About a month after my conversion, I again caught typhoid fever. For twelve days I experienced the same tortures and agonies as in 1837. But this time, I was really happy to die; there was no fear of seeing my good works as a grain of sand, and the mountains of my iniquities in the balance of God against me. I was trusting in Jesus alone to be saved. It was the blood of Jesus, the Lamb slain from the foundation of the world for me, which was in the balance. I had no fear then, for I knew that I was saved by Jesus, and that that salvation was a perfect act of His love, His mercy, and His power; consequently I was glad to die.

The thirteenth day of my sufferings the doctor had left me, saying the very same words of the doctors of Quebec: "He has only a few minutes to live, if he be not already dead." Although for three or four days I had not given any sign of life, I was perfectly conscious. I had heard the words of the doctor, and I was glad to exchange the miseries of this short life for that eternity of glory which my Saviour had bought for me. I only regretted to die before bringing more of my dear countrymen out of the idolatrous religion of Rome. From the lips of my soul I said: "Dear Jesus, I am glad to go with Thee just now, but if it be Thy will to let me live a few years more, that I may spread the light of the Gospel among my countrymen, and I will bless Thee eternally, with my converted countrymen, for Thy mercy."

This prayer had scarcely reached the mercy seat, when I saw a dozen bishops marching toward me, sword in hand to kill me. As the first sword was raised to split my head, I made a desperate effort, wrenched it from the hand of my would-be murderer, and struck such a blow on his neck that his head rolled on to the floor. The second, third, fourth, and so on to the last, rushed to kill me; but I struck such terrible blows on the necks of every one of them, that twelve heads were rolling on the floor and swimming in a pool of blood. In my excitement I cried to my friends around me: "Do you not see the heads rolling and the blood flowing on the floor?"

And suddenly I felt a kind of electric shock from head to foot. I was cured! perfectly cured!! I asked my friends for something to eat; I had not taken any food for twelve days. And with tears of joy and gratitude to God, they complied with my request. This last was not only the perfect cure of the body, but it was a perfect cure of the soul. I understood then clearly that the first was not more miraculous than the second. I had a perfect understanding of the diabolical forgeries and miracles of Rome. In both cases I was not cured or saved by the saints, the bishops or the popes, but by my God, through His Son Jesus.

CHAPTER XXX

The 21st of September, 1838, was a day of desolation for me, I received the letter of my bishop appointing me curate of Beauport. That parish was justly considered the very nest of the drunkards of Canada.. The natural resources of that parish were extraordinary. Yet, the people of Beauport were among the poorest and most wretched people of Canada. For almost every cent they earned went into the hands of the saloon-keepers. How many times I heard them fill the air with their cries and blasphemies; and saw the streets reddened with their blood when fighting with one another, like mad dogs!

The Rev. Mr. Gegin, who was their curate since 1825, had accepted the moral principles of the great Roman Catholic theologian Liguori, who says, "that a man is not guilty of the sin of drunkenness, so long as he can distinguish between a small pin and a load of hay." I immediately went to the palace to persuade his lordship to select another priest for Beauport.

He listened to my arguments and answered: "My dear Mr. Chiniquy, you forget that implicit and perfect obedience to his superiors is the virtue of a good priest. Your obstinate resistance to your superiors is one of your weak points. If you continue to follow your own mind rather than obey those whom God has chosen to guide you, I really fear for your future. Your name is entered in our official registers as the curate of Beauport; it will remain there till I change my mind." I saw there was no help, I had to obey.

My predecessor was selling all his furniture before taking charge of his distant parish. He kindly invited me to go and buy, on long credit, what I wished for my own use. The whole parish was there long before me, partly to show their friendly sympathy for their last pastor, and partly to see their new curate. My small stature and leanness cut a poor figure by the side of my tall and jolly predecessor.

"He is hardly bigger than my tobacco box," said one not far from me: "I think I could put him in my vest pocket."

"Has he not the appearance of a salted sardine?" whispered a woman to her neighbor, with a hearty laugh.

After a couple of hours, a large cloth was suddenly removed from a long table, presenting an incredible number of wine and beer glasses, empty decanters and bottles. This brought a burst of laughter and clapping from almost every one. All eyes were turned towards me, and I heard from hundreds of lips: "This is for you, Mr. Chiniquy." I instantly answered: "I do not come to Beauport to buy wine glasses and bottles, but to break them."

These words fell upon their ears as a spark into gunpowder. A deluge of insults and cursings overwhelmed me; and I soon saw that the best thing I could do was to leave.

I immediately returned to the bishop's palace to try and change his mind. I told him what had occurred, stating "I feel that I have neither the moral or the physical power to do any good there."

"I differ with you," replied the bishop. "Evidently the people wanted to try your mettle by inviting you to buy those glasses and you would have lost had you yielded to their desire. You are just what the people of Beauport want. You took them by surprise with your bold rebuke. Believe me, they will bless you, if by the grace of God you fulfill your prophecy; though it will be a miracle if you succeed in making the people of Beauport sober."

Next Sunday was a splendid day, and the church of Beauport was filled. My first sermon was on the text: "Woe is unto me, if I preach not the Gospel." (I Cor. 9:16) With a voice many times suffocated by sobs, I explained some of the awful responsibilities of a pastor. The effect of the sermon was felt to the last day of my priestly ministry in Beauport.

After the sermon, I told them: "I have a favor to ask of you. I have just given you some of the duties of your poor young curate towards you; I want you to return this afternoon at 2:30 that I may teach you some of your duties towards your pastor." At the appointed hour the church was even more crowded.

The text was: "When he (the shepherd) putteth forth his own sheep, he goeth before them, and the sheep follow him; for they know his voice." (John 10:4)

My intensions were to keep my people away from the taverns the greater part of the Sabbath and to impress on their minds the great saving truths by presenting them twice on the same day under different aspects. I continued the practice during the four years I remained in Beauport.

I had not been more than three months at the head of that parish when I decided to form a Temperance Society on the same principles as Father Mathew, in Ireland. First I approached the bishop on the subject, but to my great dismay he absolutely forbade me to even think about it. "Preach against drunkenness, but let the respectable people who are not drunkards alone. St. Paul advised his disciple Timothy to drink wine. Do not try to be more zealous than the Apostles."

Next, I tried gaining support from the neighboring priests. But without a single exception, they laughed at me and forbade me to speak anymore to them of giving up their social glass of wine. I was determined, at any cost, to form the temperance society, but was frightened by the idea, not only of the wrath of the whole clergy, but of the ridicule of the whole country which would overwhelm me in case of a failure.

Perplexed, I decided to write to Father Mathew and ask his advice. That noble apostle of temperance answered, pressing me to begin the work immediately, relying on God, without paying any attention to the opposition of man.

I took his advice and began at once to prepare. Before starting I prayed to God and all His saints, almost day and night. I studied all the best books written in England, France and the U.S.A. on the subject and I had taken a course in anatomy under the learned Dr. Douglas.

At last I felt ready for battle.

CHAPTER XXXI

On March 21, 1839 I gave my first sermon on temperance. I explained how alcohol was destroying not only their lives, but that of their starving children.

"I cannot fight this battle alone," I challenged. "We must raise up a great army with Jesus Christ as our general. He will bless us and lead us to victory. For the next three days we will fill our ranks; so that giant destroyer of your bodies and souls can be driven from our midst!"

The next day 75 men who were considered to be among the most desperate drunkards of Beauport, enrolled themselves under the banner of temperance. On the second day 200 joined the battle. By the third day 300 more took the pledge. During these three days more than two-thirds of my people had publicly taken the pledge of temperance solemnly said in the presence of God, before their altars.

As a great number of people from the surrounding parishes, and even from Quebec, had come to hear me the third day through curiosity, the news of that marvelous work spread very quickly throughout the whole country. The press, both French and English, were unanimous in their praises and felicitations. But when the Protestants of Quebec were blessing God for that reform, the French Canadians, at the example of their priests, denounced me as a fool and heretic.

The indignation of the bishop knew no bounds. A few days after, he ordered me to his palace. "You have compromised our holy religion by introducing a society whose origin is clearly heretical. Last evening the venerable Grand Vicar Demars told me that you would sooner or later become a Protestant, and that this was your first step. Do you not see that the Protestants only praise you? My first thought, when an eye-witness told me yesterday what you had done, was to interdict you. I have been prevented only by the hope that you will yourself dissolve that anti-Catholic association, which smells of heresy and will not be tolerated by your bishop."

I answered: "My lord, have you forgotten I was absolutely against being appointed curate of Beauport; and God knows that you have only to say a word, and I will give you my resignation. But I will put a condition to the resignation: that I will be allowed to publish before the world that the Rev. Mr. Begin, my predecessor, has never been troubled by his bishop for having allowed his people, during twenty-three years, to swim in the mire of drunkenness; and that I have been disgraced by my bishop, and turned out from that same parish, for having been the instrument, by the mercy of God, in making them the most sober people in Canada."

The poor bishop felt, at once, that he could not stand his ground. He also saw that his threats had no influence over me, and that I was not ready to undo what I had done. After a painful silence of a minute or two, he said: "Do you not see that the solemn promises you have extorted from those poor drunkards are rash and unwise; they will break them at the first opportunity? Their future state of degradation, after such an excitement, will be worse than the first."

I answered: "I would partake of your fears if that change were my work; but as it is the Lord's work, we have nothing to fear. About the prophecy of the venerable Mr. Demars, that I have taken my first step towards Protestantism by turning a drunken into a sober people, the venerable Grand Vicar would do better to come and see what the Lord is doing in Beauport, than to slander me and turn false prophets against its curate and people. My only answer is that Protestants, on this question, understand the Word of God, and have more respect for it than we Roman Catholics. It is high time we open our eyes to our false position.

"Would your lordship be kind enough to tell me why I am denounced and abused when Father Mathew is publicly praised by his bishops and blessed by the pope for covering Ireland with temperance societies?"

At that very moment, the sub-secretary entered to tell the bishop that a gentleman wanted to see him immediately on pressing business, and the bishop abruptly dismissed me, to my great comfort and his apparent relief.

With the exception of the Secretary, Mr. Cazeault, all the priests I met that day and the next month, either gave me the cold shoulder or overwhelmed me with their sarcasms. One of them who had friends in Beauport was bold enough to try to go through the whole parish ridiculing me by saying that I was half crazy, and the best thing the people could do was to drink moderately to my health when they went to town.

But at the third house he met a woman, who, after listening to the bad advice he was giving to her husband, said to him: "I do not know if our pastor is a fool in making people sober, but I know you are a messenger of the devil, when you advise my husband to drink again. You know that he was one of the most desperate drunkards of Beauport. You personally know of the blows I have received from him when he was drunk; how poor and miserable we were; how the children had to run on the streets half naked and beg in order not to starve with me!

"Now that my husband has taken the pledge of temperance, we have every comfort. My dear children are well fed and clothed, and I find myself as in a little paradise. If you do not go out of this house at once, I will turn you out with my broomstick." And she would have fulfilled her promise, had not the priest had the good sense to disappear "double quick."

Four months after the foundation of the society in Beauport, peace, happiness, abundance and industry took the place of the riots, fighting, blasphemies and squalid misery. The gratitude and respect of that noble people for their young curate knew no bounds.

CHAPTER XXXII

Within a year, the owners of the seven taverns of Beauport were forced to try some more honorable trade for a living. When this was published by the whole press of Quebec, several of the best thinking people of the surrounding parishes began to say to one another: "Why should we not try to bring into our midst this temperance reformation which is doing so much good in Beauport?" The wives of drunkards would say: "Why does not our curate do here what the curate of Beauport has done?"

One day one of those unfortunate women whose husband had spent a rich inheritance in dissipation came to me. She explained how she had asked her curate to establish a temperance society in his parish, but he had told her "to mind her own business." She had then respectfully requested him to invite me to come and help but had been sternly rebuked at the mention of my name.

The poor woman was weeping when she said: "Is it possible that our priests are so indifferent to our sufferings, and that they will let the demon of drunkenness torture us as long as we live, when God gives us such an easy and honorable way to destroy his power forever?"

My heart was touched by the tears of that lady, and I said to her: "I know a way to put an end to the opposition of your curate, and force him to bring among you the reformation you so much desire, but I must rely upon your most sacred promise of secrecy before opening my mind to you on that subject."

She answered, "I will never reveal your secret. For God's sake tell me what to do."

I replied: "The first time you go to confession, say to your priest that you have a new sin to confess which is very difficult to reveal to him. He will press you more to confess it. You will then say: 'Father, I confess I have lost confidence in you.' Being asked 'Why?' You will tell him: 'Father, you know the bad treatment I have received from my drunken husband, as have hundreds of other wives in your parish. You know the tears we have shed on the ruin of our children, who are destroyed by the bad examples of their drunken fathers. You know the daily crimes and unspeakable abominations caused by drunkenness. You could dry our tears, benefit our husbands and save our children by establishing the society of temperance here as it is in Beauport. But you refuse to do it. How, then, can I believe you are a good priest, with charity and compassion for us?'

"Listen with a respectful silence to what he will tell you, accept his penance, and when he asks you if you regret that sin, answer that you cannot regret it till he has taken the means which God offers him to persuade the drunkards. Get as many other women as you can to go and confess the same thing."

A fortnight later she returned to tell me that more than fifty other respectable women had confessed to the priest that they had lost confidence in him. The poor priest was beside himself, forced every day to hear from his most respectable female parishioners that they were losing confidence in him. He feared lest he lose his fine parish near Quebec and be sent to the backwoods of Canada.

Three weeks later he was knocking at my door. He was very pale and anxious. However, I was happy to see him. He was considered a good priest and had been one of my best friends. I invited him to dine with me and made him feel at home as much as possible, for I knew by his embarrassed manner that he had a very difficult proposition to make. I was not mistaken.

At last he said: "Mr. Chiniquy, would you be kind enough to preach a retreat of temperance, during three days, to my people, as you have done here?"

I answered: "Yes, sir, with the greatest pleasure. But it is on condition that you be the first to take the solemn pledge of temperance, in the presence of your people."

"Certainly," he answered; "for the pastor must be an example to his people."

Three weeks later his parish had nobly followed the example of Beauport. Without losing a day, he went to the two other curates and persuaded them to do what he had done. Six weeks later all the saloons from Beauport to St. Joachim were closed.

Little by little, the country priests were rallying around our glorious banners of temperance. But my bishop, though less severe, was still very cold toward me. At last the good providence of God forced him, through a great humiliation, to count our society among the greatest spiritual and temporal blessings of the age.

At the end of August, 1840, we learned that the Count de Forbin Janson, Bishop de Nancy, in France, was just leaving for Montreal. Father Mathew had told me, in one of his letters, that this bishop had visited him, and blessed his work in Ireland, and had also persuaded the pope to send him his apostolical benediction.

I asked and obtained leave of absence for a few days, and went to Montreal. I went immediately to pay my homage to him and ask him, in the name of God to bravely throw the weight of his great name and position in favor of our temperance societies. He promised he would, adding "The social habit of drinking is so general and strong, that it is almost impossible to save the people from becoming drunkards. I have seen Father Mathew in Ireland and be sure that I shall do all in my power to strengthen your position. But do tell no one that you have seen me."

Some days later in Quebec a grand dinner was given in his honor. As one of the youngest curates I had taken the last seat just opposite the four bishops. When the rich viands and delicate fruits had been well disposed of, bottles of the choicest wines were brought. The Rev. Mr. Demars knocked on the table to command silence, rose and said, "Please, my lord bishops, and gentlemen, let us drink to the health of my Lord Count de Forbin Janson, Primate of Lorraine and Bishop of Nancy."

When the wine was handed to me I passed it to my neighbor and filled my glass with water, hoping none noticed. I was mistaken. The eyes of my bishop, my Lord Signaie, were upon me. With a stern voice, he said: "Mr. Chiniquy, put wine in your glass, to drink with us the health of Mgr. de Nancy."

Paralyzed with terror, I could not utter a word. To openly resist my bishop in the presence of such an august assembly seemed impossible. But to obey him was also impossible, for I had promised my God and my country never to drink any wine. All eyes were upon me.

My heart began to beat so violently that I could not breathe. I wished I had never come to that dinner. A few tears rolled down from my eyes. The Rev. Mr. Lafrance, who was by me, nudged me, and said, "Do you not hear the order of my Lord Signaie?" I remained mute, as if nobody had spoken to me. My eyes were cast down; I wished I were dead. The silence told me that everyone was waiting for my answer; but my lips were sealed. After a minute of that silence, the bishop, with a loud and angry voice repeated: "Why do you not put wine in your glass, and drink to the health of my Lord Forbin Janson, as the rest of us are doing?"

"My lord," I said, with a subdued and trembling voice, "I have put in my glass what I want to drink. I have promised my God and my country that I would never drink any more wine."

The bishop, forgetting where he was, said: "You are nothing but a fanatic, and you want to reform us."

I forgot that I was the subject of that bishop, and remembered that I was a man, in the presence of another man. I raised my head and opened my eyes, and as quick as lightning I rose to my feet, and addressing the Grand Vicar Demars I said, with calmness, "Sir, was it that I might be insulted at your table that you have invited me here? Is it not your duty to defend my honor when I am your guest? But, as you seem to forget what you owe to your guests, I will make my own defense against my unjust aggressor."

Then, turning towards the Bishop de Nancy, I said: "My Lord de Nancy, I appeal to your lordship from the unjust sentence of my own bishop. In the name of God, and of His Son, Jesus Christ, I request you to tell us here if a priest cannot, for His Saviour's sake, and for the good of his fellow-men, as well as for his own self-denial, give up for ever the use of wine and other intoxicating drinks, without being abused, slandered, and insulted, as I am here, in your presence?"

It was evident that my words had made a deep impression on the whole company. A solemn silence followed for a few seconds, which was interrupted by my bishop, who said to the Bishop de Nancy, "Yes, yes, my lord; give us your sentence."

No words can express the excitement of that multitude of priests, accustomed from infancy to abject submission to their bishop, who now found themselves for the first time in the presence of a hand-to-hand conflict between a powerless, humble, unprotected, young curate, and his all-powerful, proud, and haughty archbishop.

The Bishop of Nancy at first refused, but pressed by Bishop Signaie and nine-tenths of that vast assembly of priests, raised his eyes and hands to heaven, and made a silent but ardent prayer to God. Then he said with unspeakable dignity: "My lord of Quebec! Here, before us, is our young priest, Mr. Chiniquy, who, once on his knees, in the presence of God and His angels, for the love of Jesus Christ, the good of his own soul and the good of his country, has promised never to drink! We are the witnesses that he is faithful to his promise.

"And because he keeps his pledge with such heroism, your lordship has called him a fanatic! Now, I am requested to pronounce my verdict on that painful occurrence. Here it is: If I look through the past ages when God Himself was ruling His own people through His prophets, I see Samson, who, by the special order of God, never drank wine or any other intoxicating drink.

"From the Old Testament, I pass to the New, I see John the Baptist, the precursor of our Savior, Jesus Christ, who, to obey the command of God, never drank any wine! When I look at Mr. Chiniquy, and see Samson at his right hand to protect him, and John the Baptist at his left to bless him, I find his position so strong and impregnable, that I would not dare attack or condemn him!"

Bishop de Nancy then sat down, emptied his wine glass into a tumbler, filled it with water and drank to my health.

Nobody thought of drinking his wine; and the health of the Bishop de Nancy was left undrunk. But a good number of priests filled their glasses with water, and giving me a silent sign of approbation, drank to my health.

It was at that table that temperance began her triumphant march through Canada.

CHAPTER XXXIII

Has God given us ears to hear, eyes to see, and intelligence to understand? The pope says, no! But the Son of God says, yes. "Perceive ye not yet, neither understand? Have ye your heart yet hardened? Having eyes, see ye not? and having ears, hear ye not? and do not ye remember?" (Mark 8:17-18)

This solemn appeal of our Saviour to our common sense could demolish the whole fabric of Rome. The pope knows it; hence Roman Catholics are warned not to trust the testimony of their ears, eyes, or intelligence.

There was living at "La Jeune Lorette" an old retired priest, who was blind. To help him, the curates around Quebec used to keep him by turn in their parsonages. The Councils of Rome have forbidden blind priests to say their mass; but on account of high piety, he had gotten from the pope the privilege of celebrating the short mass of the Virgin, which he knew perfectly by heart.

One morning, the old priest was at the altar saying his mass; I was in the vestry hearing confessions when the young servant boy came to me and said, "Father Daule calls you; please come quick."

Fearing something had happened to my old friend, I ran to him. I found him nervously tapping the altar with his hands, as in anxious search of some very precious thing. When very near to him, I said: "What do you want?" He answered with a shriek of distress: "The good god has disappeared from the altar. He is lost!" Hoping that he was mistaken, and that he had only dropped the good god, "Le Bon Dieu," on the floor, by some accident, we made a most minute search but the good god could not be found.

At first, remembering the thousand miracles I had read of the disappearance, and marvelous changes of form of the wafer god, it came to my mind that we were in the presence of some great miracle. But I soon changed my mind. The church of Beauport was inhabited by the boldest and most insolent rats I have ever seen.

Many times when saying mass I had seen the ugly noses of several of them, who, attracted by the smell of the fresh wafer, wanted to make their breakfast with the body, blood, soul, and divinity of my Christ. But, as I was constantly in motion, or praying with a loud voice, the rats had invariably been frightened and fled into their secret quarters.

Father Daule sincerely believed what all the priests of Rome are bound to believe, that he had the power to turn the wafer into God. Leaning my head towards the distressed old priest, I asked him: "Have you not remained, as you are used, a long time motionless, in adoring the good god, after the consecration?"

He quickly answered, "Yes; but what has this to do with the loss of the good god?"

I replied in a low voice, but with an honest accent of distress and awe, "Some rats have dragged away and eaten the good god!"

"What do you say?" replied Father Daule. "The good god carried away and eaten by rats!"

"Yes," I replied, "I have not the least doubt about it."

"My God! my God! what a dreadful calamity upon me!" The old man raised his hands and his eyes to heaven and cried: "My God! my God! Why have you not taken away my life before such a misfortune could fall upon me!" He could not speak any longer; his voice was choked by his sobs.

At first I did not know what to say; a thousand thoughts, some very grave, some exceedingly ludicrous, crossed my mind. The old priest was weeping as a child. He asked me, with a voice broken by his sobs, "What must I do now?" I answered him: "The Church has foreseen occurrences of that kind, and provided for them. The only thing you have to do is to get a new wafer, consecrate it, and continue your mass as if nothing strange had occurred. I will go and get you new bread."

I ran to the vestry and brought a new wafer, which he consecrated and turned into a new god, and finished his mass, as I had told him. After it was over I took the disconsolate old priest by the hand to my parsonage. I tried to calm his feelings by telling him that it was no fault of his; that this strange and sad occurrence was not the first; and that it had been calmly foreseen by the Church which had told us what to do in these circumstances; that there was no fault, no offense against God or man on his part.

I had hoped that the common sense of my words would help him to overcome his feelings, but I was mistaken; his lamentations were as bitter and as long as those of Jeremiah.

At last I lost patience and said: "My dear Father Daule, our great and just God cannot like such an excess of sorrow and regret about a thing which was only, and entirely, under the control of His power and eternal wisdom."

"Mr. Chiniquy," he replied, "I see you lack the attention and experience so often lacking among young priests. You do not comprehend the awful calamity which has just occurred in your church. If you had more faith and piety you would weep with me. How can you speak so lightly of a thing which makes the angels of God weep? Our dear Saviour dragged and eaten by rats! Oh! great God! does not this surpass the humiliation and horrors of Calvary?"

"My dear Father Daule," I replied, "allow me respectfully to tell you that I understand, as well as you do, the nature of the deplorable event of this morning. I would have given my blood to prevent it. But let us look at that fact in its proper light. It did not depend on our will. Our God is the only one who could foresee and prevent it. And, to give you plainly my own mind, if I were God Almighty, and a miserable rat would come to eat me, I would strike him dead before he could touch me."

As you can see, my former robust faith in my priestly power of changing the wafer into my God had largely evaporated. Evidently God wanted to open my eyes to the awful absurdities of a religion whose god could be dragged and eaten by rats. Had I been faithful to the saving insights which were in me then, I would have been saved that very hour; and before the end of that day I would have broken the shameful chains of the pope. In that hour it seemed evident that the dogma of transubstantiation was a most monstrous lie, and my priesthood an insult to God and man.

My intelligence said to me with a thundering voice: "Do not remain any longer the priest of a god whom you make every day, and whom the rats can eat."

Though blind, Father Daule understood very well, by the stern accents of my voice, that my faith in the god whom he had created that morning had been seriously modified, if not entirely crumbled. He remained silent for some time after which he invited me to sit by him and he spoke to me with a pathos and an authority which my youth and his old age alone could justify. He gave me the most awful rebuke I ever had. He overwhelmed me with a deluge of Holy Fathers, Councils, and infallible popes who had believed and preached before the whole world, the dogma of transubstantiation.

If I had paid attention to the voice of my intelligence, and accepted the light which my merciful God was giving me, I could easily have smashed the arguments of the old priest of Rome. But what could my intelligence say against the Church of Rome? I was forbidden to hear it, for it carried no weight against so many learned, holy, infallible intelligences!

Alas! I was not aware then that the weight of the intelligence of God was on my side; and that, weighed against the intelligence of the popes, was greater than all the worlds against a grain of sand.

One hour later, shedding tears of regret, I was at the feet of Father Daule, in the confessional box, confessing the great sin I had committed by doubting, for a moment, the power of the priest to change a wafer into God. He gave me my pardon. For my penance he forbade me ever to say a word about the sad end of the god he had created that morning; for, said he, "This would destroy the faith of the most sincere Roman Catholics."

The other part of the penance was that for nine days I had to go on my knees before the 14 stations of the cross, and say a penitential psalm before every picture, which I did. By the sixth day the skin of my knees was pierced, and the blood was flowing freely. I suffered real torture every time I knelt down, and at every step I made. But it seemed to me that these terrible tortures were nothing compared to my great iniquity!

CHAPTER XXXIV

Several days prior to the victory won during the dinner party honoring Bishop de Forbin Janson . . . I found myself in a state of great despair over the wrath I had incurred by establishing a temperance society. My feelings of isolation were becoming unbearable. It was indeed one of the darkest hours of my life.

While gazing through my window I noticed a stranger coming to my door. From his demeanor I perceived him to be a gentleman of quality. Clasping my hand as though we were old friends, he introduced himself and with great joy, proceeded to explain the purpose of his visit.

He had been chosen to personally inform me that the vast majority of English speaking people, not only of Quebec, but throughout Canada were filled with the deepest admiration for the great reform I had accomplished in Beauport. And that the people he represented were well aware of the stern opposition I was facing from my superiors.

He said, "God is on your side," quoting Proverbs 23:31,32, "Take courage sir, for you have on your side Jesus Christ Himself, for He has said; 'Blessed are they who do hunger after righteousness for they shall be filled. Blessed are ye when men shall revile you and persecute you and say all manner of evil against you falsely for my sake.' (Matt. 5:6,11)

"Though many oppose you there are many more praying for you day and night. Asking our Heavenly Father to pour upon you His most abundant blessings." He then proceeded to give me his views on temperance. They were identical to my own! I marveled at his sincerity of purpose and clarity of understanding.

His words of encouragement were truly prophetic; "Though you stand alone today and the seeds you sow are often watered with your own tears, I know that before long a grateful country will bless your name."

Hardly giving me time to express gratitude, he said, "I know you must be very busy and I shan't take up anymore of your time. Good-bye sir, and may the Lord bless you and be your keeper in all your ways."

The unexpected news that the English speaking people were praying for me filled my heart with joy and surprise. My first thought was to fall on my knees and thank God for sending me such a messenger. Every word from his lips had fallen on my wounded soul as the oil of the Good Samaritan upon the bleeding wounds of the traveler to Jericho.

When suddenly my mind recoiled in horror accompanied by a sense of unspeakable humiliation. That man was a Protestant!

A person who my Church had taught to anathematize and curse as slaves of Satan, rebels against Christ. I was so ashamed to think of those people praying for me!

Yet, a voice rose up within me; try as I might to silence it, the louder it grew, "Who is nearer God?"

The answers coming from my soul could not be silenced. I was forced to listen and blush at the reality before my eyes. Pride! yes diabolical pride! is the vice, (par excellence) of every priest of Rome. Just as he is taught to believe and say that his Church is far above every other church, the same is taught of the priesthood. As a priest, he is above all the kings, emperors, governors, and presidents of the world. Pride is the daily bread of the pope, bishops, priests and even the lowest layman in the Church of Rome. It's the great secret of their power and strength. It nerves them with an iron will to bring everything to their feet, subject every human being to their will. The priest of Rome believes that he is called by God Almighty to rule, subdue and govern the world.

If anyone suspects I exaggerate, read the following words which Cardinal Manning puts in the lips of the pope in one of his lectures: "I acknowledge no civil power; I am the subject of no prince. I am more than this. I claim to be the supreme judge and director of the conscience of men: of the peasant who tills his field, and of the prince who sits upon the throne; of the household that lives in the shade of privacy, and the legislator that makes laws for the kingdom. I am the sole, last, supreme judge of what is right or wrong."

That pride which was in me, though I didn't see it then, had received a rude check indeed, from my Protestant visitor.

What a strange being man is! How fickle are his judgments! In 1842, they had no words sufficiently flattering to praise the very man they had spit upon in 1838 for doing the very same thing. This sudden passage from condemnation to that of praise, when I was doing the very same work, had the good effect to cure me of that natural pride which one is apt to feel when publicly applauded by men.

CHAPTER XXXV

By the great mercy of God the parish of Beauport, which at first had appeared to me as a bottomless abyss in which I was to perish, had been changed for me into an earthly paradise. There was only one desire in my heart: that I never should be removed from it.

Suddenly the carriage of the Bishop of Quebec came to the door of the parsonage. The sub-secretary, directed his steps towards the garden, where I was, and handed me the following letter from the Right Rev. Turgeon, Coadjutor of Quebec:

My Dear Mons. Chiniquy:

His lordship Bishop Signaie and I wish to confer with you on a most important matter. We have sent our carriage to bring you to Quebec. Please come without the least delay.

Truly yours,
FLAV. TURGEON

One hour after, I was with the two bishops. My Lord Signaie said: "Monseigneur Turgeon will tell you why we have sent for you in such haste."

"Mons. Chiniquy," said Bishop Turgeon, "is not Kamouraska your birthplace?"

"Yes, my lord."

"Do you like that place, and do you interest yourself much in its welfare?"

"Of course, my lord, the most happy hours of my youth were spent there."

"You know," rejoined the bishop, "that Rev. Mons. Varin has been too infirm, these last years, to superintend the spiritual interest of that important place. Hundreds of the best families of Quebec and Montreal resort there every summer. Drunkenness, luxury, and immoralities of the most degrading kind are eating up the very life of Kamouraska today."

These words passed through my soul as a two-edged sword: "My lord, I hope it is not your intention to remove me from my dear parish of Beauport."

"No, Mons. Chiniquy, we will not use our authority to break the sacred and sweet ties which unite you to the parish of Beauport. But we will put before your conscience the reasons we wish you at the head of that great and important parish."

For more than an hour the two bishops made strong appeals to my charity for the multitudes who were sunk into the abyss of drunkenness and every vice, and had no one to save them.

Bishop Signaie added, "Will not a double crown be put upon your forehead by your bishops, your country, and your God, if you consent to be the instrument of the mercies of God towards the people of your own birthplace, and the surrounding country? Can you rest and live in peace now in Beauport, when you hear day and night the voice of the multitudes, who cry: 'Come to our help, we are perishing'? What will you answer to God, at the last day, when He will show you the thousands of precious souls lost at Kamouraska, because you refused to go to their rescue?"

Their paternal friendly appeals had more power over me than orders. I consented to go, well aware of the endless troubles and warfare I would have to face.

The people of Beauport did all in their power to induce the bishops to let me remain among them some time longer. But the sacrifice had to be made. I gave my farewell address in the midst of indescribable cries, sobs, and tears; and on the 17th of September, I departed for Kamouraska.

When I took leave of the Bishop of Quebec, they showed me a letter just received by them from Mons. Varin, filled with the most bitter expressions of indignation on account of the choice of such a fanatic and firebrand as Chiniquy, for a place as well known for its peaceful habits and harmony among all classes. The last words of the letter were as follows:

"The clergy and people of Kamouraska and vicinity consider the appointment of Mons. Chiniquy to this parish as an insult, and we hope and pray that your lordship may change your mind on the subject."

In showing me the letter, my lords Signaie and Turgeon said: "We fear that you will have more trouble than we expected with the old curate and his partisans, but we commend you to the grace of God and the protection of the Virgin Mary, remembering that our Savior has said: 'Be of good cheer; I have overcome the world.'" (John 16:33)

I arrived at Kamouraska the 21st of September, 1842, on one of the finest days of the year. But my heart was filled with an unspeakable desolation, for all along the way the curates had told me that the people, with their old pastor, were unanimous in their opposition to my going there. I dismissed my driver, took my satchel in my hand, entered the church and I spent more than an hour in fervent prayers, or rather in cries and tears. I felt so heart-sick that I needed that hour of rest and prayer. The tears I shed there relieved my burdened spirit.

There is a marvelous power in the prayers and tears which come from the heart. I felt as a new man. I seemed to hear the trumpet of God calling me to the battlefield. My only business then was to go and fight, relying on Him alone for victory. I took my traveling bag, went out of the church and walked slowly towards the parsonage.

At my knocking, an angry voice called out: "Walk in."

I entered, made a step toward the old and infirm curate. As I was about to salute him, he angrily said: "The people of Beauport have made great efforts to keep you in their midst, but the people of Kamouraska will make as great efforts to turn you out of this place."

"Mons. le Cure," I answered calmly, "God knoweth that I never desired to leave Beauport for this place. But I think it is that great and merciful God who has brought me here by the hand; and I hope He will help me to overcome all opposition, from whatever quarter it may come."

He replied angrily: "Is it to insult me that you call me 'Mons. le Cure?' I am no more the curate of Kamouraska. You are the curate now, Mr. Chiniquy."

"I beg your pardon, my dear Mr. Varin; you are still, I hope you will remain all your life, the honored and beloved curate of Kamouraska. The respect and gratitude I owe you have caused me to refuse the titles and honors which our bishop wanted to give me."

"But, then, if I am the curate, what are you?" replied the old priest, with more calmness.

"I am nothing but a simple soldier of Christ, and a sower of the good seed of the Gospel!" I answered. "When I fight the common enemy in the plain, as Joshua did, you, like Moses, will stand on the top of the mountain, lift up your hands to heaven, send your prayers to the mercy seat, and we will gain the day. Then both will bless the God of our salvation for the victory."

"Well! well! this is beautiful, grand, and sublime," said the old priest, with a voice filled with friendly emotions. "But where is your household furniture, your library?"

"My household furniture," I answered, "is in this little bag, which I hold in my hand. I do not want any of my books as long as I have the pleasure and honor to be with the good Mons. Varin, who will allow me, I am sure of it, to ransack his splendid library, and study his rare and learned books."

"But what rooms do you wish to occupy?" rejoined the good old curate.

"As the parsonage is yours and mine," I answered, "please tell me where you want me to sleep and rest. I will accept, with gratitude. I do not want to bother you in any way. When I was young, a poor orphan in your parish, some twenty years ago, were you not a father to me? Please continue to look upon me as your own child, for I have always loved and considered you as a father, and I still do. You were my guide and adviser in my first steps in the ways of God? Please continue to guide and advise me to the end of your life."

I had not finished the last sentence when the old man burst into tears, threw himself into my arms, pressed me to his heart, and said, with a voice half-suffocated by his sobs: "Dear Mr. Chiniquy, forgive me the evil things I have written and said about you. You are welcome in my parsonage, and I bless God to have sent me such a young friend, who will help me to carry the burden of my old age."

I then handed him the bishop's letter, which had confirmed all I had said about my mission of peace towards him.

From that day to his death, which occurred six months after, I never had a more sincere friend than Mr. Varin.

The principal opposition the people had to my coming was that I was the nephew of the Hon. Amable Dionne, who had made a colossal fortune at their expense. The Rev. Mr. Varin, who was always in his debt, was forced by the circumstances, to buy everything, both for himself and the church, from him, and had to pay without murmur the most exorbitant prices for everything.

The very next day after my arrival, the beadle told me that the church needed a few yards of cotton to make some repairs, and asked me if he would not go, as usual, to Mr. Dionne's store. I told him to go there first, ask the price of that article, and then go to the other stores, ordering him to buy at the cheapest one. Thirty cents was asked at Mr. Dionne's, and only fifteen cents at Mr. St. Pierre's; of course, we bought at the latter's store.

The day was not over, before this apparently insignificant fact was known all over the parish, and was taking the most extraordinary and unforeseen proportions. Farmers would meet with their neighbors and congratulate themselves that, at last, the taxes they had to pay the store were at an end. Many came to Mr. St. Pierre to hear from his own lips that their new curate had, at once, freed them from what they considered the long and ignominious bondage. For the rest of this week this was the only subject of conversation. They congratulated themselves that they had, at last, a priest with such an independent and honest mind, that he would not do them any injustice even to please a relative in whose house he had spent the years of his childhood. This simple act of fair play towards that people won over their affection. Only one little dark spot remained in their minds against me. They had been told that the only subject on which I could preach was: rum, whiskey, and drunkenness.

There was an immense crowd at church, the next Sunday. My text was: "As the Father has loved Me, so have I loved you." (John 15:9) Showing them how Jesus had proved that He was their friend. But their sentiments of piety and pleasure at what they had heard were nothing compared to their surprise when they saw that I preached nearly an hour without saying a word on whiskey, rum or beer.

CHAPTER XXXVI

At the invitation of all the curates to establish temperance societies among their people, I had the sad opportunity, as no priest ever had in Canada, to know the secret and public scandals of each parish. When I went to the Eboulements, on the north side of the river, invited by the Rev. Noel Toussignant, I learned from the very lips of that young priest, and the ex-priest Tetreau, the history of a most shameful scandal.

In 1830, a young priest of Quebec called Derome had fallen in love with one of his young female penitents of Vercheres, where he had preached a few days. He had persuaded her to follow him to the parsonage of Quebec. To better conceal their iniquity from the public, he persuaded his victim to dress herself as a young man and throw her dress in the river to make her parents and the whole parish believe that she was drowned.

I had seen her many times at the parsonage of Quebec, under the name of Joseph, and had much admired her refined manners, though more than once I was very much inclined to think that the smart Joseph was no one else than a lost girl. But the respect I had for the curate of Quebec (who was the coadjutor of the bishop) and his young vicars, caused me to reject those suspicions. Things went on pretty smoothly between Joseph and the priest for several years, till some suspicions arose in the minds of the sharp-sighted people of the parish, who told the curate that it would be safer and more honorable for him to get rid of his servant. In order to put an end to those suspicions, and to retain him in the parsonage, the curate persuaded him to marry the daughter of a poor neighbor.

The two girls were duly married by the curate, who continued his criminal intimacies, in the hope that no one would trouble him any more on that subject. But not long after he was removed to La Petite Riviere, in 1838 the Rev. M. Tetreau was appointed curate. This new priest, knowing nothing of the abominations which his predecessor had practised, continued to employ Joseph. One day, when Joseph was working at the gate of the parsonage, in the presence of several people, a stranger came and asked him if Mr. Tetreau was at home.

"Yes, sir, Mr. Curate is at home," answered Joseph; "but as you seem a stranger to the place, would you allow me to ask you from what parish you come?"

"I am not ashamed of my parish," answered the stranger. "I come from Vercheres."

At the word "Vercheres," Joseph turned so pale that the stranger was puzzled. He looked carefully at him, and exclaimed:

"Oh! my God! What do I see here? Genevieve! Genevieve! over whom we have mourned so long as drowned! Here you are disguised as a man!"

"Dear uncle" (it was her uncle); "for God's sake, not a word more here!"

But it was too late; the people who were there had heard the uncle and the niece. Their long and secret suspicions were well-founded. One of their former priests had kept a girl, under the disguise of a man, in his house; and to blind his people more thoroughly, he had married that girl to another, in order to have them both in his house when he pleased, without awakening any suspicions!

The news went, almost as quickly as lightning, from one end to the other of the parish, and spread all over the country, on both sides of the St. Lawrence. I had heard of that horror, but could not believe it. However, I had to believe it, when, on the spot, I heard from the lips of the ex-curate, M. Tetreau, and the new curate, M. Noel Toussignant, and from the lips of the landlord, the Honorable Laterriere, the following details, which had come to light only a short time before.

The justice of the peace had investigated the matter, in the name of public morality. Joseph was brought before the magistrates, who decided that a physician should be charged to make, not a *post-mortem*, but an *ante-mortem* inquest. The Honorable Laterriere, who made the inquest, declared that Joseph was a girl, and the bonds of marriage were legally dissolved.

The bishop and his vicars immediately sent a trustworthy man with two thousand dollars to induce the girl to leave the country without delay. She accepted the offer and crossed to the United States where she was soon married, and where she still lives.

I wished that this story had never been told me, or at least that I might be allowed to doubt some of its circumstances; but there was no help. I was forced to acknowledge that in my Church of Rome there was such corruption from head to foot which could scarcely be surpassed in Sodom. I remember what the Rev. Mr. Perras had told me of the tears and desolation of Bishop Plessis when he had discovered that all the priests of Canada, with the exception of three, were atheists.

But the abominations of which Joseph was a victim seemed to overstep the conceivable limits of infamy. For the first time, I sincerely regretted that I was a priest. The priesthood of Rome seemed then, to me, the very fulfillment of the prophecy of Revelation, about the great prostitute who made the nations drunk with the wine of her prostitutions. (Rev. 17:1-5)

The auricular confession, which I knew to be the cause of these abominations, appeared to me, what it really is, a school of perdition for the priest and his female penitents. The priest's oath of celibacy was to my eyes in those hours of distress but a shameful mask to conceal a corruption which was unknown in the most depraved days of old paganism.

I still believed there was no salvation outside the Church of Rome, but my soul was filled with trouble and anxiety. I not only distrusted myself, but I lost confidence in the rest of the priests and bishops. To whatever side I turned my eyes, I saw nothing but the most seducing examples of perversion. I wished to depart from this deceitful and lost world.

The Rev. Mr. Guignes, Superior of the Monastery of the Fathers of Oblates of Mary Immaculate, at Longueil, near Montreal, came to pass a few days with me, for the benefit of his health. I confessed my fears to him. The Reverend Superior answered me: "I understand your fears perfectly. They are legitimate and too well-founded. I know the formidable dangers which surround the priest. I have not dared to be a secular priest a single day. I knew the humiliating and disgraceful history of Joseph. Nay! I know many things still more horrible and unspeakable which I have learned when preaching and hearing confessions in France and in

Canada. The fact is, that it is morally impossible for a secular priest to keep his vows of celibacy, except by a miracle of the grace of God. Our holy church would be a modern Sodom long ago had not our merciful God granted her grace through the many priests who have always enrolled themselves in the different religious orders. Only the priests whom God calls, in His mercy, to become members of those orders, are safe. For they are under the paternal care and surveillance of superiors whose zeal and charity are like a shield to protect them. Their holy and strict laws are like strong walls and high towers which the enemy cannot storm."

The last Sabbath of September I gave my farewell address to my dear parish to go to Longueil and become a novice of the Oblates of Mary Immaculate.

CHAPTER XXXVII

On the first Sabbath of November, 1846, I asked to be received as a novice of the religious order of the Oblates of Mary Immaculate of Longueuil, whose object is to preach retreats (revivals) among the people. No child of the Church of Rome ever entertained more exalted views of the beauty and holiness of the monastic life than I had the day I enrolled myself under its mysterious banners.

How easy to secure salvation now! I had only to look to Father Guigues and obey him as my Father in Heaven. Yes! His will was to be for me, the will of my God. Though I might err in obeying him, my errors would not be laid to my charge. To save my soul, I would have only to be like a corpse in the hands of my father superior. Without any anxiety or any responsibility whatever of my own, I was to be led to heaven as the new-born child in the arms of his loving mother.

But how short were to be these fine dreams of my poor deluded mind! When on my knees, Father Guigues handed me, with great solemnity, the Latin books of the rules of that monastic order which is their real gospel, warning me that it was a *secret book,* and he made me solemnly promise that I would never show it to anyone outside of the order.

Alone in my cell the next morning I said to myself: "Have you not a thousand times heard and said that the Holy Church of Rome absolutely condemns and anathematizes secret societies?" After having, in vain, tried, in my mind, to reconcile these two things, I happily remembered that I was a corpse, that I had forever given up my private judgment — that my only business now was to obey.

As I read with the utmost attention, I soon understood why this book was kept from the eyes of the curates and the secular priests.

To my unspeakable amazement, I found that, from the beginning to the end, it speaks with the most profound contempt for them all.

The Oblate who studies his book of rules, his only gospel, must have his mind filled with the idea of his superior holiness, not only over the poor sinful, secular priest, but over everyone else. The Oblate alone is Christian, holy, and sacred; the rest of the world is lost! The Oblate alone is the salt of the earth, the light of the world! I said to myself: "Is it to attain to this pharisaical perfection that I have left my beautiful and dear parish?"

However, after some time spent in these despondent reflections, I remembered the frightful, unsuspected, and numberless scandals I had known in almost every parish I had visited. I remembered the drunkenness of that curate, the impurities of this one, the ignorance of another, the worldliness, and absolute want of faith of others, and concluded that, after all, the Oblates were not far from the truth.

Finally I said to myself: "After all, if the Oblates live a life of holiness, as I expect to find here, is it a crime that they should feel and express among themselves the difference which exists between a regular and a secular clergy? Am I come here to judge and condemn these holy men? No! I came here to save myself by the practice of the most heroic Christian virtues, the first of which, is that I should absolutely and forever, give up my *private judgment* — consider myself as a corpse in the hand of my superior."

With all the fervor of my soul, I prayed to God and to the Virgin Mary day and night that first week that I might attain that supreme state of perfection, where I would have no will, no judgment of my own. The days of that first week passed very quickly, spent in prayer, reading and meditation of the Scriptures, study of ecclesiastical history and ascetical books, from half-past five in the morning till half-past nine at night.

The meals were taken at the regular hours of seven, twelve, and six o'clock, during which, with rare exceptions, silence was kept, and pious books were read. The quality of the food was good; but, at first, before they got a female cook to preside over the kitchen, everything was so unclean that I had to shut my eyes at meals. I would have complained, had not my lips been sealed by that strange monastic view of perfection that every religious man is a corpse! What does a corpse care about the cleanness or uncleanliness of what is put into its mouth?

The third day, having drank at breakfast a glass of milk which was literally mixed with the dung of the cow, my stomach rebelled; a circumstance which I regretted exceedingly, attributing it to my want of monastic perfection. I envied the high state of holiness of the other fathers who had so perfectly attained to the sublime perfection of submission that they could drink that impure milk just as if it had been clean.

One day after tea we were going from the dining room to the chapel to pass five or ten minutes in adoration of the wafer god. We had two doors to cross, and it was pretty dark. Being the last who had entered the monastery, I had to walk first, the other monks following me. We were reciting, with a loud voice, a Latin Psalm. We were all marching rapidly when suddenly my feet met a large, unseen object, and down I fell, rolling on the floor; my next companion did the same, and rolled over me, and so did five or six others, who, in the dark, had also struck their feet on that object.

In a moment, we were five or six "Holy Fathers" rolling on each other on the floor, unable to raise up, splitting our sides with convulsive laughter. It turned out that Father Brunette, in one of his fits of humility, had left the table a little before the rest, with the permission of the Superior, to lay himself flat on the floor across the door.

No words can describe my shame when I saw almost every day, some performance of this kind under the name of Christian humility. In vain I tried to silence the voice of my intelligence, which spoke louder, day after day, that such acts of humility were a mockery.

In vain I said to myself, "Chiniquy, thou art not come here to philosophize but to sanctify thyself by becoming like a corpse, which has no preconceived ideas, no acquired store of knowledge, no rule of common sense to guide it! Poor, wretched, sinful Chiniquy, thou art here to save thyself by admiring every iota of the holy rules of your superiors, and to obey every word of their lips." I envied the humble piety of the other good Fathers, who were apparently so happy, having conquered that haughty reason which was constantly rebelling in me.

Twice a week I went to my guide and confessor, Father Allard, the master of novices, with my vain efforts to subdue my rebellious reason. He always gladdened me with the promise that, sooner or later, I should have that perfect peace which is promised to the humble monk when he has attained the supreme monastic perfection of considering himself a corpse in the hands of his superiors.

My sincere and constant efforts to reconcile myself to the rules of the monastery were, however, soon to receive a new and rude check. I had read in the book of rules, that a true monk must closely watch those who live with him, and secretly report to his superior the defects and sins which he detects in them. The first time I read that strange rule, my mind was so taken up by other things that I did not pay much attention to it. But the second time I studied that clause I said: "Is it possible that we are a band of spies?"

I was not long in seeing its disastrous effects. One of the fathers for whom I had a particular affection, and who had many times proven his sincere friendship, said to me one day: "For God's sake, my dear Father Chiniquy, tell me if it is you who denounced me to the Superior for having said that the conduct of Father Guigues towards me was uncharitable?"

"No! my dear friend," I answered, "I never said such a thing against you."

"I am glad to know that," he rejoined, "for I was told by some of the fathers that you were the one who had reported me to the Superior as guilty, though I am innocent of that offense. I could not believe it." He added with tears, "I regret having left my parish to be an Oblate. That abominable law makes a real hell of this monastery, and, I suppose, of all the monastic orders. When you have passed more time here, you will see that that law of detection puts an insurmountable wall between us all; it destroys every spring of Christian and social happiness."

"I understand perfectly well what you say," I answered him; "the last time I was alone with Father Superior he asked me why I had said that the present Pope was an old fool; he persisted in telling me that I must have said it, 'for'; he added, 'one of our most reliable fathers has assured me you said it.' 'Well, my dear Father Superior,' I answered him, 'that reliable father has told you a big lie; I never said such a thing, because I sincerely think that our present Pope is one of the wisest that ever ruled the church.'"

I added, "Now I understand why the conversations are colorless and without life in the hours we are allowed to talk. Nobody dares to speak his mind on any grave subject."

"That is just the reason," answered my friend. "When some of the fathers, like you and me, would prefer to be hung rather than become spies, the great majority of them, particularly among the French priests recently imported from France, will not hear ten words from your lips on any subject without finding an opportunity of reporting eight of them as unbecoming and unchristian, to the superiors.

"I do not say that it is always through malice that they give such false reports; it is more through want of judgment. They are very narrow minded; they do not understand the half of what they hear in its true sense; and they give their false impressions to the superiors, who, unfortunately, encourage that system of spying as the best way of transforming every one of us into corpses. As we are never confronted with our false accusers, we can never know them, and we lose confidence in each other; thus it is that the sweetest and holiest springs of true Christian love are forever dried up."

Because of this spying system a celebrated French writer, who had been a monk himself, wrote: "Monks enter a monastery without knowing each other; they live there without loving each other; and they depart from each other without any regret."

Not long after my reception as a novice, the superior of the Seminary of St. Sulpice, and grand vicar of the Diocese of Montreal, the Rev. Mr. Quiblier, knocked at our door, to rest an hour, and take breakfast with us. This unfortunate priest, who was among the best orators and the best looking men Montreal had ever seen, had lived such a profligate life with his penitent nuns and ladies of Montreal, that a cry of indignation from the whole people had forced Bishop Bourget to send him back to France. Our father superior took the opportunity of his visit to make us bless God for having gathered us behind the walls of our monastery where the efforts of the enemy were powerless.

It was not long after the public fall of the grand vicar of Montreal, when a fine-looking widow was engaged to preside over our kitchen. She was more than forty years old, and had very good manners. Unfortunately, she had not been four months in the monastery, when she fell in love with her father confessor, one of the most pious of the French father Oblates. Both were found, in an evil hour, forgetting one of the holy laws of God. The guilty priest was punished and the weak woman dismissed. But an unspeakable shame remained upon us all!

From that day forward, the strange and beautiful illusions which had brought me to that monastery faded away. I studied the Oblates with my eyes opened, and I saw them just as they were.

In the spring of 1847, having a severe illness, the doctor ordered me to go to the Hotel Dieu of Montreal near the splendid St. Mary's Church. I made there the acquaintance of a venerable old nun, who was very talkative. She was one of the superiors of the house; her family name was Urtubise. Her mind was still full of indignation at the bad conduct of two father Oblates, who, under the pretext of sickness, had lately come to her monastery to seduce the young nuns who were serving them.

She told me how she had turned them out, forbidding them ever to come again, under any pretext, into the hospital. After she had given me several other spicy stories, I asked her if she had known Maria Monk when she was in their house, and what she thought of her book, "Awful Disclosures?"

"I have known her well," she said. "She spent six months with us. I have read her book, which was given me that I might refute it. But after reading it, I refused to have anything to do with that deplorable *exposure*. There are surely some inventions and suppositions in that book. But there is a sufficient amount of truth to cause all our nunneries to be pulled down by the people, if only the half of them were known to the public!"

She then said to me: "For God's sake, do not reveal these things to the world, till the last one of us is dead, if God spares you." She then covered her face with her hands, burst into tears, and left the room.

I remained horrified. I regretted having heard her words, though I was determined to respect her request not to reveal the terrible secrets she had entrusted to me. My God knows that I never repeated a word of it till now. But I think it is my duty to reveal to my country and the whole world the truth on that grave subject, as it was given me by a most unimpeachable eye-witness.

Though not quite recovered I left the same day for Longueuil, where I entered the monastery with a heavy heart. The day before, two of the fathers had come back from a two or three months' evangelical excursion among the lumber men who were cutting wood in the forests along the Ottawa River. I was glad to hear of their arrival. I hoped that the interesting history of their evangelical excursions would cause a happy diversion from the deplorable things I had recently learned.

But only one of those fathers could be seen, and his conversation was anything but interesting and pleasant. There was evidently a dark cloud around him. And the other Oblate? The very day of his arrival he had been ordered to keep to his room and make a retreat of ten days, during which time he was forbidden to speak to anyone.

I inquired from a devoted friend among the old Oblates the reason of such a strange thing. "Poor Father D— — has seduced one of his fair penitents on the way. She was a married woman, the lady of the house where our missionaries used to receive the most cordial hospitality. The husband having discovered the infidelity of his wife, came very near killing her; he ignominiously turned out the two fathers and wrote a terrible letter to the superior.

"Do these deplorable acts occur often among the father Oblates?" I asked. My friend raised his eyes filled with tears and with a deep sigh, he answered: "Dear Father Chiniquy, would to God that I could tell you that it is the first. But alas! you know by what has occurred with our female cook that it is not. And you know also the abominable life of Father Telmont with the two nuns at Ottawa!"

"If it be so," I replied, "where is the spiritual advantage of the regular clergy over the secular?"

"The only advantage I see," answered my friend, "is that the regular clergy gives himself with more impunity to every kind of debauch and licentiousness than the secular. The monks being concealed from the eyes of the public inside the walls of their monastery where nobody, or at least very few people, have any access, are more easily conquered by the devil, and more firmly kept in his chains, than the secular priests. The sharp eyes of the public, and the daily contact the secular priests have with their relations and parishioners, form a powerful restraint upon our depraved nature. In the monastery there is no restraint except the childish and ridiculous punishments of retreats, kissing of the floor, or of the feet, prostration upon the ground, as Father Brunette did, a few days after your coming among us.

"That great and divine law of self-respect, which God Himself has implanted in the heart of every man and woman who live in a Christian society, is completely destroyed in the monastery and nunnery. The foundation of perfection in the monk and the nun is that they must consider themselves as corpses. Do you not see that this principle strikes at the root of all that God has made good, grand, and holy in man?

"If you study the true history, *not the lying history,* of monasticism you will find the details of a corruption impossible anywhere else, not even among the lowest houses of prostitution. Read the Memoirs of Scipio de Ricci, one of the most pious and intelligent bishops our Church has ever had, and you will see that the monks and the nuns of Italy live the very life of the brutes in the fields. Yes! read the terrible revelations of what is going on among those unfortunate men and women, whom the iron hand of monasticism keeps tied in their dark dungeons, you will hear from the very lips of the nuns that the monks are more free with them than husbands are with their legitimate wives. You will see that every one of those monastic institutions is a new Sodom! Everything is mechanical, material, false, in the life of a monk and a nun. Even the best virtues are deceptions and lies.

"Have you not remarked how those so-called monks speak with the utmost contempt of the rest of the world! I have had opportunities to see the profound hatred which exists among all monastic orders against each other. How the Dominicans have always hated the Franciscans, and how they both hate the Jesuits, who pay them back in the same coin! What a strong and nameless hatred divides the Oblates, to whom we belong, from the Jesuits! The Jesuits never lose an opportunity of showing us their supreme contempt! You are aware that it is absolutely forbidden to an Oblate to confess to a Jesuit. It is forbidden for a Jesuit to confess to an Oblate, or to any other priest.

"I have found among the monks of Canada the very same things I have seen among those of France and Italy. With very few exceptions they are all corpses, absolutely dead to every sentiment of true honesty and real Christianity; they are putrid carcasses, which have lost the dignity of manhood."

I regret that the remarkable monk whose abridged views on monasticism I have here given, should have requested me never to give his name. He was eventually able to obtain an assignment to preach to the savages of the Rocky Mountains and there, without noise, he slipped out of their hands; broke his chains to live the life of a freed man in Christ, in the holy bonds of Christian marriage with a respectable American lady.

I had, a year earlier, been a weak and timid soldier, frightened by the ruins spread everywhere on the battle field. I looked around to find a shelter against the impending danger and thought that the monastery of the Oblates of Mary Immaculate was one of those strong towers, built by my God, where the arrows of the enemy could not reach me, and I threw myself into it.

Suddenly the high towers and walls around me fell to the ground and turned into dust. And I heard a voice saying to me: "Soldier! come out and get in the light of the sun; trust no more in the walls built by the hand of man; they are nothing but dust. Come and fight in the open day, under the eyes of God, protected only by the gospel banner of Christ! Come out from behind those walls — they are a diabolical deception, a snare, a fraud!"

I listened to that voice, and on the 1st of November, 1847 I bade adieu to the inmates of the monastery of the Oblates of Mary Immaculate.

CHAPTER XXXVIII

The eleven months spent in the monastery of the Oblates of Mary Immaculate were among the greatest favors God has granted me. No testimony whatever could have convinced me that the monastic institutions were not one of the most blessed of the Gospel. But just as the eyes of Thomas were opened only after he had seen Christ's wounds, so I could never have believed that the monastic institutions were of heathen and diabolical origin if my God had not forced me to see with my own eyes their unspeakable corruptions.

Though I remained for some time longer a sincere Catholic priest, I dare say that God Himself had just broken the strongest tie of my affections and respect for that Church.

Long before my leaving the Oblates, many influential priests of the district of Montreal had told me that my only chance of success, if I wanted to continue my crusade against the demon of drunkenness, was to work alone. At the head of the French Canadian curates who thus spoke, was my venerable personal friend and benefactor the Rev. Mr. Brassard, curate of Longueuil. He had not only been one of my most devoted friends and teachers when I was studying in the college of Nicolet, but he had helped me with his own money to go through the last four years of my studies.

No one had thought more highly than he of the Oblates of Mary Immaculate when they first settled in Canada. But their monastery was too near his parsonage for their own benefit. His sharp eyes, high intelligence, and integrity of character soon detected that there was more false varnish than pure gold on their glittering escutcheon.. Several love scrapes between some of the Oblates and the pretty young ladies of his parish had filled him with disgust.

But what had absolutely destroyed his confidence was the discovery that Father Guigues, the superior, was opening the letters of Mr. Brassard which many times had passed from the post office through his hands. That criminal action had come very near to being brought before the legal courts by Mr. Brassard. This was avoided only by Father Guigues acknowledging his guilt, asking pardon in the most humiliating way before me and several other witnesses.

Long before I left the Oblates, Mr. Brassard had said to me: "The Oblates are not the men you think them to be. I have been sorely disappointed in them, and your disappointment will be no less than mine when your eyes are opened. I know that you will not remain long in their midst. I offer you, in advance, the hospitality of my parsonage, when your conscience calls you out of their monastery!"

I availed myself of this kind invitation on the evening of the 1st of November, 1847. The next week was spent in preparing the memo which I intended to present to my Lord Bourget, Bishop of Montreal, as an explanation of my leaving the Oblates. I knew that he was disappointed and displeased with the step I had taken.

This did not surprise me. I knew that those monks had been imported by him from France and that they were pets of his. When I entered their monastery eleven months before, he was just starting for Rome, and expressed to me the pleasure he felt that I was to join them. My reasons for leaving, however, were so good, and the memo I was preparing so full of undoubted facts and unanswerable arguments, that I was pretty sure it would appease the wrath of my bishop and gain his esteem more firmly than before. I was not disappointed.

A few days later I called upon his lordship, and was received very coldly. He said: "I cannot conceal from you my surprise and pain at the rash step you have just taken. What a shame for all your friends to see your want of consistency and perseverance! You have lost the confidence of your best friends by leaving, without good reasons, the company of such holy men. Some bad rumors are already afloat against you, which give us to understand that you are an unmanageable man, a selfish priest, whom the superiors have been forced to turn out."

I remained perfectly calm. I had, in advance, resolved to hear all his unfriendly, insulting remarks just as if they were addressed to another person. I answered: "My lord, please read this important document, and you will see that I have kept my good name during my stay in that monastery." I handed him the following testimonial letter which the superior had given me when I left:

"I, the undersigned, Superior of the Novitiate of the Oblates of Mary Immaculate at Longueuil, do certify that the conduct of Mr. Chiniquy, when in our monastery, has been worthy of the sacred character which he possesses, and after this year of solitude, he does not less deserve the confidence of his brethren in the holy ministry than before. We wish, moreover, to give our testimony of his persevering zeal in the cause of temperance. We think that nothing will give a character of stability to that admirable reform, and to secure its perfect success, than the profound reflections and studies of Mr. Chiniquy, when in the solitude of Longueuil, on the importance of that work."

T.F. ALLARD,
Superior of the Novitiate O.M.I.

It was really most pleasant for me to see that every line of that document read by the bishop was blotting out some of the stern and unfriendly lines which were on his face. Amiably he handed it back to me, saying: "I thank God to see that you are still as worthy of my esteem and confidence as when you entered that monastery. But would you be kind enough to give me the real reasons why you have so abruptly separated from the Oblates?"

"Yes, my lord, I will give them to you." I handed him the memo, about thirty pages long, which I had prepared. The bishop read very carefully five or six pages and said: "Are you positive as to the exactness of what you write here?"

"Yes, my lord! They are as true and real as I am here."

The bishop turned pale and remained a few minutes silent,

biting his lips, and after a deep sigh, said: "Is it your intention to reveal those sad mysteries to the world, or can we hope that you will keep that secret?"

"My lord," I answered, "I consider myself bound, in conscience and honor, to keep those things secret, provided I am not forced to reveal them in self-defense against any abuse or persecutions emanating from the Oblates, or any other party!"

"But the Oblates cannot say a word against you after the honorable testimony they have given you," promptly answered the bishop.

"That is true, my lord, but you know another who has my future destinies in his hands." I answered.

"I understand you. But I pledge myself that you have nothing to fear from that quarter. Though I frankly would have preferred seeing you work as a member of the Oblates, it may be more according to the will of God that you work in that glorious temperance of which you are evidently the blessed apostle in Canada. I am glad to tell you that I have spoken of you to the Pope, and he requested me to give you a precious medal, which bears his most perfect features, with a splendid crucifix. His holiness has graciously attached three hundred days for indulgences to every one who will take the pledge of temperance in kissing the feet of that crucifix. Wait a moment," added the bishop, "I will go and get them and present them to you."

When the bishop returned, I fell on my knees to receive them and pressed them both to my lips with the utmost respect. He granted me the power to preach and hear confessions all over his diocese, and he dismissed me only after having put his hand on my head and asked God to pour upon me His most abundant benedictions everywhere I should go work in the holy cause of temperance in Canada.

CHAPTER XXXIX

In resuming my battle for temperance, I again studied the best works on the subject from the learned naturalist, Pliny, to the celebrated Sir Astley Cooper. I compiled a multitude of scientific notes, arguments, and facts from these books and prepared a "Manual of Temperance," which was so great a success that it went through four editions of twenty-five thousand copies in less than four years. But my best source of information and wisdom was from letters received from Father Mathew, and my personal interviews with him, when he visited the United States.

I never lectured on temperance in any place without first inquiring from the most reliable sources about: (1) The number of
deaths and accidents caused by drunkenness the last fifteen or
twenty years. (2) The number of orphans and widows made by
drunkenness. (3) The number of rich families ruined, and the
number of poor families made poorer. (4) The approximate sum of
money spent by the people for alcohol during the last twenty years.

Our merciful God had visibly blessed the work and His unprofitable servant. In the first parish of Longueuil, 2,300 citizens enrolled under the banners of temperance. Instead of inviting them
to sign any written pledge, I asked them to come to the foot of the
altar and kiss the crucifix I was holding (given to me and blessed
by the pope).

During the next four years, I gave 1,800 public addresses in 200
parishes with the same fruits and enrolled more than 200,000
people under the banners of temperance. Everywhere the taverns,
the distilleries and breweries were shut, and their owners forced to
take other trades to make a living; not on account of any stringent
law, but because the whole people had ceased drinking their
beverages, after having been fully persuaded that they were in-
jurious to their bodies, opposed to their happiness, and ruinous to
their souls.

The convictions were so unanimous in many places, that the
last evening I spent in their midst the merchants would make a
pyramid of all their barrels of rum, beer, wine and brandy in the
public squares and I was invited to set them on fire. While the husbands and wives, the parents and children of the redeemed drunkards rent the air with their cries of joy at the destruction of their
enemy, and the fire was in full blaze, one of the merchants would
give me an axe to stave in the last barrel of rum. After the last
drop was emptied, I usually stood on it to address some parting
words to the people.

The only thing which marred that joy were the exaggerated
honors and unmerited praises with which I was really
overwhelmed. I was, at first, forced to receive an ovation from the
curates and people of Longueuil which filled me with confusion,
for I felt so keenly that I did not deserve such honors. But it was
still worse at the end of May, 1849. Judge Mondelet was deputed
by the bishop and the priests and the city of Montreal, accompanied by 15,000 people, to present me with a gold medal, and a gift
of four hundred dollars.

But the greatest surprise came at the end of June, 1850 when I
was deputed by 40,000 teetotalers to present a petition to the Par-

liament of Toronto to make the rum sellers responsible for the ravages caused to the families of the poor drunkards to whom they had sold their poisonous drugs. The House of Commons kindly appointed a committee of ten members to help me to frame that bill which passed easily through the three branches. I was present when that bill became law giving the innocent victims of the drunken father or husband an indemnity from the landsharks who were fattening on their poverty and unspeakable miseries.

When in May, 1850, Archbishop Turgeon, of Quebec, sent the Rev. Charles Baillargeon, curate of Quebec, to Rome, to become his successor, he advised him to come to Longueuil, and get a letter from me which he might present to the pope, with a volume of my "Temperance Manual." I complied with his request, and wrote to the pope. Some months later, I received the following lines:

ROME, Aug. 10th, 1850

REV. MR. CHINIQUY:
SIR AND DEAR FRIEND:

Monday, the 12th was the first opportunity given me to have a private audience with the Sovereign Pontiff. I presented Him your book, with your letter, which he received with all special marks of satisfaction and approbation, while charging me to state to you that he accords his apostolic benediction to you and to the holy work of temperance you preach. I consider myself happy to have had to offer on your behalf, to the Vicar of Jesus Christ, a book which, after it had done so much good to my countrymen, had been able to draw from his venerable lips, such solemn words of approbation of the temperance society and of blessings on those who are its apostles; and it is also, for my heart, a very sweet pleasure to transmit them to you.

Your Friend,
CHARLES BAILLARGEON,
Priest

A short time before I received that letter from Rome, Bishop Bourget of Montreal had officially given me the title of "Apostle of Temperance" in the following document:

"IGNATIUS BOURGET, By the Divine Mercy and Grace of the Holy Apostolic See, Bishop of Montreal."

"To all who inspect the present letters, we make known and certify that the venerable Charles Chiniquy, "Apostle of Temperance," Priest of our Diocese, is very well known to us, and we regard him as proved, to lead a praiseworthy life, and one agreeable to his ecclesiastical profession. Through the tender mercies of our God, he is under no ecclesiastical censures, at least, which have come to our knowledge.

"We entreat each and all, Archbishop, Bishop, and other dignitaries of the Church, to whom it may happen that he may go, that they, for the love of Christ, entertain him kindly and courteously, and as often as they may be asked by him, permit him to celebrate the holy sacrifice of the mass, and exercise other ecclesiastical privileges of piety, being ourselves ready to grant him these and other greater privileges. In proof of this we have ordered the present letters to be prepared under our sign and seal, and with subscription of our secretary, in our palace of the blessed James, in the year one thousand eight hundred and fifty, on the sixth day of the month of June.

✠ IGNATIUS, Bishop of Marianopolis.

By order of the most illustrious and most Reverend Bishop of Marianopolis, D.D.

J.O. Pare, Canon, Secretary.

No words from my pen can give an idea of the distress and shame I felt at these unmerited praises and public honors. For, when my natural pride was near to deceive me, there was my conscience crying with a louder voice: "Chiniquy, thou art a sinner, unworthy of such praises and honors."

Another serious anxiety for me was the large sums of money constantly flowing from the hands of my too kind and grateful reformed countrymen into mine. Those sums would have soon made of me one of the richest men of Canada. But I confess that, when in the presence of God, I went to the bottom of my heart to see if it were strong enough to carry such a glittering weight, and found it far too weak. When only eighteen years old my venerable and dear benefactor the Rev. Mr. Leprohon, director of the College of Nicolet had told me a thing I never had forgotten: "Chiniquy," he said, "I am sure you will be what we call a successful man in the world. It is probable that you will have many opportunities of becoming rich. But when the silver and gold flows into your hands, do not pile and keep it. For if you set your affections on it, you will be miserable in this world and damned in the next. Give it while you are living. Then you will be blessed by God and man, and you will be blessed by your own conscience. You will lie in peace and die in joy."

These solemn warnings from one of the wisest and best friends God had ever given me has never gone out of my mind. I found them corroborated in every page of that Bible which I loved and studied every day. I found them also written, by God, in my heart. I then, on my knees, took the resolution, without making an absolute vow of it, to keep only what I needed for my daily support and give the rest to the poor, or some Christian or patriotic project. I kept my promise. The money given me by Parliament did not remain three weeks in my hands. I never put a cent in Canada in the vaults of any bank and when I left for Illinois, in the fall of 1851, instead of taking with me a fortune which I could have had so easily, I had hardly 1,500 dollars in hand, the price of a part of my library which was too heavy to be carried so far away.

CHAPTER XL

August 15, 1850 I preached in the Cathedral of Montreal on the Blessed Virgin Mary's power in heaven when interceding for sinners. Nothing seemed more natural than to pray to her, and rely on her protection. Of course, my address was more sentimental than scriptural, but I sincerely believed what I said.

"Who among you, my dear brethren," I said to the people, "will refuse any of the reasonable demands of a beloved mother? Who will sadden her loving heart by refusing a petition which you have the power to grant? For my own part, were my beloved mother still living, I would prefer to have my right hand crushed and burned into cinders, to have my tongue cut out, than to say, No! to my mother, asking me any favor which I could bestow.

"This respect and obedience to our mothers, Christ Jesus, the Son of God, practised to perfection. Although God and man, He was still in perfect submission to the will of His mother. The Gospel says, in reference to His parents, Joseph and Mary, He 'was subject unto them.' (Luke 2:51) What a grand and shining revelation we have in these few words: Jesus was subject unto Mary! Is it not written, that Jesus is the same today as He was yesterday, and will be forever? (Heb. 13:8) He has not changed. He is still the Son of Mary, as He was when only twelve years old.

"This is why our holy Church invites us to put our unbounded confidence in her intercession. Remembering that Jesus has always granted her petitions, let us put our petitions in her hands, if we want to receive the favors we need.

"The second reason why we must all go to Mary is that we are sinners — rebels in the sight of God. Jesus Christ is our Saviour. Yes! but He is also our God, infinitely just, infinitely holy. He hates our sins with an infinite hatred.

"Had we loved and served Him faithfully we might go to Him with the hope and assurance of being welcomed. But we have forgotten and offended Him; we have trampled His blood under our feet; we have joined with those who nailed Him on the cross, pierced His heart with the lance, and shed His blood to the last drop. How can we dare to look at Him and meet His eyes? This is why our holy Church, speaking through her infallible supreme pontiff, the Vicar of Christ, Gregory XVI, has told us, in the most solemn manner, that 'Mary is the only hope of sinners.'"

Winding up my arguments, I added: "Jesus has a thousand good reasons to refuse our petitions, if we are impudent enough to speak to Him ourselves. But look to the right hand of our offended King, and behold His dear and divine mother. She is your mother also. For it is to every one of us, as well as to John, that Christ said on the cross, speaking of Mary, 'Behold thy mother.' (John 19:27) Jesus has never refused any favor asked by that Queen of Heaven. He cannot rebuke His mother. Let us go to her; let us ask her to be our advocate and plead our cause, and she will do it. Let us request her to ask for our pardon, and she will get it."

My sermon had made a visible and deep impression. Bishop Prince thanked and congratulated me for the good effect it would have on the people, and I sincerely thought I had said what was true and right before God.

Before going to bed, I took my Bible as usual, knelt down before God. I read the twelfth chapter of Matthew with a praying heart and a sincere desire to understand. Strange to say! when I reached the 40th verse, I felt a mysterious awe, as if I had entered for the first time into a new and most holy land.

Though I had read that verse and the following many times, they came to my mind with a freshness as if I had never seen them before. Slowly, and with breathless attention, I contemplated approaching the house with Mary to meet her divine Son, who had been so long absent from her. My heart beat with joy at the privilege of witnessing that interview, and of hearing the respectful words Jesus would address to His mother!

With heart and soul throbbing with these feelings, I slowly read: "While He yet talked to the people, behold His mother and His brethren stood without, desiring to speak with Him. Then one said unto Him: 'Behold, Thy mother and Thy brethren stand without, desiring to speak to Thee. But He answered and said unto him that told Him: Who is My mother! and Who are My brethren! And He stretched forth His hands towards His disciples, and said: Behold My mother and My brethren! For whosoever shall do the will of My Father which is in Heaven, the same is My brother, and sister, and mother.'"

I had hardly finished reading the last verse, when big drops of sweat began to flow from my face, my heart beat with a tremendous speed, and I came near fainting. I sat in my large armchair, expecting any minute to fall on the floor. Only those who have heard the thundering noise of Niagara Falls and felt the shaking of the rocks under their feet have an idea of what I felt in that hour of agony.

My conscience was thundering like the voice of a thousand Niagaras telling me: "You have preached a sacrilegious lie this morning when you said to your ignorant and deluded people that Jesus always granted the petitions of His mother, Mary. Are you not ashamed to deceive yourself and your poor countrymen with such silly falsehoods?

"Read again and understand that, far from granting all the petitions of Mary, Jesus has always, except when a child, said No! to her requests. He has always rebuked her when she asked Him anything in public! Was it lack of love and respect when He gave her that rebuke? No! Never a son loved and respected a mother as He did. But it was a solemn protest against the blasphemous worship of Mary as practised in the Church of Rome."

I felt so confounded by the voice which was shaking my very bones that I thought for a moment that I was possessed of a demon. "My God," I cried, "have mercy on me! Come to my help! Save me from my enemy's hands!" As quick as lightning the answer came: "It is not Satan's voice you hear. It is I, thy Saviour and thy God, who speaks to thee. Read what Mark, Luke, John tell you about the way I received her petitions, from the very day I began to work, and speak publicly as the Son of God, and the Saviour of the world."

I took my Bible and read: "There came then His brethren and His mother, and standing without, sent unto Him, calling Him. And the multitude sat about Him and they said unto Him, Behold, Thy mother and Thy brethren without, seek for Thee. And He answered them, saying, Who is My mother, or My brethren? And He looked round about on them which sat about Him, and said, Behold My mother and My brethren. For whosoever shall do the will of God, the same is My brother, and My sister, and mother." (Mark 3:31-35)

The voice continued: "Do you not see you have presented a blasphemous lie, every time you said that Jesus always granted the petitions of His mother?"

Again unable to fight down the thoughts which were so mercilessly shaking my faith, and demolishing the respect I held for my Church, it came to mind that St. Luke had narrated this interview in a very different way. But how shall I find words to express my distress when I saw that the rebuke of Jesus Christ was expressed in a still sterner way by St. Luke!

These three seemed to be saying to me: "How dare you preach with your apostate and lying Church that Jesus has always granted all of Mary's petitions, when we were ordered by God to write and proclaim that all the public petitions she had presented to Him, when working as the Son of God, and the Saviour of the world, had been answered by a public rebuke?"

What could I answer? Trembling from head to foot, I fell upon my knees, crying to the Virgin Mary to come to my help and pray that I might not succumb to this temptation, and lose my faith and confidence in her. But the more I prayed, the louder the voice seemed to say: "How dare you preach such a lie when we tell you the contrary by the order of God Himself?"

In vain I wept, prayed, cried, and struggled from ten at night till three in the morning. Suddenly the miraculous change of water into wine, by Christ, at the request of His mother, came to mind. I felt a momentary hope that in this case the Saviour had obeyed the demands of His holy mother. I eagerly opened my Bible and read:

"And the third day there was a marriage in Cana of Galilee; and the mother of Jesus was there. And both Jesus was called, and His disciples, to the marriage. And when they wanted wine, the mother of Jesus saith unto Him, They have no wine. Jesus saith unto her, Woman, what have I to do with thee? Mine hour is not yet com... His mother saith unto the servants, Whatsoever He saith unto you, do it." (John 2:1-5)

I had always accepted that text as proving that the very first miracle of Jesus Christ was wrought at the request of His mother. And I was preparing to answer the three witnesses: "Here is proof of my confidence in her intercession; here is the seal of her irresistible superhuman power over her divine Son; here is the undeniable evidence that Jesus cannot refuse anything asked by His mother!"

But when, armed with these explanations of the church, I was preparing to meet what St. Matthew, St. Mark, and St. Luke had just told me, a sudden distressing thought came to my mind as though the three witnesses were saying: "How can you be so blind as not to see that instead of being a favor granted to Mary, this first miracle is the first opportunity chosen by Christ to protest against her intercession. It is a solemn warning to Mary never to ask anything from Him, and to us, never to put any confidence in her requests. Here, Mary, evidently full of compassion for those poor people who had not the means to provide the wine for the guests who had come with Jesus, wants her Son to give them the wine they wanted. How does Christ answer her requests? He answers it by a rebuke, a most solemn rebuke. Instead of saying: 'Yes, mother, I will do as you wish,' He says, 'Woman, what have I to do with thee?' which clearly means, 'Woman, thou hast nothing to do in this matter. I do not want you to put yourself between the wants of humanity and Me. I do not want the world to believe that you had any right, any power or influence over me, or more compassion on the miseries of man than I have. Is it not to Me and Me alone, the lost children of Adam must look to be saved? Woman, what have I to do with thee in My great work of saving this perishing world? Nothing, absolutely nothing. I know what I have to do to fulfill, not your will, but My Father's will!'"

This is what Jesus meant by the solemn rebuke given to Mary. He wanted to banish all idea of her ever becoming an intercessor between man and Christ. He wanted to protest against the doctrine of the Church of Rome and Mary understood it well when she said, "Whatsoever He saith unto you, do it." Never come to me, but go to Him. "For there is none other name under heaven given among men, whereby we must be saved." (Acts 4:12)

Every one of these thoughts passed over my distressed soul like a hurricane. Every sentence was like a flash of lightning in a dark night. Till the dawn, I felt powerless against the efforts of God to pull down and demolish the huge fortress of sophisms, falsehoods, idolatries, which Rome had built around my soul. What a fearful thing it is to fight against the Lord!

During the long hours of that night, my God was contending with me, and I was struggling against Him. But though brought down to the dust, I was not conquered. My understanding was very nearly convinced. My rebellious and proud will was not yet ready to yield.

That morning my eyes were red, and my face swollen. At breakfast, Bishop Prince, asked: "Your eyes are as if you had wept all night!"

"Your lordship is not mistaken, I have wept the whole night!" I answered. Bishop Prince, had been my personal friend from the time I entered the college at Nicolet, where he was professor of Rhetoric.

The bishop replied, "Might I know the cause of your sorrow?"

"Yes, my lord. The most horrible temptations against our holy religion have assailed me all night. You congratulated me yesterday on proving that Jesus had always granted the requests of His mother, and that He cannot refuse any of her petitions. The whole night it has been told me that this was a blasphemous lie. From the Holy Scriptures themselves I have been nearly convinced that you and I, nay, that our holy church, are preaching a blasphemous falsehood every time we proclaim the doctrines of the worship of Mary."

The poor bishop quickly answered: "I hope you have not yielded to these temptations, and become a Protestant as so many of your enemies whisper."

"It is my hope, my lord, that our merciful God will keep me, to the end of my life, a dutiful and faithful priest of our holy church.

However, I cannot conceal from your lordship that my faith was terribly shaken last night. As a bishop your portion of light and wisdom must be greater than mine. Please tell me how you reconcile that proposition with this text." I handed him the Gospel of Matthew, pointing to the last five verses of the twelfth chapter.

He read them and said: "Now, what do you want from me?"

"My lord, I want respectfully to ask you how we can say that Jesus has always granted the requests of His mother, when this evangelist tells us the exact opposite. Must we not fear that we proclaim a blasphemous falsehood when we support a proposition directly opposed to the Gospel?"

The poor bishop seemed absolutely confounded by this simple honest question. I also felt confused and sorry for his humiliation. Beginning a phrase, he would give it up; trying arguments, he could not push to their conclusion. It seemed to me that he had never read that text, or like myself and the rest of the priests of Rome, had never noted that they entirely demolish the worship of Mary.

In order to help him out of the inextricable difficulties into which I had at once pushed him, I said: "My lord, will you allow me to put a few more questions to you?"

"With pleasure," he answered.

"Well! my lord, who came to this world to save you and me? Is it Jesus or Mary?"

The bishop answered, "It was Jesus."

I then asked, "When Jesus and Mary were on earth, who loved sinners with a more efficacious and saving love?"

"Jesus, being God, His love was evidently more efficacious and saving than Mary's," answered the bishop.

"And to whom did Jesus invite sinners to go for their salvation; was it to Himself or Mary?" I asked again.

The bishop answered: "Jesus; 'Come unto Me.' He never said, come or go to Mary."

"Have we any examples, in the Scriptures, of sinners, who, fearing to be rebuked by Jesus, have gone to Mary and obtained access to Him through her, and been saved through her intercessions?"

"I do not remember of any such cases," replied the bishop.

I then asked: "To whom did the penitent thief on the cross address himself to be saved; was it to Jesus or Mary?"

"It was to Jesus," replied the bishop.

"Did that penitent thief do well to address himself to Jesus on the cross, rather than to Mary who was at his feet?" said I.

"Surely he did better," answered the bishop.

"Now, my lord, allow me only one question more. Please tell me if you think that Jesus in heaven, since He is sitting at the right hand of His Father, has lost any of His superior love and mercy for sinners? And if so can you show me that what Jesus has lost has been gained by Mary?"

"I do not think that Christ has lost any of His love and power to save us now that He is in heaven," answered the bishop.

"Now, my lord, if Jesus is still my best friend, my most powerful, merciful, and loving friend, why should I not go directly to Him? Why should we, for a moment, go to any one who is infinitely inferior, in power, love, and mercy, for our salvation?"

The bishop was stunned by my questions. He stammered some unintelligible answer, excused himself on account of some pressing business. Extending his hand to me before leaving, he said: "You will find an answer to your questions and difficulties in the Holy Fathers."

"Can you lend me the Holy Fathers, my lord?"

He replied: "No, sir, I have them not."

This last answer, from my bishop left my mind in a state of great distress. With the sincere hope of finding in the Holy Fathers some explanations which would dispel my painful doubts, I immediately went to Mr. Fabre, the great bookseller of Montreal, who was able to obtain from France the splendid edition of the Holy Fathers by Migne. I studied, with the utmost attention, every page where I might find what they taught of the worship of Mary, and the doctrines that Jesus Christ had never refused any of her prayers.

What was my desolation and my shame to find that the Holy Fathers of the first six centuries had never advocated the worship of Mary. The many eloquent pages on the power of Mary in heaven and her love for sinners, found in my theologians, and other ascetic books I had read till then, were but impudent lies; additions interpolated in their works, a hundred years after their death. After discovering these forgeries of which my church was guilty, how many times in the silence of my long nights of study and prayerful meditations, did I hear a voice telling me: "Come out of Babylon!"

But where could I go? Out of the Church of Rome, where could I find that salvation which was to be found only within her walls? I said to myself, "Surely there are some errors in my dear church! But will I not find still more damnable errors among those hundreds of Protestant churches, which, under the name of Episcopalians, Presbyterians, Baptists, Methodists, etc., etc., are divided and subdivided into scores of contemptible sects, anathematizing and denouncing each other before the world?"

My ideas of the great family of evangelical churches, comprised under the broad name of Protestantism, were so exaggerated then, that it was absolutely impossible for me to find in them that unity, which I considered the essentials of the church of Christ. The hour was not yet to come, when my dear Saviour would make me understand His sublime words: "I am the vine, and ye are the branches."

It was later, when under a beautiful vine I had planted in my own garden, I saw no two branches alike in that prolific vine. Some branches were very big, some very thin, some very long, some very short, some going up, some going down, some straight as an arrow, some crooked as a flash of lightning, some turning to the west, some to the east. But, although the branches were so different from each other in so many ways, they all gave me excellent fruit, so long as they remained united to the vine.

CHAPTER XLI

The most desolate work of a sincere Catholic priest is the study of the Holy Fathers. He does not make a step in the labyrinth of their discussions and controversies without seeing the dreams of his theological studies and religious views disappear! Bound by a solemn oath, to interpret the Holy Scriptures only according to the unanimous consent of the Holy Fathers, the first thing which distresses him is their absolute want of unanimity on the greater part of the subjects which they discuss. The fact is, that more than two-thirds of what one Father has written is to prove that what some other Holy Father has written is wrong and heretical.

The student of the Fathers also finds that many of them do not even agree with themselves. Often they confess that they were mistaken when they said this or that; that they have lately changed their minds; that they now hold for saving truth what they formerly condemned as a damning error! What becomes of the solemn oath of every priest in the presence of this undeniable fact?

It is true, that in my Roman Catholic theological books I had long extracts of Holy Fathers, very clearly supporting and confirming my faith in those dogmas. For instance, I had the apostolic liturgies of St. Peter, St. Mark, and St. James, to prove that the sacrifice of the mass, purgatory, prayers for the dead, transubstantiation, were believed and taught from the very days of the apostles. But what was my dismay when I discovered that those liturgies were nothing but vile, audacious forgeries presented to the world, by my popes and my church, as gospel truths. I could not find words to express my sense of shame and consternation.

What right has my church to be called holy and infallible, when she is publicly guilty of such lies?

From my infancy I had been taught, with all the Roman Catholics, that Mary is the mother of God, and many times, every day, when praying to her, I used to say, "Holy Mary, mother of God, pray for me." But what was my distress when I read in the "Treatise on Faith and Creed," by Augustine, these very words: "When the Lord said, 'Woman, what have I to do with thee? Mine hour is not yet come.' (John 2:4) He rather admonishes us to understand that, in respect of His being God, there was no mother for Him."

This was so completely demolishing the teachings of my church, and telling me that it was blasphemy to call Mary mother of God, that I felt as if struck with a thunderbolt.

Several volumes might be written, if my plan were to give the story of my mental agonies, when reading the Holy Fathers. Thus wounded, I showed them to Mr. Brassard, saying: "Do you not see here the incontrovertible proof of what I have told you many times, that, during the first six centuries of Christianity, we do not find the least proof that there was anything like our dogma of the supreme power and authority of the Bishop of Rome, or any other bishop, over the rest of the Christian world?"

"My dear Chiniquy," answered Mr. Brassard, "did I not tell you, when you bought the Holy Fathers, that you were doing a foolish and dangerous thing? As you are the only priest in Canada who has the Holy Fathers, it is thought and said, in many quarters, that it is through pride you got them; that it is to raise yourself above the rest of the clergy. I see, with regret, that you are fast losing the respect of the bishop and of the priests in general on account of your indomitable perseverance in giving all your spare time to their study. You are also too free and imprudent in speaking of what you call the contradictions of the Holy Fathers, and their lack of harmony with some of our religious views.

"Many say that this too great application to study, without a moment of relaxation, will upset your intelligence and trouble your mind. They even whisper that they would not be surprised if the reading of the Bible and the Holy Fathers would drive you into the abyss of Protestantism. I know that they are mistaken, and I do all in my power to defend you. But, I thought, as your most devoted friend, that it was my duty to tell you those things, and warn you before it is too late."

I replied: "Bishop Prince told me the very same things, and I will give you the answer he got from me; 'When you ordain a priest, do you not make him swear that he will never interpret the Holy Scriptures except according to the unanimous consent of the Holy Fathers? How can we know their unanimous consent without studying them? Is it not more than strange that, not only the priests do not study the Holy Fathers, but the only one in Canada who is trying to study them, is turned into ridicule and suspected of heresy? Is it my fault if that precious stone, called 'unanimous consent of the Holy Fathers,' which is the very foundation of our religious belief and teaching, is to be found nowhere in them? Is it my fault if Origen never believed in the eternal punishment of the damned; if St. Cyprian denied the supreme authority of the Bishop of Rome; if St. Augustine positively said that nobody was obliged to believe in purgatory; if St. John Chrysostom publicly denied the obligation of auricular confession, and the real presence of the body of Christ in the eucharist? Is it my fault if one of the most learned and holy popes, Gregory the Great, has called by the name of Antichrist, all his successors, for taking the name of supreme Pontiff, and trying to persuade the world that they had, by divine authority, a supreme jurisdiction and power over the rest of the church?'"

"And what did Bishop Prince answer you?" rejoined Mr. Brassard.

"Just as you did, by expressing his fears that the study of the Bible and the Holy Fathers would either send me to the lunatic asylum, or drive me into the bottomless abyss of Protestantism."

I answered him very seriously, "So long as God keeps my intelligence sound, I cannot join the Protestants, for the numberless and ridiculous sects of these heretics are a sure antidote against their poisonous errors. I will not remain a good Catholic on account of the unanimity of the Holy Fathers, which does not exist, but I will remain a Catholic on account of the grand and visible unanimity of the prophets, apostles, and the evangelists with Jesus Christ. My faith will not be founded upon the fallible, obscure, and wavering words of Origin, Tertullian, Chrysostom, Augustine, or Jerome; but on the infallible word of Jesus, the Son of God, and of His inspired writers: Matthew, Mark, Luke, John, Peter, James, and Paul. It is Jesus, and not Origen, who will now guide me; for the second was a sinner, like myself, and the first is forever my Saviour and my God. I know enough of the Holy Fathers to assure your lordship that the oath we take of accepting the Word of God according to their unanimous consent is a miserable blunder, if not a blasphemous perjury. It is evident that Pius IV, who imposed the obligation of that oath upon us all, never read a single volume of the Holy Fathers. He would not have been guilty of such an incredible blunder if he had known that the Holy Fathers are unanimous in only one thing, which is to differ from each other on almost everything."

"And what did my Lord Prince say to that?" asked Mr. Brassard.

"Just as when he was cornered by me, on the subject of the Virgin Mary, he abruptly put an end to the conversation by looking at his watch and saying that he had a call to make at that very hour."

Not long after that painful conversation about the Holy Fathers, it was the will of God that a new arrow should be thrust into my Roman Catholic conscience. I had been invited to give a course of three sermons at Varennes. I was coming from the church with the curate, when we were met by a poor man, covered with rags. His pale, trembling lips indicated that he was reduced to the last degree of human misery. Taking off his hat through respect for us, he said to Rev. Primeau, with a trembling voice: "You know, sir, that my poor wife was buried ten days ago. I was too poor to have a funeral service sung the day she was buried. I fear she is in purgatory, for almost every night I see her in my dreams wrapped in burning flames. She cries to me for help and asks me to have a high mass sung for the rest of her soul. I come to ask you to be so kind as to sing that high mass for her."

The curate answered: "Of course, your wife is in the flames of purgatory and suffers there the most unspeakable tortures, which can be relieved only by the offering of the holy sacrifice of mass. Give me five dollars and I will sing that mass tomorrow morning."

"You know very well, Mr. le Cure," answered the poor man in a most supplicating tone, "that my wife has been sick, as well as myself, a good part of the year. I am too poor to give you five dollars!"

"If you cannot pay, you cannot have any mass sung. You know it is the rule. It is not in my power to change it."

These words were said by the curate with a high and unfeeling tone, in absolute contrast with the solemn distress of the poor sick man. They made a very painful impression upon me, for I felt for him. I knew the curate was well-off, at the head of one of the richest parishes of Canada; that he had several thousand dollars in the bank. I hoped at first he would kindly grant the petition without speaking of the pay, but I was disappointed.

My first thought, after hearing this hard rebuke, was to put my hand in my pocket and take out one of the several five-dollar gold pieces I had, and give it to the poor man, but I was prevented by fear of insulting that priest, who was older than myself, and for whom I had always entertained great respect. I knew that he would have taken my action as a condemnation of his conduct.

When I was feeling ashamed of my own cowardice, he said to the disconcerted poor man: "That woman is your wife, not mine. It is your business, and not mine, to see how to get her out of purgatory."

Turning to me, he said, in the most amiable way: "Please, sir, come to tea."

We hardly started, when the poor man, raising his voice, said in a most touching way: "I cannot leave my poor wife in the flames of purgatory; if you cannot sing a high mass, will you please say five low masses to rescue her soul from those burning flames?"

The priest turned to him and said: "Yes, I can say five masses to take the soul of your wife out of purgatory, but give me five shillings; for you know the price of a low mass is one shilling."

The poor man answered: "I can no more give one dollar than I can five. I have not a cent; and my three poor little children are naked and starving."

"Well! well," answered the curate, "when I passed this morning before your house, I saw two beautiful sucking pigs. Give me one of them, and I will say your five low masses."

The poor man said: "These small pigs were given me by a charitable neighbor, that I might raise them to feed my poor children next winter. They will surely starve to death, if I give my pigs away."

I could not listen any longer to that strange dialogue; I was beside myself with shame and disgust. I abruptly left the merchant of souls finishing his bargains, went to my sleeping-room, locked the door, and fell upon my knees to weep to my heart's content.

A quarter of an hour later, the curate knocked at my door, and said: "Tea is ready; please come down!"

I answered: "I am not well; I want some rest. Please excuse me if I do not take my tea tonight."

It would require a more eloquent pen than mine, to give the correct history of that sleepless night. The hours were dark and long.

"My God! my God!" I cried, a thousand times, "is it possible that, in my so dear Church of Rome, there can be such abominations as I have seen and heard today? And how cruel, how merciless, we, Thy priests, are. But are we really Thy priests? Is it not blasphemous to call ourselves Thy priests, when not only will we not sacrifice anything to save that soul, but will starve the poor husband and his orphans? What right have we to extort such sums of money from Thy poor children to help them out of purgatory? Do not Thy apostles say that Thy blood alone can purify the soul?

"Is it possible that there is such a fiery prison for the sinners after death, and that neither Thyself nor any of Thy apostles has said a word about it? Several of the Fathers consider purgatory as of pagan origin. Tertullian spoke of it only after he had joined the sect of the Montanists, and he confesses that it is not through the Holy Scriptures, but through the inspiration of the Paraclete of Montanus that he knows anything about purgatory. Augustine, the most learned and pious of the Holy Fathers, does not find purgatory in the Bible, and positively says that its existence is dubious; that every one may believe what he thinks proper about it. Is it possible that I am so mean as to have refused to extend a helping hand to that poor distressed man, for fear of offending the cruel priest?

"We priests believe, and say that we can help souls out of the burning furnace of purgatory, by our prayers and masses: but instead of rushing to their rescue, we turn to the parents, friends, the children of those departed souls, and say: 'Give me five dollars; give me a shilling, and I will put an end to those tortures; but if you refuse us that money, we will let your father, husband, wife, child, or friend endure those tortures, hundreds of years more!'"

It would take too long to give the thoughts which tortured me during that terrible night.

I spent the morning hearing confessions, then I delivered a very exciting sermon on the malice of sin, proved by the sufferings of Christ on the cross. This address gave a happy diversion to my mind. After the sermon, the curate took me by the hand to his dining-room, where he gave me, in spite of myself, the place of honor.

He had the reputation of having one of the best cooks of Canada. The dishes before our eyes did not diminish his good reputation. The first dish was a sucking pig roasted with an art and perfection as I had never seen; it looked like a piece of pure gold, and its smell would have brought water to the lips of the most penitent anchorite.

I had not tasted anything for the last twenty-four hours. Besides, that was a favorite dish with me. My knife and fork had soon done their work. I was carrying to my mouth the first succulent mouthful when suddenly the remembrance of the poor man's sucking pig came to my mind. I laid the piece on my plate and with painful anxiety said to the curate: "Will you allow me to put a question about this dish?"

"Oh! yes, ask me not only one, but two questions, and I will be happy to answer you to the best of my ability," answered he, with his fine manners.

"Is this the sucking pig of the poor man of yesterday?" I asked.

With a convulsive fit of laughter, he replied: "Yes, it is just it. If we cannot take away the soul of the poor woman out of the flames of purgatory, we will, at all events, eat a fine sucking pig!" The other thirteen priests filled the room with laughter, to show their appreciation of their host's wit.

However, their laughter was not of long duration. With a feeling of shame and uncontrollable indignation, I pushed away my plate with such force, that it crossed the table and nearly fell on the floor; saying, with disgust which no pen can describe: "I would rather starve to death than eat of that execrable dish; I see in it the tears of the poor man; I see the blood of his starving children; it is the price of a soul.

"No! no, gentlemen, do not touch it. You know, Mr. Curate, how 30,000 priests and monks were slaughtered in France in the bloody days of 1792. It was for such iniquities as this that God Almighty visited the church in France. The same future awaits us here in Canada the very day that people will awaken from their slumber and see that, instead of being ministers of Christ, we are the vile traders of souls, under the mask of religion."

The poor curate, stunned by the solemnity of my words, as well as by the consciousness of his guilt, lisped some excuse. The sucking pig remained untouched; and the rest of the dinner had more the appearance of a burial ceremony than of a convivial repast. By the mercy of God, I had redeemed my cowardice of the day before. But I had mortally wounded the feelings of the curate and his friends, and forever lost their good-will.

CHAPTER XLII

On December 15, 1850 I received a letter from the Bishop of Chicago, Oliv Vandeveld, requesting me to join him and become his successor.

He told me of the rich fertile lands of Illinois and the Mississippi Valley. "It is our intention, without noise, to take possession of those vast and magnificent regions in the name of our holy Church," he wrote. His plan was to gather the flow of French, Canadian and Belgium Catholic immigrants who were scattering in the U.S. cities and direct them toward settlement in the new regions.

"Why should we not, for instance, induce them to come and take possession of these fertile states of Illinois, Missouri, Iowa,

Kansas, etc. They can get those lands now, at a nominal price. If we succeed, as I hope we will, our holy Church will soon count her children here by ten and twenty millions, and through their numbers, their wealth and unity, they will have such a weight in the balance of power that they will rule everything," the bishop reasoned.

He went on to explain how this power would be obtained and how this plan would also prevent loss of faith by the immigrants: "The Protestants, always divided among themselves, will never form any strong party without the help of the united vote of our Catholic people. Then, in reality, though not in appearance, our holy Church will rule the United States, as she is called by our Saviour Himself to rule the whole world. There is, today, a wave of emigrants from Canada towards the United States, which, if not stopped or well directed, is threatening to throw the good French Canadian people in the mire of Protestantism. Your countrymen, when once mixed with the numberless sects which try to attract them, are soon shaken in their faith."

I answered him that the Bishops of Boston, Buffalo, and Detroit had already advised me to put myself at the head of the French Canadian immigration, in order to direct its tide towards the vast and rich regions of the West. I wrote him that I felt as he did, that it was the best way to prevent my countrymen from falling into the snares laid before them by Protestants.

I told him that I would consider it a great honor and privilege to spend the last part of my life in extending the power and influence of our holy Church over the United States, and that I would, in June next, pay my respects to him in Chicago, when on my way towards the colony of my countrymen at Bourbonnais Grove. I added that after I should have seen those territories of Illinois and the Mississippi valley with my own eyes it would be more easy to give him a definite answer.

I ended my letter by saying: "But I respectfully request your lordship to give up the idea of selecting me for your coadjutor, or successor. I have already twice refused to become a bishop. That high dignity is too much above my merits and capacities to be ever accepted by me. I am happy and proud to fight the battles of our holy Church; but let my superiors allow me to continue to remain in her ranks as a simple soldier, to defend her honor and extend her power. I may, then, with the help of God, do some good. But I feel, and know that I would spoil everything, if raised to an elevated position for which I am not fit."

Without speaking to anybody of the proposition of the Bishop of Chicago, I was preparing to go and see the new field where he wanted me to work, when, in the beginning of May, 1851, I received a very pressing invitation from my Lord Lefebre, Bishop of Detroit, to lecture on temperance to the French Canadians who were, then, forming the majority of the Roman Catholics of that city.

That bishop had taken the place of Bishop Rese, whose public scandals and infamies had covered the whole Catholic Church of America with shame. During the last years he had spent in his diocese, very few weeks had passed without his being picked up beastly drunk in the lowest taverns, and even in the streets of Detroit, and dragged, unconscious to his palace.

After long and vain efforts to reform him, the pope and the bishops of America had happily succeeded in persuading him to go to Rome and pay his respects to the so-called vicar of Jesus Christ. He had hardly set his feet in Rome when the inquisitors threw him in one of their dungeons, where he remained till the republicans set him at liberty in 1848, after Pope Pius IX had fled to Civita Vecchia.

In order to blot out from the face of his Church the black spots with which his predecessor had covered it, Bishop Lefebre made the greatest display of zeal for the cause of temperance. As soon as he was inducted, he invited his people to follow his example and enroll themselves under its banners, in a very powerful address on the evils caused by the use of intoxicating drinks. At the end of his eloquent sermon, laying his right hand on the altar, he made a solemn promise never to drink any alcoholic liquors.

His telling sermon on temperance, with his solemn and public promise, were published through almost all the papers of that time, and I read it many times to the people with good effect. So, on my way to Illinois in the first week of June, I stopped in the city of Detroit to give the course of lectures demanded by the bishop. Though the bishop was absent, I immediately began to preach to an immense audience in the Cathedral. I had agreed to give five lectures, and it was only during the third one that Bishop Lefebre arrived. After paying me great compliments for my zeal and success in the temperance cause, he took me by the hand to his dining-room, and said: "Let us go and refresh ourselves."

I shall never forget my surprise and dismay when I perceived the long dining table, covered with bottles of brandy, wine, beer, etc., prepared for himself and his six or seven priests, who were already around it, joyfully emptying their glasses. My first thought was to express my surprise and indignation, and leave the room in disgust, but by a second and better thought I waited a little to see more of that unexpected spectacle. I accepted the seat offered me by the bishop at his right hand.

"Father Chiniquy," he said, "this is the sweetest claret you ever drank." And before I could utter a word, he had filled my large glass with the wine, and drank his own to my health.

Looking at the bishop in amazement, I said, "What does this mean, my lord?"

"It means that I want to drink with you the best claret you ever tasted."

"Do you take me for a comedian? and have you called me here to play such a strange comedy?" I replied, with lips trembling with indignation.

"I did not invite you to play a comedy," he answered. "I invited you to lecture on temperance to my people, and you have done it in a most admirable way, these last three days. Though you did not see me, I was present at this evening's address. I never heard anything so eloquent on that subject as what you said. But now that you have fulfilled your duty, I must do mine, which is to treat you as a gentleman, and drink that bottle of wine with you."

"But, my lord, allow me to tell you that I would not deserve to be called or treated as a gentleman, were I vile enough to drink wine after the address I gave this evening."

"I beg your pardon for differing from you," answered the bishop. "Those drunken people to whom you spoke so well against the evils of intemperance, are in need of the stringent and bitter remedies you offer them in your teetotalism. But here we are sober men and gentlemen, we do not want such remedies. I never thought that the physicians were absolutely bound to take the pills they administer to their patients."

"I hope your lordship will not deny me the right you claim for yourself, to differ with me in this matter. I entirely differ from you, when you say that men who drink as you do with your priests, have a right to be called sober men."

"I fear, Mr. Chiniquy, that you forget where you are, and to whom you speak just now," replied the bishop.

"It may be that I have made a blunder, and that I am guilty of some grave error in coming here, and speaking to you as I am doing, my lord. In that case, I am ready to ask your pardon. But before I retract what I have said, please allow me to respectfully ask you a very simple question."

Then taking from my pocketbook his printed address, and his public and solemn promise never to drink, neither to offer any intoxicating drinks to others, I read it aloud, and said:

"Are you the same Bishop of Detroit, called Lefebre, who had made this solemn promise? If you are not the same man, I will retract and beg your pardon, but if you are the same, I have nothing to retract."

My answer fell upon the poor bishop as a thunderbolt.

He lisped some unintelligible and insignificant explanation, which, however, he ended by a *coup d'etat,* in saying:

"My dear Mr. Chiniquy, I did not invite you to preach to the bishop, but only to the people of Detroit."

"You are right, my lord, I was not called to preach to the bishop, but allow me to tell you, had I known sooner that when the Bishop of Detroit, with his priests, solemnly, publicly, and with their right hand on the altar, promised that they would never drink any intoxicating drinks, it means that they will drink and fill themselves with those detestable liquors, till their brains shiver, I would not have troubled you with my presence or my remarks here. However, allow me to tell your lordship to be kind enough to find another lecturer for your temperance meetings. For I am determined to take the train tomorrow morning for Chicago."

There is no need to say that during that painful conversation the priests (with only one exception) were as full of indignation against me as they were full of wine. I left the table and went to my sleeping apartment overwhelmed with sadness and shame.

Half an hour later, the bishop was with me urging me to continue my lectures, on account of the fearful scandals which would result from my sudden and unexpected exit from Detroit. I acknowledged that there would be a great scandal, but I told him that he was the only one responsible for it by his want of faith and consistency.

He, at first, tried to persuade me that he was ordered to drink by his own physicians for his health; but I showed him that this was a miserable illusion. He then said that he regretted what had occurred and confessed that it would be better if the priests practised what they preached to the people. After which, he asked me, in the name of our Lord Jesus Christ, to forget the errors of the bishops and priests of Detroit, in order to think only of the good which the conversion of the numberless drunkards of that city would do to the people.

He spoke to me with such earnestness that he touched the most sensitive chords of my heart, and got from me the promise that I would deliver the other two expected lectures.

When alone, I tried to drown in a sound sleep the sad emotions of that evening; but it was impossible. That night was to be again a sleepless one to me. The intemperance of that high dignitary and his priests filled me with an unspeakable horror and disgust. Many times, during the dark hours of that night, I heard as if it were a voice saying to me, "Do you not see that the bishops and priests of your church do not believe a word of their religion? Their only object is to throw dust in the eyes of the people, and live a jolly life. Do you not see that you do not follow the Word of God, but only the vain and lying traditions of men in the Church of Rome? Come out of it. Break the heavy yoke which is upon you, and follow the simple, pure religion of Jesus Christ."

I tried to silence that voice by saying to myself: "These sins are not the sins of my holy church; they are the sins of individuals. It was not the fault of Christ if Judas was a thief! It is not more the fault of my holy Church if this bishop and his priests are drunkards and worldly men. Where will I go if I leave my church? Will I not find drunkards and infidels everywhere I may go in search of a better religion?"

Hoping that the first fresh air of the morning would do me good, I went to the beautiful garden around the episcopal residence. But what was my surprise to see the bishop leaning on a tree, with his handkerchief over his face, and bathed in tears. I said to him: "My dear bishop, what is the matter? Why do you weep and cry at such an early hour?"

Pressing my hand convulsively in his, he answered: "Dear Father Chiniquy, you do not yet know the awful calamity which has befallen me this night?"

"What calamity?" I asked.

"Do you not remember," he answered, "that young priest who was sitting at your right hand last evening? Well! he went away during the night with a young man's wife whom he had seduced, and stole 4,000 dollars from me before he left."

"I am not at all surprised. When the blood of a man is heated by those fiery liquors, it is sheer absurdity to think that he will keep his vow of chastity," I answered.

"You are right! You are right! God Almighty has punished me for breaking the public pledge I had taken. We want a reform in our midst, and we will have it," he answered.

Of course, the next two days that I was the guest of Bishop Lefebre, not a single drop of intoxicating drink was seen on the table. But I know that not long after, that representative of the pope forgot again his solemn vows, and continued drinking with his priests still he died a most miserable death in 1875.

CHAPTER XLIII

The journey from Detroit to Chicago, in the month of June, 1851, was not so pleasant as it is today. On the 15th of June, I first landed, with the greatest difficulty, on a badly wrecked wharf, at the mouth of the river. Some of the streets I had to cross in order to reach the bishop's palace were almost impassable. In many places loose planks had been thrown across them to prevent people from sinking in the mud and quicksands.

The first sight of Chicago, was then far from giving an idea of what that city has become in 1884.

When I entered the miserable house called the "bishop's palace," I could hardly believe my eyes. The planks of the lower floor in the dining room were floating, and it required a great deal of ingenuity to keep my feet dry while dining with him for the first time. But the Christian kindness and courtesy of the bishop made me more happy in his poor house than I felt later in the white marble palace built by his haughty successor, C. Regan.

There were, then, in Chicago about 200 French Canadian families, under the pastorate of the Rev. M.A. Lebel, who, like myself, was born in Kamouraska. The drunkenness and other immoralities of the clergy, pictured to me by that priest, surpassed all I had ever heard or known.

After getting my promise that I would never reveal the fact before his death, he assured me that the last bishop had been poisoned by one of his grand vicars. He said the grand vicar, being father confessor of the nuns of Loretto, had fallen in love with one of the so-called virgins, who died a few days after becoming the mother of a still-born child.

This threatened a great scandal so the bishop thought it was his duty to make an inquest, and punish his priest, if he should be found guilty. But the grand vicar found that the shortest way to escape exposure was to put an end to the inquest by murdering the bishop. A poison very difficult to detect was administered and the death of the prelate soon followed without exciting any surprise in the community.

Horrified by this mystery of iniquity, I came very near returning to Canada immediately. But after more mature consideration, it seemed to me that these awful iniquities on the part of the priests of Illinois was just the reason why I should not shut my ears to the voice of God, if it were His will that I should come to take care of the precious souls He would trust to me. I spent a week in Chicago lecturing on temperance every evening and listening during the days to the grand plans the bishop was maturing to make our Church of Rome the mistress and ruler of the magnificent valley of the Mississippi.

He clearly demonstrated to me, that once mistress of the incalculable treasures of those rich lands through the millions of her obedient children, our church would easily command the respect and the submission of the less favored states of the East. I felt really happy and thankful to God that He should have chosen me to help the pope and the bishops realize such a noble and magnificent project.

Leaving Chicago, it took me nearly three days to cross the vast prairies, which were then a perfect wilderness between Chicago and Bourbonnais. I spent three weeks in preaching and exploring the country, extending from the Kankakee River to the southwest, towards the Mississippi. Only then did I plainly understand the greatness of the plans of the bishop. I determined to sacrifice the exalted position God had given me in Canada to guide the steps of the Roman Catholic emigrants from France, Belgium and Canada, towards the regions of the West, in order to extend the power and influence of my church all over the United States.

On my return to Chicago, in the second week of July, all was arranged with the bishop for my coming back in the autumn. However, it was understood between us that my leaving Canada for the United States would be kept a secret till the last hour, on account of the stern opposition I expected from my bishop. The last thing to be done, on my return to Canada, in order to prepare the emigrants to go to Illinois, rather than any other part of the United States, was to tell them through the press the unrivaled advantages which God had prepared for them in the West. I did so by a letter, which was published not only by the press of Canada, but also in many papers of France and Belgium. The importance of that letter is such, that I hope my readers will bear with me in reproducing the following extracts from it.

Montreal, Canada East
August 13th, 1851

It is impossible to give our friends, by narration, an idea of what we feel, when we cross, for the first time, the immense prairies of Illinois. It is a spectacle which must be seen to be well understood. You see around you the most luxuriant verdure; flowers of every kind, and magnificent above description. But, if in the silence of meditation, you look with new attention on those prairies, so rich, so magnificent, you feel an inexpressible sentiment of sadness.

You remember your friends in Canada, and more particularly those who, crushed down by misery, are watering with the sweat of their brow a sterile and desolated soil, you say: "Ah! if such and such of my friends were here, how soon they would see their hard and unrewarded labors changed into the most happy position."

Perhaps I will be accused then of trying to depopulate my country, and drive my countrymen from Canada to the United States. No! no. I never had so perverse a design. Here is my mind about the subject of emigration, and I see no reason to be ashamed of it, or to conceal it. It is a fact that a great number (and much greater than generally believed) of French Canadians are yearly emigrating from Canada, and nobody regrets it more than I do; but as long as those who govern Canada will not pay more attention to that evil, it will be an incurable one, and every year Canada will lose thousands and thousands of its strongest arms and noblest hearts, to benefit our happy neighbors.

The greatest part of them, for the want of roads to the markets of Quebec and Montreal, and still more by the tyranny of their cruel landlords, will soon be obliged to bid an eternal adieu to their country, and with an enraged heart against their haughty oppressors, they will seek, in exile to a strange land, the protection they could not find in their own country. Yes! If our Canadian government continues a little longer to show the same incomprehensible apathy for the welfare of its own subjects, emigration will increase every year from Canada, to swell the ranks of the American people.

Since we cannot stop that emigration, is it not our first duty to direct it in such a way that it will be, to the poor emigrants, as beneficial as possible? Let us do everything to hinder them from going to the large cities of the United States. Drowned in the mixed population of American cities, our unfortunate emigrating countrymen would be too much exposed to losing their morality and their faith.

Surely there is not another country under the heavens where space, bread, and liberty are so universally assured to every member of the community, as the United States. But it is not in the great cities of the United States that our poor countrymen will sooner find these three gifts. The French Canadian who will stop in the large cities, will not, with a very few exceptions, raise himself above the unenviable position of a poor journeyman. But those among them who will direct their steps toward the rich and extensive prairies of Bourbonnais, will certainly find a better lot.

Many in Canada would believe that I am exaggerating, were I to publish how happy, prosperous, and respectable is the French Canadian population of Bourbonnais. The French Canadians of Bourbonnais have had the intelligence to follow the good example of the industrious American farmers, in the manner of cultivating the lands. On their farms as well as on those of their neighbors, you will find the best machinery to cut crops, to thresh their grain. They enjoy the just reputation of having the best horses of the country, and very few can beat them for the number and quality of their cattle.

Now, what can be the prospect of a young man in Canada, if he has not more than two hundred dollars? A whole life of hard labor and continued privation is his too certain lot. But, let that young man go directly to Bourbonnais, and if he is industrious, sober, and religious, before a couple of years he will see nothing to envy in the most happy farmer of Canada.

As the land he will take in Illinois is entirely prepared for the plow, he has no trees to cut or eradicate, no stones to move, no ditch to dig; his only work is to fence and break his land and sow it, and the very first year the value of the crop will be sufficient to pay for his farm. Holy Providence has prepared everything for the benefit of the happy farmers of Illinois. That fertile country is well watered by a multitude of rivers and large creeks, whose borders are generally covered with the most rich and extensive groves of timber of the best quality, as black oak, maple, white oak, burr oak, ash, etc. The seeds of the beautiful acacia (locust), after five or six years, will give you a splendid tree. The greatest variety of fruits are growing naturally in almost every part of Illinois; coal mines have been discovered in the very heart of the country, more than sufficient for the wants of the people. Before long, a railroad from Chicago to Bourbonnais will bring our happy countrymen to the most extensive market, the queen city of the West — Chicago.

I will then say to my young countrymen who intend emigrating from Canada: "My friend, exile is one of the greatest calamities that can befall a man. Young Canadian, remain in the country, keep thy heart to love it, thy intelligence to adorn it, and thine arms to protect it. Young and dear countrymen, remain in thy beautiful country; there is nothing more grand and sublime in the world than the waters of the St. Lawrence. It is on its deep and majestic waters that, before long, Europe and America will meet and bind themselves to each other by the blessed bonds of an eternal peace; it is on its shores that they will exchange their incalculable treasures. Remain in the country of your birth, my dear son. Let the sweat of thy brow continue to fertilize it, and let the perfume of thy virtues bring the blessing of God upon it. But, my dear son, if thou hast no more room in the valley of the St. Lawrence, and if, by the want of protection from the government, thou canst not go to the forest without running the danger of losing thy life in a pond, or being crushed under the feet of an English or Scotch tyrant, I am not the man to invite thee to exhaust thy best days for the benefit of the insolent strangers, who are the lords of the eastern lands. I will sooner tell thee, 'go my child,' there are many extensive places still vacant on the earth, and God is everywhere. That great God calleth thee to another land, submit thyself to His Divine will. But, before you bid a final adieu to thy country, engrave on thy heart and keep as a holy deposit, the love of thy holy religion, of thy beautiful language, and of the dear and unfortunate country of thy birth. On thy way to the land of exile, stop as little as possible in the great cities, for fear of the many snares thy eternal enemy has prepared for thy perdition. But go straight to Bourbonnais. There you will find many of thy brothers who have erected the cross of Christ; join thyself to them, thou shalt be strong of their strength; go and help them to conquer, to the Gospel of Jesus, those rich countries which shall very soon weigh more than is generally believed, in the balance of the nations.

"Yes, go straight to Illinois. Thou shalt not be entirely in a strange and alien country. Holy Providence has chosen thy fathers to find that rich country, and to reveal to the world its admirable resources. More than once that land of Illinois has been sanctified by the blood of thy ancestors. In Illinois thou shalt not make a step without finding indestructible proof of the perseverance, genius, bravery, and piety of the French forefathers. Go to Illinois; and the many names of Bourbonnais, Joliet, Dubuque, La Salle, St. Charles, St. Mary, etc., that you will meet everywhere, will tell you more than my words, that that country is nothing but the rich inheritance which your fathers have found for the benefit of their grandchildren."

C. CHINIQUY

I would never have published this letter if I had foreseen its effects on the farmers of Canada. In a few days after its appearance their farms fell to half their value. In some parishes every one wanted to sell their lands and emigrate to the West. It was only for want of purchasers that we did not see an emigration which would have surely ruined Canada. I was frightened by its immediate effect on the public mind. However, while some were praising me to the skies for having published it, others were cursing me and calling me a traitor. The very day after its publication I was in Quebec. The first one I met was my Lord De Charbonel, Bishop of Toronto. After having blessed me, he pressed my hand in his, and said:

"I have just read your admirable letter. It is one of the most beautiful and eloquently written articles I ever read. The Spirit of God has surely inspired every one of its sentences. I have, just now, forwarded six copies of it to different journals in France and Belgium, where they will be republished, and do an incalculable amount of good by directing the French-speaking Catholic emigrants towards a country where they will run no risk of losing their faith, with the assurance of securing a future of unbounded prosperity for their families. Your name will be put among the names of the greatest benefactors of humanity."

Though these compliments seemed to me much exaggerated and unmerited, I cannot deny that they pleased me, by adding to my hopes and convictions that great good would surely come from the plan. I thanked the bishop for his kind and friendly words, and left him to go and present my respectful salutations to Bishop Bourget, of Montreal, and give him a short sketch of my voyage to the far West. I found him alone in his room, in the very act of reading my letter. A lioness who had just lost her whelps would not have looked upon me with more angry and threatening eyes.

"Is it possible, Mr. Chiniquy," he said, "that your hand has written and signed such a perfidious document? How could you so cruelly pierce the bosom of your own country after her dealing so nobly with you? Do you not see that your treasonable letter will give such an impetus to emigration that our most thriving parishes will soon be turned into solitude?"

Surprised by this unexpected burst of bad feeling, I answered: "Your lordship has surely misunderstood me, if you have found in my letter any treasonable plan to ruin our country. Please read it again, and you will see that every line has been inspired by the purest motives of patriotism, and the highest views of religion." The abrupt answer the bishop gave clearly indicated that my absence would be more welcome than my presence. I left him, after asking his blessing, which he gave me in the coldest manner possible.

On the 25th of August, I was back at Longueuil, from my voyage to Quebec, which I had extended as far as Kamouraska, to see again the noble-hearted parishioners, whose unanimity in taking the pledge of temperance, and admirable fidelity in keeping it then, had filled my heart with such joy.

I related my last interview with Bishop Bourget to my faithful friend Mr. Brassard. He answered me: "The present bad feelings of the Bishop of Montreal against you are not a secret to me. Unfortunately the low-minded men who surround and counsel him are as unable as the bishop himself to understand your exalted views in directing the steps of the Roman Catholics towards the splendid valley of the Mississippi. Now, I am sure of what I say, though I am not free to tell you how it came to my knowledge, there is a plot somewhere to dishonor and destroy you at once. Those who are at the head of that plot hope that if they can succeed in destroying your popularity, nobody will be tempted to follow you to Illinois. For, though you have concealed it as well as you could, it is evident to everyone now, that you are the man selected by the bishops of the West to direct the uncertain steps of the poor immigrants towards those rich lands."

"Do you mean, my dear Mr. Brassard," I replied, "that there are priests around the Bishop of Montreal, cruel and vile enough to forge calumnies against me, and spread them before the country in such a way that I shall be unable to refute them?"

"It is just what I mean," answered Mr. Brassard; "mind what I tell you; the bishop has made use of you to reform his diocese. He likes you for that work. But your popularity is too great today for your enemies; they want to get rid of you, and no means will be too vile or criminal to accomplish your destruction, if they can attain their object."

"But, my dear Mr. Brassard, can you give me any details of the plots which are in store against me?" I asked.

"No! I cannot, for I know them not. But be on your guard; for your few, but powerful enemies, are jubilant. They speak of the absolute impotency to which you will soon be reduced, if you accomplish what they so maliciously and falsely call your treacherous objects."

I answered: "Our Saviour has said to all His disciples: 'In the world ye shall have tribulation. But be of good cheer, I have overcome the world.' (John 15:33) I am more determined than ever to put my trust in God, and to fear no man."

Two hours after this conversation, I received the following from the Rev. M. Pare, secretary to the bishop:

To the Rev. Mr. Chiniquy,
Apostle of Temperance

My Dear Sir — My lord Bishop of Montreal would like to see you upon some important business. Please come at your earliest convenience.

Yours truly,
JOS. PARE, *Secretary*

The next morning I was alone with Monseigneur Bourget, who received me very kindly. He seemed at first to have entirely banished the bad feelings he had shown in our last interview at Quebec. After making some friendly remarks on my continual labors and success in the cause of temperance, he stopped for a moment, and seemed embarrassed how to resume the conversation. At last he said: "Are you not the father confessor of Mrs. Chenier?"

"Yes, my lord. I have been her confessor since I lived in Longueuil."

"Very well, very well," he rejoined, "I suppose that you know that her only child is a nun, in the Congregation Convent?"

"Yes! my lord, I know it," I replied.

"Could you not induce Mrs. Chenier to become a nun also?" asked the bishop.

"I never thought of that, my lord," I answered, "and I do not see why I should advise her to exchange her beautiful cottage, washed by the fresh and pure waters of the St. Lawrence, where she looks so happy and cheerful, for the gloomy walls of the nunnery."

"But she is still young and beautiful; she may be deceived by temptations when she is there, in that beautiful house, surrounded by all the enjoyments of her fortune," replied the bishop.

"I understand your lordship. Yes, Mrs. Chenier has the reputation of being rich; though I know nothing of her fortune; she has kept well the charms and freshness of her youth. However, I think that the best remedy against the temptations you seem to dread so much for her, is to advise her to marry. A good Christian husband seems to me a much better remedy against the dangers to which your lordship alludes, than the cheerless walls of a nunnery."

"You speak just as a Protestant," rejoined the bishop, with an evident nervous irritation. "We remark that, though you hear the confessions of a great number of young ladies, there is not a single one of them who has ever become a nun. You seem to ignore that the vow of chastity is the shortest way to a life of holiness in this world and happiness in the next."

"I am sorry to differ from your lordship, in that matter," I replied. "But I cannot help it, the remedy you have found against sin is quite modern. The old remedy offered by our God Himself, is very different and much better, I think."

"'It is not good that the man should be alone; I will make an help meet for him' (Gen. 2:18), said our Creator in the earthly paradise. 'Nevertheless, to avoid fornication, let every man have his own wife, and let every woman have her own husband' (I Cor. 7:2), said the same God, through His Apostle Paul."

"I know too well how the great majority of nuns keep their vows of chastity, to believe that the modern remedy against the temptations you mention, is an improvement on the old one found and given by our God!" I answered.

With an angry look, the bishop replied: "This is Protestantism, Mr. Chiniquy. This is sheer Protestantism."

"I respectfully ask your pardon for differing from your lordship. This is not Protestantism. It is simply and absolutely the 'pure Word of God.' But my lord, God knows that is is my sincere desire, as it is my interest and my duty, to do all in my power to deserve your esteem. I do not want to vex nor disobey you. Please give me a good reason why I should advise Mrs. Chenier to enter a monastery, and I will comply with your request the very first time she comes to confess."

Resuming his most amiable manner, the bishop answered me, "My first reason is, the spiritual good which she would receive from her vows of perpetual chastity and poverty in a nunnery. The second reason is, that the lady is rich, and we are in need of money. We would soon possess her whole fortune; for her only child is already in the Congregation Convent."

"My dear bishop," I replied, "you already know what I think of your first reason. After having investigated that fact, from the lips of the nuns themselves, as well as from their father confessors, I am fully convinced that the real virtue of purity is much better kept in the homes of our Christian mothers, married sisters, and female friends than in the secret rooms, not to say prisons, where the poor nuns are enchained by the heavy fetters assumed by their vows, which the great majority curse when they cannot break them. And for the second reason, your lordship gave me to induce Mrs. Chenier becoming a nun, I am again sorry to say that I cannot conscientiously accept it. I have not consecrated myself to the priesthood to deprive respectable families of their legal inheritance in order to enrich myself, or anybody else. I know she has poor relations who need her fortune after her death.".

"Do you pretend to say that your bishop is a thief?" angrily rejoined the bishop.

"No, my lord! By no means. No doubt, from your high standpoint of view, your lordship may see things in a very different aspect, from what I see them, in the low position I occupy in the church. But, as your lordship is bound to follow the dictates of his conscience in everything, I also feel obliged to give heed to the voice of mine."

This painful conversation had already lasted too long. I rose up to take leave of him, and said: "My lord, I beg your pardon for disappointing your lordship."

He coldly answered me: "It is not the first time; though I would it were the last, that you show such a want of respect and submission to the will of your superiors. But, as I feel it is a conscientious affair on your part, I have no ill-will against you, and I am happy to tell you that I entertain for you all my past esteem. The only favor I ask from you just now is, that this conversation may be kept secret."

I answered: "It is still more to my interest than yours to keep this unfortunate affair a secret between us. I hope that neither your lordship nor the great God, who alone has heard us, will ever make it an imperious duty for me to mention it."

"What good news do you bring me from the bishop's palace?" asked my venerable friend, Mr. Brassard, when I returned, late in the afternoon.

"I would have very spicy, though unpalatable news to give you, had not the bishop asked me to keep what has been said between us a secret."

Mr. Brassard laughed outright at my answer, and replied: "A secret! a secret! Ah! but it is a gazette secret; for the bishop has bothered me, as well as many others, with that matter, frequently, since your return from Illinois. Several times he has asked us to persuade you to advise your devoted penitent, Mrs. Chenier, to become a nun. I knew he invited you to his palace yesterday for that object. The eyes and heart of our poor bishop," continued Mr. Brassard, "are too firmly fixed on the fortune of that lady. Hence, his zeal about the salvation of her soul through the monastic life.

In vain I tried to dissuade the bishop from speaking to you on that subject, on account of your prejudices against our good nuns. He would not listen to me. No doubt you have realized my worst anticipations; you have, with your usual stubbornness, refused to yield to his demands. I fear you have added to his bad feelings, and consummated your disgrace."

"What a deceitful man that bishop is!" I answered, indignantly. "He has given me to understand that this was a most sacred secret between him and me, when I see, by what you say, that it is nothing else than a farcical secret, known by the hundreds who have heard of it. But, please, my dear Mr. Brassard, tell me, is it not a burning shame that our nunneries are changed into real traps, to steal, cheat, and ruin so many unsuspecting families? I have no words to express my disgust and indignation, when I see that all those great demonstrations and eloquent tirades about the perfection and holiness of the nuns, on the part of our spiritual rulers, are nothing else, in reality, than a veil to conceal their stealing operations. Do you not feel, that those poor nuns are the victims of the most stupendous system of swindling the world has ever seen? I know that there are some honorable exceptions. For instance, the nunnery you have founded here is an exception. You have not built it to enrich yourself, as you have spent your last cent in its erection. But you and I are only simpletons, who have, till now, ignored the terrible secrets which put that machine of the nunneries and monkeries in motion. I am more than ever disgusted and terrified, not only by the unspeakable corruptions, but also by the stupendous system of swindling, which is their foundation stone. If the cities of Quebec and Montreal could know what I know of the incalculable sums of money secretly stolen through the confessional, to aid our bishops in building the famous cathedrals and splendid palaces; or to cover themselves with robes of silk, satin, silver, and gold; to live more luxurious than the Pashas of Turkey; they would set fire to all those palatial buildings; they would hang the confessors, who have thrown the poor nuns into these dungeons under the pretext of saving their souls, when the real motive was to lay hands on their inheritance, and raise their colossal fortunes. The bishop has opened before me a most deplorable and shameful page of the history of our church. It makes me understand many facts which were a mystery to till today. Now I understand the terrible wrath of the English people in the days of old, and of the French people more recently, when they so violently wrenched from the hands of the clergy the enormous wealth they had accumulated during the Dark Ages. I have condemned those great nations till now. But, today, I absolve them. I am sure that those men, though blind and cruel in their vengeance, were the ministers of the justice of God. The God of Heaven could not, forever, tolerate a sacrilegious system of swindling, as I know, now, to be in operation from one end to the other, not only of Canada, but of the whole world, under the mask of religion. I know that the bishop and his flatterers will hate and persecute me for my stern opposition to his rapacity. But I do feel happy and proud of his hatred. The God of truth and justice, the God of the gospel, will be on my side when they attack me. I do not fear them; let them come. That bishop surely did not know me, when he thought that I would consent to be the instrument of his hypocrisy, and that, under the false pretext of a delusive perfection, I would throw that lady into a dungeon for her life, that he might become rich with her inheritance."

Mr. Brassard answered me: "I cannot blame you for your disobeying the bishop, in this instance. I foretold him what has occurred; for I knew what you think of the nuns. Though I do not go so far as you in that, I cannot absolutely shut my eyes to the facts which stare us in the face. Those monkish communities have, in every age, been the principal cause of the calamities which have befallen the church. For their love of riches, their pride and laziness, with their other scandals, have always been the same. Had I been able to foresee what has occurred inside the walls of the nunnery I built up here, I never would have erected it. However, now that I have built it, it is as the child of my old age, I feel bound to support it to the end. This does not prevent me from being afflicted when I see the facility with which our poor nuns yield to the criminal desires of their too weak confessors. Who could have thought, that that lean, ugly superior of the Oblates, Father Allard, could have fallen in love with his young nuns. Have you heard how the young men of our village, indignant at his spending the greater part of the night with the nuns, have whipped him, when he was crossing the bridge, not long before his leaving Longueuil for Africa? It is evident that our bishop multiples too fast those religious houses. My fear is that they will, sooner than we expect, bring upon our Church of Canada the same cataclysms which have so often desolated her in England, France, Germany, and even in Italy."

The clock struck twelve just when this last sentence fell from the lips of Mr. Brassard. It was quite time to take some rest. When leaving me for his sleeping room he said:

"My dear Chiniquy, gird your loins well, sharpen your sword for the impending conflict. My fear is that the bishop and his advisers will never forget your wrenching from their hands the booty they

were coveting so long. They will never forgive the spirit of independence with which you have rebuked them. In fact, the conflict is already begun, may God protect you against the open blows, and the
secret machinations they have in store for you."

I anwered him: "I do not fear them. I put my trust in God. It is
for His honor I am fighting and suffering. He will surely protect
me from those sacrilegious traders in souls."

CHAPTER XLIV

The first week of September, 1851, I was hearing confessions in
one of the churches of Montreal, when a fine-looking girl came to
confess sins, whose depravity surpassed anything I had ever heard.
Though I forbade her twice to do it, she gave me the names of
several priests who were the accomplices of her orgies. The details
of her iniquities were told with such cynical impudence, that the
idea struck me at once that she was sent by someone to ruin me. I
abruptly stopped her disgusting stories by saying: "The way you
confess your sins is a sure indication that you do not come here to
reconcile yourself to God, but to ruin me. By the grace of God, you
will fail. I forbid you to come any more to my confessional. If I see
you again among my penitents, I will order the beadle to turn you
out of the church."

I instantly shut the door of the small aperture through which
she was speaking to me. She answered something which I could
not understand. But the manner in which she left the confessional
indicated she was beside herself with rage, as she went to speak a
few words to a carter who was in the church preparing himself to
confess.

The next evening, I said to Rev. Mr. Brassard that I suspected
that a girl was sent to my confessional to ruin me. He agreed with
me and expressed great anxiety over the incident. I replied that I
could not partake of his fears; that God knew my innocence and
the purity of my motives; He would defend and protect me.

"My dear Chiniquy," replied Mr. Brassard, "I know your
enemies. They are not numerous but their power for mischief
knows no limits. Surely God can save you from their hands; but I
cannot share your security for the future. Your answer to the
bishop, in reference to Mrs. Chenier has forever alienated him.
Bishop Bourget has a merited reputation of being the most
revengeful man in Canada. He will avail himself of the least opportunity to strike you without mercy."

I answered, "Though there should be a thousand Bishops Bourget to plot against me, I will not fear them, so long as I am in the right, as I am today."

By month's end I found on my table a short letter from Bishop Bourget telling me that, for a criminal action which he did not want to mention, committed with a person he would not name, he had withdrawn all my priestly powers and interdicted me. I handed the letter to Mr. Brassard and said: "Is not this the fulfillment of your prophecies? What do you think of a bishop who interdicts a priest without giving him a single fact, and without even allowing him to know his accusers?"

"It is just what I expected from the implacable vengeance of the Bishop of Montreal. He will never give you the reasons of your interdict for he knows well you are innocent and he will never confront you with your accusers for it would be too easy for you to confound them."

"But is not this against all the laws of God, man, and church?" I replied.

"Of course it is," answered he, "but do you not know that on this continent of America the bishops have long ago thrown overboard all the laws of God, man and the church, to rule and enslave the priests?"

"Mind what I tell you," I replied. "I will not allow the bishop to deal with me in that way. If he dares to trample the laws of the Gospel under his feet to accomplish my ruin and satisfy his vengeance, I will teach him a lesson that he will never forget. I am innocent; God knows it. My trust is in Him; He will not forsake me. I will go immediately to the bishop. If he never knew what power there is in an honest priest, he will learn it today."

Two hours later, I was knocking at the bishop's door. He received me with icy politeness. "My lord," I said, "you already know why I am in your presence. Here is a letter from you accusing me of a crime which is not specified, under the testimony of accusers whom you refuse to name! And before hearing me, and confronting me with my accusers, you punish me as guilty! I come in the name of God, and of His Son, Jesus Christ, to respectfully ask you to tell me the crime of which I am accused, that I may show you my innocence. I want to be confronted with my accusers, that I may confound them."

The bishop was at first, obviously embarrassed by my presence; his lips were pale and trembling but his eyes were dry and red like the tiger's eyes in the presence of his prey. He answered: "I cannot grant your request, sir."

Opening then my New Testament, I read: "Receive no accusation against a priest, except under two or three witnesses." (I Tim. 5:19) I added: "It was after I had heard this voice of God, and of His holy church, that I consented to be a priest. I hope it is not the intention of your lordship to put aside this Word of God and of His church. Is it your intention to break that solemn covenant made by Christ with His priests, and sealed with His blood?"

With an air of contempt and tyrannical authority which I had never suspected to be possible in a bishop, he answered: "I have no lesson of Scripture or canonical law to receive from you, sir, and no answer to give to your impertinent questions. You are interdicted!"

These words, uttered by the man whom I was accustomed to consider as my superior, had a strange effect upon me. I felt as if awakening from a long and painful dream. For the first time I understood the sad prophecies of the Rev. Mr. Brassard and I realized the horror of my position. My ruin was accomplished. Though I knew that that high dignitary was a monster of hypocrisy, injustice and tyranny, he had, among the masses, the reputation of a saint. His unjust sentence would be considered as just and equitable by the multitude over whom he was reigning supremely; at a nod of his head the people would fall at his feet, and obey his commands to crush me. All ears would be shut and all hearts hardened against me. In that fatal hour, for the first time in my life my moral strength and courage failed me. I felt as if I had just fallen into a bottomless abyss, out of which it was impossible to escape. What would my innocence, known only to God, avail me, when the whole world would believe me guilty? No words can give an idea of the mental torture of that horrible hour.

For more than a quarter of an hour, not a word was exchanged between us. He seemed very busy writing letters, while I was resting my head between my hands in despair. At last I fell on my knees, took the hands of the bishop in mine, and, with a voice half-choked with sighs I said: "My lord, in the name of our Lord Jesus Christ, and in the presence of God, I swear that I have done nothing which could bring such a sentence against me. I again implore your lordship to confront me with my accusers, that I may show you my innocence."

With a savage insolence, the bishop withdrew his hands, as if I had contaminated them, and said, after rising from his chair: "You are guilty; go out of my presence."

A thousand times since I have thanked my God that I had no dagger with me, for I would have plunged it into his heart. But, strange to say, the diabolical malice of that depraved man suddenly brought back my former self-respect and courage. At once I resolved to face the storm. I felt, in my soul, that giant strength which often God Himself imparts to the oppressed in the presence of his merciless tyrants. It seemed that a flash of lightning had passed through my soul, after having written in letters of fire on the walls of the palace: "Mystery of iniquity."

Relying entirely on the God of truth and justice, who knew my innocence and the great perversity of my oppressor, I left the room without saying a word and hastened back to Longueuil, to acquaint the Rev. Mr. Brassard with my firm resolution to fight the bishop to the end. He burst into tears when I told him what had occurred in the bishop's palace.

"Though innocent, you are condemned," he said. "The infallible proof of your innocence is the cruel refusal to be confronted with your accusers. Were you guilty they would be too glad to show it by confounding you before those witnesses. But the perversity of your accusers is so well known that they are ashamed to give their names. The bishop prefers to crush you under the weight of his unmerited reputation for justice and holiness, for very few know him as we do. I fear he will succeed in destroying you. Though innocent, you will never be able to contend against such a mighty adversary."

"My dear Mr. Brassard, you are mistaken," I replied. "I never was so sure of coming out victorious. The monstrous iniquity of the bishop carries its own antidote. It was not a dream I saw when he so ignominiously turned me out of his room. A flash of lightning passed before my eyes, and wrote, as if on the walls of the palace: 'Mystery of iniquity!' When Canada, the whole of Christendom, shall know the infamous conduct of that dignitary; when they shall see the 'mystery of iniquity,' which I shall stamp upon his forehead, there will be a unanimous cry of indignation against him!

"Oh! If I can only find out the names of my accusers, I will force that mighty tyrant to withdraw that sentence, double quick. I am determined to show, not only to Canada, but to the whole world, that this infamous plot is but the work of the vile male and female slaves by whom the bishop is surrounded.

"My first thought is to start immediately for Chicago, where Bishop Vandeveld expects me. But I am resolved not to go until I have forced my merciless oppressor to withdraw his unjust sentence. I will immediately go to the Jesuit College where I plan to spend the next eight days in prayer and retreat. The Jesuits are the ablest men under heaven to detect the most hidden things. I hope they will help me to unearth that dark mystery of iniquity and expose it to the world."

"I am glad to see that you do not fear the terrible storm which is upon you, and that your sails are so well trimmed," answered Mr. Brassard. "You do well in putting your trust in God first, and in the Jesuits afterwards. The fearless way in which you intend to meet the attacks of your merciless enemies will give you an easy victory. My hope is that the Jesuits will help you hurl back in the face of the bishop the shame and dishonor he had prepared for you."

At six p.m., in a modest, well-lighted and ventilated room of the Jesuit College, I was alone with the venerable Mr. Schneider, its director. I told him how the Bishop of Montreal, four years before, after giving up his prejudices against me when I had left the Oblates, had earnestly supported me in my labors. I acquainted him also with the sudden change of those good feelings into the most uncontrollable hatred, from the day I had refused to force Mrs. Chenier to become a nun, that he might secure her fortune. I told him also how those bad feelings had found new food in my plan of consecrating the rest of my life to direct the tide of the French Catholic emigration towards the Mississippi Valley. I exposed to him my suspicions about that miserable girl I had turned out from my confessional. "I have a double object in view," I added. "The first is to spend the last eight days of my residence in Canada in prayer. But my second is to ask the help of your charity, wisdom, and experience in forcing the bishop to withdraw his unjust sentence against me. I am determined, if he does not withdraw it, to denounce him before the whole country and to challenge him publicly to confront me with my accusers."

"If you do that," answered Mr. Schneider, "I fear lest you not only do an irreparable damage to the Bishop of Montreal, but to our holy Church also."

I replied: "Our holy church would suffer greater damage if she sanctions the infamous conduct of the bishop."

"You are correct," rejoined the Jesuit. "Our holy Church cannot sanction such criminal conduct. She has hundreds of times condemned those tyrannical and unjust actions in other bishops. Such want of common honesty and justice will be condemned everywhere as soon as it is known. The first thing we have to do is to find out the names of your accusers. My impression is that the miserable girl you have so abruptly and so wisely turned out of your confessional knows more than the bishop wants us to find out about the plot. It is a pity you did not ask her name and residence.

"At all events, you may rely on my efforts to persuade our bishop that he has taken a position against you which is absolutely untenable. Before your retreat is at an end, no doubt he will be too happy to make his peace with you. Only trust in God, and in the blessed Virgin Mary and you have nothing to fear. Our bishop has put himself above all the laws of man and God to condemn the priest he had himself officially named 'the Apostle of Temperance of Canada.' The 200,000 soldiers you have enrolled under the holy banners of temperance will force him to retract his too hasty and unjust sentence."

It would be too long to repeat here all the encouraging words which that wise Jesuit uttered. Father Schneider was a European priest, who was in Montreal only since 1849. He had won my confidence the very first time I met him, and I had chosen him, at once, for my confessor and adviser. The third day of my retreat, Father Schneider came to my room earlier than usual, and said:

"I have found out the name and residence of the carter to whom that miserable girl spoke in the church. If you have no objection I will send for him. He may know that girl and induce her to come here."

"By all means, dear father," I answered, "do it without losing a moment."

Two hours later the carter was with me. I recognized him as one of those dear countrymen whom our society of temperance had transformed into a new man. I asked him if he remembered the name of the girl who, a few days before, had spoken to him in the church, after going out of my confessional.

"Yes sir! I know her well. She has a very bad name though she belongs to a respectable family."

I added: "Do you think you can induce her to come here by telling her that a priest in the Jesuit College wants to see her? But do not give her my name."

He answered: "Nothing is more easy. She will be here in a couple of hours, if I find her at home."

At three p.m., the carter was again knocking at my door, and said, with a low voice: "The girl you want is in the parlor; she has no idea you are here, for she told me that you were now preaching in St. Constant. She seems to be very angry against you, and bitterly complains against your want of courtesy the very first time she went to confess to you."

"Is it possible that she told you that?" I replied.

"Yes sir! She told me that when coming out of your confessional the other day; she then requested me to drive her home. She was really beside herself, and swore that she would make you pay for your harsh words and rude manners towards her. You will do well to be on your guard. She is one of the most depraved girls of Montreal and has a most dangerous tongue, though to the shame of our holy religion she is daily seen in the bishop's palace."

I immediately went to Father Schneider, and said: "My dear

father, by the mercy of God, the girl we want to see is in the parlor. By what I have just heard from the carter who drove her, I have not the least doubt that she is the one employed by the bishop to slander me. Please come with me to witness my innocence. But take your Gospel, ink, paper and pen with you."

"All right," answered the wise Jesuit.

Two minutes later we were in her presence. It is impossible to describe her dismay when she saw me. She came near fainting. I feared she would not be able to utter a word. I spoke to her very kindly, and ran to get a glass of cold water, which did her good. When she recovered, I said to her, with a tone of mixed authority and kind firmness: "You are here in the presence of God and of two of His priests. That great God will hear every word which will fall from your lips. You must speak the truth. You have denounced me to the bishop as guilty of some great iniquity. You are the cause of my being interdicted. You, alone, can repair the injury you have done me. That injury is very great; but it can be easily repaired by you. In the presence of this venerable priest, say whether or not I am guilty of the crime you have brought to my charge!"

At these words the unfortunate girl burst into tears. She hid her face in her handkerchief and with a voice half-suffocated with sighs, she said: "No sir! You are not guilty."

I added: "Confess another thing. Is it not a fact that you came to my confessional more with the intention of tempting me to sin than to reconcile yourself to God?"

"Yes sir!" she added, "that was my wicked intention."

"Continue to tell the truth, and our great and merciful God will forgive you. Is it not for revenge that you have brought the false accusations to the bishop in order that he might interdict me?"

"Yes sir! that is the only reason I had for accusing you."

After Father Schneider had made four copies of those declarations, signed by him as witness, and after she had sworn on the Gospel, I forgave her the injury she had done me, I gave her some good advice and dismissed her.

"Is it not evident," I said to Father Schneider, "that our merciful God never forsakes those who trust in Him?"

"Yes, I never saw the interposition of God so marvelously manifested. But please tell me why you requested me to make four copies of her sworn declaration of your innocence; was not one sufficient?" asked Mr. Schneider.

I answered: "One of those copies was for the bishop; another will remain in your hands, Mr. Brassard will have one, and I need one for myself. For the dishonesty of the bishop is so evident to me, now, that I think him able to destroy the copy I will send him, with the hope, after its destruction, of keeping me at his feet. If he does that new act of iniquity, I will confound him with the three other authentic copies. Besides, this unfortunate girl may die sooner than we expect. In that case, I would find myself again with the bishop's knife on my throat, if I had no other copies of the retraction."

"You are right," replied Father Schneider; "now the only thing for you to do is to send that retraction to the bishop, with a firm and polite request to retract his unjust sentence against you. Let me do the rest with him. Thanks be to God, you have a most complete victory over your unjust aggressors. The bishop will do all in his power, no doubt, to make you forget the darkest page of his life."

The shrewd Jesuit was correct. Never did any bishop receive me with such kindness and respect as he, when I went to take leave of him before my departure from Canada for the United States.

CHAPTER XLV

I arrived at Chicago on the 29th of October, 1851 and spent six days with Bishop Vandeveld in maturing the plans of our Catholic colonization. He gave me the wisest advice, with the most extensive powers which a bishop can give a priest, and urged me to begin at once by selecting the most suitable spot for such an important and vast prospect. My heart was filled with uncontrollable emotions when the hour came to leave my superior and go to the conquest of the magnificent state of Illinois for the benefit of my Church. I fell at his knees to ask his benediction, and requested him never to forget me in his prayers. He was not less affected than I was, and pressing me to his bosom, bathed my face with his tears, and blessed me.

It took me three days to cross the prairies from Chicago to Bourbonnais. Those prairies were then a vast solitude with almost impassable roads. At the invitation of their priest, Mr. Courjeault, several people had come long distances to receive and overwhelm me with the public expressions of their joy and respect.

After a few days of rest in the midst of their interesting young colony, I explained to Mr. Courjeault that, having been sent by the bishop to found a settlement for Roman Catholic immigrants, on a sufficiently grand scale to rule the government of Illinois, it was my duty to go further south, to find the most suitable place for the first village. But to my unspeakable regret, the very moment I told him the object of my coming to Illinois, I felt the spirit of jealousy turn him into an implacable enemy. It had been just the same thing with Rev. Mr. Lebel, at Chicago.

So long as they believed that I had left Canada to help them increase their small congregations by inducing the immigrants to settle among them, they loaded me, both in public and in private, with marks of their esteem. But the moment they saw that I was going to found, in the very heart of Illinois, settlements on such a large scale, they banded together to paralyze and ruin my efforts. Had I suspected such opposition from the very men on whose moral help I had relied for the success of my colonizing schemes, I would have never left Canada, for Illinois. But it was now too late to stop my onward march.

Trusting in God alone for success, I persuaded six of the most respectable citizens of Bourbonnais to accompany me, in three wagons, in search of the best site for the center of my future colony. I had a compass to guide me through those vast prairies, spread before me like a boundless ocean. I wanted to select the highest point in Illinois for my first town, in order to secure the purest air and water for the new immigrants. I was fortunate enough, under the guidance of God, to succeed better than I expected, for the government surveyors have lately acknowledged that the village of St. Anne occupies the very highest point of that splendid state.

To my great surprise, ten days after I had selected that spot, fifty families from Canada had planted their tents around mine, on the beautiful site which forms today the town of St. Anne. We were at the end of November, and though the weather was still mild, I felt I had not an hour to lose in order to secure shelters for every one of those families, before winter could spread sickness and death among them. The greater part were illiterate and poor without any idea of the dangers and incredible difficulties of establishing a new settlement. There were, at first, only two small houses, one 25 by 30, and the other 16 by 20 feet, to lodge us. With the rest of my dear immigrants, wrapped in buffalo robes, with my overcoat for my pillow, I slept soundly, many nights on the bare floor, during the three months which it took to get my first house erected.

Having taken the census of the people on the first of December, I found two hundred souls, one hundred of whom were adults. I said to them: "There are not three of you, if left alone, able to prepare a shelter for your families, this winter; but if, forgetting yourselves, you work for each other as true friends and brethren, you will increase your strength tenfold and in a few weeks there will be a sufficient number of small, but solid buildings, to protect you against the storms and snow of the winter which is fast coming upon us.

"Let us go to the forest together and cut the wood today; and tomorrow we will draw that timber to one of the lots you have selected, and you will see with what marvelous speed the house will be raised. But before going to the forest, let us kneel down to ask our Heavenly Father to bless the work of our hands, and grant us to be of one heart, and to protect us against the too common accidents of those forests and building works." We all knelt on the grass, and, as much with our tears as with our lips, we sent to the mercy seat a prayer and we started for the forest.

How quickly the first forty small, but neat houses were put up on our beautiful prairies. Whilst the men were cutting timber and raising one another's houses with unity, joy, goodwill and diligence, the women would prepare the common meals. We obtained our flour and pork from Bourbonnais and Momence at a very low price; and, as I was a good shot, one or two friends and I used to kill, every day, enough prairie chickens, quails, ducks, wild geese, brants and deer to feed more people than there were in our young colony.

When I saw that a sufficient number of houses had been built to give shelter to every one of the first immigrants, I called a meeting, and said: "My dear friends, I think that we now must build a two-story house. The upper part will be used as the schoolhouse for your children on week days, and for a chapel on Sundays, and the lower part will be my parsonage. I will furnish the money for the flooring, shingles, nails, etc., and you will give your work gratis to cut and draw the timber and put it up. I will also pay the architect, without asking a cent from you. What do you think of this?"

They unanimously answered: "Yes! after you have worked so hard to give a home to every one of us, it is just that we should help you to make one for yourself. We are happy to hear that it is your intention to secure a good education for our children. Let us begin the work at once." This was the 16th of January, 1852. The sun was as warm as on a beautiful day of May in Canada. We again fell upon our knees to implore the help of God.

The next day, we were seventy-two men in a neighboring forest, felling the great oaks. On the 17th of April, only three months later, that fine two-story building, nearly forty feet square, was blessed by Bishop Vandeveld. It was surmounted by a thirty foot steeple with a bell weighing 250 pounds, whose solemn sound was to tell our joys and sorrows over the boundless prairies. By then we numbered more than one hundred families with more than five hundred adults. The chapel which we thought at first would be too large, was filled to its utmost capacity on the day of its consecration to God.

Not a month later, we had to speak of making an addition of forty feet more, which, when finished six months later, was found to be still insufficient for the accommodation of the constantly increasing flood of immigration which came, not only from Canada, but from Belgium and France. It soon became necessary to make a new center, and expand the limits of my first colony which I did by planting a cross at l'Erable, about fifteen miles southwest of St. Anne, and another at a place we call St. Mary, twelve miles southeast, in the county of Iroquois. These settlements were soon filled, for that very spring more than one thousand new families came from Canada to join us.

No words can express the joy of my heart, when I saw how quickly my (then) dear Church of Rome was taking possession of those magnificent lands, and how soon she would be unrivaled mistress, not only of the state of Illinois, but of the whole valley of the Mississippi. But the ways of men are not the ways of God. I had been called by the bishops of Rome to Illinois, to extend the power of that Church. But my God called me there, that I might give to that Church the most deadly blow she has ever received on this continent.

My task is now to tell my readers how the God of Truth, and Light, and Life, broke, one after another, all the charmed bonds by which I was kept a slave at the feet of the pope; and how He opened my eyes and those of my people, to the unsuspected and untold abominations of Romanism.

CHAPTER XLVI

"Please accompany me to Bourbonnais; I have to confer with you and the Rev. Mr. Courjeault on important matters," said the bishop, half an hour before leaving St. Anne, after having blessed the chapel.

"I intended, my lord, to ask your lordship to grant me that honor, before you offered it," I answered.

Two hours of good driving took us to the parsonage of the Rev. Mr. Courjeault, who had prepared a sumptuous dinner, to which several of the principal citizens of Bourbonnais had been invited.

When all the guests had departed, and the bishop, Mr.

Courjeault, and I, were alone, he drew from his trunk a bundle of weekly papers of Montreal, Canada, in which several letters, very insulting for the bishop, were published, signed R.L.C. Showing them to me, he said:

"Mr. Chiniquy, can I know the reasons you had for writing such insulting things against your bishop?"

"My lord," I answered, "I have no words to express my surprise and indignation, when I read those letters. But, thanks be to God I am not the author."

"Are you positive in that denial; and do you know the contents of these lying communications?" replied the bishop.

"Yes, my lord, I know the contents. I have read them several times with supreme disgust and indignation."

"Then, can you tell me who did write them?" said the bishop.

I answered: "Please, my lord, put that question to the Rev. Mr. Courjeault; he is more able than anyone to satisfy your lordship on that matter."

I looked at Mr. Courjeault with an indignant air which told him that he had been discovered. The eyes of the bishop were also turned and firmly fixed on the wretched priest.

Never had I seen anything so strange as the countenance of that guilty man. His face, though usually ugly, suddenly took a cadaverous appearance; his eyes were fixed on the floor, as if unable to move.

The only signs of life left in him were in his knees which were shaking convulsively; and in the big drops of sweat rolling down his unwashed face; for, I must say here, that, with very few exceptions, that priest was the dirtiest man I ever saw.

The bishop, with unutterable expressions of indignation, exclaimed: "Mr. Courjeault; you are the writer of those infamous and slanderous letters! Three times you have written, and twice you told me verbally, that they were coming from Mr. Chiniquy! I do not ask you if you are the author of these slanders against me, I see it written in your face. Your malice against Mr. Chiniquy is really diabolical. How is it possible that a priest can so completely give himself to the Devil?"

Addressing me the bishop said: "Mr. Chiniquy, I beg your pardon for having believed that you were depraved enough to write those calumnies against your bishop: I was deceived by that deceitful man. I will immediately retract what I have written and said against you."

Then addressing Mr. Courjeault he said: "The least punishment I can give you is to turn you out of my diocese and write to all the bishops of America, that you are the vilest priest I ever saw, that they may never give you any position on this continent."

These last words had hardly fallen from the lips of the bishop when Mr. Courjeault fell on his knees before me, and convulsively pressing my hands in his, said: "Dear Mr. Chiniquy, I see the greatness of my iniquity against you and against our bishop. For the dear Saviour, Jesus' sake, forgive me. I take God to witness that you will never have a more devoted friend than I will be. And you, my lord, allow me to tell you, that I thank God that my malice and my great sin against both you and Mr. Chiniquy is known and punished at once. However, in the name of our crucified Saviour, I ask you to forgive me. God knows that, hereafter, you will not have a more obedient and devoted priest than I."

It was a most touching spectacle to see the tears and hear the sobs of that repentant sinner. I could not contain myself nor refrain my tears. I answered: "Yes, Mr. Courjeault, I forgive you with all my heart, as I wish my merciful God to forgive me my sins. May the God who sees your repentance forgive you also!"

Bishop Vandeveld, who was gifted with a most sensitive and kind nature, was also shedding tears. He asked me: "What do you advise me to do? Must I forgive also? and can I continue to keep him at the head of this important mission?"

"Yes, my lord. Please forgive and forget the errors of that dear brother, he has already done so much good to my countrymen of Bourbonnais. I pledge myself that he will hereafter be one of your best priests."

And the bishop forgave him, after some very appropriate and paternal advice, admirably mixed with mercy and firmness.

It was then about three o'clock in the afternoon. We separated to say our vespers and matins (prayers which took nearly an hour). I had just finished reciting them in the garden, when I saw the Rev. Mr. Courjeault walking from the church towards me with such an expression of terror and sadness, that he was hardly recognizable. He muttered something that I could not understand, his voice was drowned in his tears and sobs. Supposing that he was coming to ask me, again, to pardon him, I felt an unspeakable compassion for him. I said to him: "My dear Mr. Courjeault, come and sit here with me; and do not think any more of the past. I will never think any more of your momentary errors, you may look upon me as your devoted friend."

"Dear Mr. Chiniquy," he answered, "I have to reveal to you another dark mystery of my miserable life. Since more than a year, I have lived with the beadle's daughter as if she were my wife! She has just told me that she is to become a mother, and that I have to see to that, and give her five hundred dollars. She threatens to denounce me publicly if I do not support her and her offspring. Would it not be better for me to flee away, this night, and go back to France to live in my family and conceal my shame? Sometimes, I am even tempted to throw myself in the river, to put an end to my miserable and dishonored existence. Do you think that the bishop would forgive this new crime, if I threw myself at his feet and asked pardon? Would he give me some other place in his vast diocese, where all my misfortunes and my sins are not known? Please tell me what to do?"

Absolutely stupefied, I did not know what to answer. Though I had compassion, I must confess that this new development of hypocrisy filled me with unspeakable horror and disgust. He had, till then, wrapped himself in such a thick mantle of deception, that many of his people looked upon him as an angel of purity. His infamies were so well concealed under an exterior of extreme moral rigidity, that several of his parishioners looked upon him as a saint, whose relics could perform miracles. Not long before, two young couples, of the best families of Bourbonnais, having danced in a respectable social gathering, had been condemned by him, and compelled to ask pardon, publicly in the church. This pharisaical rigidity caused the secret vices of that priest to be still more conspicuous and scandalous. I felt that the scandal which would follow the publication of this mystery of iniquity would be awful; that it would even cause many forever to lose faith in our Church. So many sad thoughts filled my mind, that I was confused and unable to give him any advice. I answered:

"Your misfortune is really great. If the bishop were not here, I might, perhaps, tell you my mind about the best thing to do. But the bishop is here; he is the only man to whom you have to go. He is your proper counselor; go and tell him, frankly, everything, and follow his advice."

With staggering steps, and in such deep emotion that his sobs and cries could be heard for quite a distance, he went to the bishop. I remained alone, half-petrified at what I had heard.

Half an hour later, the bishop came to me. He was pale and his eyes reddened with his tears. He said to me: "Mr. Chiniquy, what an awful scandal! What a new disgrace for our holy Church! That Mr. Courjeault is an incarnate devil; what shall I do? Please help me by your advice; tell me what you consider the best way of preventing the scandal, and protecting the faith of the good people against the destructive storm which is coming upon them."

"My dear bishop," I answered, "the more I consider these scandals here, the less I see how we can save the Church from becoming a dreadful wreck. I feel too much the responsibility of my advice to give it. Let your lordship, guided by the Spirit of God, do what you consider best for the honor of the church and the salvation of so many souls, which are in danger of perishing when this scandal becomes known. For me, the only thing I can do is to conceal my shame, go back to my young colony, to pray, and weep and work."

The bishop replied: "Here is what I intend to do: Mr. Courjeault tells me that there is the least suspicion among the people of his sin, and that it is an easy thing to send that girl to the house provided in Canada for priests' offenses, without awakening any suspicion. He seems so penitent that I hope, hereafter, we have nothing to fear from him. He will now live the life of a good priest here, without giving any scandal. But if I remove him, then there will be some suspicions of his fall, and the awful scandal we want to avoid will come. What do you think of that plan?"

"If your lordship is sure of the conversion of Mr. Courjeault, and that there is no danger of his great iniquity being known by the people, evidently the wisest thing you can do is to send that girl to Canada and keep Mr. Courjeault here. Though I see great dangers even in that way of dealing in this sad affair."

Five days later, four of the principal citizens of Bourbonnais knocked on my door. They were sent as a deputation for the whole village, to ask me what to do about their curate, Mr. Courjeault. They told me that several of them had, long since, suspected what was going on between the priest and the beadle's daughter, but they had kept that secret. However, yesterday, they said the eyes of the parish had been opened to the awful scandal.

The disgusting demonstrations and attention of the curate, when the victim of his lust took the stagecoach, left no doubt in the mind of any one, that she is to have a child in Montreal.

"Now, Mr. Chiniquy, we are sent here to ask your advice. Please tell us what to do?"

"My dear friends," I answered, "it is not from me, but from our common bishop, that you must ask what is to be done, in such deplorable affairs."

But they replied, "Would you not be kind enough to come to Bourbonnais with us, and go to our unfortunate priest to tell him that his criminal conduct is known by the whole people, and that we cannot decently keep him a day longer as our Christian teacher. He has rendered us great services in the past, which we will never forget. We do not want to abuse or insult him in any way. Though guilty, he is still a priest. The only favor we ask from him now, is that he quits the place without noise and scandal, in the night, to avoid any disagreeable demonstrations which might come from his personal enemies, whom his pharisaical rigidity has made pretty numerous and bitter."

"I do not see any reason to refuse you that favor," I answered.

Three hours later, in the presence of those four gentlemen, I was delivering my sad message to the unfortunate curate. He received it as his death warrant. But he was humble and submitted to his fate.

After spending four hours with us in settling his affairs, he fell on his knees, with torrents of tears, he asked pardon for the scandal he had given, and requested us to ask pardon from the whole parish. At twelve o'clock at night he left for Chicago. That hour was a sad one indeed, for us all. But my God had a still sadder hour in store for me. The people of Bourbonnais had requested me to give them some religious evening services the next week, and I was just at the end of one of them, the 7th of May, when suddenly the Rev. Mr. Courjeault entered the church, walked through the crowd, saluting this one, smiling on that one, and pressing the hands of many. His face bore the marks of impudence and debauchery.

From one end of the church to the other, a whisper of amazement and indignation was heard: "Mr. Courjeault! Mr. Courjeault! Great God! what does this mean?"

I observed that he was advancing towards me, probably with the intention of shaking hands, before the people, but I did not give him time to do it. I left by the back door, and went to the parsonage. He then went back to the door to have a talk with the people, but very few gave him that chance. Every one, particularly the women, were filled with disgust at his impudence. Seeing himself nearly deserted at the church door, he turned his steps toward the parsonage, which he entered, whistling. When he beheld me he laughed and said:

"Oh oh! our dear little Father Chiniquy here? How do you do?"

"I am quite unwell," I answered, "since I see that you are so miserably destroying yourself."

"I do not want to destroy myself," he answered; "but it is you who want to turn me out of my beautiful parish of Bourbonnais, to take my place. With the four blockheads who accompanied you the other day, you have frightened and persuaded me that my misfortune with Mary was known by all the people: but our good bishop has understood that this was a trick of yours and that it was one of your lying stories. I came back to take possession of my parish, and turn you out."

"If the bishop has sent you back here to turn me out, that I may go back to my dear colony, he has just done what I asked him to do; for he knows better than any man, for what great purpose I came to this country, and that I cannot do my work as long as he asks me to take care of Bourbonnais. I go, at once, and leave you in full possession of your parsonage. But I pity you, when I see the dark cloud which is on the horizon. Good-bye!"

"You are the only dark cloud on my horizon," he answered. "When you are begone, I will be in as perfect peace as I was before you set your feet in Illinois. Good-bye; and, please, never come back here, except I invite you."

I left to drive back to St. Anne, but when crossing the village, I saw that there was a terrible excitement among the people. Several times they stopped me, and requested me to remain in their midst to advise them what to do. But I refused, saying to them: "It would be an insult on my part to advise you anything in a matter where your duty as men and Catholics is so clear. Consult the respect you owe to yourselves, to your families, and to your Church, and you will know what to do."

It took me all night, which was very dark, to come back to St. Anne, where I arrived at dawn, the 9th of May, 1852. The next Sabbath day the service in my chapel was crowded. I made no illusion to that deplorable affair. On the Monday following, four citizens of Bourbonnais came to tell me what they had done, and asked me not to desert them in that hour of trial, but to remember that I was their countryman, and that they had nobody else to whom they could look, to help to fulfill their religious duties. Here is the substance of their message:

"As soon as you had left our village without telling us what to do, we called a public meeting where we passed the following resolutions:

1st. No personal insult shall be given to Mr. Courjeault.

2nd. We cannot consent to keep him a single hour as our pastor.

3rd. Next Sabbath, when he begins his sermon, we will instantly leave the church, and go out the door, that he may remain absolutely alone, and understand our stern determination not to have him any more for our spiritual leader.

4th. We will send these resolutions to the bishop, and ask him to allow Mr. Chiniquy to divide his time and attention between his new colony and us, till we have a pastor able to instruct and edify us."

Strangely, poor Mr. Courjeault, shut up in his parsonage, knew nothing of that meeting. He had not found a single friend to warn him of what was to happen the next Sunday. That Sunday the weather was magnificent, and there never had been such a multitude of people at the church. The miserable priest, thinking by the unusual crowd that everything was to be right with him that day, began his mass and went to the pulpit to deliver his sermon.

But he had hardly pronounced the first words when the whole

people ran out of the church as if it had been on fire, and he remained alone. Of course, this fell upon him as a thunderbolt, and he came very near fainting. However, recovering himself, he went to the door, and with his tears and sobs, persuaded the people to listen, he said: "I see that the hand of God is upon me, and I deserve it. I have sinned by coming back. You do not want me any more to be your pastor. I cannot complain of that; this is your right, you will be satisfied. I will leave the place forever tonight. I only ask you to forgive my past errors and pray for me."

This short address was followed by the most deadly silence. Not a voice was heard to insult him. Many, on the contrary, were so much impressed with the sad solemnity of this occurrence that they could not refrain their tears. The whole people went back to their homes with broken hearts. Mr. Courjeault left Bourbonnais that very night, never to return again. But the awful scandal he had given did not disappear with him.

Our Great and Merciful God, who, many times, has made the very sins and errors of His people to work for good, caused that public iniquity of the priest to remove the scales from many eyes, and prepare them to receive the light, which was already dawning at the horizon. A voice from heaven was as if heard by many of us. "Do you not see that in your Church of Rome, you do not follow the Word of God, but the lying traditions of men? Is it not evident that your priests' celibacy is a snare and an institution of Satan?"

Many asked me to show them in the Gospel where Christ had established the law of celibacy. "I will do better," I added, "I will put the Gospel in your hands, and you will look for yourselves in that holy book, what is said on that matter." The very same day I ordered a merchant from Montreal to send me a large box filled with New Testaments, printed by the order of the Archbishop of Quebec. Very soon it was known by every one of my immigrants that not only had Jesus never forbidden His apostles and priests to marry, but He had left them free to have their wives, and live with them, according to the very testimony of Paul. "Have we not power to lead about a sister, a wife, as well as other apostles, and as the brethren of the Lord, and Cephas?" (I Cor. 9:5) They saw, by their Gospel, that the doctrine of celibacy of the priests was not brought from heaven by Christ, but had been forged in darkness to add to the miseries of man. They read and read over again these words of Christ: "If ye continue in My word, then are ye My disciples indeed. And ye shall know the truth, and the truth shall make you free . . . If the Son, therefore, shall make you free, ye shall be free indeed." (John 8:31,32,36)

And those promises of liberty which Christ gave to those who read and followed His Word, made their hearts leap with joy. They fell upon their minds as music from heaven. They also soon found, by themselves, that every time the disciples of Christ had asked Him who would be the first ruler, or the pope, in His Church, He had always solemnly and positively said that, in His Church, nobody would ever become the first, the ruler or the pope. And they began to seriously suspect that the great powers of the pope and his bishops were nothing but a sacrilegious usurpation. I soon saw that the reading of the Holy Scriptures by my dear country-men was changing them into other men. Their minds were ob-viously enlarged and raised to higher spheres of thought. They were beginning to suspect that the heavy chains which were wounding their shoulders, were preventing them from making progress in wealth, intelligence, and liberty, as enjoyed by their more fortunate fellowmen, called Protestants.

This was not yet the light of the day, but it was the blessed dawn.

CHAPTER XLVII

During the next six months, more than 500 families from France, Belgium, and Canada, came to our colony. My joy was much diminished, however, by the sudden news that Mr. Cour-jeault had come back from France, where he spent only one month. Not daring to visit Bourbonnais again, he was lurking on the fron-tiers of Indiana, only a few miles distant. Driven to madness by his jealousy and hatred, he addressed to me, on the 23rd of January, 1853, the most abusive letter I ever received, and ended it by tell-ing me that the fine (though unfinished) church of Bourbonnais, which he had built, was to be burned, and that my life would be in danger if I remained at the head of that mission.

I immediately sent that letter to the bishop, asking his advice. In his answer, he told me that he thought that Mr. Courjeault was wicked enough to fulfill his threats. He added: "Though I lack clear evidence, I fear that Mr. Lebel is united with Mr. Courjeault, in the diabolical plot of burning your church of Bourbonnais. Several people have reported that he says that your presence there will be the ruin of that people, and the destruction of their church. I would advise you, my dear Mr. Chiniquy, to insure that church without delay. I have tried to do it here, but they have refused, under the pretext that it is an unfinished, frame building, and that there are too many dangers of fire when people are still working at it. My impression is, that Mr. Lebel is on intimate terms with some insurance gentlemen, and has frightened them by speaking of that rumor, of which he is probably the father, with that miserable Courjeault. Perhaps you may have a better chance, by addressing yourself to some insurance company at Joliet, or Springfield."

After vain efforts to insure the church, I wrote to the bishop, "The only way to escape the impending danger, is to finish the church at once, and insure it after. I have just made a collection of four hundred dollars among the people of Bourbonnais, to which I added three hundred dollars from my own private resources; and will go to work immediately if your lordship has no objections."

He agreed and we worked almost day and night till it was finished. I dare affirm, that for a country place, that church was unsurpassed in beauty. The inside frame work and altar was all made of the splendid black oak of Bourbonnais, polished and varnished by most skillful men. It was late at night, when we could say with joy the solemn words, "It is finished!" Afterwards we sung the Te Deum. Had I had an opportunity at that late hour, I would have insured it. But I was forced to wait till the next Monday.

The next day (the first Sabbath of May, 1853), the church had never been so crowded. The words of gratitude which I addressed to my God, when I thanked Him for the church He had given us, had never been so sincere and earnest. Alas! who would suspect that, six hours later, that same people, gathered around the smoking ruins of their church, would rend the air with their cries of desolation! Such, however was the case.

After the public service, two little boys, who had remained in the church to wait for the hour of the catechism, ran to the parsonage, crying: "Fire! Fire!! Fire!!!" Bare headed, and half-paralyzed I rushed to the church with a pail of water in hand. But it was too late, the flames were already running and leaping over the fresh varnish. In less than two hours our beautiful church was gone. We had no doubt that this was the work of an incendiary, for we had left no fire in the church after the service.

Though stunned by that awful calamity, the noble-hearted people of Bourbonnais did not lose their minds. As they gathered around the smoking ruins, I encouraged them that it was only in the midst of great trials and difficulties that men could show their noblest qualities and their true manhood. If we were true men, instead of losing our time in shedding tears and rending the air with our cries of desolation, we would immediately put our hands to the work the very next day to raise up a stone church, which would not burn, but stand before God and man as an imperishable monument of their faith, indomitable courage and liberality.

We immediately started a collection. In less than one hour, four thousand dollars in money, and more than five thousand dollars in time, timber and stone and other material, were pledged and faithfully given to erect that fine stone church of Bourbonnais.

The next Thursday, Bishop Vandeveld came from Chicago to see what could be done to repair that terrible loss, and to inquire confidentially of me as to the author of the fire. All the facts indicated that the miserable Courjeault, with Lebel, the French Canadian priest of Chicago, had done it through their emissaries. No doubt of this remained in my mind when I learned that soon after, Mr. Courjeault had thrown himself into one of those dark dungeons called a monastery of La Trappe.

I had hoped my bishop would bring me words of encouragement. Instead he said to me: "Mr. dear Mr. Chiniquy, I must reveal to you a thing that I have not yet made known to anyone. Please do not say a word about it until it is accomplished. I cannot remain any longer bishop of Illinois! It is beyond my power to fulfill my duties. The conduct of the priests of this diocese is such, that, should I follow the regulations of the canon, I would be forced to interdict all my priests except you and two or three others. They are all either notorious drunkards, or given to public or secret concubinage; several of them have children by their own nieces, and two by their own sisters. I do not think that ten of them believe in God. Religion is nothing to them but a well paying comedy. Where can I find a remedy to such a general evil? Can I punish one of them and leave the others free in their abominable doings? Would not the general indiction of these priests be the death blow of our Church in Illinois? Besides, how can I punish them, when I know that many of them are ready to poison me the very moment I raise a finger against them. I intend to go to Rome, as soon as I receive my permit from the pope, to renounce at his feet the Bishopric of Chicago, which I will not keep on any consideration! The awful responsibility of my position here, I cannot any longer endure it."

I determined to wait till the next morning, when I should have plenty of time, I hoped, to expel his dark thoughts, and give him more courage. Besides, I was myself so discouraged by those awful disclosures, that I was in need of mental as well as bodily rest. But, alas! the next day was to be one of the darkest of my priestly life! When the hour for breakfast came the next morning, I went to awaken the bishop. What was my dismay when I found him drunk?

I had been told that Bishop Vandeveld was a drunkard, as well as the greater part of the bishops of the United States, but I had never believed it.

The destruction of my dear church by the hands of incendiaries, was surely a great calamity for me; but the fall of my bishop, from the high position he had in my heart and mind, was still greater. My love and respect for Bishop Vandeveld were very strong chains by which I was bound to the feet of the idols of Rome. I will eternally bless God for having Himself broken these chains, on that day of supreme desolation. The remaining part of the day I remained almost mute in his presence. He was not less embarrassed when he asked me my views about his project of leaving the diocese. I answered him, in a few words, that I could not disapprove the purpose; for I would myself prefer to live in a dark forest, in the midst of wild animals, than among drunken, atheist priests and bishops.

Some months later I learned, without regret, that the pope had accepted his resignation of the Bishopric of Chicago, and appointed him Bishop of Natchez, in Louisiana. His successor in Chicago was Rev. O'Regan. One of the very first things which this new bishop did was to bring Bishop Vandeveld before the criminal tribunals as a thief, accusing him of having stolen 100,000 dollars from the Bishopric of Chicago. This action caused a terrible scandal, not only in Illinois, but through all the United States. The two bishops, employing the best lawyers to fight each other, came very near proving to the world that both of them were equally swindlers and thieves; when the pope forced them both to stop and bring the affair before his tribunal at Rome. There it was decided that the one hundred thousand dollars taken from Chicago to the Natchez diocese, should be equally divided between the two bishops.

How many sleepless nights did the voice of my conscience cry out: "What are you doing here, extending the power of a Church which is a den of thieves, drunkards, and impure atheists? A Church, governed by men whom you know to be godless swindlers, and vile comedians? Do you not see that you do not follow the Word of God, but the lying traditions of men, when you consent to bow your knees before such men? Is it not blasphemy to call such men the ambassadors, and the disciples of the humble, pure, holy, peaceful, and loving Jesus? Come out of that Church! Break the fetters, by which you are bound as a vile slave to the feet of such men! Take the Gospel for thine only guide and Christ for thine only Ruler!"

In desolation I found my faith in my Church was, in spite of myself, shaken by these scandals. On my knees I asked my God to preserve it from ruin. But I remained the whole night, as a ship drifting on an unknown sea, without a compass or a rudder. Much later I learned that the divine and sure Pilot was directing my course towards the port of salvation!

It seemed, though I had been very busy finding homes for the new immigrants, that my duty was to go and pay my respects to my new bishop, and open to him my heart as to my best friend, and the guide whom God Himself had chosen to heal the wounds of my soul with the oil and wine of charity.

I will never forget the day (the 11th of December, 1854), when I saw Bishop O'Regan for the first time. He was of medium stature, with a repugnant face, and his head always in motion; all its motions seemed the expression of insolence, contempt, tyranny, and pride; there was absolutely nothing pleasant, either in his words or in his manners. I fell on my knees to ask his benediction and kissed his hand, which seemed as cold as a corpse. "Ah! ah! you are Father Chiniquy," he said. "I am glad to see you, though you have deferred your visit a long time; please sit down. I want some explanation from you about a certain very strange document, which I have just read today." And he went, at the double quick, to his room to get the document. There were two Irish priests in the room, who came a few minutes before me. When we were alone, one of them said: "We had hoped that we would gain by changing Bishop Vandeveld for this one. But my fear is that we have only passed from Charybdis into Scylla," and they laughed outright. But I could not laugh. I was more inclined to weep. The bishop returned, holding in his hand a paper, which I understood to be the deed of the eleven acres of land which I had purchased and built my chapel of St. Anne.

"Do you know this paper?" he asked me in an angry manner.

"Yes, my lord, I know it," I answered.

"But, then," he quickly replied, "you must know that that title is a nullity — a fraud, which you ought never to have signed."

"Your venerable and worthy predecessor has accepted it," I answered.

"I do not care a straw about what my predecessor has done," he abruptly answered, "We have not to deal with my lord Vandeveld, but with a document which is a nullity, a deception, which must be thrown in the fire; you must give me another title of that property!"

And saying this, he flung my deed on the floor. I calmly picked it up and said: "I exceedingly regret, my lord, that my first interview with your lordship should be the occasion of such an unexpected act. But I hope that this will not destroy the paternal sentiments which God must have put into the heart of my bishop, for the last and least of his priests. I see that your lordship is very busy; I do not want to trespass on your valuable time; I take this rejected document with me, to make another one, which I hope will be more agreeable to your views," and I then took my departure.

It seemed that my most pressing duty, after my first interview, was to bring my heart nearer to my God than ever; to read and study my Bible with more attention, and to get my people to take more than ever the Word of God as their daily bread. I began, also, to speak more openly of our Christian rights, as well as of our duties, as these are set forth in the Gospel of Christ.

Some time before this, I had respectfully sent my resignation of Bourbonnais to the bishop, which had been accepted. A priest had been called by him to take my place there. But he too, was, ere long, guilty of a public scandal with his servant girl. The principal citizens of Bourbonnais protested against his presence in their midst, and forced the bishop to dismiss him. His successor was the miserable priest, Lebel, who had been turned out of Chicago for a criminal offense with his own niece, and was now to be the curate of Bourbonnais. But his drunkenness and other public vices caused him to be interdicted, and expelled from that place in the month of September, 1855. About the same time, a priest who had been expelled from Belgium for a great scandal, was sent to Kankakee, as the curate of the French Canadians of that interesting young city. After his expulsion from Belgium he had come to Chicago, where, under another name, he had made a fortune, and for five or six years kept a house of prostitution. Tired of that, he offered five thousand dollars to the bishop if he would accept him as one of his priests and give him a parish. Bishop O'Regan, being in need of money, accepted the gift, and sent him to Kankakee.

Soon he came with Mr. Lebel to pay me a visit. I received them politely as possible, though they were both half drunk when they arrived. After dinner, they went to shoot prairie chickens, and got so drunk that one of them, Mr. Lebel, lost his boots in the slough, and came back barefooted, without noticing his loss. I had to help them get into their carriage, and the next day I wrote them, forbidding them to ever set foot in my house again.

But what was my surprise and sadness, (not long before these two infamous priests were ignominiously turned out by their people), to receive a letter from my bishop, which ended in these words: "I am sorry to hear that you refuse to live on good terms with your two neighboring brother priests. This ought not to be, and I hope to hear soon that you have reconciled yourself with them."

It came to be a public fact that the bishop had said before many people: "I would give anything to the one who would help me to get rid of that unmanageable Chiniquy." Among those who heard the bishop was a land shark, who had been found guilty of perjury in Iroquois county. He was very angry against me for protecting my poor countrymen against him. He said to the bishop, "If you pay the expense of the suit, I pledge myself to have Chiniquy put in jail." The bishop had publicly answered him: "No sum of money will be too great to be delivered from a priest who alone gives me more trouble than the rest of my clergy." This speculator dragged me before the criminal court of Kankakee on the 16th day of May, 1855, but he lost his action and was condemned to pay the cost.

It was my impression that the bishop, having so often expressed in public his bad feelings against me, would not visit my colony. But I was mistaken. On the 11th of June, taking the Rev. Mr. Lebel and Carthuval for his companions, he came to St. Anne to administer the sacrament of confirmation.

In private I energetically protested the presence of these two degraded men in my house. "My lord, allow me respectfully to tell you, that the Gospel of Christ tells us to avoid the company of publicly vicious and profligate men. My conscience tells me that through respect for myself and my people, and through respect for the Gospel I preach, I must avoid the company of men, one of whom has lived with his niece as his wife, and the other has, till very lately, been guilty of keeping a house of prostitution in Chicago. Your lordship may ignore these things, and, in consequence of that, may give your confidence to these men; but nothing is more apt to destroy the faith of our French Canadian people, than to see such men in your company when you come to administer the sacrament of confirmation. It is through respect for your lordship that I take the liberty of speaking thus."

He angrily answered me: "I see it is true what people say about you. It is to the Gospel you constantly appeal. The Gospel! The Gospel is surely a holy book; but remember that it is the *Church* which must guide you. Christ has said, 'Hear My church.' I am here the interpreter, ambassador — the representative of the Church — when you disobey me, it is the Church you disobey."

"Now, my lord, that I have fulfilled a conscientious duty, through respect for your lordship I will deal with these two priests as if they were worthy of the honorable position you have given them."

"All right! all right!" replied the bishop. "But it must be near the hour for dinner."

"Yes, my lord, I have just heard the bell calling us to the dining room."

After the blessing of the table by the bishop, he looked at the Rev. Carthuval, who was sitting just before him, and said:

"What is the matter with you, Mr. Carthuval, you do not look well?"

"No, my lord," he answered, "I am not well; I want to go to bed."

He was correct. He was not well, for he was drunk. During the public services he had left the chapel to come down and ask for a bottle of the wine I kept to celebrate mass. The housekeeper, thinking he wanted the wine in the chapel, handed him the bottle, which he drank in her presence in less than five minutes. After which he went to the chapel to help the bishop in administering the confirmation to the 150 people whom I had prepared for the reception of that rite.

As soon as dinner was finished, the bishop requested me to take a walk with him. After giving me some compliments on the beauty of the site I had chosen for my first village and chapel, he saw at a short distance a stone building, which was raised only a little above the windows, and directing his steps towards it, he stopped only twenty or thirty feet distant, and asked me:

"Whose house is this?"

"It is mine, my lord."

"It is yours!" he replied; "and to whom does that fine garden belong?"

"It is mine also, my lord."

"Well! well!" he rejoined; "where did you get the money to purchase that fine piece of land and build that house?"

"I got the money where every honest man gets what he possesses, in my hard labor, and in the sweat of my brow," I replied.

"I want that house and that piece of land!" rejoined the bishop, with an imperative voice.

"So do I," I replied.

"You must give me that house, with the land on which it is built," said the bishop.

"I cannot give them as long as I am in need of them, my lord," I replied.

"I see that you are a bad priest, as I have often been told, since you disobey your bishop," he rejoined with an angry manner.

I replied: "I do not see why I am a bad priest, because I keep what my God has given me."

"Are you ignorant of the fact that you have no right to possess any property?" he answered.

"Yes! my lord, I am ignorant of any law in our holy Church that deprives me of any such rights. If, however, your lordship can show me any such law, I will give you the title of that property just now."

"If there is not such a law," he replied, stamping on the ground with his feet, "I will get one passed."

"My lord," I replied, "you are a great bishop. You have great power in the Church, but allow me to tell you that you are not great enough to have such a law passed in our holy Church!"

"You are an insolent priest," he answered with terrible anger, "and I will make you repent for your insolence."

He then turned his face towards the chapel, without waiting for my answer, and ordered the horses to be hitched to the carriage, that he might leave in the shortest possible time. A quarter of an hour later he had left St. Anne, where he was never to come again. The visit of that mitred thief, with his two profligate priests, though very short, did much by the mercy of God, to prepare our minds to understand that Rome is the great harlot of the Bible, which seduces and intoxicates the nations with the wine of her prostitution. (Rev. 17:2)

CHAPTER XLVIII

The 8th of December, 1854, Pope Pius IX was sitting on his throne; a triple crown of gold and diamonds was on his head; silk and damask — red and white vestments on his shoulders; five hundred mitred prelates were surrounding him; and more than fifty thousand people were at his feet in the incomparable St. Peter's Church of Rome. After a few minutes of most solemn silence, a cardinal, dressed with his purple robe, left his seat, and gravely walked towards the pope, humbly prostrating himself at his feet, and said:

"Holy Father, tell us if we can believe and teach that the Mother of God, the Holy Virgin Mary, was immaculate in her conception."

The Supreme Pontiff answered: "I do not know; let us ask the light of the Holy Ghost."

The cardinal withdrew; the pope and the numberless multitude fell on their knees; and the harmonious choir sang the "Veni Creator Spiritus."

The last note of the sacred hymn had hardly rolled under the vaults of the temple, when the same cardinal left his place, and again advanced towards the throne of the pontiff, prostrated himself at his feet, and said:

"Holy Father, tell us if the Holy Mother of God, the blessed Virgin Mary, was immaculate in her conception."

The pope again answered: "I do not know; let us ask the light of the Holy Ghost."

And again the "Veni Creator Spiritus" was sung.

Again the eyes of the multitude followed the grave steps of the purple-robed cardinal for the third time to the throne of the successor of St. Peter, to ask again:

"Holy Father, tell us if we can believe that the blessed Virgin Mary, the Mother of God was immaculate."

The pope, as if he had just received a direct communication from God, answered with a solemn voice:

"Yes! we must believe that the Blessed Virgin Mary was immaculate in her conception . . . There is no salvation to those who do not believe this dogma!"

And, with a loud voice, the pope intoned the Te Deum; the bells of the three hundred churches of Rome rang; the cannons of the citadel were fired. The last act of the most ridiculous and sacrilegious comedy the world had ever seen, was over; the doors of heaven were forever shut against those who would refuse to believe the antiscriptural doctrine that there is a daughter of Eve who has not inherited the sinful nature of Adam.

She was redeclared exempt when the God of Truth said, "There is none righteous; no, not one: for all have sinned!" (Rom. 3:10, 23)

No trace of this teaching is found in the first centuries of the Church. Only in the twelfth century was it openly preached by some brainless monks. But then it was opposed by the most learned men of the time. We have a very remarkable letter of St. Bernard to refute some monks of Lyons who were preaching this new doctrine. A little later, Peter Lombard adopted the views of the monks of Lyons, and wrote a book to support that opinion; but he was refuted by St. Thomas Aquinas, who is justly considered by the Church of Rome as the best theologian of that time.

After that, the Franciscans and the Dominicans attacked each other without mercy on that subject, and filled the world with the noise of their angry disputes, condemning each other as heretics. They succeeded in driving the Roman Catholics of Europe into two camps of fierce enemies. It was discussed, attacked and defended, not only in the chairs of universities, and the pulpits of the cathedrals, but also in the fields, and in the very streets of the cities. And when the two parties had exhausted their ingenuity, their learning, or their ignorant fanaticism, they often had recourse to the stick and to the sword to sustain their arguments.

Incredibly, some of the large cities of Europe, particularly in Spain, were reddened with the blood of the supporters and opponents of that doctrine. To resolve the conflicts, the kings of Europe sent deputation after deputation to the popes to know, from their infallible authority, what to believe on the subject. Philip III and Philip IV made supreme efforts to force the popes, Paul V, Gregory XV, and Alexander VII to stop the shedding of blood, and disarm the combatants, by raising the opinion in favor of the Immaculate Conception to the dignity of a Catholic dogma. But they failed.

The only answer they could get from the infallible head of the Church of Rome was that "that dogma was not revealed in the Holy Scriptures, had never been taught by the Apostles, nor by the Fathers, and had never been believed or preached by the Church of Rome as an article of faith!"

The only thing the popes could do to please the supplicant kings and bishops, and nations of Europe in those days, was to *forbid* both parties to call the other *heretics;* and to *forbid* to say that it was an article of faith which ought to be believed to be saved. At the Council of Trent, the Franciscans, and all the partisans of the Immaculate Conception, gathered their strength to have a decree in favor of the new dogma; but the majority of the bishops were against it and they failed.

It was reserved to the unfortunate Pius IX to drag the Church of Rome to that last limit of human folly. In the last century, a monk, called Father Leonard, had a dream in which he heard the Virgin Mary telling him: "That there would be an end to the wars in the world, and to the heresies and schisms in the Church, only after a pope should have obliged, by a decree, all the faithful to believe she was immaculate in her conception." The dream, under the name of a "celestial vision," had been extensively circulated by means of little tracts.

Many believed it to be a genuine revelation from heaven; and, unfortunately, the good natured but weak-minded Pius IX was among the number. When he was an exile in Gaeta, he had himself a dream, which he took for a vision, on the same subject. He saw the Virgin, who told him that he would come back to Rome, and get an eternal peace for the Church, only after he promised to declare that the Immaculate Conception was a dogma, which every one had to believe to be saved. He awoke from his dream much impressed by it and vowed to promulgate the new dogma as soon as he could return to Rome. The world has seen how he has fulfilled that vow.

But, by the promulgation of this new dogma, Pius IX, far from securing an eternal peace to his Church, far from destroying what he is pleased to call the heresies which are attacking Rome on every side, has done more to shake the faith of the Roman Catholics than all their enemies. By trying to force this new article of faith on the consciences of his people, in a time that so many can judge for themselves and read the records of past generations, he has pulled down the strongest column supporting his Church.

With dignified and supreme contempt the priests of Rome had been speaking of the "new articles of faith, the novelties of the arch-heretics, Luther, Calvin, Knox, etc., etc!" How eloquently they said: "In our holy Church of Rome there is no change, no innovations, no novelties, no new dogmas. We believe today just what our fathers believed and only what the Apostles believed and preached." And the ignorant multitudes were saying: "Amen!"

But, alas, for the poor priests of Rome today! They must confess that their unchangeable creed is mere shameful lies; that the Church of Rome is FORGING NEW DOGMAS, NEW ARTICLES OF FAITH. Their conscience says: "Where was your religion before the 8th of December, 1854?" and they cannot answer.

I will never forget my sadness when I received the order from Bishop O'Regan to proclaim that new dogma to my people. It was as if an earthquake had destroyed the ground under my feet. My most cherished illusions about the immutability and the infallibility of my Church were crumbling down in spite of my efforts to keep them up. I have seen old priests, to whom I opened my mind on that subject, shed tears of sorrow on the injury this new dogma would do to their Church.

A few days after I had read to my congregation the decree of the pope proclaiming the new dogma, and damning all those who would not believe it, one of my most intelligent and respectable farmers came to visit me, and put to me the following questions on the new articles of faith: "Mr. Chiniquy, please tell me, have I correctly understood the letter from the pope you read us last Sabbath? Does the pope tell us in that letter that we can find this new dogma of the Immaculate Conception in the Holy Scriptures, that it has been taught by the Fathers, and that the Church has constantly believed it from the days of the Apostles?"

I answered, "Yes, my friend, the pope tells us all those things in his letter which I read in the church last Sabbath."

"But, sir, will you be so kind as to read me the verses of the Holy Scriptures which are in favor of the Immaculate Conception of the Holy Virgin Mary?"

"My dear friend," I answered, "I am sorry to say that I have never found in the Holy Scriptures a single word to tell us that Mary is immaculate; but I have found many words, and very clear words, which say the very contrary thing."

"Now, please tell me the name of the Holy Fathers who have preached that we must believe in the Immaculate Conception, or be forever damned, if we do not believe in it?"

I answered to my parishioner: "I would have preferred, my dear friend, that you should never come to put to me these questions; but as you ask me the truth, I must tell you the truth. I have studied the Fathers with a pretty good attention, but I have not yet found a single one of them who was of that opinion in any way."

"I hope," added the good farmer, "you will excuse me if I put to you another question on this subject. Perhaps you do not know it, but there is a great deal of talking about this new article of faith among us since last Sabbath; I want to know a little more about it. The pope says in his letter that the Church of Rome has always believed and taught that dogma of Immaculate Conception. Is that correct?"

"Yes, my friend, the pope says that in his Encyclical; but these last nine hundred years, more than one hundred popes have declared that the Church had never believed it. Even several popes have forbidden anyone to say 'that the Immaculate Conception was an article of faith.'"

"If it be so with this new dogma, how can we know it is not so with the other dogmas of our Church, as the confession, the purgatory, etc.?" added the farmer.

"My dear friend, do not allow the devil to shake your faith. We are living in bad days indeed. Let us pray God to enlighten us and save us. I would have given much had you never put to me these questions!"

My honest parishioner had left me; but his awful questions and the answers I had been forced to give were sounding in my soul as thunderclaps of an irresistible storm which was to destroy all that I had cherished and respected in my then so dear and venerated Church of Rome. My head was aching. I fell on my knees; but for a time I could not utter a word of prayer; big tears were rolling on my burning cheeks; new light was coming before the eyes of my soul; but I took it for the deceitful temptation of Satan; a voice was speaking to me; it was the voice of my God, telling me, "Come out from Babylon!" (Rev. 18:4) But I took it for the voice of Satan and tried to silence it. The Lord was then drawing me away from my perishing ways; but I did not know Him then; I was struggling against Him to remain in the dark dungeons of error. But God was to be the stronger. In His infinite mercy He was to overpower His unfaithful servant. He was to conquer me, and with me many others.

CHAPTER XLIX

There are two women for whom we ought to pray daily, the Brahmin woman, who, deceived by her priests, burns herself on the corpse of her husband to appease the wrath of her wooden gods; and the Roman Catholic woman, who, not less deceived by her priests, suffers a torture far more cruel and ignominious in the auricular confessional box, to appease the wrath of her wafer-god.

Many of them prefer to throw themselves into the hands of their merciful God, and die before submitting to the defiling ordeal, rather than receive their pardon from a man, who, as they feel, would surely have been scandalized by such a recital.

How many times have I wept like a child when some noble-hearted and intelligent young girl, or some respectable married woman, told me of their invincible repugnance, their horror of such questions and answers, and they have asked me to have pity on them. But alas! I had to silence the voice of my conscience which was telling me, "Is it not a shame for you, an unmarried man, to dare to speak on these matters with a woman? Do you not blush to put such questions to a young girl? Where is your self-respect? Where is your fear of God? Do you not promote the ruin of that girl by forcing her to speak on these matters?"

How many times my God has spoken to me as He speaks to all the priests of Rome, and said with a thundering voice: "What would that young man, that father, or brother do, could he hear the questions you put to his wife, his daughter, or sister? Would he not blow out your brains?" I was compelled by all the popes, the moral theologians, and the Councils of Rome, to believe that this warning voice of my merciful God was the voice of Satan.

In the beginning of my priesthood, in Quebec, I was not a little surprised and embarrassed to see a very accomplished and beautiful young lady, whom I used to meet almost every week at her father's house, entering the box of my confessional. She usually confessed to another young priest of my acquaintance, and she was always looked upon as one of the most pious girls of the city. Though she had disguised herself as much as possible, in order that I might not know her, I felt I was not mistaken.

Not being absolutely certain who she was, I did not disclose that I thought I knew her. At the beginning she could hardly speak; her voice was suffocated by her sobs. After much effort, she said: "Dear Father, I hope you do not know me, and that you will never try to know me. I am a desperately great sinner. Oh! I fear that I am lost! But if there is still hope for me to be saved, for God's sake do not rebuke me.

"Before I begin my confession, allow me to ask you not to pollute my ears by questions which our confessors are in the habit of putting to their female penitents; I have already been destroyed by those questions. Before I was seventeen years old, God knows that His angels are not more pure than I was; but the chaplain of the nunnery where my parents had sent me for my education, though approaching old age, put to me, in the confessional, a question which, at first, I did not understand, but was later explained to me by one of my young classmates.

"This first unchaste conversation of my life plunged my thoughts into a sea of iniquity till then absolutely unknown to me. Temptations of the most humiliating character assailed me for a week, day and night; after which, sins which I would blot out with my blood, if it were possible, overwhelmed my soul as with a deluge. But the joys of the sinners are short. Struck with terror at the thought of the judgments of God, after a few weeks of the most deplorable life, I determined to give up my sins and reconcile myself to God.

"Covered with shame, and trembling from head to foot, I went to confess to my old confessor, whom I respected as a saint and cherished as a father. It seems to me that, with sincere tears of repentance, I confessed to him the greatest part of my sins, though I concealed one of them, through shame and respect for my spiritual guide. But I did not conceal from him that the strange questions he had put to me at my last confession, were, with the natural corruption of my heart, the principal cause of my destruction.

"He spoke to me very kindly, encouraged me to fight against my bad inclinations, and at first gave me very kind and good advice. But when I thought he had finished speaking, and as I was preparing to leave the confessional box, he put to me two new questions of such a polluting character that I fear neither the blood of Christ, nor all the fires of hell will ever be able to blot them out from my memory. Those questions have achieved my ruin; they have stuck to my mind like two deadly arrows; they are day and night before my imagination; they fill my very arteries and veins with a deadly poison.

"It is true that, at first, they filled me with horror and disgust; but alas! I soon got so accustomed to them that they seemed to be incorporated with me, and as if becoming a second nature. Those thoughts have become a new source of innumerable criminal thoughts, desires, and actions.

"A month later, we were obliged by the rules of our convent to go and confess; but by this time I was so completely lost that I no longer blushed at the idea of confessing my shameful sins to a man. I had a real, diabolical pleasure in the thought that I should have a long conversation with my confessor on those matters, and that he would ask me more of his strange questions. In fact, when I told him everything without a blush, he began to interrogate me, and God knows what corrupting things fell from his lips into my poor criminal heart! Every one of his questions was thrilling my nerves and filling me with the most shameful sensations! After an hour of this criminal *tête-à-tête* with my old confessor, I perceived that he was as depraved as I was myself. With some half-covered words he made a criminal proposition, which I accepted with covered words also; and during more than a year we have lived together on the most sinful intimacy. Though he was much older than I, I loved him in the most foolish way. When the course of my convent instruction was finished, my parents called me back to their home. I was really glad of that change of residence, for I was beginning to be tired of my criminal life. My hope was that, under the direction of a better confessor, I should reconcile myself to God and begin a Christian life.

"Unfortunately for me, my new confessor, who was very young, began also his interrogations. He soon fell in love with me, and I loved him in a most criminal way. I have done with him things which I hope you will never request me to reveal to you, for they are too monstrous to be repeated, even in the confessional, by a woman to a man.

"I do not say these things to take away the responsibility of my iniquities with this young confessor, for I think I have been more criminal than he was. I believe that he was a good and holy priest before he knew me; but the questions he put to me, and the answers I had to give him, melted his heart just as boiling lead would melt the ice on which it flows.

"I know this is not such a detailed confession as our holy Church requires me to make, but I have thought it necessary for me to give you this short history of the life of the greatest and most miserable sinner who ever asked you to help her to come out from the tomb of her iniquities. This is the way I have lived these last few years. But last Sabbath, God, in His infinite mercy, looked down upon me. He inspired you to give us the Prodigal Son as a model of true conversion, and as the most marvelous proof of the infinite compassion of the dear Saviour for the sinner. I have wept day and night since that happy day, when I threw myself into the arms of my loving, merciful Father. Even now I can hardly speak, because my regret for my past iniquities, and my joy that I am allowed to bathe the feet of the Saviour with tears, are so great that my voice is as choked.

"You understand that I have forever given up my last confessor. I come to ask you to do me the favor to receive me among your penitents. Oh! do not reject nor rebuke me, for the dear Saviour's sake! Be not afraid to have at your side such a monster of iniquity! But before going further, I have two favors to ask from you.

"The first is, that you will never do anything to ascertain my name; the second is, that you will never put to me any of those questions by which so many penitents are lost and so many priests destroyed. Twice I have been lost by those questions. Oh! dear father, let me become your penitent, that you may help me to go and weep with Magdalene at the Saviour's feet! Do respect me, as He respected that true model of all the sinful, but repenting women! Did our Saviour put to her any question? did He extort from her the history of things which a sinful woman cannot say without forgetting the respect she owes to herself and to God! No! you told us not long ago, that the only thing our Saviour did was to look at her tears and her love. Well, please do that, and you will save me!"

I was then a very young priest, and never had any words so sublime come to my ears in the confessional box. Her tears and her sobs, mingled with the frank declaration of the most humiliating actions, had made such a profound impression upon me that I was, for some time, unable to speak. It had come to my mind also that I might be mistaken about her identity, and that perhaps she was not the young lady that I had imagined. I could, then, easily grant her first request, which was to do nothing by which I could know her. The second part of her prayer was more embarrassing; for the theologians are very positive in ordering the confessors to question their penitents, particularly those of the female sex.

I encouraged her in the best way I could to persevere in her good resolutions by invoking the blessed Virgin Mary and St. Philomene. I told her that I would pray and think over the subject of her second request; and I asked her to come back in a week for my answer.

The very same day I went to my own confessor, the Rev. Mr. Baillargeon. I told him the singular and unusual request she had made and I did not conceal from him that I was much inclined to grant her that favor; for I repeated what I have already several times told him, that I was supremely disgusted with the infamous and polluting questions which the theologians forced us to put to our female penitents. I told him frankly that several old and young priests had already come to confess to me; and that, with the exception of two, they had told me that they could not put those questions and hear the answers they elicited without falling into the most damnable sins.

My confessor seemed to be much perplexed and asked me to come the next day, that he might review some theological books in the interval. The next day I took down in writing his answer:

"Such cases of the destruction of female virtue by the questions of the confessors is an unavoidable evil. It cannot be helped; for such questions are absolutely necessary in the greater part of the cases with which we have to deal. Men generally confess their sins with so much sincerity that there is seldom any need for questioning them, except when they are very ignorant. But St. Liguori, as well as our personal observation, tells us that the greatest part of girls and women, through a false and criminal shame, very seldom confess the sins they commit against purity. It requires the utmost charity in the confessors to prevent those unfortunate slaves of their secret passions from making sacrilegious confessions and communions. With the greatest prudence and zeal he must question them on those matters, beginning with the smallest sins, and going, little by little, as much as possible by imperceptible degrees, to the most criminal actions. As it seems evident that the penitent referred to in your questions of yesterday is unwilling to make a full and detailed confession of all her iniquities, you cannot promise to absolve her without assuring yourself by wise and prudent questions that she has confessed everything.

"You must not be discouraged when, through the confessional or any other way, you learn the fall of priests into the common frailties of human nature with their penitents. Our Saviour knew very well that the occasions and the temptations we have to encounter in the confessions of girls and women, are so numerous, and sometimes so irresistible, that many would fall. But He has given them the Holy Virgin Mary, who constantly asks and obtains their pardon; He has given them the sacrament of penance, where they can receive their pardon as often as they ask for it. The vow of perfect chastity is a great honor and privilege; but we cannot conceal from ourselves that it puts on our shoulders a burden which many cannot carry forever. St. Liguori says that we must not rebuke the penitent priest who falls only once a month; and some other trustworthy theologians are still more charitable."

This answer far from satisfied me. It seemed to me composed of soft soap principles. I went back with a heavy heart and an anxious mind; and God knows that I made many fervent prayers that this girl should never come again to give me her sad history. I was then hardly twenty-six years old, full of youth and life. It seemed to me that the stings of a thousand wasps to my ears could not do me so much harm as the words of that dear, beautiful, accomplished, but lost girl.

I do not mean to say that the revelations which she made had, in any way, diminished my esteem and my respect for her. It was just the contrary. Her tears and her sobs at my feet; her agonizing expressions of shame and regret; her noble words of protest against the disgusting and polluting interrogations of the confessors, had raised her very high in my mind. My sincere hope was that she would have a place in the kingdom of Christ with the Samaritan woman, Mary Magdalene, and all the sinners who have washed their robes in the blood of the Lamb.

At the appointed day, I was in my confessional listening to the confession of a young man, when, though incognito, I recognized Miss Mary entering the vestry, and coming directly to my confessional box, where she knelt by me.

Oh! I would have given every drop of my blood in that solemn hour, that I might have been free to deal with her just as she had so eloquently requested me to do.

But, there, in that confessional box, I was not the servant of Christ, I was the slave of the pope! I was not there to save, but to destroy; for, under the pretext of purifying, the real mission of the confessor, often, if not always, in spite of himself, is to scandalize and damn the souls.

Without noise, I turned myself towards her, and said, through the little aperture, "Are you ready to begin your confession?"

But she did not answer me. All that I could hear was: "Oh, my Jesus, have mercy upon me! I come to wash my soul in Thy blood; wilt Thou rebuke me?" During several minutes she raised her hands and eyes to heaven, and wept and prayed. My tears were flowing with her tears, and my ardent prayers were going to the feet of Jesus with her prayers. I would not have interrupted her for any consideration, in this, her sublime communion with her merciful Saviour.

But after a pretty long time, I made a little noise with my hand, and putting my lips near the opening of the partition which was between us, I said in a low voice, "Dear sister, are you ready to begin your confession?"

She turned her face a little towards me, and said, with trembling voice, "Yes, dear father, I am ready. My dear father, do you remember the prayers which I made to you the other day? Can you allow me to confess my sins without forcing me to forget the respect that I owe to myself, to you, and to God, who hears us? And can you promise that you will not put to me any of those questions which have already done me such irreparable injury? I frankly declare to you that there are sins in me that I cannot reveal to anyone, except to Christ, because He is my God, and that He already knows them all. Let me weep and cry at His feet: can you not forgive me without adding to my iniquities by forcing me to say things that the tongue of a Christian woman cannot reveal to a man?"

"My dear sister," I answered, "were I free to follow the voice of my own feelings I would be only too happy to grant your request; but I am here only as the minister of our holy Church, and bound to obey the laws. Through her most holy popes and theologians she tells me that I cannot forgive your sins if you do not confess them all, just as you have committed them. The Church tells me also that you must give the details, which may add to the malice or change the nature of your sins. I am sorry to tell you that our most holy theologians make it a duty of the confessor to question the penitent on the sins which he has good reason to suspect have been voluntarily omitted."

With a piercing cry she exclaimed, "Then, O my God, I am lost — forever lost!"

This cry fell upon me like a thunderbolt; but I was still more terror-stricken when, looking through the aperture, I saw she was fainting. I heard the noise of her body falling upon the floor, and of her head striking against the sides of the confessional box.

Quick as lightning I ran to help her, took her in my arms, and called a couple of men, who were at a little distance, to assist me in laying her on a bench. I washed her face with some cold water and vinegar. She was as pale as death, but her lips were moving, and she was saying something which nobody but I could understand: "I am lost forever!"

We took her home to her disconsolate family, where for a month she lingered between life and death. Her two first confessors came to visit her; but having asked everyone to go out of the room, she politely, but firmly, requested them to go away, and never come again. She asked me to visit her every day, "For," she said, "I have only a few more days to live. Help me to prepare myself for the solemn hour which will open to me the gates of eternity!"

Every day I visited her, and I prayed and I wept with her. Many times, when alone, with tears I requested her to finish her confession; but, with a firmness which then seemed to be mysterious and inexplicable, she politely rebuked me.

One day, when alone with her, I was kneeling by the side of her bed to pray, I was unable to articulate a single word, because of the inexpressible anguish of my soul on her account, she asked me, "Dear father, why do you weep?"

I answered, "How can you put such a question to your murderer! I weep because I have killed you, dear friend."

This answer seemed to trouble her exceedingly. She was very weak that day. After she had wept and prayed in silence, she said, "Do not weep for me, but weep for so many priests who destroy their penitents in the confessional. I believe in the holiness of the sacrament of penance, since our holy Church has established it. But there is, somewhere, something exceedingly wrong in the confessional. Twice I have been destroyed, and I know many girls who have also been destroyed by the confessional. I pity the poor priests the day that our fathers will know what becomes of the purity of their daughters in the hands of their confessors. Father would surely kill my two last confessors, if he could only know they have destroyed his poor child."

I could not answer except by weeping. We remained silent for a long time, then she said, "It is true that I was not prepared for the rebuke you have given me the other day in the confessional; but you acted conscientiously as a good and honest priest. I know you must be bound by certain laws."

She then pressed my hand with her cold hand and said, "Weep not, dear father, because that sudden storm has wrecked my too fragile bark. This storm was to take me out from the bottomless sea of my iniquities to the shore where Jesus was waiting to receive and pardon me. The night after you brought me, half dead, here to my father's house, I had a dream. Oh, no! it was not a dream, it was a reality. My Jesus came to me, He was bleeding; His crown of thorns was on His head, the heavy cross was bruising His shoulders. He said to me, with a voice so sweet that no human tongue can imitate it, 'I have seen thy tears, I have heard thy cries, and I know thy love for Me: thy sins are forgiven; take courage, in a few days thou shalt be with Me!'"

She had hardly finished her last word when she fainted. I called her family, who rushed into the room. The doctor was sent for. He found her so weak that he thought proper to allow only one or two persons to remain in the room with me. He requested us not to speak at all, "For," said he, "the least emotion may kill her instantly; her disease is, in all probability, an aneurism of the aorta, the big vein which brings the blood to the heart: when it breaks, she will go as quick as lightning."

It was nearly ten at night when I left the house to go and take some rest. But it was a sleepless night. My dear Mary was there, pale, dying from the deadly blow which I had given her in the confessional. She was there, on her bed of death, her heart pierced with the dagger which my Church had put into my hands! and instead of rebuking and cursing me for my savage, merciless fanaticism, she was blessing me! She was dying from a broken heart! and I was not allowed by my Church to give her a single word of consolation and hope, for had she not made her confession? I had mercilessly bruised that tender plant, and there was nothing in my hands to heal the wounds I had made!

It was very probable that she would die the next day, and I was forbidden to show her the crown of glory which Jesus has prepared in His kingdom for the repenting sinner.

Before the dawn of day, I arose to read my theologians again, and see if I could not find someone who would allow me to forgive the sins of that dear child, without forcing her to tell me anything she had done. But they seemed to me, more than ever, unanimously inexorable, and I put them back on the shelves of my library with a broken heart.

At nine a.m. the next day, I was at Mary's bedside. I cannot sufficiently tell the joy I felt, when the doctor and whole family said to me, "She is much better; the rest of last night has wrought a marvelous change, indeed."

With a really angelic smile she extended her hand towards me, and said, "I thought, last evening, that the dear Saviour would take me to Him, but He wants me, dear father, to give you a little more trouble; however, be patient, it cannot be long before the solemn hour of the appeal will strike. Will you please read me the history of the suffering and death of the beloved Saviour, which you read me the other day? It does me so much good to see how He has loved me, such a miserable sinner."

There was a calm and solemnity in her words which struck me singularly, as well as all those who were there.

After I had finished reading, she exclaimed, "He has loved me so much that He died for my sins!" And she shut her eyes as if to meditate in silence, but there was a stream of big tears rolling down her cheeks.

I knelt down by her bed, with her family, to pray; but I could not utter a single word. The idea that this dear child was there, dying from the cruel fanaticism of my theologians and my own cowardice in obeying them, was as a millstone to my neck. It was killing me.

After we had silently prayed and wept by her bedside, she requested her mother to leave her alone with me.

When I saw myself alone, under the irresistible impression that this was her last day, I fell on my knees again, and with tears of the most sincere compassion for her soul, I requested her to shake off her shame and to obey our holy Church, which requires everyone to confess their sins if they want to be forgiven.

She calmly, but with the air of dignity which no human words can express, said, "Is it true that, after the sins of Adam and Eve, God Himself made coats and skins and clothed them, that they might not see each other's nakedness?"

"Yes," I said, "this is what the Holy Scriptures tell us."

"Well, then, how is it possible that our confessors dare to take away from us that holy, divine coat of modesty and self-respect? Has not Almighty God Himself made, with His own hands, that coat of womanly modesty and self-respect that we might not be to you and to ourselves a cause of shame and sin?"

I was really stunned by the beauty, simplicity, and sublimity of that comparison. I remained absolutely mute and confounded. Though it was demolishing all the traditions and doctrines of my Church, and pulverizing all my holy doctors and theologians, that noble answer found such an echo in my soul, that it seemed to me a sacrilege to try to touch it with my finger.

After a short time of silence, she continued, "Twice I have been destroyed by priests in the confessional. They took away from me that divine coat of modesty and self-respect which God gives to every human being who comes into this world, and twice I have become for those very priests a deep pit of perdition, into which they have fallen, and where I fear they are forever lost! My merciful heavenly Father has given me back that coat of skins, that nuptial robe of modesty, self-respect, and holiness which had been taken away from me. He cannot allow you or any other man to tear again and spoil that vestment which is the work of His hands."

These words had exhausted her; it was evident to me that she wanted some rest. I left her alone, but I was absolutely beside myself. Filled with admiration for the sublime lessons which I had received from the lips of that regenerated daughter of Eve, who, it was evident, was soon to fly away from us, I felt a supreme disgust for myself, my theologians — shall I say it? Yes, I felt in that solemn hour a supreme disgust for my Church, which was cruelly defiling me and all her priests, in the confessional box. I felt, in that hour, a supreme horror for that auricular confession, which is so often a pit of perdition and supreme misery for the confessor and penitent.

At 4:00 p.m. I returned to the house. When alone with her, I again fell on my knees, and, amidst torrents of tears, I said, "Dear sister, it is my desire to give you the holy viaticum and the extreme unction: but tell me, how can I dare to do a thing so solemn against all the prohibitions of our holy Church? How can I give you the holy communion without first giving you absolution? and how can I give you absolution when you earnestly persist in telling me that you have so many sins which you will never declare to me or any other confessor?

"You know that I cherish and respect you as if you were an angel sent to me from heaven. I bless every hour we have passed together in looking to the wounds of our beloved, dying Saviour; I bless you for having forgiven me your death! for I know it, and I confess it in the presence of God, I have killed you, dear sister. But now I prefer a thousand times to die than to say to you a word which would pain you in any way, or trouble the peace of your soul. Please, my dear sister, tell me what I can and must do for you in this solemn hour."

Calmly, and with a smile of joy such as I had never seen before, nor since, she said, "I thank and bless you, dear father, for the parable of the Prodigal Son, on which you preached a month ago. You have brought me to the feet of the dear Saviour; there I have found a peace and a joy surpassing anything that human heart can feel; I have thrown myself into the arms of my Heavenly Father, and I know He has mercifully accepted and forgiven His poor prodigal child! Oh, I see the angels with their golden harps around the throne of the Lamb! Do you not hear the celestial harmony of their songs? I go — I go to join them in my Father's house. I SHALL NOT BE LOST!"

Her hands were crossed on her breast, and there was on her face the expression of a really superhuman joy; her beautiful eyes were fixed as if they were looking on some grand and sublime spectacle; it seemed to me, at first, that she was praying. But I was mistaken. The redeemed soul had gone, on the golden wings of love, to join the multitude of those who have washed their robes in the blood of the Lamb, to sing the eternal Alleluia.

The revelation of the unmentionable corruptions directly and unavoidably engendered by auricular confession, had come to me from the lips of that young lady, as the first rays of the sun which were to hurl back the dark clouds of night by which Rome had wrapped my intelligence on that subject.

She was brought there by the merciful hand of God, to right my course. Her words, filled with a superhuman wisdom, and her burning tears, came to me, by the marvelous Providence of God, as the first beams of the Sun of Righteousness, to teach me that auricular confession was a Satanic invention.

Had she been the only one I might still have held some doubt about the diabolical origin of that institution. But thousands and thousands, before and after her, have been sent by my merciful

God to tell me the same tale, till after twenty-five years of experience it became certain to me that that modern invention of Rome must, sooner or later, with very few exceptions, drag both the confessor and his female penitents into a common and irreparable ruin.

Those who would like to know all about the abominations of auricular confession should have my volume "The Priest, the Woman and the Confessional."

CHAPTER L

On the first of August, 1855, I received a letter from my bishop in Chicago, instructing me to attend a spiritual retreat to be given the next month at the college, in Chicago, for the clergy of the diocese of Chicago and Quincy.

Wishing to study the *personnel* of that Irish clergy of which Bishop Vandeveld had told such frightful things, I went to St. Mary's University, two hours ahead of time.

Never did I see such a band of jolly fellows. Their dissipation and laughter, their exchange of witty, and too often, unbecoming expressions, the tremendous noise they made in addressing each other, at a distance: Their "Hallo, Patrick!" "Hallo, Murphy!" "Hallo, O'Brien! How do you do? How is Bridget? Is Marguerite still with you?" The answers: "Yes ! yes ! She will not leave me;" or "No! no! the crazy girl is gone," were invariably followed by outbursts of laughter.

What stranger, in entering that large hall, would have suspected that those men were about to begin one of the most solemn and sacred actions of a priest! With the exception of five or six, they looked more like a band of carousing raftsmen.

About an hour before the opening of the exercises, I saw one of the priests with hat in hand, accompanied by two others, going to every one, collecting money. I supposed that this collection was intended to pay for our board, during the retreat, and I prepared to give fifteen dollars. The big hat was literally filled with five and ten dollar bills. I asked: "What is the object of that collection?"

"Ah! ah!" they answered with a hearty laugh. "Dear Father Chiniquy, is it possible that you do not know it yet? Don't you know that, when we are so crowded as we will be here, the rooms are apt to become too warm, and we get thirsty? Then a little drop to cool the throat and quench the thirst, is needed," and the collectors laughed outright.

I answered politely, but seriously: "Gentlemen, I came here to meditate and pray; I have given up, long ago, the use of intoxicating drinks. Please excuse me, I am a teetotaler."

"So we are!" they answered, with a laugh; "we have all taken the pledge from Father Mathew; but this does not prevent us from taking a little drop to quench our thirst and keep up our health. Father Mathew is not so merciless as you are."

"I know Father Mathew well," I answered. "I have written to him and seen him many times. Allow me to tell you that we are of the same mind about the use of intoxicating drink."

"Is it possible you know Father Mathew and you are exchanging letters with him? What a holy man he is, and what good he has done in Ireland, and everywhere!" they answered.

"But the good he has done will not last long," I said, "if all his disciples keep their pledges as you do."

As we were talking, a good number of priests came around us to hear what was said; for it was evident to all that the bark of their collectors, not only had come to shallow waters, but had struck on a rock.

One of the priests said: "I thought we were to be preached to by Bishop Spaulding. I had no idea that it was Father Chiniquy who had that charge."

"Gentlemen," I answered, "I have as much right to preach to you in favor of temperance as you have to preach to me in favor of intemperance. You may do as you please about the use of strong drink, during the retreat; but I hope I also may have the right to think and do as I please in that matter."

They then left me, saying something which I could not understand, but they were evidently disgusted with what they considered my stubbornness and want of good manners.

I must, however, say that two of them, Mr. Dunn, and another unknown to me, came to congratulate me on the stern rebuke I had given.

After apologizing for the behavior of his fellow priests, Mr. Dunn expressed his disgust over what had just occurred; informing me the total amount collected was 500 dollars . Stepping closer he said, "Do not think that you are friendless here, in our midst. You have more friends than you think among the Irish priests; and I am one of them, though you do not know me. Bishop Vandeveld has often spoken to me of your grand colonization work."

Then he pressed my hand in his, and taking me a short distance from the others, said: "Consider me, hereafter, as your friend, you have lost a true friend in Bishop Vandeveld. I fear that our present bishop will not do you justice. Lebel and Carthuval have preju-

diced him against you. But I will stand by you, if you are ever unjustly dealt with, as I fear you will, by the present administration
of the diocese.

"After the mild and paternal ruling of Bishop Vandeveld, neither the priests nor the people of Illinois will long bear the iron
chains which the present bishop has in store for us all."

I thanked Mr. Dunn for his kind words, and told him that I had
already tasted the paternal love of my bishop by being twice
dragged by Spink before the criminal courts for having refused to
live on good terms with the two most demoralized priests I have
ever known.

At that moment, the bell called us to the chapel to hear the
regulations of the bishop in reference to the retreat. At 8 p.m. we
had our first sermon by Bishop Spaulding, from Kentucky. He was
a fine-looking man, a giant in stature, and a good speaker. But the
way in which he treated his subjects, though very clever, left, in
my mind, the impression that he did not believe a word of what he
said. He delivered two sermons each day; and the Rev. Mr.
Vanhulest, a Jesuit, gave us two meditations, each of them lasting
from forty to fifty minutes.

The rest of the time was spent in reading aloud the life of a
saint, reciting the breviarum, examination of conscience, and
going to confession. We had half-an-hour for meals, followed by
one hour of recreation. Thus were the days spent. But the nights!
the nights! what shall I say of them? My pen refuses to write all of
what my eyes saw and my ears heard during the long hours of
those nights.

The drinking used to begin about nine o'clock, but within a half-
an-hour the alcohol was beginning to unloose the tongues, and
upset the brain. Then it began, the witty stories, followed by the
most indecent and shameful recitals. The lascivious songs and the
most infamous anecdotes were flying from bed to bed, from room to
room, till one or two o'clock in the morning.

One night, three priests were taken with delirium tremens
almost at the same time. One cried out that he had a dozen rattle-
snakes at his shirt; the second was fighting against thousands of
bats, which were trying to tear his eyes from their sockets; and the
third, with a stick, was repulsing millions of spiders, which, he
said, were as big as wild turkeys, all at work to devour him. In
addition, dozens of them were ejecting their overloaded stomachs
in the beds and all around! The third day I was so disgusted and indignant that I determined to leave, without noise, under the pretext that I was sick.

There was, however, another thing which was still more

overwhelming. It was the terrible moral struggle in my soul; the voice of my conscience, (which I had to take for the voice of Satan), was crying in my ears: "Do you not clearly see that your Church is the devil's Church — that those priests, instead of being the Lamb's priests, are the successors of the old Bacchus priests?

"Read your Bible a little more attentively, and see if this is not the reign of the great harlot, which is defiling the world with her abominations? How long will you remain in this sea of Sodom? Come out! come out of Babylon, if you do not want to perish with her! Can the Son of God come down every morning in body, in soul, and divinity, into the hands and stomach of such men? Can the nations be led into the ways of God by them? Are you not guilty of an unpardonable crime when you are planting, with your own hands, over this magnificent country, a tree bearing such fruits? How dare you meet your God, after you have so deceived yourself and the people to believe that these are the representatives, the leaders, the priests of the Church outside of which there is no salvation!"

Oh! what an awful thing it is to resist the voice of God! To take Him for the evil one, when, by His warnings, He seeks to save your soul! Fearing lest I should entirely lose my faith in my religion, and become an absolute infidel by remaining any longer in the midst of such profligacy, I determined to leave; but before doing so, I wanted to consult the new friend whom the providence of God had given me in Mr. Dunn.

I went to him, after dinner, and taking him aside, I told him what had occurred last night, and asked his advice on my determination not to continue the retreat.

He answered: "You teach me nothing, for I spent last night in the same dormitory where you were. One priest told me all about those orgies, yesterday; I could hardly believe what he said, and I determined to see and hear for myself. You do not exaggerate, you do not even mention half of the horrors of last night. It baffles any description. It is simply incredible for anyone who has not himself witnessed them.

"However, I do not advise you to leave. It would forever ruin you in the mind of the bishop. The best thing you can do is to go and say everything to Bishop Spaulding. I have done it this morning; but I felt that he did not believe the half of what I told him. When the same testimony comes from you, then he will believe it, and will probably take some measures, with our own bishop, to put an end to those horrors. I have something to tell you, confidentially, which surpasses anything you know of abominations of these last three nights.

"A respectable policeman who belongs to my congregation, came to me this morning to tell me that the first night, six prostitutes, dressed as gentlemen, and last night twelve came to the university, after dark, entered the dormitory, and went, directed by signals, to those who had invited them, each being provided with the necessary key.

"I have just reported the thing to Bishop O'Regan; but instead of paying any attention to what I said, he became furious against me, saying, 'Do you think that I am going to come down from my dignity of bishop to hear the reports of degraded policemen, or vile spies? If they want to damn themselves, there is no help, let them go to hell! I am not more obliged or able than God Himself to stop them! Does God stop them? Does He punish them? No! Well! you cannot expect from me more zeal and power than in our common God!'"

"With these fine words ringing in my ears," said good Mr. Dunn, "I had to leave his room double quick. It is of no use for us to speak to Bishop O'Regan on that matter. It will do no good. He wants to get a large subscription from those priests, at the end of the retreat, and he is rather inclined to pet than punish them, till he obtains the hundred thousand dollars he wants to build his white marble palace on the lake shore."

I replied: "Though you add to my desolation, instead of diminishing it, by what you say of the strange principles of our bishop, I will speak to my lord Spaulding as you advise me." Without a moment's delay, I went to his room. He received me very kindly, and did not at all seem surprised at what I said. It was as if he had been accustomed to see the same, or still worse abominations.

However, when I told him the enormous quantity of liquor drank, and that the retreat would be only a ridiculous comedy if no attempt at reform was tried, he agreed it would be advisable to try. "Though this is not in our program, we might give one or two sermons on the necessity of priests giving an example of temperance to their people. Will you please come with me to the room of my lord O'Regan, that we may confer on the matter, after you have told him what is going on?"

"Yes!" said Bishop O'Regan, "it is very sad to see that our priests have so little self-respect, even during such solemn days as those of public retreat. The Rev. Mr. Dunn has just told me the same sad story as Father Chiniquy. But what remedy can we find for such a state of things? Perhaps it might do well to give them a good sermon on temperance. Mr. Chiniquy, I am told that you are called 'the temperance apostle of Canada,' and that you are a powerful speaker on that subject; would you not like to give them one or two addresses on the injury they are doing to themselves and to our holy Church by their drunkenness?"

"If those priests could understand me in French," I replied, "I would accept the honor you offer me with pleasure; but to be understood by them, I would have to speak in English; and I am not sufficiently free in that language to attempt it. My broken English would only bring ridicule upon the holy cause of temperance. But my lord Spaulding has already preached on that subject in Kentucky and an address from his lordship would be listened to with more attention and benefit from him than from me."

It was then agreed he should change his program and give two addresses on temperance. But though these addresses were really eloquent, they were pearls thrown before swine. The drunken priests slept, as usual; and even snored, almost through the whole length of the delivery. It is true that we could notice a little improvement, and less noise the following nights; the change, however, was very little.

On the fourth day of the retreat, the Rev. Mr Lebel came to me with his bag in hand. He looked furious. He said: "Now, you must be satisfied. I am interdicted and turned out ignominiously from this diocese. It is your work! But mind what I tell you; you will, also, soon be turned out from your colony by the mitred tyrant who has just struck me down. He told me several times that he would, at any cost, break your plans of French colonization, by sending you to the southwest of Illinois, along the Mississippi, to an old French settlement, opposite St. Louis. He is enraged against you for your refusing to give him your fine property at St. Anne."

I answered him: "You are mistaken when you think that I am the author of your misfortunes. You have disgraced yourself by your own acts. Nobody is more sorry than I am for your misfortune, and my most sincere wish is that the past may be a lesson to guide your steps in the future. The desire of the bishop to turn me out of my colony does not trouble me. If it is the will of God to keep me at the head of that great work, the Bishop of Chicago will go down from this episcopal throne before I go down the beautiful hill of St. Anne." He soon disappeared. But how the fall of this priest, whom I had so sincerely loved, saddened me!

The next Sabbath was the last day of the retreat. All the priests went in procession to the cathedral, to receive the holy communion, and every one of them ate, what we had to believe was the true body, soul, and divinity of Jesus Christ. This, however did not prevent thirteen of them from spending the greater part of the next night in jail, to which they had been taken by the police, from houses of ill-fame, where they were rioting and fighting. The next morning they were released after paying large fines for the trouble of the night!

The next day, I went to Mr. Dunn's parsonage to ask him if he could give me any explanation of the rumor which Mr. Lebel had mentioned that I was to be removed by the bishop from my colony to a distant part of his diocese.

"It is unfortunately too true," said he. "Bishop O'Regan thinks that he has a mission from heaven to undo all his predecessor has done. One of the best and grandest schemes of Bishop Vandeveld was to secure the possession of this magnificent state of Illinois to our Church, by inducing all Roman Catholic emigrants from France, Belgium, and Canada, to settle here.

"Our present bishop opposes that plan and will remove you to such a distance that your colonization plans will be at an end. He says that the French are generally rebels and disobedient to their ecclesiastical superiors. I have, in vain, tried to change his mind.

"I told you before he often asks my opinion on what I think is best for the diocese. But my impression now is that he wants to know our views only for the pleasure of acting opposite to what we advise."

At the end of the retreat Bishop O'Regan's plea for funds was a success; even though everyone present felt it was ludicrous to build a 100,000 dollar palace in such a young and poor diocese. We immediately raised amongst ourselves 7,000 dollars in cash and promissory notes as a show of good will. Then, promising that we would do all in our power to raise the balance of that ridiculous sum, we were simultaneously blessed and dismissed from our retreat.

I was but a few steps from the university, when an Irish priest, unknown to me, ran after me to say, "My lord O'Regan wants to see you immediately." Five minutes later I was alone with my bishop, who, without any preface, told me, "Mr. Chiniquy, I hear very strange and damaging things about you, from every quarter. But the worst of all is that you are a secret Protestant emissary; that, instead of preaching the true doctrines of our holy Church, about the Immaculate Conception, purgatory, etc., you spend a part of your time in distributing Bibles and New Testaments among your immigrants; I want to know from your own lips, if this be true or not."

I answered, "A part of what the people told you about the matter is not true, the other is true. It is not true that I neglect the preaching of the doctrines of our holy Church, about purgatory, Immaculate Conception of Mary, auricular confession, or the respect due to our superiors. But it is true that I do distribute the Holy

Bible and the Gospel of Christ among my people."

"And instead of blushing at such unpriestly conduct, you seem to be proud of it," angrily replied the bishop.

"I do not understand, my lord, why a priest of Christ could blush for distributing the Word of God among his people; as I am bound to preach that Holy Word, it is not only my right but my duty to give it to them. I am fully persuaded that there is no preaching so efficacious and powerful as the preaching of our God Himself, when speaking to us in His Holy Book."

"This is sheer Protestantism, Mr. Chiniquy, this is sheer Protestanism," he answered me angrily.

"My dear bishop," I answered calmly, "if to give the Bible to the people and invite them to read and meditate on it is Protestanism, our holy Pope Pius VI was a good Protestant. In his letter to Martini, which is probably in the first pages of the beautiful Bible I see on your lordship's table, he not only blesses him for having translated that Holy Book into Italian, but invites the people to read it."

The bishop, assuming an air of supreme contempt, replied: "Your answer shows your complete ignorance on the subject on which you speak so boldly. If you were a little better informed on that grave subject, you would know that the translation by Martini, which the pope advised the Italian people to read, formed a work of twenty-three big volumes which, of course, nobody, except very rich and idle people could read. Not one in ten thousand Italians have the means of purchasing such a voluminous work; and not one in twenty thousand have the time or the will to peruse such a mass of endless commentaries. The pope would never have given such an advice to read a Bible, as the one you distribute so imprudently."

"Then, my lord, do you positively tell me that the pope gave permission to read Martini's translation, because he knew that the people could never get it on account of its enormous size and price, and do you assure me that he would never have given such advice, had the same people been able to purchase and read that holy work."

"Yes, sir! It is what I mean," answered the bishop, with an air of triumph, "for I know positively that this is the fact."

I replied, calmly: "I hope your lordship is unwillingly mistaken; for if you were correct, the stern and unflinching principles of logic would force me to think and say that the pope and all his followers were deceivers, and that encyclical a public fraud in his own hands; for we Catholic priests make use of it, all over the world, and reprint it at the head of our own Bibles, to make the people, both Protestants and Catholics believe that we approve of their reading our own versions of that Holy Book."

Had I thrown a spark of fire in a keg of powder, the explosion would not have been more prompt and terrible than the rage of that prelate. Pointing his finger to my face, he said: "Now, I see the truth of what I have been told, that you are a disguised Protestant, since the very day that you were ordained a priest. The Bible! The Bible is your motto! For you the Bible is everything, and the holy Church, with her popes and bishops nothing! What an insolent, I dare say, what a blasphemous word, I have just heard from you! You dare call an encyclical letter of one of our most holy popes, a fraud!"

In vain, I tried to explain. He would not listen; and he silenced me by saying: "If our holy Church has, in an unfortunate day, appointed you one of her priests in my diocese, it was to preach the doctrines, and not to distribute the Bible! If you forget that, I will make you remember it!" And with that remark, I had to take the door which he had opened. Thanks be to God this first persecution I received for my dear Bible's sake did not diminish my love, my respect for God's Holy Word nor my confidence in it. On the contrary, on reaching home, I took it, fell on my knees, and pressing it to my heart, I asked my heavenly Father to grant me the favor to love it more sincerely, and follow its divine teachings with more fidelity till the end of my life.

CHAPTER LI

Within a month after the retreat, all the cities of Illinois were filled by the most humiliating clamors against Bishop O'Regan. Numerous articles appeared in the principal papers, signed by the most respectable names, accusing him of theft, simony, and perjury. Bitter complaints came from almost every congregation: "He has stolen the beautiful and costly vestments we bought for our church," cried the French Canadians of Chicago. "He has swindled us out of a fine lot given us to build our church, sold it for 40,000 dollars and pocketed the money for his own private use without giving us any notice," said the Germans. "His thirst for money is so great," said the whole Catholic people of Illinois, "that he is selling even the bones of the dead to fill his treasures!"

I had not forgotten the bold attempt of the bishop to wrench my little property from my hands, on his first visit to my colony. But I had hoped that this act was an isolated and exceptional case in the life of my superior; and I did not whisper a word of it to anybody. I began to think differently, however. I had hoped these reports were exaggerations and the clamor against the bishop would soon die out. However the outcry grew louder with each passing day.

I determined to go to Chicago and see for myself. I went directly to the French Canadian church. To my unspeakable dismay it was true! The bishop had stolen their vestments for his own personal use. The outrage of my fellow countrymen knew no bounds. Several spoke of prosecuting him before the civil courts. There was even talk of mobbing and insulting him publicly in the streets, or even in his palace. The only way I could appease them was to promise to go to his lordship and ask to have those vestments restored.

My next stop was the Roman Catholic graveyard. On the way I met a great many cart loads of sand. At the very door of the consecrated spot I found three carts just leaving the grounds. I obtained permission from the drivers to search the sand to see if there were not some bones. I could not find any in the first cart, but, to my horror and shame, I found the lower jaw of a child in the second, and part of the bones of an arm, and almost the whole foot of a human being, in the third cart!

I politely requested to know where they had dug the sand. To my unspeakable regret and shame, I found that the bishop had told an unmitigated falsehood. To appease the public indignation against his sacrilegious trade, he had published that he was selling only the sand which was outside of the fence.

In order to make his case good he had ordered the old fence replaced by a new one many feet inside the old one. To make matters worse the bishop had received that piece of land from the city for a burial ground only after he had taken a solemn oath to use it only for burying the dead. Every load of sand sold then, was not only an act of simony, but the breaking of a solemn oath!

I then went directly to the bishop to fulfill the promise I had made to the French Canadians. It didn't take me long to realize that my request would not be well received. However, I thought it my duty to do all in my power to open the eyes of my bishop to the pit he was digging for himself and for all us Catholics, by his conduct. "My lord," I said, "I shall not surprise your lordship, when I tell you that all the true Catholics of Illinois are filled with sorrow by the articles they find, every day, in the press, against their bishop."

"Yes! yes!" he abruptly replied, "the good Catholics must be sad indeed to read such disgusting diatribes against their superior; and I presume that you are one of those that are sorry. But, then, why do you not prevent your insolent and infidel countrymen from writing those things! I see that a great part of those libels are signed by the French Canadians."

I answered, "It is to try, as much as it is in my power, to put an end to those scandals that I am in Chicago today, my lord."

"Very well, very well," he replied, "as you have the reputation of having a great influence over your countrymen, make use of it to stop them in their rebellious conduct against me, and I will then believe that you are a good priest."

I answered, "I hope that I will succeed in what your lordship wants me to do. But there are two things to be done, in order to secure my success."

"What are they?" quickly asked the bishop.

"The first is, that your lordship give back the fine church vestments which you have taken from the French Canadian congregation of Chicago. The second is that your lordship abstain, absolutely, from this day, to steal the sand of the burying ground, which covers the tombs of the dead."

The bishop striking his fist violently upon the table, crossed the room two or three times; then turning towards me, and pointing his finger in my face, he exclaimed with indescribable rage:

"Now, I see the truth of what Mr. Spink told me! You are not only my bitterest enemy, but you are at the head of my enemies. You take sides with them against me. You approve of their libelous writings against me! I will never give back those church vestments. They are mine, as the French Canadian church is mine! Do you not know that the ground on which the churches are built, as well as the churches themselves, and all that belongs to the church, belongs to the bishop? Was it not a burning shame to use those fine vestments in a poor miserable church of Chicago, when the bishop of that important city was covered with rags! It was in the interest of the episcopal dignity, that I ordered those rich and splendid vestments, which were mine by law, to be transferred from that small and insignificant congregation, to my cathedral of St. Mary, and if you had an ounce of respect for your bishop, Mr. Chiniquy, you would immediately go to your countrymen and put a stop to their murmurs and slanders against me, by simply telling them that I have taken what was mine from that church, which is mine also, to the cathedral, which is altogether mine. Tell your countrymen to hold their tongues, and respect their bishop, when he is in the right, as I am today."

I had, many times, considered the infamy and injustice of the law which the bishops have had passed all over the United States, making every one of them a corporation, with the right of possessing personally all the church properties of the Roman Catholics.

But I had never understood the infamy and tyranny of that law so clearly as in that hour.

I answered: "My lord, I confess that this is the law in the United States; but this is a human law, directly opposed to the Gospel. I do not find a single word in the Gospel which gives this power to the bishop. Such a power is an abusive, not a divine power, which will sooner or later destroy our holy Church in the United States, as it has already mortally wounded her in Great Britain, France, and in many other places. When Christ said, in the Holy Gospel, that He had not enough of ground whereon to lay His head, He condemned, in advance, the pretensions of the bishops who lay their hands on our church properties as their own. Such a claim is an usurpation and not a right, my lord. Our Saviour Jesus Christ protested against that usurpation, when asked by a young man to meddle in his temporal affairs with his brothers; He answered that 'He had not received such power.' The gospel is a long protest against that usurpation, in every page, it tells us that the kingdom of Christ is not of this world. I have myself given fifty dollars to help my countrymen to buy those church vestments. They belong to them and not to you!"

My words, uttered with an expression of firmness which the bishop had never yet seen in any of his priests, fell upon him, at first, as a thunderbolt. They so puzzled him, that he looked at me a moment, as if he wanted to see if it were a dream or a reality, that one of his priests had the audacity to use such language in his presence. But soon recovering from this stupor, he interrupted me by striking his fist again on the table, and saying in anger: "You are half a Protestant! Your words smell of Protestanism! The Gospel! the Gospel! that is your great tower of strength against the laws and regulations of our holy Church! If you think, Mr. Chiniquy, that you frighten me with your big words of the Gospel, you will soon see your mistake, at your own expense. I will make you remember that it is the Church you must obey, and it is through your bishop that the Church rules you!"

"My lord," I answered, "I want to obey the Church. Yes! but it is a church founded on the Gospel; a church that respects and follows the Gospel that I want to obey.!"

My words threw him into a fit of rage, and he answered: "I am too busy to hear your impertinent babbling any longer. Please let me alone, and remember that you will soon hear from me again if you cannot teach your people to respect and obey their superiors!" The bishop kept his promise.

My lord O'Regan had determined to interdict me; but, not being able to find any cause in my private or public life as a priest to found such a sentence, he pressed the land speculator, Spink, to prosecute me again; promising to base his interdict on the condemnation which, he had been told, would be passed against me by the criminal court of Kankakee. But the bishop and Peter Spink were again to be disappointed; for the verdict of the court, given on the 13th of November, 1855, was gain in my favor.

My joy was short lived when my two lawyers, Messrs. Osgood and Paddock, came to me and said: "Our victory, though great, is not so decisive as was expected; for Mr. Spink has just taken an oath that he has no confidence in this Kankakee court, and he has appealed, by a change of venue, to the court of Urbana, in Champaign County. We are sorry to have to tell you that you must remain a prisoner, under bail, in the hands of the sheriff, who is bound to deliver you to the sheriff of Urbana, the 19th of May, next spring."

I came very near fainting when I heard this. The court of Urbana was nearly 110 miles away. The expense of bringing my 15-20 witnesses that great distance was completely beyond my means!

The very moment I was leaving the court with a heavy heart, a stranger came to me and said: "I have followed your suit from the beginning. It is more formidable than you suspect. Your prosecutor, Spink, is only an instrument in the hands of the bishop. The real prosecutor is the land shark who is at the head of the diocese, and who is destroying our holy religion by his private and public scandals. As you are the only one among his priests who dares to resist him, he is determined to get rid of you. He will spend all his treasures and use the almost irresistible influence of his position to crush you. The misfortune for you is that, when you fight a bishop, you fight all the bishops of the world. They will unite all their wealth and influence to Bishop O'Regan's to silence you, though they hate and despise him. There was no danger of any verdict against you in this part of Illinois, where you are too well known for the perjured witnesses they have brought to influence your judges. But when you are among strangers, mind what I tell you: the false oaths of your enemies may be accepted as gospel truths by the jury, and then, though innocent, you are lost. Though your two lawyers are expert men, you will want something better at Urbana. Try to secure the services of Abraham Lincoln, of Springfield. If that man defends you, you will surely come out victorious from that deadly conflict!"

I answered: "I am much obliged to you for your sympathetic words: but would you please allow me to ask your name?"

"Be kind enough to let me keep my incognito here," he replied.

"The only thing I can say is that I am a Catholic like you, and one who, like you, cannot bear any longer the tyranny of our American bishops. With many others, I look to you as our deliverer, and for that reason I advise you to engage the services of Abraham Lincoln."

"But," I replied, "who is that Abraham Lincoln? I never heard of that man before."

He replied: "Abraham Lincoln is the best lawyer and the most honest man we have in Illinois."

I went immediately, with that stranger, to my two lawyers and asked if they would have any objection that I should ask the services of Abraham Lincoln, to help them to defend me at Urbana.

They both answered: "Oh! if you can secure the services of Abraham Lincoln, by all means do it. We know him well; he is one of the best lawyers and one the most honest men we have in our state."

Without losing a minute, I went to the telegraph office with that stranger and telegraphed Abraham Lincoln to ask him if he would defend my honor and my life (though I was a stranger to him) at the next May term of court at Urbana.

About twenty minutes later I received the answer:

"Yes, I will defend your honor and your life at the next May term at Urbana.

ABRAHAM LINCOLN"

My unknown friend then paid the operator, pressed my hand, and said: "May God bless and help you, Father Chiniquy. Continue to fight fearlessly for truth and righteousness against our mitred tyrants; and God will help you to the end." He then took a train for the north and soon disappeared, as a vision from heaven. I have not seen him since, though I have not let a day pass without asking my God to bless him. A few minutes later Spink came to the office to telegraph to Lincoln, asking his services at the next May term of the court at Urbana. But it was too late.

On the 19th of May, 1856, I met Mr. Abraham Lincoln for the first time. He was a giant in stature; but I found him still more a giant in his noble mind and heart. It was impossible to converse five minutes with him without loving him. There was such an expression of kindness and honesty in that face, and such an attractive magnetism in the man, that after a few moments' conversation one felt tied to him by all the noblest affections of the heart. When pressing my hand he told me: "You were mistaken when you telegraphed that you were unknown to me. I know you, by reputation, as the stern opponent of the tyranny of your bishop, and the fearless protector on your countrymen in Illinois; I have heard much of you from two priests; and, last night, your lawyers, Messrs. Osgood and Paddock have acquainted me with the fact that your bishop is employing some of his tools to get rid of you. I hope it will be an easy thing to defeat his projects, and protect you against his machinations." He then asked me how I had been induced to desire his services. I answered by giving him the story of that unknown friend who had advised me to have Mr. Abraham Lincoln for one of my lawyers, for the reason that "he was the best lawyer and the most honest man in Illinois." He smiled at my answer and replied: "That unknown friend would surely have been more correct had he told you that Abraham Lincoln was the ugliest lawyer in the country!" and he laughed outright.

I spent six long days at Urbana as a criminal, in the hands of the sheriff, at the feet of my judges. During the greatest part of that time, all that human language can express of abuse and insult was heaped upon my poor head. God only knows what I suffered in those days; but I was providentially surrounded, as by a strong wall. I had Abraham Lincoln for my defense — "the best lawyer and the most honest man of Illinois," and the learned and upright David Davis for my judge. The latter became vice-president of the United States in 1882; and the former its most honored president from 1861 to 1865.

I never heard anything like the eloquence of Abraham Lincoln when he demolished the testimonies of the two perjured priests, Lebel and Carthuval, who, with ten or twelve other false witnesses, had sworn against me. I would have surely been declared innocent after that eloquent address and the charge of the learned Judge Davis, had not my lawyers, by a sad blunder, left a Roman Catholic on the jury. Of course, that Irish Roman Catholic wanted to condemn me, when the eleven honest and intelligent Protestants were unanimous in voting "not guilty." The court, having at last found that it was impossible to persuade the jury to give an unanimous verdict, discharged them. But Spink again forced the sheriff to keep me under bail, by obtaining from the court the permission to continue the prosecution the 19th of October, 1856. Humanly speaking, I would have been one of the most miserable men, had I not had my dear Bible, which I was meditating and studying day and night in those dark days of trial.

Though the world did not suspect it, I knew from the beginning that all my tribulations were coming from my unconquerable attachment and my unfaltering love and respect for the Bible, as the root and source of every truth given by God to man; and I felt assured that my God knew it also. That assurance supported my courage in the conflict. Every day my Bible was becoming dearer to me. I was then constantly trying to walk in its marvelous light and divine teaching. I wanted to learn my duties and rights. I like to acknowledge that it was the Bible which gave me the power and wisdom I then so much needed to face fearlessly so many foes. That power and wisdom I felt were not mine. On this very account my Bible enabled me to remain calm in the very lions' den; and it gave me, from the very beginning of that terrible conflict, the assurance of a final victory; for every time I bathed my soul in its Divine light, I heard my merciful heavenly Father's voice, saying, "Fear not, for I am with thee." (Isaiah 43:5)

CHAPTER LII

The focus of Bishop O'Regan's tyrannical wrath fell primarily upon the French Canadian congregations of Chicago and St Anne. His diabolical plan was nothing less than their complete destruction.

Shortly after Easter, 1856, the bishop put his plan into action; the Rev. Mons. Lemaire was interdicted and ignominiously driven from the Chicago diocese without cause, leaving the French Canadians without a pastor. A few days later the parsonage was sold for 1,200 dollars to an American. The beautiful little church which stood on the lot next to the parsonage was removed 5 or 6 blocks southwest, and rented by the bishop to the parish Catholics for about 2,000 dollars per annum. Not one word was given my countrymen, who incidentally had built those fine buildings with their own money.

On August 19th, 1856 the bishop, having heard that I was in Chicago, sent for me. Though not absolutely drunk, I found him full of wine, and terribly excited.

"Mr. Chiniquy," he said, "you had promised me to make use of your influence to put an end to the rebellious conduct of your countrymen against me. But I find that they are more insolent and unmanageable than ever; and my firm belief is that it is your fault. You, and the handful of French Canadians of Chicago, give me more trouble than all the rest of my priests and my people of Illinois. You are too near Chicago, sir, your influence is too much felt on your people here. I must remove you to a distant place, where you will have enough to do without meddling in my administration. I want your service in Kahokia, in my diocese of Quincy; and if you are not there by the 15th of September next, I will interdict and excommunicate you, and forever put an end to your intrigues."

"My lord, you speak of interdict and excommunication! Allow me to respectfully tell you that if you can show me that I have done anything to deserve to be interdicted or excommunicated, I will submit in silence to your sentence. But before you pass that sentence, I ask you, in the name of God, to make a public inquest about me, and have my accusers confront me. I warn your lordship, that if you interdict or excommunicate me without holding an inquest, I will make use of all the means which our holy Church puts in the hands of her priests to defend my honor and prove my innocence; I will also appeal to the laws of our great republic, which protects the character of all her citizens against anyone who slanders them. It will, then, be at your risk and peril that you will pass such a sentence against me."

My calm answer greatly excited his rage. He violently struck the table with his fist, and said: "I do not care a straw about your threats. I repeat it, Mr. Chiniquy, if you are not at Kahokia by the 15th of next month, I will interdict and excommunicate you."

Feeling that it was a folly on my part to argue with a man who was beside himself by passion and excess of wine, I immediately left the room to take the train to St. Anne.

Having spent a part of the night praying God to change the heart of my bishop, and keep me in the midst of my people, I addressed the following letter to the bishop: —

To the Rt. Rev. O'Regan, Bishop of Chicago.

My Lord. — The more I consider your design to turn me out of the colony which I have founded, and of which I am the pastor, the more I believe it a duty which I owe to myself, my friends, and to my countrymen, to protest before God and man against what you intend to do.

Not a single one of your priests stands higher than I do in the public mind, neither is more loved and respected by his people than I am. I defy my bitterest enemies to prove the contrary. And that character which is my most precious treasure, you intend to despoil me of by ignominiously sending me away from among my people! Certainly, I have enemies, and I am proud of it. The chief ones are well known in this country as the most depraved of men. The cordial reception they say they have received from you, has not taken away the stains they have on their foreheads.

By this letter, I again request you to make a public and most minute inquest into my conduct. My conscience tells me that nothing can be found against me. Such a public and fair dealing with me would confound my accusers. But I speak of accusers, when I do not really know if I have any. Where are they? What are their names? Of what sin do they accuse me? All these questions which I put to you last Tuesday were left unanswered! and would to God that you would answer them today, by giving me their names. I am ready to meet them before any tribunal. Before you strike the last blow on the victim of this most hellish plot, I request you, in the name of God, to give a moment's attention to the following consequences of my removal from this place at present.

You know I have a suit with Mr. Spink at the Urbana court, for the beginning of October. My lawyers and witnesses are all in Kankakee and Iroquois Counties; and in the very time I want most to be here to prove my innocence and guard my honor, you order me to go to a place more than three hundred miles distant! Did you ever realize that by that strange conduct, you help Spink against your own priest? When at Kahokia, I will have to bear the heavy expenses of traveling more than three hundred miles, many times, to consult my friends, or be deprived of their valuable help! Is it possible that you thus try to tie my hands and feet, and deliver me into the hands of my remorseless enemies? Since the beginning of that suit, Mr. Spink proclaims that you help him, and that, with the perjured priests, you have promised to do all in your power to crush me down! For the sake of the sacred character you bear, do not show so publicly that Mr. Spink's boastings are true. For the sake of your high position in the Church, do not so publicly lend a helping hand to the heartless land speculator of L'Erable. He has already betrayed his Protestant friends to get a wife; he will, ere long, betray you for less. Let me then live in peace here, till that suit is over.

By turning me away from my settlement, you destroy it. More than nine tenths of the emigrants come here to live near me; by striking me you strike them all.

Where will you find a priest who will love that people so much as to give them, every year, from one to two thousand dollars, as I have invariably done? It is at the price of those sacrifices that, with the poorest class of emigrants from Canada, I have founded, here, in four years, a settlement which cannot be surpassed, or even equaled, in the United States, for its progress? And now that I have spent my last cent to form this colony, you turn me out of it. Our college, where one hundred and fifty boys are receiving such a good education, will be closed the very day I leave. For, you know very well the teachers I got from Montreal will leave as soon as I do.

Ah! if you are merciless towards the priest of St. Anne, have pity on these poor children. I would rather be condemned to death than to see them destroy their intelligence by running in the streets. Let me then finish my work here, and give me time to strengthen these young institutions which would fall to the ground with me.

If you turn me out or interdict me, as you say you will do if I disobey your order, my enemies will proclaim that you treat me with that rigor because you have found me guilty of some great iniquity; and this necessarily will prejudice my judges against me. They will consider me as a vile criminal. For who will suppose, in this free country, that there is a class of men who can judge a man and condemn him as our bishop of Chicago is doing today, without giving him the names of his accusers, or telling him of what crimes he is accused?

In the name of God, I again ask you to not force me to leave my colony before I prove my innocence, and the iniquity of Spink, to the honest people of Urbana.

But, if you are deaf to my prayers, and if nothing can deter you from your resolution, I do not wish to be in the unenviable positon of an interdicted priest among my countrymen; send me, by return mail, my letters of mission for the new places you intend trusting to my care. The sooner I get there the better for me and my people. I am ready! When on the road of exile, I will pray the God of Abraham to give me the fortitude and the faith He gave to Isaac, when laying his head on the altar, he willingly presented his throat to the sword. I will pray my Saviour, bearing His heavy cross to the top of Calvary, to direct and help my steps towards the land of exile you have prepared for your

Devoted Priest,
C. CHINIQUY

The following day we heard that the drunkard priests around us were publishing that the bishop had interdicted me, and they had received orders from him to take charge of the colony of St. Anne. I immediately called a meeting of the whole people and told them: "The bishop has not interdicted me as the neighboring priests publish; he has only threatened to do so, if I do not leave this place for Kahokia, by the 15th of next month. But though he has not interdicted me, it may be that he does falsely publish that he has done it. We can expect anything from the destroyer of the fine congregation of the French Canadians of Chicago. He wants to destroy me and you as he has destroyed them. But before he immolates us, I hope that, with the help of God, we will fight as Christian soldiers, for our life, and we will use all the means which the laws of our Church, the Holy Word of God, and the glorious Constitution of the United States allow us to employ against our merciless tyrant.

"I ask you, as a favor, to send a deputation of four members of our colony, in whom you place the most implicit confidence, to carry this letter to the bishop. But before delivering it, they will put to him the following questions, the answers of which they will write down with great care in his presence, and deliver them to us faithfully. It is evident that we are now entering into a momentous struggle. We must act with prudence and firmness."

Messrs. J. B. Lemoine, Leon Mailloux, Francis Bechard, and B. Allaire, having been unanimously chosen for that important mission, we gave them the following questions to put to the bishop: —

1st. "Have you interdicted Mr. Chiniquy?

2nd. "Why have you interdicted him? Is Mr. Chiniquy quilty of any crime to deserve to be interdicted? Have those crimes been proved against him in a canonical way?

3rd. "Why do you take Mr. Chiniquy away from us?"

(Our deputies came back from Chicago with the following answers which they swore to some time later before the Kankakee court.)

1st. "I have suspended Mr. Chiniquy on the 19th inst., on account of his stubbornness and want of submission to my orders when I ordered him to Kahokia.

2nd "If Mr. Chiniquy has said mass since, as you say, he is irregular, and the pope alone can restore him in his ecclesiastical and sacerdotal functions.

3rd "I take him away from St. Anne despite his prayers and yours, because he has not been willing to live in peace and friendship with the Rev. Messrs. Lebel and Carthuval.

(The bishop, being asked if those two priests had not been interdicted by him for public scandals, was forced to say: "Yes!")

4th "My second reason for taking Mr. Chiniquy from St. Anne, and sending him to his new mission, is to stop the lawsuit Mr. Spink has instituted against him.

(The bishop being asked if he would promise that the suit would be stopped by the removal of Mr. Chiniquy, answered: "I cannot promise that.")

5th "Mr. Chiniquy is one of the best priests in my diocese, and I do not want to deprive myself of his services, no accusation against his morality has been proved before me.

6th "Mr. Chiniquy has demanded an inquest to prove his innocence against certain accusations made against him; he asked me the names of his accuser, to confound them; I have refused to grant this request.

(After the bishop had made those declarations, the deputation presented him the letter of Mr. Chiniquy; it evidently made a deep impression upon him. As soon as he read it, he said:)

7th "Tell Mr. Chiniquy to come and meet me to prepare for his new mission, and I will give him the letters he wants, to go and labor there.

FRANCIS BECHARD,
J. B. LEMOINE,
BASILIQUE ALLAIRE,
LEON MAILLOUX."

(Those gentlemen, with the exception of Mr. Allaire, are still living, 1885.)

After the above had been read and delivered to the people, I showed them the evident falsehood and contradictions of the bishop's responses.

Now, my friends, here is the law of our holy Church: "If a man had been unjustly condemned, let him pay no attention to the unjust sentence: let him even do nothing to have that unjust sentence removed." (Canon of the Church, by Pope Gelasins)

"It strikes me, today, for the first time, that it is more your destruction, as a people, than mine, which the bishop wants to accomplish. It is my desire to remain in your midst to defend your rights as Catholics. If you are true to me, as I will be to you in the impending struggle, we have nothing to fear; for our holy Catholic Church is for us; all her laws and canons are in our favor; the Gospel of Christ is for us. The God of the Gospel is for us. Even the pope, to whom we will appeal, will be for us. The archbishop of St. Louis, to whom I brought my complaint in April last, advised me to write the pope and tell him of the criminal deeds of Bishop O'Regan. If you are true to yourselves as Catholics and Americans you will not allow that mitred tyrant to accomplish here the same atrocities he has committed against our fellow countrymen in Chicago. If you promise to stand by your rights, I will tell that avaricious bishop: 'Come and sell our parsonage and our church here, if you dare!' We have a glorious battle to fight. It is the battle of freedom against the most cruel tyranny the world has ever seen: it is the battle of truth again falsehood; it is the battle of the old Gospel of Christ against the new gospel of Bishop O'Regan. Let us be true to ourselves to the end, and our holy Church, which that bishop dishonors, will bless us. Our Saviour Jesus Christ, whose Gospel is despised by that adventurer, will be for us, and give us a glorious victory. Have you not read your Bibles that Jesus wanted His disciples to be free, when He said: 'If the Son therefore shall make you free, ye shall be free indeed.' (John 8:36) Does that mean that the Son of God wants us to be slaves of Bishop O'Regan?"

"No!" cried out the whole people.

"May God bless you for your understanding of your Christian rights. Let all those who want to be free, with me, raise their hands. Thanks be to God," I again exclaimed, "There is not a traitor among us! You are all the true, brave and noble soldiers of liberty, truth and righteousness! May the Lord bless you all!"

It is impossible to describe the enthusiasm of the people. Before dismissing them, I said: "We will, no doubt, very soon, witness one of the most ludicrous comedies ever played on this continent: that comedy is generally called excommunication. Some drunkard priests, sent by the drunkard bishop of Chicago, will come to excommunicate us. I expect their visits in a few days. That performance will be worth seeing; and I hope that you will see and hear the most amusing thing in your life."

I was not mistaken. The very next day, we heard that the 3rd of September had been chosen by the bishop to excommunicate us. I said to the people: "When you see the flag of the free and the brave floating from the top of our steeple, come and rally around that emblem of liberty."

There were more than 3,000 people on our beautiful hill when the priests made their appearance. A few moments before, I had said to that immense gathering:

"I bless God that you are so many to witness the last tyrannical act of Bishop O'Regan. But I have a favor to ask of you. It is, that no insult whatever will be made to the priests who come to play that comedy. Please do not say an angry word; do not move a finger against the performers. They are not responsible for what they will do, for two reasons. 1. They will probably be drunk. 2. They are bound to do that work by their master, Lord Bishop O'Regan."

The priests arrived at about two o'clock p.m., and never such shouting and clapping of hands had been heard in our colony as on their appearance. Never had I seen my dear people so cheerful and good humored, as when one of the priests, trembling from head to foot with terror and drunkenness, tried to read the following sham act of excommunication; which he nailed on the door of the chapel:

"The Reverend Monsieur Chiniquy, heretofore curate of St. Anne, Colony of Beaver, in the Diocese of Chicago, has formally been interdicted by me for canonical causes.

"The said Mr. Chiniquy, notwithstanding that interdict, has maliciously performed the functions of the holy ministry, in administrating the holy sacraments and saying mass. This has caused him to be irregular, and in direct oppostion to the authority of the Church, consequently, he is a schismatic.

"The said Mr. Chiniquy, thus named by my letters and verbal injunction, has absolutely persisted in violating the laws of the Church, and disobeyed her authority, and is by this present letter excommunicated.

I forbid any Catholic having any communication with him, in spiritual matters, under pain of excommunication. Every Catholic who goes against this suspense, is excommunicated."

(Signed)   ✠ ANTHONY,

Bishop of Chicago, and administrator of Quincy.

Sept. 3rd., 1856.

As soon as the priests, who had nailed this document to the door of our chapel, had gone away at full speed, I went to see it, and found what I had expected, that it was not signed by the bishop, neither by this grand vicar, nor any known person, and, consequently it was a complete nullity, according to the laws of the Church. Fearing I would prosecute him, as I threatened, he shrank from the responsibility of his own act, and had not signed it. He was probably ignorant of the fact that he was himself excommunicated, *ipso facto,* for not having signed the document himself, or by his known deputies. I learned afterwards, that they had gotten a boy twelve years old to write and sign it. In this way, it was impossible for me to bring that document before any court, on account of its want of legal and necessary forms. That act was also void for being brought by three priests who were not mentally capable, due to the fact they were drunk!

The people understood very well that the whole affair was a miserable farce, designed to separate them from their pastor. By the good providence of God, it had just the contrary effect. They had never shown me such sincere respect and devotedness as since that never-to-be-forgotten day.

CHAPTER LIII

The Sabbath afternoon after the three drunken priests nailed their unsigned, unsealed, untestified, and consequently void sentence of excommunication to the door of our chapel, the people had gathered from every part of our colony into the large hall of the court house of Kankakee City to hear several addresses on their duties of the day, and they unanimously passed the following resolution:

"Resolved, — That we, French Canadians of the County of Kankakee, do hereby decide to give our moral support to Rev. C. Chiniquy, in the persecution now exerted against him by the Bishop of Chicago, in violation of the laws of the Church, expressed and sanctioned by the Councils."

The stern and unanimous determination of my countrymen to stand by me in the impending struggle is one of the greatest blessings which God has ever given me. It filled me with a courage which nothing could hereafter shake. But the people of St. Anne did not think that it was enough to show to the bishop that nothing could ever shake the resolution they had taken to live and die free men. They gathered in an immense public meeting on the Sabbath after the sham excommunication, to adopt the following address to the Bishop of Chicago, a copy which was sent to every bishop of the United States and Canada, and to Pope Pius IX:

"TO HIS LORDSHIP, ANTHONY O'REGAN OF CHICAGO: — We, the undersigned, inhabitants of the parish of St. Anne, Beaver settlement, seeing with sorrow that you have discarded our humble request, which we have sent you by the four delegates, and have persisted in trying to drive away our honest and worthy priest, who has edified us in all circumstances by this public and religious conduct, and having, contrary to the rules of our holy Church and common sense, struck our worthy pastor, Mr. Chiniquy, with excommunication, having caused him to be announced as a schismatic priest, and having forbidden us to communicate with him in religious matters, are hereby protesting against the unjust and iniquitous manner in which you have struck him, refusing him the privilege of justifying himself and proving his innocence.

"Consequently, we declare that we are ready at all times as good Catholics, to obey all your orders and ordinances that are in accordance with the laws of the Gospel and the Church, but that we are not willing to follow you in all your errors of judgments, in your injustices and covetous caprices. Considering Mr. Chiniquy as a good and virtuous priest, we have unanimously decided to keep him among us as our pastor; therefore praying your lordship not to put yourself to the trouble of seeking another priest for us. More yet; we have unanimously decided to sustain him and furnish him the means to go as far as Rome, if he cannot have justice in America.

"We further declare that it has been dishonorable and shameful for our bishop and for our holy religion to have seen, coming under the walls of our chapel, bringing the orders of the prince of the Church, a representative of Christ, three men covered with their sacerdotal garments, having their tongues half paralyzed by the effect of whiskey, and who, turning their backs to the Church, went to the house and the barn of one of our settlers and there emptied their bottles. And from there, taking their seats in the buggies, went toward the settlement of L'Erable, singing drunken songs and hallooing like wild Indians. Will your lordship be influenced by such a set of men, who seem to have for their mission to degrade the priesthood and Catholicism?

"We conclude, hoping that, changing your determination, you will work to the welfare of our holy religion, and not to its degradation, into which your intolerant conduct would lead us, and that you will not persist in trying to drive our worthy pastor, Rev. Charles Chiniquy, from the flourishing colony that he has founded at the cost of the abandonment of his native land, of the sacrifice of the high position he had in Canada; that you will bring peace between you and us, that we shall have in the Bishop of Chicago not a tyrant, but a father, and that you will have in us not rebels, but faithful children. Subscribing ourselves the obedient children of the Church.

"THEODORE DORIEN,	J.B. LEMOINE, N.P.,
"DET. VANIER,	OLIVER SENECHALL,
"J.B. BELANGER,	BASILIQUE ALLAIR,
"CAMILE BETOURNEY,	MICHEL ALLAIR,
"STAN'LAS GAGNE,	JOSEPH GRISI,
"ANTOINE ALLAIN,	JOSEPH ALLARD,

"And five hundred others."

This address was reproduced by almost the whole press in the United States. It fell as a thunderclap on the head of the heartless destroyer of our people. But it did not change his destructive plans. He published the most lying stories to explain his conduct, and to show the world that he had good reasons for destroying the French congregation of Chicago, and trying the same experiment on St. Anne.

With very few exceptions, the press of the state of Illinois, whose columns had so often echoed the cries of indignation raised everywhere against the tyranny of Bishop O'Regan, took sides with me. Hundreds of priests, not only from Illinois, but from every corner of the United States, addressed their warmest thanks to me for the stand I had taken, and asked me, in the name of God and for the honor of the Church, not to yield an inch of my rights. Unfortunately those priests disclosed their cowardice by putting in their letters "absolutely confidential."

However, this did not disturb me, my trust was not in my own strength, but in His protection. I was sure that I was in the right, that the Gospel of Christ was on my side, that all the canons and laws of the councils were in my favor. My library was filled with the best books on the canons and laws passed in the great councils of my Church and all stood in agreement with the course I had taken.

Above all, knowing the unanimous will of my people that I should remain with them and continue the great and good works so providentially entrusted to me in my colony, and regarding this as an indication of the Divine Will, I determined to remain, in spite of the Bishop of Chicago.

But if he were spiritually powerless against me, it was not so in temporal matters. His power and his desire to injure us had increased with his hatred, since he had read our letters and seen them in all the papers of Chicago. The first thing he did was to reconcile himself to the priest Lebel, whom he had turned out ignominiously from his diocese some time before. That priest had since obtained a fine situation in the diocese of Michigan.

He invited him to his palace, and petted him several days. I felt that the reconciliation of those two men meant nothing good for me. The air was soon filled with the strangest rumors against me. It was said everywhere that Mr. Lebel was to bring such charges against my character that I would be sent to the penitentiary.

What were the new iniquities to be laid to my charge? No one could tell. But the few partisans and friends of the bishop, Messrs. Lebel and Spink, were jubilant and sure that I was to be forever destroyed.

At last the time arrived when the Sheriff of Kankakee had to drag me again as a criminal and a prisoner to Urbana, and deliver me into the hands of the sheriff of that city. I arrived there on the 20th of October, with my lawyers, Messrs. Osgood and Paddock, and a dozen witnesses. Mr. Abraham Lincoln had preceded me only by a few minutes from Springfield.

The jury having been selected and sworn, the Rev. Mr. Lebel was the first witness called to testify and say what he knew against my character. Mr. Lincoln objected to that kind of testimony, and tried to prove that Mr. Spink had no right to bring his new suit against me by attacking my character. But Judge Davis ruled that the prosecution had that right in the case that was before him. Mr. Lebel had, then, full liberty to say anything he wanted. His testimony lasted nearly an hour, and was too long to be given here. I will only say that he began by declaring that "Chiniquy was one of the vilest men of the day — that every kind of bad rumors were constantly circulating against him."

He gave a good number of those rumors, though he could not positively swear if they were founded on truth or not, for he had not investigated them. But he said there was one of which he was sure, for he had authenticated it thoroughly. He expressed a great deal of apparent regret that he was forced to reveal to the world such things which were not only against the honor of Chiniquy, but, to some extent, involved the good name of a dear sister, Madame Bossey. But as he was to speak the truth before God, he could not help it — the sad truth was to be told. "Mr. Chiniquy," he said, "had attempted to do the most infamous thing with my own sister, Madame Bossey. She herself has told me the whole story under oath, and she would be here to unmask the wicked man today before the whole world, if she were not forced to silence at home with severe illness."

Though every word of that story was a perjury, there was such a color of truth and sincerity in my accuser that his testimony fell upon me and my lawyers and all my friends as a thunderbolt. My God only knows the weight and the bitterness of the waves of desolation which then passed over my soul.

After that testimony was given, there was a lull, and a most profound silence in the court room. All the eyes were turned upon me, and I heard many voices speaking of me, whispering, "The villain!" Though innocent, I wished that the ground would open under my feet to conceal me from the eyes of my friends and the whole world.

However, Mr. Lincoln soon interrupted the silence by addressing to Lebel such cross-questions that his testimony, in the minds of many, soon lost much of its power. And he did still more damage to Lebel's false oath, when he brought my twelve witnesses, who were among the most respectable citizens of Bourbonnais, formerly the parishioners of Mr. Lebel. Those twelve gentlemen swore that Mr. Lebel was such a drunkard and vicious man, that he was so publicly my enemy on account of many rebukes I had given to his private and public vices, that they would not believe a word of what he said, even upon his oath.

At ten p.m. the court adjourned, to meet again the next morning and I went to the room of Mr. Lincoln, with my two other lawyers. I could see in the face of my lawyers, though they tried to conceal it, that they were also full of anxiety.

"My dear Mr. Chiniquy," said Mr. Lincoln, "though I hope

tomorrow to destroy the testimony of Mr. Lebel against you, I must concede that I see great dangers ahead. There is not the least doubt in my mind that every word he has said is a sworn lie; but my fear is that the jury thinks differently. I am a pretty good judge in these matters. I feel that our jurymen think that you are guilty. There is only one way to perfectly destroy the power of a false witness — it is by another direct testimony against what he has said, or by showing from his very lips that he has perjured himself. I failed to do that last night, though I have diminished, to a great extent, the force of his testimony. Can you not prove an alibi, or can you not bring witnesses who were there in the same house that day, who would flatly and directly contradict what your remorseless enemy has said against you?"

I answered him: "How can I try to do such a thing when they have been shrewd enough not to state the date of the alleged crime against me?"

"You are correct, you are perfectly correct, Mr. Chiniquy," answered Mr. Lincoln, "as they have refused to precise the date, we cannot try that. I have never seen two such skillful rogues as those two priests. There is really a diabolical skill in the plan they have concocted for your destruction. It is evident that the bishop is at the bottom of the plot. You remember how I have forced Lebel to confess that he was now on the most friendly terms with the Bishop of Chicago, since he has become the chief of your accusers. Though I do not give up the hope of rescuing you from the hands of your enemies, I do not like to conceal from you that I have several reasons to fear that you will be declared guilty, and condemned to a heavy penalty, or to the penitentiary, though I am sure you are perfectly innocent.

"It is very probable that we will have to confront that sister of Lebel tomorrow. Her sickness is probably a feint, in order not to appear here except after the brother will have prepared the public mind in her favor. At all events, if she does not come, they will send some justice of the peace to get her sworn testimony, which will be more difficult to rebut than her own verbal declarations.

"That woman is evidently in the hands of the bishop and her brother priest, ready to swear anything they order her, and I know nothing so difficult as to refute such female testimonies, particularly when they are absent from the court. The only way to be sure of a favorable verdict tomorrow is, that God Almighty would take our part and show your innocence! Go to Him and pray, for He alone can save you." Mr. Lincoln was exceedingly solemn when he addressed those words to me, and they went very deep into my soul.

I have often been asked if Abraham Lincoln had any religion?

But I never had any doubt about his profound confidence in God, since I heard those words falling from his lips in that hour of anxiety. Unable to conceal my distress, burning tears were rolling on my cheeks while he was speaking, and there was on his face the expression of friendly sympathy which I shall never forget. Without being able to say a word, I left him to go to my little room.

From eleven p.m. to three in the morning I cried to God, and raised my supplicating hands to His throne of mercy. But I confess, to my confusion, it seemed to me in certain moments, that it was useless to pray and cry, for though innocent, I was doomed to perish. I was in the hands of my enemies. My God had forsaken me!

What an awful night I spent! I hope none of my readers will ever know by their own experience of the agony of spirit I endured. I had no other expectation than to be forever dishonored, and sent to the penitentiary next morning! But God had not forsaken me! He had again heard my cries, and was once more to show me His infinite mercy!

At three a.m. I heard three knocks at my door, and I quickly went to open it. Who was there? Abraham Lincoln, with a face beaming with joy! I could hardly believe my eyes. But I was not mistaken. It was my noble-hearted friend, the most honest lawyer of Illinois! — one of the noblest men Heaven had ever given to earth! — it was Abraham Lincoln. On seeing me bathed with tears, he exclaimed, "Cheer up, Mr. Chiniquy, I have the perjured priests in my hands. Their diabolical plot is all known, and if they do not fly away before the dawn of day, they will surely be lynched. Bless the Lord, you are saved."

The sudden passage of extreme desolation to an extreme joy came near killing me; unable to utter a single word, I took his hand, pressed it to my lips, and bathed it with tears of joy. I said: "May God forever bless you, dear Mr. Lincoln. But please tell me how you can bring me such glorious news!"

Here is the simple but marvelous story, as told me by that great and good man, whom God had made the messenger of His mercies towards me: "As soon as Lebel had given his perjured testimony against you yesterday," said Mr. Lincoln, "one of the agents of the Chicago press telegraphed to some of the principal papers of Chicago: 'It is probable that Mr. Chiniquy will be condemned; for the testimony of Rev. Mr. Lebel seems to leave no doubt that he is guilty.' And the little Irish boys, to sell their papers, filled the streets with cries: 'Chiniquy will be hung! Chiniquy will be hung!' The Roman Catholics were so glad to hear that, that ten thousand extra copies have been sold. Among those who bought those papers was a friend of yours called Terrien, who went to his wife and told her that you were to be condemned, and when the woman heard that, she said, 'It is too bad, for I know Mr. Chiniquy is not guilty.'"

"'How do you know that?' said the husband. She answered: 'I was there when the priest Lebel made the plot, and promised to give his sister two eighties of good land if she would swear a false oath and accuse him of a crime which that woman said he had not even thought of with her.'

"'If it be so,' said Terrien, 'we cannot allow Mr. Chiniquy to be condemned. Come with me to Urbana.'

"'But that woman being quite unwell,' said to her husband, 'You know well I cannot go; but Miss Philomene Moffat was with me then. She knows every particular of that wicked plot as well as I do. She is well; go and take her to Urbana. There is no doubt that her testimony will prevent the condemnation of Mr. Chiniquy.'

"Narcisse Terrien started immediately, and when you were praying God to come to your help, He was sending your deliverer at the full speed of the railroad cars. Miss Moffat has just given me the details of that diabolical plot. I have advised her not to show herself before the court is opened. I will then send for her, and when she will have given, under oath, before the court, the details she has just given me, I pity Spink with his perjured priests. As I told you, I would not be surprised if they were lynched; for there is a terrible excitement in town among many people, who from the beginning suspect that the priests have perjured themselves to destroy you. Now your suit is gained, and, tomorrow, you will have the greatest triumph a man ever got over his confounded foes. But you are in need of rest as well as myself. Good bye." After thanking God for that marvelous deliverance, I went to bed and took the needed rest.

But what was the priest Lebel doing in that very moment? Unable to sleep after the awful perjury he had just made, he had watched the arrival of the trains from Chicago with an anxious mind; for he was aware, through the confessions he had heard, that there were two persons in that city who knew his plot and his false oath; and though he had the promises from them that they would never reveal it to anybody, he was not without some fearful apprehension that I might, by some way or other, become acquainted with his abominable conspiracy. Not long after the arrival of the trains from Chicago, what was his dismay when he saw the first name entered was "Philomene Moffat!" That very name, Philomene Moffat, who some time before, had gone to confess to him that she had heard the whole plot from his own lips, when he had promised 160 acres of land to persuade his sister to perjure herself in order to destroy me. A deadly presentiment chilled the blood in his veins! "Would it be possible that this girl is here to reveal and prove my perjury before the world?"

He immediately sent for her, when she was just coming from meeting Mr. Lincoln.

"Miss Philomene Moffat here!" he exclaimed, when he saw her. "What are you coming here for this night?" he said.

"You will know it, sir, tomorrow morning," she answered.

"Ah! wretched girl! you come to destroy me?" he exclaimed.

She replied: "I do not come to destroy you, for you are already destroyed. Mr Lincoln knows everything."

"Oh! my God! my God!" he exclaimed, striking his forehead with his hands. Then taking a big bundle of bank notes from his pocket book, he said: "Here are one hundred dollars for you if you take the morning train and go back to Chicago."

"If you would offer me as much gold as this house could contain, I would not go," she replied.

He then left her abruptly, ran to the sleeping room of Spink, and told him: "Withdraw your suit against Chiniquy; we are lost; he knows all." Without losing a moment, he went to the sleeping room of his co-priest, and told him: "Make haste — dress yourself and let us take the train; we have no business here: Chiniquy knows all our secrets."

When an hour of opening the court came, there was an immense crowd, not only inside, but outside its walls. Mr. Spink, pale as a man condemned to death, rose before the judge and said: "Please the court, allow me to withdraw my prosecution against Mr. Chiniquy. I am now persuaded that he is not guilty of the faults brought against him before this tribunal."

Abraham Lincoln, having accepted that reparation in my name, made a short, but one of the most admirable speeches I have ever heard, on the cruel injustices I had suffered from my merciless persecutors. His terrible denouncement of the rascality of the priests who had perjured themselves proved how wise they had been to fly away and disappear before the opening of the court, for the whole city was ransacked for them by hundreds who blamed me for forgiving them and refusing to have my revenge for the wrong they had done me. But I really thought that my enemies were sufficiently punished by the awful public disclosures of their infernal plot. It seemed that the dear Saviour, who had so visibly protected me, was to be obeyed, when He was whispering in my soul, "Forgive them and love them as thyself."

Was not Spink sufficiently punished by the complete ruin which was brought upon him by the loss of the suit? For having gone to Bishop O'Regan to be indemnified for the enormous expenses of such a long prosecution, at such a distance, the bishop coldly answered him: "I had promised to indemnify if you would put Chiniquy down, as you promised me. But as it is Chiniquy who has put you down, I have not a cent to give you."

Abraham Lincoln had not only defended me with the zeal and talent of the ablest lawyer I have ever known, but as the most devoted and noblest friend I ever had. After pleading during two long sessions of the court of Urbana, without receiving a cent from me, I considered that I was owing him a great sum of money. My two other lawyers, who had not done the half of his work, asked me a thousand dollars each, and I had not thought that too much. After thanking him for the inappreciable services he had rendered me, I requested him to show me his bill, assuring him that, though I would not be able to pay the whole cash, I would pay him to the last cent, if he had the kindness to wait a little for the balance.

He answered me with a smile and an air of inimitable kindness, which was peculiar to him: "My dear Mr. Chiniquy, I feel proud and honored to have been called to defend you. But I have done it less as a lawyer than as a friend. The money I should receive from you would take away the pleasure I feel at having fought your battle. Your case is unique in my whole practice. I have never met a man so cruelly persecuted as you have been, and who deserves it so little. Your enemies are devils incarnate. The plot they had concocted against you is the most hellish one I ever knew. But the way you have been saved from their hands, the appearance of that young and intelligent Miss Moffat, who was really sent by God in the very hour of need, when, I confess it again, I thought everything was nearly lost, is one of the most extraordinary occurrences I ever saw. It makes me remember what I have too often forgotten, and what my mother often told me when young — that our God is a prayer-hearing God. This good thought, sown into my young heart by that dear mother's hand, was just in my mind when I told you, 'Go and pray, God alone can save you.' But I confess to you that I had not faith enough to believe that your prayer would be so quickly and so marvelously answered. Now let us speak of what you owe me. Well! Well! how much do you owe me? You owe me nothing! for I suppose you are quite ruined. The expense of such a suit, I know, must be enormous. Your enemies want to ruin you. Will I help them to finish your ruin, when I hope I have the right to be put among the most sincere and devoted of your friends?"

"You are right," I answered him, "you are the most devoted and noblest friend God ever gave to me, and I am nearly ruined by my enemies. But you are the father of a pretty large family; you must support them. Your traveling expenses in coming twice here for me from Springfield; your hotel bills during the two terms you have defended me, must be very considerable. It is not just that you should receive nothing in return for such work and expenses."

"Well! well!" he answered, "I will give you a promissory note which you will sign." Taking then a small piece of paper, he wrote:

Urbana, May 23-1857
Due A Lincoln
fifty dollars,
for value received.
C Chiniquy

He handed me the note, saying, "Can you sign that?"

After reading it, I said, "Dear Mr. Lincoln, this is a joke. It is not possible that you ask only fifty dollars for services which are worth at least two thousand dollars."

He then tapped me with the right hand on the shoulder and said: "Sign that; it is enough. I will pinch some rich men for that, and make them pay the rest of the bill," and he laughed outright.

The relaxation of the great strain upon my mind, and the great kindness of my benefactor and defender in charging me so little for such a service, and the terrible presentiment that he would pay with his life what he had done for me caused me to break into sobs and tears.

"Father Chiniquy, what are you crying for?

"Dear Mr. Lincoln," I answered, "allow me to tell you that the joy I should naturally feel for such a victory is destroyed in my mind by the fear of what it may cost you. There were in the court not less than ten or twelve Jesuits from Chicago and St. Louis, who came to hear my sentence of condemnation to the penitentiary. But it was on their heads that you have brought the thunders of heaven and earth! nothing can be compared to the expression of their rage against you, when you not only wrenched me from their cruel hands, but you were making the walls of the courthouse tremble under the awful and superhumanly eloquent denunciation of their infamy, diabolical malice, and total want of Christian and human principle, in the plot they had formed for my destruction. What troubles my soul just now and draws my tears, is that it seems to me that I have read your sentence of death in their fiendish eyes. How many other noble victims have already fallen at their feet!"

He tried to divert my mind, at first, with a joke, "Sign this," said he, "it will be my warrant of death."

But after I had signed, he became more solemn, and said, "I know that Jesuits never forget nor forsake. But man must not care how and where he dies, provided he dies at the post of honor and duty," and he left me.

CHAPTER LIV

In 1851 I was contacted by an Irishman, D'Arcy McGee, editor of *The Freeman's Journal,* official Journal of the Bishop of New York. Mr. McGee was very interested not only in my colonization work but the temperance movement as well. Through our correspondence it became apparent we were of the same mind.

Mr. McGee had determined to head a colonization project guiding his fellow countrymen to the fertile lands of the west, as the living conditions of the majority of Irish Roman Catholics were on a par with the people of Beauport prior to my arrival in that city.

I attended a large assembly, principally composed of priests, who met at Buffalo, in the spring of 1852. But what was his disappointment, when he saw that the greatest part of those priests were sent by the bishops of the United States to oppose and defeat his plans!

Though he spoke with burning eloquence, the majority coldly answered him: "We are also determined to take possession of the United States; but we must proceed with the utmost secrecy and wisdom. What does a skillful general do when he wants to conquer a country? Does he scatter his soldiers over the farm lands, and spend their energy in plowing the fields? No! he keeps them close to his flanks and marching toward the strongholds: the rich and powerful cities. The farming countries then submit and become the price of this victory without moving a finger to subdue them.

"So it is with us. Silently and patiently, we must mass our Roman Catholics in the great cities of the United States, remembering that the vote of a poor journeyman, though he be covered with rags, has as much weight in the scale of power as the millionaire Astor, and that if we have two votes against his one, he will become as powerless as an oyster. Let us then multiply our votes; let us call our poor but faithful Irish Catholics from every corner of the world, and gather them into the very hearts of the cities of Washington, New York, Boston, Chicago, Buffalo, Albany, Troy, Cincinnati, etc.

"Under the shadows of those great cities, the Americans consider themselves a giant unconquerable race. They look upon the poor Irish Catholics wth supreme contempt, as only fit to dig their canals, sweep their streets and work in their kitchens. Let no one awake those sleeping lions, today. Let us pray God that they continue to sleep a few years longer, waking only to find their votes outnumbered as we will turn them forever, out of every position of honor, power and profit! When not a single judge or policeman, will be elected if he be not a devoted Irish Catholic! What will those so-called giants think when not a single senator or member of Congress will be chosen, unless he has submitted to our holy father the pope!

"We will not only elect the president, but fill and command the armies, man the navies and hold the keys of the public treasury. It will then be time for our faithful Irish people to give up their grog shops, in order to become the judges and governors of the land.

"Then, yes! then, we will rule the United States, and lay them at the feet of the Vicar of Jesus Christ, that he may put an end to their godless system of education, and impious laws of liberty of conscience which are an insult to God and man!"

D'Arcy McGee was left almost alone when the votes were taken. From that, the Catholic priests gathered their Irish legions into the great cities of the United States of America. The day is very near when the Jesuits will rule every aspect of their country. They are already the masters of New York, Baltimore, Chicago, St. Paul, New Orleans, Mobile, Savannah, Cincinnati, Albany, Troy, Milwaukee, St. Louis, San Francisco, etc. Yes! San Francisco the rich, the great queen of the Pacific, is in the hands of the Jesuits!

From the very first days of the discovery of the gold mines of California, the Jesuits had the hopes of becoming masters of those inexhaustible treasures, and they secretly laid their plans, with the most profound ability and success. The Jesuits saw at a glance that if they could persuade the Irish Catholics to settle and remain there, they would soon be the masters and rulers of that golden city whose future is so bright and great!

The consequence is, that while you find only a few Americans, Germans, Scotch, and English millionaires in San Francisco, you find more than fifty Catholic Irish millionaires in that city. Its richest bank (Nevada Bank) is in their hands, and so are all the street railways. The principal offices of the city are filled with Irish Roman Catholics. Almost all the police are composed of the same class, as well as the volunteer military associations. Their compact unity, in the hands of the Jesuits, with their enormous wealth, make them almost supreme masters of the mines of California and Nevada.

When one knows the absolute, abject submission of the Irish Roman Catholics, rich or poor, to their priests, how the mind, the soul, the will, the conscience, are firmly and irrevocably tied to the feet of their priests, he can easily understand that the Jesuits of the United States form one of the richest and most powerful corporations the world ever saw. It is well known that those fifty Catholic millionaires, with their myriads of employees are, through their wives, and by themselves, continually at the feet of their Jesuit confessors. Where the Jesuits rule, there is little hope for a true Protestant to ever have a lucrative office in the United States today.

It is to San Francisco that you must go to have an idea of the number of secret and powerful organizations with which the Church of Rome prepares for the impending conflict, through which she hopes to destroy the schools, and every vestige of human rights and liberties in the United States.

In order to more easily drill the Roman Catholics and prepare them for this struggle, the Jesuits have organized them into a great number of secret societies, the principal of which are: Ancient Order of Hibernian, Irish American Society, Knights of St. Patrick, St. Patrick's Cadets, St. Patrick Mutual Alliance, Apostles of Liberty, Benevolent Sons of the Emerald Isle, Knights of St. Peter, Knights of the Red Branch, Knights of the Columskill, The Secret Heart, etc., etc.

Almost all these secret associations are military ones. They have their headquarters at San Francisco, but their rank and file are scattered all over the United States. They number 700,000 soldiers, who, under the name of U.S. Volunteer Militia, are officered by some of the most skillful generals and officers of this republic.

Another fact, to which the American Protestants do not sufficiently pay attention, is that the Jesuits have been shrewd enough to have a vast majority of Roman Catholic generals and officers to command the army and man the navy of the United States.

Long before I was ordained a priest, I knew that my Church was the most implacable enemy of this republic. My professors of philosophy, history, and theology had been unanimous in telling me that the principles and laws of the Church of Rome were absolutely antagonistic to the laws and principles which are the foundation stones of the Constitution of the United States.

1st. The most sacred principle of the United States Constitution is the equality of every citizen before the law. But the fundamental principle of the Church of Rome is the denial of that equality.

2nd. Liberty of conscience is proclaimed by the United States, a most sacred principle which every citizen must uphold, even at the price of his blood. But liberty of conscience is declared by all the popes and councils of Rome, a most godless, unholy, and diabolical thing, which every good Catholic must abhor and destroy at any cost.

3rd. The American Constitution assures the absolute independence of the civil from the the ecclesiastical or church power; but the Church of Rome declares, through all her pontiffs and councils, that such independence is an impiety and revolt against God.

4th. The American Constitution leaves every man free to serve God according to the dictates of his conscience; but the Church of Rome declares that no man has ever had such a right, and that the pope alone can know and say what man must believe and do.

5th. The Constitution of the United States denies the right in any body to punish any other for differing from him in religion. But the Church of Rome says that she has the right to punish with the confiscation of their goods, or the penalty of death, those who differ in faith from the pope.

6th. The United States have established schools all over their immense territories, where they invite the people to send their children, that they may cultivate their intelligence and become good and useful citizens. But the Church of Rome has publicly cursed all those schools, and forbidden their children to attend them, under pain of excommunication in this world and damnation in the next.

7th. The Constitution of the United States is based on the principle that the people are the primary source of all civil power. But hundred of times, the Church of Rome has proclaimed that this principle is impious and heretical. She says that "all government must rest upon the foundation of the Catholic faith; with the pope alone as the legitimate and infallible source and interpreter of the law."

I could cite many other facts, proving the Church of Rome to be an irreconcilable enemy of the United States; but it would be too long. Rome is a viper, sooner or later that viper will bite and kill this republic. This was foretold by Lafayette, and is now promulgated by the greatest thinkers of our time.

The great inventor of electric telegraphy, Samuel Morse, found it out when in Rome, and published it in 1834, in his remarkable work, "Conspiracies Against the Liberties of the United States." The learned Dr. S. Ireneus Prime, in his life of Professor Morse, says, "When Mr. Morse was in Italy, he became acquainted with several ecclesiastics of the Church of Rome, and he was led to believe, from what he learned from them, that a political conspiracy, under the cloak of a religious mission, was formed against the United States. When he came to Paris and enjoyed the confidence and friendship of Lafayette, he stated his convictions to the general, who fully concurred with him in the reality of such a conspiracy."

That great statesman and patriot, Richard W. Thompson, Secretary of the Navy, in his admirable work, *The Papacy and the Civil Power,* says, "Nothing is plainer than that, if the principles of the Church of Rome prevail here, our Constitution would necessarily fall. The two cannot exist together. They are in open and direct antagonism with the fundamental theory of our government and of all popular government everywhere."

The eloquent Spanish orator, Castelar, speaking of his own Church of Rome, said, in 1869: "There is not a single progressive principle that has not been cursed by the Catholic Church. This is true of England and Germany, as well as all Catholic countries. The Church cursed the French Revolution, the Belgian Constitution, and the Italian Independence. Not a constitution has been born, not a step of progress made, not a solitary reform effected, which has not been under terrific anathemas of the Church.

Why ask the testimony of Protestants or Liberals to warn the American people against that conspiracy, when we have the public testimony of all the bishops and priests to prove it? Read for yourselves the position taken by the Church of Rome today. I give you the following unimpeachable documents.

"The Church is of necessity intolerant. Heresy she endures when and where she must, but she hates it and directs all her energies to destroy it."

"If Catholics ever gain a sufficient numerical majority in this country, religious freedom is at an end. So our enemies say, so we believe." *(The Shepherd of the Valley,* official journal of the Bishop of St. Louis, Nov. 23, 1851.)

"No man has a right to choose his religion." *(New York Freeman,* official journal of Bishop Hughes, Jan. 26, 1852.)

"The Church . . . does not, and cannot accept, or in any degree favor, liberty in the Protestant sense of liberty." *(Catholic World,* April, 1870.)

"The Catholic Church is the medium and channel through

which the will of God is expressed. While the State has rights, she has them only in virtue and by permission of the Superior Authority, and that authority can be expressed only through the Church." *(Catholic World,* July, 1870.)

"Protestanism has not, and never can have, any right where Catholicity has triumphed." *(Catholic Review,* June, 1875.)

"Religious Liberty is merely endured until the opposite can be carried into effect without peril to the Catholic Church." (Rt. Rev. O'Connor, Bishop of Pittsburgh.)

"There is, ere long, to be a state religion in this country, and that state religion is to be the Roman Catholic.

"1st. The Roman Catholic is to wield his vote for the purpose of securing Catholic ascendancy in this country.

"2nd. All legislation must be governed by the will of God, unerringly indicated by the pope.

"3rd. Education must be controlled by Catholic authorities, and under education the opinions of the individual and the utterances of the press are included, and many opinions are to be forbidden by the secular arm, under the authority of the Church, even to war and bloodshed." (Father Hecker, *Catholic World,* July, 1870.)

"It was proposed that all religious persuasions should be free and their worship publicly exercised. But we have rejected this article as contrary to the canons and councils of the first Catholic Church." (Pope Pius VII, *Encyclical,* 1808.)

One of the first and most solemn acts of the present Pope, Leo XIII, was to order that the theology of St. Thomas Aquinas be taught in all colleges, seminaries, and universities of the Church of Rome, as the most accurate teaching of the doctrines of his Church. On the 30th December, 1880, I forced the Rt. Rev. Foley, Bishop of Chicago, to translate from Latin into English, before the court of Kankakee, and to swear that the following law was among those promulgated by St. Thomas as one of the present and unchangeable laws of the Church of Rome:

"Though heretics must not be tolerated because they deserve it, we must bear with them, till, by a second admonition, they may be brought back to the faith of the Church. But those who, after a second admonition, remain obstinate in their errors, must not only be excommunicated, but they must be delivered to the secular power to be exterminated." (St. Thomas Aquinas, *Summa Theologia,* Vol. iv. p. 90.)

After the bishop had sworn that this was the true doctrine of the Church of Rome expressed by St. Thomas, and taught in all the colleges, seminaries, and universities of the Church of Rome, I forced him to declare, under oath, that he, and every priest of

Rome, once a year, under pain of eternal damnation, is obliged to say, in the presence of God, in his Breviarum (his official prayer book), that that doctrine was so good and holy, that every word of t has been inspired by the Holy Ghost to St. Thomas.

The same Bishop Foley was again forced by me, before the same court of Kankakee, to translate from Latin into English, the following decree of the Council of Lateran, and to acknowledge, under oath, that it was as much the law of the Church of Rome today as on the day it was passed in the year 1215.

"We excommunicate and anathematize every heresy that exalts itself against the holy orthodox and Catholic faith, condemning all heretics, by whatever name they may be known, for though their faces differ, they are tied together by their tails. Such as are condemned are to be delivered over to the existing secular powers to receive due punishment. If laymen, their goods must be confiscated. If priests, they shall be degraded from their respective orders, and their property applied to the church in which they officiated. Secular powers of all ranks and degrees are to be warned, induced, and, if necessary, compelled by ecclesiastical censure, to swear that they will exert themselves to the utmost in the defense of the faith, and extirpate all heretics denounced by the Church, who shall be found in their territories. And whenever any person shall assume government, whether it be spiritual or temporal, he shall be bound to abide by this decree.

"If any temporal lord, after having been admonished and required by the Church, shall neglect to clear his territory of heretical depravity, the Metropolitan and Bishop of the Province, shall unite in excommunicating him. Should he remain contumacious a whole year, the fact shall be signified to the Supreme Pontiff, who will declare his vassals released from their allegiance from that time, and will bestow his territory on Catholics, to be occupied by them, on condition of exterminating the heretics and preserving the said territory in the faith.

"Catholics who shall assume the cross for the extermination of heretics, shall enjoy the same indulgence, and be protected by the same privileges as are granted to those who go to the help of the Holy Land. We decree further that all those who have dealings with heretics, and especially such as receive, defend and encourage them, shall be excommunicated. He shall not be eligible to any public office. He shall not be admitted as a witness. He shall neither have the power to bequeath his property by will, nor succeed to an inheritance. He shall not bring any action against any person, but any one can bring action against him. Should he be a judge, his decision shall have no force, nor shall any cause be brought before him. Should he be an advocate, he shall not be allowed to plead. Should he be a lawyer, no instruments made by him shall be held valid, but shall be condemned with their authors."

Cardinal Manning, speaking in the name of the pope, said: "I acknowledge no civil power; I am the subject of no prince; and I claim more than this. I claim to be the supreme judge and director of the conscience of men — of the peasants that till the fields, and of the prince that sits upon the throne; of the household that lives in the shade of privacy, and the legislator that makes laws for kingdoms — I am sole, last, supreme judge of what is right and wrong. Moreover, we declare, affirm, define, and pronounce it to be necessary to salvation to every human creature, to be subject to the Roman Pontiff!!" *(Tablet,* Oct. 9, 1864.)

"Undoubtedly it is the intention of the pope to possess this country. In this intention he is aided by the Jesuits, and all the Catholic prelates and priests." *(Brownson's Review,* May, 1864.)

"No good government can exist without religion, and there can be no religion without an Inquisition, which is wisely designed for the promotion and protection of the true faith." *(Boston Pilot,* official journal of the Bishop.)

"The power of the Church exercised over sovereigns in the Middle Ages was not a usurpaton, was not derived from the concessions of princes or the consent of the people, but was and is held by divine right, and whoso resists it rebels against the King of kings and Lord of lords." *(Brownson's Review,* June, 1851.)

The Council of Constance, held in 1414, declared, "That any person who has promised security to heretics shall not be obliged to keep his promise, by whatever he may be engaged." Under this principle John Huss was publicly burned the 6th July, 1415, in the city of Constance, though he had a safe passport from the Emperor.

"Negroes have no rights which the white man is bound to respect." (Roman Catholic Chief-Justice Taney, in his Dred Scot Decision.)

"If the liberties of the American people are ever destroyed, they will fall by the hands of the Catholic clergy." — Lafayette.

"See, sir, from this chamber, I govern, not only to Paris, but to China; not only to China, but to all the world, without anyone knowing how I do it." *(Tamburini,* General of the Jesuits.)

"A man who has been excommunicated by the Pope may be killed anywhere." (Busembaum.— Lacroix, *Theologia Moralis,* 1757.)

"If, then, you receive a command from one who holds the place of God, you should observe it as if it came from God Himself. It may be added that there is more certainty of doing the will of God by obedience to our superiors than by obedience to Jesus Christ, should He appear in person and give His command." (Saint Liguori, *The Nun Sanctified.*)

"The Jesuits are a *military organization,* not a religious order. Their chief is a general of an army, not the mere father abbot of a monastery. And the aim of this organization is: POWER. Power in its most despotic exercise. Absolute power, universal power, power to control the world by the volition of a single man. Jesuitism is the most absolute of despotisms; and at the same time the greatest and the most enormous of abuses." (*Memorial of the Captivity of Napoleon at St. Helena,* by General Montholon, Vol. ii p. 62.)

In the allocution of September, 1851, Pope Pius IX said:

"That he had taken the principle for basis: That the Catholic religion, with all its votes, ought to be exclusively dominant in such sort that every other worship shall be banished and interdicted.!

"You ask if the Pope were lord over this land and you were in a minority, what he would do to you? That, we say, would entirely depend on circumstances. If it would benefit the cause of Catholicism, he would tolerate you: if expedient, he would imprison, banish you, probably he might even hang you. But be assured of one thing, he would never tolerate you for the sake of your glorious principles of civil and religious liberty." (*Rambler,* one of the most prominent Catholic papers of England, Sept., 1851.)

Lord Acton, one of the Roman Catholic peers of England, reproaching her bloody and anti-social laws to his own church, wrote: "Pope Gregory VII decided it was no murder to kill excommunicated persons. This rule was incorporated in *the canon law.* During the revision of the code, which took place in the 16th century, and which produced a whole volume of corrections, the passage was allowed to stand. It appears in every reprint of the *Corpus Juris.* It has been for 700 years, and continues to be, part of the ecclesiastical law. Far from being a dead letter, it obtained a new application in the days of the Inquisition; and one of the later Popes has declared that the murder of a Protestant is so good a deed that it atones, and more than atones, for the murder of a Catholic." (*The London Times,* July 20, 1872.)

In the last council of the Vatican, has the Church of Rome expressed any regret for having promulgated and executed such bloody laws? No! On the contrary, she has anathematized all those who think or say that she was wrong when she deluged the world with the blood of the millions she ordered to be slaughtered to quench her thirst for blood; she positively said that she had the right to punish those heretics by tortures and death.

Those bloody and anti-social laws, were written on the banners of the Roman Catholics, when slaughtering 100,000 Waldenses in the mountains of Piedmont, and more than 50,000 defenseless men, women and children in the city of Bezieres. It is under the inspiration of those diabolical laws of Rome, that 75,000 Protestants were massacred the night and following week of St. Bartholomew.

It was to obey those bloody laws that Louis XIV revoked the Edict of Nantes, caused the death of half a million of men, women, and children, who perished in all the highways of France, and caused twice that number to die in the land of exile, where they had found a refuge.

Those anti-social laws, today, are written on her banners with the blood of ten millions of martyrs. It is under those bloody banners that 6,000 Roman Catholic priests, Jesuits and bishops, in the United States, are marching to the conquest of this republic, backed by their seven millions of blind and obedient slaves.

Those laws, which are still the ruling laws of Rome, were the main cause of the last rebellion of the Southern States.

Yes! without Romanism, the last awful Civil War would have been impossible. Jeff Davis would never have dared to attack the North, had he not had assurance from the Pope, that the Jesuits, the bishops, the priests and the whole people of the Church of Rome, under the name and mask of democracy, would help him.

These diabolical and anti-social laws of Rome caused a Roman Catholic (Beauregard) to be the man chosen to fire the first gun at Fort Sumter, against the flag of Liberty, on the 12th of April, 1861. Those anti-christian and anti-social laws caused the Pope of Rome to be the only crowned prince in the whole world, so depraved as to publicly shake hands with Jeff Davis, and proclaim him president of a legitimate government.

These are the laws which led the assassins of Abraham Lincoln to the house of a rabid Roman Catholic woman, Mary Surratt, which was not only the rendezvous of the priests of Washington, but the very dwelling-house of some of them.

Those bloody and infernal laws of Rome nerved the arm of the Roman Catholic, Booth, when he slaughtered one of the noblest men God has ever given to the world.

Those bloody and anti-social laws of Rome, after having covered Europe with ruins, tears, and blood for ten centuries, have crossed the oceans to continue their work of slavery and desolation, blood and tears, ignorance and demoralization on this continent. Under the mask and name of democracy they have raised the standard of rebellion of the South against the North, and caused more than half a million of the most heroic sons of America to fall on the fields of carnage.

In a very near future, if God does not miraculously prevent it, those laws of dark deeds and blood will cause the prosperity, the rights, the education, and the liberties of this too confident nation to be buried under a mountain of smoking and bloody ruins. On the top of that mountain, Rome will raise her throne and plant her victorious banners.

Then she will sing her *Te Deums* and shout her shouts of joy, as she did when she heard the lamentations and cries of desolation of the millions of martyrs in the capitals and great cities of Europe.

CHAPTER LV

Rome saw at once that the very existence of the United States was a formidable menace to her own life. From the very beginning she perfidiously sowed the germs of division and hatred between the two great sections of this country and succeeded in dividing South from North on the burning question of slavery. That division was her golden opportunity to crush one by the other, and reign over the bloody ruins of both, a favored, long-standing policy. She hoped that the hour of her supreme triumph over this continent was come. She ordered the Emperor of France to be ready with an army in Mexico ready to support the South, and she bade all Roman Catholics to enroll themselves under the banners of slavery by joining themselves to the Democratic party. Only one bishop dared to disobey.

Above everything, the order was handed down to oppose the election of Lincoln at all cost. The Democratic press, almost entirely under Roman Catholic control and a devoted tool of the Jesuits, deluged the country with the most fearful denunciations. They called him an ape, a stupid brute, a most dangerous lunatic, a bloody monster, a merciless tyrant, etc.,etc. Rome ransacked the English dictionary to find the most suitable expressions to fill the people with contempt, hatred, and horror against him. But God decreed that honest Abraham Lincoln should be proclaimed President of the United States, the 4th of March, 1861.

At the end of August, I learned from a Roman Catholic priest, whom, by the mercy of God, I had persuaded to leave the errors of popery, that there was a plot among them to assassinate the president, I thought it was my duty to go and tell him what I knew.

He received me with greatest cordiality and kindness. "I am so glad to meet you again," he said: "you see that your friends, the Jesuits, have not yet killed me. But they would have surely done it when I passed through their most devoted city, Baltimore, had I not passed by incognito a few hours before they expected me. We have proof that the company which had been selected and organized to murder me was led by a rabid Roman Catholic, called Byrne; it was almost entirely composed of Roman Catholics; more than that, there were two disguised priests among them, to lead and encourage them. I am sorry to have so little time to see you: but I will not let you go before telling you that, a few days ago, I saw Mr. Morse, the learned inventor or electric telegraphy: he told me that when he was in Rome, not long ago, he found out the proofs of a most formidable conspiracy against this country and all its institutions. It is evident that it is to the intrigues and emissaries of the pope that we owe, in great part, the horrible civil war which is threatening to cover the country with blood and ruins.

"I am sorry that Professor Morse had to leave Rome before he could know more about the secret plans of the Jesuits against the liberties and the very existence of this country. But do you know that I want you to take his place and continue that investigation? My plan is to attach you to my ambassador of France, as one of the secretaries. In that honorable position you would go from Paris to Rome, where you might find, through the directions of Mr. Morse, an opportunity of reuniting the broken threads of his researches. 'It takes a Greek to fight a Greek.' As you have been twenty-five years a priest of Rome, I do not know any man in the United States so well acquainted as you are with the tricks of the Jesuits, and on whom I could better rely. What do you think of that?"

"My dear president," I answered, "I feel overwhelmed by your kindness. Surely nothing could be more pleasant to me than to grant your request. The honor you want to confer upon me is much above my merit, but my conscience tells me that I cannot give up the preaching of the Gospel to my poor French Canadian countrymen. I feel that I am the servant, the ambassador of One who is above even the good and great president of the United States. I appeal to your own Christian and honorable feelings to know if I can forsake the one for the other."

The president became very solemn, and replied: "You are right! There is nothing so great under heaven as to be the ambassador of Christ."

Then with one of his fine jokes, he said: "Yes! yes! You are the ambassador of a greater Prince than I am, but He does not pay you with so good cash as I would do." He then added: "I am exceedingly pleased to see you. However, I am so pressed by most important affairs; could you please come again tomorrow at ten o'clock. I have a very important question to ask you on a matter which has been constantly before my mind these last few weeks."

The next day at the appointed hour my noble friend said: "I could not give you more than ten minutes yesterday, but I will give you twenty today. I want your views about a thing which is exceedingly puzzling to me, and you are the only one to whom I like to speak on that subject. A great number of Democratic papers, evidently written by Roman Catholics, publish that I was born a Roman Catholic, and baptized by a priest. They call me a renegade, an apostate, and they heap upon my head mountains of abuses. At first I laughed at that, for it is a lie. Thanks be to God, I have never been a Roman Catholic. No priest of Rome has ever laid his hand on my head. But their persistency in this falsehood must have a meaning. Please tell me what you think."

"My dear president," I answered, "it was just this strange story which brought me here yesterday. I wept as a child when I read it for the first time. For I believe that it is your sentence of death and I have from the lips of a converted priest, that they have invented this falsehood to excite the fanaticism of the Roman Catholic murderers, whom they hope to find sooner or later, to strike you down. They want to brand your face with the ignominious mark of apostasy. In the Church of Rome an apostate is an outcast who has no place in society and no right to live.

"I have brought to you the theology of one of the most learned and approved of the Jesuits of his time, Busembaum, who, with many others, say that the man who will kill you will do a good and holy work. More than that, here is a copy of a decree of Gregory VII, proclaiming that the killing of an apostate, as you are declared to be, is not murder; nay, that it is a good, a Christian action. That decree is incorporated in the canon law, which every priest must study, and which every good Catholic must follow.

"My dear president, I must repeat what I said at Urbana in 1856. I fear you will fall under the blows of a Jesuit assassin if you do not pay more attention to protect yourself. Remember that because Coligny was an heretic, as you are, he was brutally murdered in the St. Bartholomew night; that Henry IV was stabbed by the Jesuit assassin, Revaillac, the 14th of May, 1610, for having given liberty of conscience to his people; and that William the Taciturn was shot dead by another Jesuit murderer, called Girard, for having broken the yoke of the pope. The Church of Rome is absolutely the same and does believe and teach today, as then, that she has the right and duty to punish by death any heretic who is an obstacle to her designs.

"The Catholic hierarchy of the United States is on the side of the rebels as incontrovertible evidence that Rome wants to destroy this republic. You are, by your personal virtues, your popularity, your love for liberty, your position, the greatest obstacle to their diabolical schemes. Their hatred is concentrated upon you. My blood chills when I contemplate the day when Rome will add to all her other iniquities the murder of Abraham Lincoln."

When saying these things to the president, I was exceedingly moved, my voice was choked, and I could hardly retain my tears. But the president was perfectly calm. When I had finished speaking, he took the volume of Busembaum from my hand, read the lines which I had marked with red and I helped him to translate them into English. He then gave me back the book, and said:

"I will repeat to you what I said at Urbana: 'Man must not care where and when he will die, provided he dies at the post of honor and duty.' But I may add today, that I have presentiment that God will call me to Him through the hand of an assassin. Let His will, and, not mine be done!" He then looked at his watch and said, "I am sorry that the twenty minutes I had consecrated to our interview have almost passed away; I will be forever grateful for the warning words you have addressed to me about the dangers ahead to my life, from Rome. I know that they are not imaginary dangers. If I were fighting against a Protestant South, as a nation, there would be no danger of assassination. The nations who read the Bible fight bravely on the battle fields, but they do not assassinate their enemies. The pope and the Jesuits, with their inferna' Inquisition, are the only organized powers in the world which have recourse to the dagger of the assassin to murder those whom they cannot convince with their arguments or conquer with the sword.

"Unfortunately, I feel more and more every day, that it is not against the Americans of the South, alone, I am fighting, it is more against the pope of Rome, his perfidious Jesuits and their blind and blood-thirsty slaves. As long as they hope to conquer the North, they will spare me; but the day we rout their armies, take their cities and force then to submit, then, it is my impression that the Jesuits, who are the principal rulers of the South will do what they have almost invariably done in the past. The dagger or the pistol will do what the strong hands of the warriors could not achieve. This civil war seems to be nothing but a political affair to those who do not see, as I do, the secret springs of that terrible drama. But it is more a religious than a civil war. It is Rome who wants to rule and degrade the North, as she has ruled and degraded the South, from the very day of its discovery. There are only very few of the Southern leaders who are not more or less under the influence of the Jesuits, through their wives, family relations, and their friends. Several members of the family of Jeff Davis belong the the Church of Rome. Even the Protestant ministers are under the influence of the Jesuits without suspecting it. To keep her ascendancy in the North, as she does in the South, Rome is doing here what she has done in Mexico, and in all the South American Republics; she is paralyzing, by civil war, the arms of the soldiers of liberty. She divides our nation in order to weaken, subdue and rule it.

"Surely we have some brave and reliable Roman Catholic officers and soldiers in our armies, but they form an insignificant minority when compared with the Roman Catholic traitors against whom we have to guard ourselves, day and night. The fact is, that the immense majority of Roman Catholic bishops, priests and laymen, are rebels in heart, when they cannot be in fact; with very few exceptions, they are publicly in favor of slavery. I understand, now, why the patriots of France, who determined to see the colors of liberty floating over their great and beautiful country, were forced to hang or shoot almost all the priests and the monks as the irreconcilable enemies of liberty. For it is now evident to me, that, with very few exceptions, every priest and every true Roman Catholic is a determined enemy of liberty. Their extermination in France was one of those terrible necessities which no human wisdom could avoid; it looks to me now as an order from heaven to save France. May God grant that the same terrible necessity be never felt in the United States! But it is very certain that if the American people could learn what I know of the fierce hatred of the priests of Rome against our institutions, our schools, our most sacred rights, and our so dearly bought liberties, they would drive them away tomorrow from among us, or they would shoot them as traitors. But you are the only one to whom I reveal these sad secrets for I know that you learned them before me. The history of these last thousand years tells us that wherever the Church of Rome is not a dagger to pierce the bosom of a free nation, she is a stone to her neck, to paralyze her, and prevent her advance in the ways of civilization, science, intelligence, happiness and liberty. But I forgot that my twenty minutes are gone long ago.

"Please accept my sincere thanks for the new light you have given me on the dangers of my position, and come again. I will always see you with a new pleasure."

My second visit to Abraham Lincoln was at the beginning of June, 1862. But I found him so busy that I could only shake hands with him. The third and last time I went to pay my respects to the doomed president was on the morning of June 8th, 1864, when he was absolutely beseiged by people who wanted to see him. After a kind and warm shaking of hands, he said:

"I am much pleased to see you again. But it is impossible, today, to say anything more than this: Tomorrow afternoon, I will receive the delegation of the deputies of all the loyal states, sent to officially announce the desire of the country that I should remain the president four years more. I invite you to be present with them at that interesting meeting. You will see some of the most prominent men of our republic, and I will be glad to introduce you to them. You will not present yourself as a delegate of the people, but only as the guest of the president; and that there may be no trouble, I will give you this card, with a permit to enter the delegation. But do not leave Washington before I see you again; I have some important matters on which I want to know your mind."

The next day, it was my privilege to have the greatest honor ever received by me. The good president wanted me to stand as his right hand when he received the delegation, and hear the address presented by Governor Dennison, the president of the convention, to which he replied in his own admirable simplicity and eloquence; finishing by one of his most witty anecdotes. "I am reminded in this convention of a story of an old Dutch farmer, who remarked to a companion, wisely, 'That it was not best to swap horses when crossing a stream.'"

The next day, he took me with him to visit the 30,000 wounded soldiers picked up on the battlefields of the seven days' battle of the Wilderness, and the thirty days' battle around Richmond, where Grant was just breaking the backbone of the rebellion. On the way to and from the hospitals, little was said, the noise of the carriage was too great. Besides, my soul was very distressed, the horrors of the fratricidal war, had stifled my voice. The only thought which seemed to occupy the mind of the president was the part which Rome had in that horrible struggle. Many times he repeated:

"This war would never have been possible without the sinister influence of the Jesuits. We owe it to popery that we now see our land reddened with the blood of her noblest sons. Though there were great differences of opinion between the South and the North on the question of slavery, neither Jeff Davis nor any of the leading men of the Confederacy would have dared to attack the North, had they not relied on the promises of the Jesuits, that, under the mask of democracy, the money and the arms of the Roman Catholics, even the arms of France, were at their disposal, if they would attack us. I pity the priests, the bishops and the monks of Rome in the United States, when the people realize that they are, in great part, responsible for the tears and the blood shed in this war. I conceal what I know, for if the people knew the whole truth, this war would turn into a religious war, and at once, take a tenfold more savage and bloody character. It would become merciless as all religious wars are. It would become a war of extermination on both sides.

"The Protestants of both the North and the South would surely unite to exterminate the priests and the Jesuits if they could hear what Professor Morse has said to me of the plots made in the very city of Rome to destroy this republic, and if they could learn how the priests, the nuns, and the monks, which daily land on our shores under the pretext of preaching their religion, instructing the people in their schools, taking care of the sick in the hospitals, are nothing else but the emissaries of the pope, of Napoleon, and the other despots of Europe, to undermine our institutions, alienate the hearts of our people from our Constitution, and our laws, destroy our schools, and prepare a reign of anarchy here as they have done in Ireland, in Mexico, in Spain, and wherever there are any people who want to be free, etc."

When the president was speaking thus, we arrived at the door of his mansion. He invited me to go with him to his study, and said: "Though I am very busy, there are many important things about the plots of the Jesuits that I can learn only from you. Have you read the letter of the pope to Jeff Davis, and what do you think of it?"

"My dear president," I answered, "it is just that letter which brought me to your presence again. That letter is a poisoned arrow thrown by the pope at you personally; it is your death warrant. Before the letter every Catholic could see that their Church as a whole, was against this free republic. However, a good number of liberty-loving Irish, German and French Catholics, following more the instincts of their noble nature than the degrading principles of their Church, enrolled themselves under the banners of liberty, and they have fought like heroes. To detach these men from the rank and file of the Northern armies, and force them to help the cause of the rebellion, became the object of the Jesuits.

"Secret pressing letters were addressed from Rome to the bishops, ordering them to weaken your armies by detaching those men from you. The bishops refused; for they would be exposing themselves as traitors and be shot. But they advised the pope to acknowledge, at once, the legitimacy of the Southern republic, and to take Jeff Davis under his supreme protection, by a letter, which would be read everywhere.

"That letter tells every Roman Catholic that you are a bloodthirsty tyrant fighting against a government which the infallible and holy pope of Rome recognizes as legitimate. The pope, by this letter, tells his blind slaves that you are outraging the God of heaven and earth, by continuing such a bloody.

"By this letter of the pope to Jeff Davis you are not only an apostate, as you were thought before, whom every man had the right to kill, according to the canonical laws of Rome; but you are more vile, criminal and cruel than the horse thief, the public bandit, and the lawless brigand, robber and murderer.

"And, my dear president, this is not a fancy imagination on my part, it is the unanimous explanation given me by a great number of the priests of Rome, with whom I have had occasion to speak on that subject. In the name of God, and in the name of our dear country, which is in so much need of your services, I plead that you to pay more attention to protect your precious life, and not continue to expose it as you have done till now."

The president listened to my words with breathless attention. He replied: "You confirm my views of the letter of the pope. Professor Morse is of the same mind. It is indeed, the most perfidious act which could occur under present circumstances. You are perfectly correct when you say it was to detach the Roman Catholics who had enrolled themselves in our armies. Since the publication of that letter, a great number of them have deserted their banners and turned traitor. One of the few who have not is Sheridan, worth a whole army by his ability, his patriotism and his heroic courage. It is true also, that Meade has remained with us, and gained the bloody battle of Gettysburg. But how could he lose it, when he was surrounded by such heroes as Howard, Reynolds, Buford, Wadsworth, Cutler, Slocum, Sickles, Hancock, Barnes, etc. But it is evident that his Romanism superseded his patriotism after the battle. He let the army of Lee escape when he could easily have cut his retreat and forced him to surrender after losing nearly the half of his soldiers in the last three days' carnage.

"When Meade was to order the pursuit after the battle, a stranger came in haste to the headquarters, and that stranger was a disguised Jesuit. After ten minutes' conversation with him, Meade made such arrangements for the pursuit of the enemy that he escaped almost untouched with the loss of only two guns!

"You are right," continued the president, "that this letter of the pope has entirely changed the nature and the ground of the war. Before they read it, the Roman Catholics could see that I was fighting against Jeff Davis and his Southern Confederacy. But now, they must believe that it is against Christ and His holy vicar, the pope, that I am raising my sacrilegious hands; we have the daily proofs that their indignation, their hatred, their malice, against me, are a hundredfold intensified. New projects of assassination are detected almost every day, accompanied with such savage circumstances that they bring to my memory the massacre of St. Bartholomew and the Gunpowder Plot. Our investigation indicates that they come from the same masters in the art of murder, the Jesuits.

"The New York riots were evidently a Romish plot from beginning to end. We have the proofs in hand that they were the work of Bishop Hughes and his emissaries. No doubt can remain about the bloody attempts of Rome to destroy New York, when we know the easy way it was stopped. I wrote to Bishop Hughes, telling him that the whole country would hold him responsible for it if he would not stop it at once. He then gathered the rioters around his palace, called them his 'dear friends', invited them to go back home peacefully, and all was finished! So Jupiter of old used to raise a storm and stop it with a nod of his head!

"From the beginning of our civil war, there has been, not a secret, but a public alliance, between the Pope of Rome and Jeff Davis. The pope and his Jesuits have advised, supported, and directed Jeff Davis on the land, from the first gun shot at Fort Sumter by the rabid Roman Catholic Beauregard. They are helping him on the sea by guiding and supporting the rabid Roman Catholic pirate, Semmes, on the ocean.

"In my interview with Bishop Hughes, I told him 'that every stranger who had sworn allegiance to our government by becoming a United States citizen, like himself, was liable to be shot or hung as a traitor and a spy. After I had put this flea in the ears of the Romish bishop, I requested him to go and report my words to the pope. My hope was that he would advise them, for their own interest, to become loyal and true to their allegiance and help us through the remaining part of the war. But the result has been the very contrary. The pope has thrown away the mask, and shown himself the public partisan and the protector of the rebellion, by taking Jeff Davis by the hand, and impudently recognizing the Southern States as a legitimate government. Now, I have the proof in hand that that very Bishop Hughes, whom I had sent to Rome to induce the pope to urge the Roman Catholics of the North at least, to be true to their oath of allegiance, and whom I thanked publicly, when, under the impression that he had acted honestly, according to the promise he had given me, is the very man who advised the pope to recognize the legitimacy of the Southern republic, and put the whole weight of his tiara in the balance against us in favor of our enemies! Such is the perfidity of those Jesuits.

"Two cankers are biting the very entrails of the United States today: the Romish and the Mormon priests. Both are equally at work to form a people of the most abject, ignorant and fanatical slaves, who will recognize no other authority but their supreme pontiffs. Both are aiming at the destruction of our schools, to raise themselves upon our ruins. Both shelter themselves under our grand and holy principles of liberty of conscience, to destroy that very liberty of conscience, and bind the world under their heavy and ignominious yoke.

"The Mormon and the Jesuit priests are equally the uncompromising enemies of our Constitution and our laws; but the more dangerous of the two is the Jesuit — the Romish priest, for he knows better how to conceal his hatred under the mask of friendship and public good; he is better trained to commit the most cruel and diabolical deeds for the glory of God.

"Till lately, I was in favor of the unlimited liberty of conscience as our Constitution gives it to the Roman Catholics. But now, it seems to me that, sooner or later, the people will be forced to put a restriction to that clause towards the papists. Is it not an act of folly to give absolute liberty of conscience to a set of men who are publicly sworn to cut our throats the very day they have the opportunity? Is it right to give the privilege of citizenship to men who are sworn and public enemies of our Constitution, our laws, our liberties, and our lives?

"The very moment that popery assumed the right of life and death on a citizen of France, Spain, Germany, England, or the United States, it assumed to be the power, the government of France, Spain, England, Germany, and the United States. Those States then committed a suicidal act by allowing popery to put a foot on their territory with the privilege of citizenship. The power to life and death is the supreme power, and two supreme powers cannot exist on the same territory without anarchy, riots, bloodshed, and civil wars without end. When popery will give up the power of life and death which it proclaims as its own divine power in all its theological books and canon laws, then, and then alone, it can be tolerated and can receive the privileges of citizenship in a free country.

"Is it not an absurdity to give to a man a thing which he has sworn to hate, curse, and destroy? And does not the Catholic Church of Rome hate, curse, and destroy liberty of conscience whenever she can do it safely? I am for liberty of conscience in its noblest, broadest, highest sense. But I cannot give liberty of conscience to the pope and to his followers, the papists, so long as they tell me, through all their councils, theologians, and canon laws, that their conscience orders them to burn my wife, strangle my children, and cut my throat when they find their opportunity! This does not seem to be understood by the people today. But sooner or later, the light of common sense will make it clear to every one that no liberty of conscience can be granted to men who are sworn to obey a pope, who pretends to have the right to put to death those who differ from him in religion.

"You are not the first to warn me against the dangers of assassination. My ambassadors in Italy, France, and England, as well as Professor Morse, have many times warned me against the plots of the murderers which they have detected in those different countries. But I see no other safeguard against those murderers but to be always ready to die, as Christ advises it. As we must all die sooner or later, it makes very little difference to me whether I die from a dagger plunged through my heart or from an inflammation of the lungs. Let me tell you I have lately read a passage in the Old Testament which had made a profound, and, I hope, a salutary impression on me. Here is that passage."

The president took his Bible, opened it at the third chapter of Deuteronomy, and read from the 22nd to the 28th verse:

"Ye shall not fear them: for the Lord your God He shall fight for you. And I besought the Lord at that time, saying, O Lord God, Thou hast begun to shew Thy servant Thy greatness and Thy mighty hand; for what God is there, in heaven or in earth, that can do according to Thy words, and according to Thy might! I pray Thee, let me go over, and see the good land that is beyond Jordan, that goodly mountain, and Lebanon. But the Lord was wroth with me for your sakes, and would not hear me: and the Lord said unto me, Let it suffice thee: speak no more unto Me of this matter. Get thee up into the top of Pisgah, and lift up thine eyes westward, and northward, and southward, and eastward, and behold it with thine eyes: for thou shalt not go over this Jordan."

After the President had read these words with great solemnity, he added: "My dear Father Chiniquy, let me tell you that I have read these strange and beautiful verses several times these last five or six weeks. The more I read them, the more it seems to me that God has written them for me as well as Moses. Has He not taken me from my poor log cabin by the hand, as He did Moses in the reeds of the Nile, to put me at the head of the greatest and the most blessed of modern nations, just as He put that prophet at the head of the most blessed nation of ancient times? Has not God granted me a privilege which was not granted to any living man, when I broke the fetters of 4,000,000 of men and made them free? Has not our God given me the most glorious victories over our enemies? Are not the armies of the Confederacy so reduced to a handful of men when compared to what they were two years ago, that the day is fast approaching when they will have to surrender?

"Now, I see the end of this terrible conflict, with the same joy of Moses at the end of his forty years in the wilderness. I pray my God to grant me to see the days of peace, and untold prosperity, which will follow this cruel war, as Moses asked God to see the other side of Jordan and enter the Promised Land. But do you know that I hear in my soul, as the voice of God, giving me the rebuke which was given to Moses?

"Yes! every time that my soul goes to God to ask the favor of seeing the other side of Jordan, and eating the fruits of that peace, after which I am longing with such an unspeakable desire, do you know that there is a still, but solemn voice, which tells me that I will see those things, only from a long distance, and that I will be among the dead, when the nation which God granted me to lead through those awful trials, will cross the Jordan, and dwell in that Land of Promise, where peace, industry, happiness, and liberty, will make every one happy; and why so? Because He has already given me favors which He never gave, I dare say, to any man, in these latter days.

"Why did God Almighty refuse to Moses the favor of crossing the Jordan, and entering the Promised Land? It was on account of this own nation's sin! That law of divine retribution and justice, by which one must suffer for another is surely a terrible mystery. But it is a fact which no man who has any intelligence and knowledge can deny. Moses, who knew that law, though he probably did not understand it better than we do, calmly says to his people, 'God was wroth with me for your sakes.'

"But though we do not understand that mysterious and terrible law, we find it written in letters of tears and blood wherever we go. We do not read a single page of history, without finding undeniable traces of its existence.

"So many plots have already been made against my life, that it is a real miracle that they have all failed, when we consider that the great majority of them were in the hands of the skillful Roman Catholic murderers, evidently trained by Jesuits. But can we expect that God will make a perpetual miracle to save my life? I believe not. The Jesuits are so expert in those deeds of blood, that Henry IV said that it was impossible to escape them, and he became their victim, though he did all that could be done to protect himself. My escape from their hands, since the letter of the pope to Jeff Davis has sharpened a million of daggers to pierce my breast, would be more than a miracle.

"But just as the Lord heard no murmur from the lips of Moses when He told him that he had to die, before crossing the Jordan, for the sins of his people; so I hope and pray that He will hear no murmur from me when I fall for my nation's sake.

"The only two favors I ask of the Lord are, first, that I may die for the sacred cause in which I am engaged, and when I am the standard bearer of the rights and liberties of my country.

"The second favor I ask of God is, that my dear son, Robert, when I am gone, will be one of those who lift up that flag of liberty which will cover my tomb, and carry it with honor and fidelity, to the end of his life, as his father did, surrounded by the millions who will be called with him to fight and die for the defense and honor of our country."

Never had I heard such sublime words. Never had I seen a human face so solemn and so prophet-like as the face of the president, when uttering these things. I was beside myself. Bathed in tears, I tried to say something, but I could not utter a word.

I knew the hour to leave had come, I asked from the president permission to fall on my knees, and pray with him that his life might be spared; and he knelt with me. But I prayed more with tears and sobs, than with words.

Then I pressed his hand on my lips and bathed it with my tears, and with a heart filled with an unspeakable desolation, I bade him adieu! It was for the last time!

The hour was fast approaching when he was to fall by the hands of a Jesuit assassin, for his nation's sake.

CHAPTER LVI

Every time I met President Lincoln I wondered how such elevation of thought and such childish simplicity could be found in the same man. After my interviews with him many times, I said to myself: "How can this rail-splitter have so easily raised himself to the highest range of human thought and philosophy?"

The secret was that Lincoln had spent a great part of his life at the school of Christ, and that he meditated His sublime teachings to an extent unsuspected by the world. I found in him the most perfect type of Christianity I ever met. Professedly, he was neither a strict Presbyterian, nor a Baptist, nor a Methodist: but he was the embodiment of all which is more perfect and Christian in them. His religion was the very essence of what God wants in man. It was from Christ Himself he had learned to love God and his neighbor, as it was from Christ he had learned the dignity and the value of man. "Ye are all brethren, the children of God," was his great motto.

It was from the Gospel that he had learned his principles of equality, fraternity, and liberty, as it was from the Gospel he had learned that sublime, childish simplicity which, alone, and forever, won the admiration and affection of all. I could cite many facts to illustrate this, but I will give only one taken from the Memoirs of Mr. Bateman, Superintendent of Public Instruction for the state of Illinois.

"Mr. Lincoln paused for long minutes, his features surcharged with emotion. Then he rose and walked up and down the reception room, in the effort to retain or regain his self-possession. Stopping at last, he said, with a trembling voice and his cheeks wet with tears: 'I know there is a God, and that He hates injustice and slavery. I see the storm coming, and I know that His hand is in it. If He has a place and work for me, and I think He has, I believe I am ready! I am nothing, but truth is everything! I know I am right, because I know that liberty is right: for Christ teaches it, and Christ is God.

"'I have told them that a house divided against itself cannot stand, and Christ and reason say the same thing. Douglas does not care whether slavery is voted up or down. But God cares, and humanity cares, and I care. And with God's help, I will not fail. I may not see the end, but it will come, and I shall be vindicated; and those men will see that they have not read their Bible right! Does it not appear strange that men can ignore the moral aspect of this contest? A revelation could not make it plainer to me that slavery, or the government, must be destroyed. The future would be something awful, as I look at it, but for this ROCK on which I stand (alluding to the Gospel book he still held in his hand). It seems as if God had borne with slavery until the very teachers of religion had come to defend it from the Bible, and to claim for it a Divine character and sanction. And now the cup of iniquity is full, and the vials of wrath will be poured out.'"

Mr. Bateman adds: "After this, the conversation was continued for a long time. Everything he said was of a very deep, tender, and religious tone, and all was tinged with a touching melancholy. After further reference to a belief in Divine Providence, and the fact of God in history, the conversation turned upon prayer. He freely stated his belief in the duty, privilege, an efficacy of prayer; and he intimated, in no unmistakable terms, that he had sought, in that way, the divine guidance and favor."

The effect of this conversation upon the mind of Mr. Bateman, a

Christian gentleman whom Mr. Lincoln profoundly respected, was to convince him that Mr. Lincoln had, in his quiet way, found a path to the Christian standpoint, that he had found God, and rested on the eternal truth of God. As the two men were about to separate, Mr. Bateman remarked: "I had not supposed that you were accustomed to think so much upon this class of subjects; certainly your friends generally are ignorant of the sentiments you have expressed to me."

He quickly replied: "I know they are, but I think more on these subjects than upon all others, and I have done so for years; and I am willing you should know it."

More than once I felt as if I were in the presence of an old prophet, when listening to his views about the future destinies of the United States. In one of my last interviews with him, I was filled with an admiration which it would be difficult to express, when I heard the following views and predictions:

"It is with the Southern leaders of this civil war as with the big and small wheels of our railroad cars. Those who ignore the laws of mechanics are apt to think that the large, strong, and noisy wheels they see are the motive power, but they are mistaken. The real motive power is not seen; it is noiseless and well concealed in the dark, behind its iron walls. The motive power are the few well-concealed pails of water heated into steam, which is itself directed by the noiseless, small, but unerring engineer's finger.

"The common people see and hear the big, noisy wheels of the Southern Confederacy's cars: they call them Jeff Davis, Lee, Toombs, Beauregard, Semmes, etc., and they honestly think they they are the motive power, the first cause of our troubles. But this is a mistake. The true motive power is secreted behind the thick walls of the Vatican, the colleges and schools of the Jesuits, the convents of the nuns, and the confessional boxes of Rome.

"There is a fact which is too much ignored by the American people, and with which I am acquainted only since I became president; it is that the best, the leading families of the South have received their education in great part, if not in whole, from the Jesuits and the nuns. Hence those degrading principles of slavery, pride, cruelty, which are as a second nature among so many of those people. Hence that strange want of fair play, humanity; that implacable hatred against the ideas of equality and liberty as we find them in the Gospel of Christ. You do not ignore that the first settlers of Louisiana, Florida, New Mexico, Texas, South California, and Missouri were Roman Catholics, and that their first teachers were Jesuits. It is true that those states have been conquered or bought by us since. But Rome had put the deadly virus of her anti-social and anti-christian maxims into the veins of the people before they became American citizens. Unfortunately, the Jesuits and the nuns have in great part remained the teachers of those people since. They have continued in a silent, but most efficacious way, to spread their hatred against our institutions, our laws, our schools, our rights and our liberties in such a way that this terrible conflict became unavoidable between the North and the South. As I have told you before, it is to popery that we owe this terrible civil war.

"I would have laughed at the man who would have told me that before I became the president. But Professor Morse has opened my eyes on that subject. And now I see that mystery; I understand that engineering of hell which, though not seen nor even suspected by the country, is putting in motion the large, heavy, and noisy wheels of the state cars of the Southern Confederacy. Our people are not yet ready to learn and believe those things, and perhaps it is not the proper time to initiate them to these dark mysteries of hell; it would throw oil on a fire which is already sufficiently destructive.

"You are almost the only one with whom I speak freely on that subject. But sooner or later the nation will know the real origin of those rivers of blood and tears, which are spreading desolation and death everywhere. And then those who have caused those desolations and disasters will be called to give an account of them."

Many of those who approached Abraham Lincoln felt that there was a prophetic spirit in him, and that he was continually walking and acting with the thought of God in his mind, and only in view to do His will and work for His glory. Speaking of slaves, he said one day before the members of his cabinet:

"I have not decided against the proclamation of liberty to the slaves, but I hold the matter under advisement. And I can assure you that the subject is on my mind, by day and by night, more than any other. Whatever shall appear to be God's will, I will do."

A few days before that proclamation, he said, before several of his counselors: "I made a solemn vow before God that if General Lee was driven back from Pennsylvania, I would crown the result by the declaration of freedom to slaves."

But I would have volumes to write, instead of a short chapter, were I to give all the facts I have collected of the sincere and profound piety of Abraham Lincoln.

I cannot, however, omit his admirable and solemn act of faith in the eternal justice of God, as expressed in the closing words of his last inaugural address of the 4th of March, 1865.

"Fondly do we hope, fervently do we pray, that this mighty

scourge of war may speedily pass away. Yet, if God wills that it continue until all the wealth piled by the bondsman's 250 years of unrequited toil shall be sunk; and until every drop of blood drawn by the lash shall be paid by another drawn by the sword, as was said 3,000 years ago, so still it must be said: 'The judgments of the Lord are true and righteous altogether.'"

These sublime words, falling from the lips of the greatest Christian whom God ever put at the head of a nation, only a few days before his martyrdom, sent a thrill of wonder through the whole world.

The 6th of April, 1865, President Lincoln was invited by General Grant to enter Richmond, the capital of the rebel states, which he had just captured. The ninth, the beaten army of Lee, surrounded by the victorious legions of the soldiers of liberty, were forced to lay down their arms and their banners at the feet of the generals of Lincoln. The tenth, the victorious president addressed an immense multitude of the citizens of Washington, to invite them to thank God and the armies of the glorious victories of the last few days, and for the blessed peace which was to follow these five years of slaughter.

But he was on the top of the mountain of Pisgah, and though he had fervently prayed that he might cross the Jordan and enter with this people into the Land of Promise, after which he had so often sighed, he was not to see his request granted. The answer had come from heaven, "You will not cross the Jordan, and you will not enter that Promised Land, which is there, so near. You must die for your nation's sake!"

The lips, the heart, and the soul of the new Moses were still repeating the sublime words, "The judgments of the Lord are true and righteous altogether," when the Jesuit assassin, Booth, murdered him the 14th of April, 1865, at ten o'clock p.m.

Let us hear the eloquent historian, Abbot, on that sad event:

"In the midst of unparalleled success, and while all the bells of the land were ringing with joy, a calamity fell upon us which overwhelmed the country in consternation and awe. On Friday evening, April 14th, President Lincoln attended Ford's Theatre, in Washington. He was sitting quietly in his box, listening to the drama, when a man entered the door of the lobby leading to the box, closing the door behind him. Drawing near to the president, he drew from his pocket a small pistol, and shot him in the back of the head. As the president fell, senseless and mortally wounded, and the shriek of his wife, who was seated at his side, pierced every ear, the assassin leaped from the box, a perpendicular height of nine feet, and as he rushed across the stage, bare-headed, brandished a dagger, exclaiming, 'Sic semper tryannis!' and disappeared behind the side scenes. There was a moment of silent consternation. Then ensued a scene of confusion which it is in vain to attempt to describe.

"The dying president was taken into a house near by and placed upon a bed. What a scene did that room present! The chief of a mighty nation lay there, senseless, drenched in blood, his brains oozing from his wound! Sumner, Farwell, and Colfax and Stanton, and many others were there, filled with grief and consternation.

"The surgeon, General Barnes, solemnly examined the wound. There was silence as of the grave, the life and death of the nation seemed dependent on the result. General Barnes looked up sadly and said, 'The wound is mortal!'

"'Oh! No! General, no! no!' cried out Secretary Stanton, and sinking into a chair, he covered his face and wept like a child. Senator Sumner tenderly held the head of the unconscious martyr.

"Though all unused to weep, he sobs as though his great heart would break. In his anguish, his head falls upon the blood-stained pillow, and his black locks blend with those of the dying victim, which care and toil has rendered grey, and which blood has crimsoned. What a scene! Sumner, who had lingered through months of agony, having himself been stricken down by the bludgeon of slavery, now sobbing and fainting in anguish over the prostrate form of his friend, whom slavery had slain! This vile rebellion, after deluging the land in blood, has culminated in a crime which appalls all nations.

"Noble Abraham, true descendant of the father of the faithful; honest in every trust, humble as a child, tender hearted as a woman, who could not bear to injure even his most envenomed foes: who, in the hour of triumph, was saddened lest the feelings of his adversaries should be wounded by their defeat, with 'charity for all, malice towards none,' endowed with 'common sense,' intelligence never surpassed, and with power of intellect which enabled him to grapple with the most gigantic opponents in debates, developing abilities as a statesman, which won the gratitude of his country and the admiration of the world, and with graces and amiability which drew to him all generous hearts; dies by the bullet of the assassin!"

But who was that assassin? Booth was nothing but the tool of the Jesuits. It was Rome who directed his arm, after corrupting his heart and damning his soul.

After I had mixed my tears with those of the grand country of my adoption, I fell on my knees and asked my God to grant me to show to the world what I knew to be the truth, that that horrible crime was the work of popery. And, after twenty years of constant and most difficult researches, I come fearlessly today before the American people, to say and prove that the president, Abraham Lincoln, was assassinated by the priests and the Jesuits of Rome.

In the book of the testimonies given in the prosecution of the assassin of Lincoln, published by Ben Pitman, and in the two volumes of the trial of John Surratt, in 1867, we have the legal and irrefutable proof that the plot of the assassins of Lincoln was matured, if not started, in the house of Mary Surratt, 561 H Street, Washington, D.C. The sworn testimonies show that it was the common rendezvous of the priests of Washington. What does the presence of so many priests in that house reveal to the world? No man of common sense, who knows anything about the priests of Rome, can doubt that they were the advisers, the counselors, the very soul of that infernal plot.

Those priests, who were the personal friends and the father confessors of Booth, John Surratt, Mrs. and Miss Surratt, could not be constantly there without knowing what was going on, particularly when we know that every one of those priests was a rabid rebel in heart. Every one of those priests, knowing that his infallible pope had called Jeff Davis his dear son, and had taken the Southern Confederacy under his protection, was bound to believe that the most holy thing a man could do, was to fight for the Southern cause by destroying those who were its enemies.

Read the history of the assassination of Admiral Coligny, Henry III and Henry IV, and William the Taciturn, by the hired assassins of the Jesuits; compare them with the assassination of Abraham Lincoln, and you will find that one resembles the other like two drops of water. You will understand that they all come from the same source, Rome!

The murderers, selected and trained by the Jesuits, were of the most exalted Roman Catholic piety, living in the company of priests, going to confess very often, receiving the communion the day before, if not the very day of the murder. You will see that the assassins were considering themselves the chosen instruments of God, to save the nation by striking its tyrant; that they firmly believed that there was no sin in killing the enemy of the people, of the holy Church, and of the infallible pope!

Booth, suffering the most horrible tortures from his broken leg, writes in his daily memorandum, the very day before his death: "I can never repent, though we hated to kill. Our country owed all her troubles to him (Lincoln), and God simply made me the instrument of his punishment."

Who can suppose that it was Jeff Davis who had filled the mind and the heart of Booth with that religious and exalted fanaticism! Surely Jeff Davis had promised the money to arm their nerves by the hope of becoming rich. The testimonies on that account say that he had promised one million dollars.

That arch-rebel could give the money; but the Jesuits alone could select the assassins, train them, and show them a crown of glory in heaven, if they would kill the author of the bloodshed, the famous renegade and apostate — the enemy of the pope and of the Church — Lincoln.

Who does not see the lessons given by the Jesuits to Booth, in their daily intercourse in Mary Surratt's house, when he reads those lines written by Booth a few hours before his death: "I can never repent; God made me the instrument of His punishment!" Compare these words with the doctrines and principles taught by the councils, the decrees of the pope, and the laws of holy Inquisition, and you will find that the sentiments and belief of Booth flow from those principles, as the river flows from its source.

And that pious Miss Surratt who, the very next day after the murder of Lincoln, said, without being rebuked, in the presence of several other witnesses: "The death of Abraham Lincoln is no more than the death of any nigger in the army." Where did she get that maxim, if not from her Church? Had not that Church recently proclaimed, through her highest legal and civil authority, the devoted Roman Catholic Judge Taney, in his Dred Scot decision, the negroes have no right which the white is bound to respect? By bringing the president on a level with the lowest nigger, Rome was saying that he had no right even to his life.

Read in the testimony concerning Mrs. Mary E. Surratt (pp.122, 123), how the Jesuits had perfectly drilled her in the art of perjuring herself. In the very moment when the government officer orders her to prepare herself, with her daughter, to follow him as prisoners, at about ten p.m., Payne, the would-be murderer of Seward, knocks at the door and wants to see Mrs. Surratt. But instead of having Mrs. Surratt to open the door, he finds himself confronted, face to face, with the government detective, Major Smith, who swears:

"I questioned him in regard to his occupation, and what business he had at the house at this late hour of the night. He stated that he was a laborer, and had come to dig a gutter at the request of Mrs. Surratt.

"I went to the parlor door, and said, 'Mrs. Surratt, will you step here a minute?' She came out, and I asked her, 'Do you know this man, and did you hire him to come and dig a gutter for you?' She answered, raising her right hand, 'Before God, sir, I do not know this man; I have never seen him, and I did not hire him to dig a gutter for me.'"

But it proved after, by several unimpeachable witnesses, that she knew very well that Payne was a personal friend of her son, who, many times had come to her house, in company of his friend and pet, Booth. She had received the communion just two or three days before that public perjury. Could Jeff Davis have imparted such a religious calm and self-possession to that woman when her hands were just reddened with the blood of the president, and she was on her way to trial?

No! Such calm in that soul, in such a terrible and solemn hour, could come only from the teachings of those Jesuits who, for more than six months, were in her house, showing her a crown of eternal glory if she could help to kill the monster, apostate Lincoln — the only cause of that horrible civil war! There is not the least doubt that the priests had perfectly persuaded Mary Surratt and Booth that the killing of Lincoln was a most holy and deserving work, for which God had an eternal reward in store.

There is a fact to which the American people have not yet given a sufficient attention: without a single exception, the conspirators were Roman Catholics. The learned and great patriot, General Baker, in his admirable report, struck and bewildered by that strange, mysterious and portentous fact said:

"I mention, as an exceptional and remarkable fact that every conspirator in custody is by education a Catholic."

Those words fell as if on the ears of deaf men. It is true that some of them, as Atzeroth, Payne and Harold, asked for Protestant ministers when they were to be hung. But on page 437 of *The Trial of John Surratt,* Louis Weichman tells us that he was going to St. Aloysian's Church with Atzeroth, and that it was there that he introduced him to Mr. Brothy (another Roman Catholic).

It is a well authenticated fact, that Booth and Weichman, who were themselves Protestant perverts to Romanism, had proselytized a good number of semi-Protestants and infidels who, either from conviction, or from hope of the fortunes promised to the successful murderers, were themselves very zealous for the Church of Rome. Payne, Atzeroth and Harold, were among those proselytes. But when those murderers were to appear before the country and receive the just punishment of their crime, the Jesuits were too shrewd to ignore that if they were all coming on the scaffold as Roman Catholics, and accompanied by their father confessors, it would, at once, open the eyes of the American people, and clearly show that this was a Roman Catholic plot. They persuaded three of their proselytes to avail themselves of the theological principles of the Church of Rome, that a man is allowed to conceal his religion, may even say that he is a heretic, a Protestant, when it is for his own interest or the best interest of this Church to conceal the truth and deceive the people. Here is the doctrine of Rome on that subject.

"It is often more to the glory of God and the good of our neighbor to cover the faith than to confess it; for example, if concealed among heretics, you may accomplish a greater amount of good; or if, by declaring our religion, more of evil would follow — for example, great trouble, death, the hostility of a tyrant."(Liguori, *Theologia Moralis,* t. ii n. 14, p. 117 Mechlin, 1845.) The Jesuits had never had better reason to suspect that the declaration of their religion would damage them and excite the wrath of their "tyrant," the American people.

Lloyds, in whose house Mrs. Surratt concealed the carbine which Booth wanted for protection, when just after the murder he was to flee towards the Southern States, was a firm Roman Catholic. Dr. Mudd, at whose place Booth stopped to have his broken leg dressed was a Roman Catholic, and so was Garrett, in whose barn Booth was caught and killed. Why so? Because, as Jeff Davis was the only man to pay one million dollars to those who would kill Abraham Lincoln, the Jesuits were the only men to select the murderers and prepare everything to protect them after their diabolical deed, and such murderers could not be found except among their blind and fanatical slaves.

The great fatal mistake of the American government in the prosecution of the assassins of Abraham Lincoln was to cover up the religious element of that terrible drama. But this was carefully avoided throughout the trial. Not long after the execution of the murderers, I went, incognito, to Washington to begin my investigation. I was not surprised to see that not a single one of the government men would discuss it with me except after I had given my word of honor that I would never mention their names. I saw, with a profound distress, that the influence of Rome was almost supreme in Washington. I could not find a single statesman who would dare to face that nefarious influence and fight it down.

Several of the government men told me in confidence: "We had not the least doubt that the Jesuits were at the bottom of that great iniquity; we even feared, sometimes, that this would come out so clearly before the military tribunal, that there would be no possibility of keeping it out of the public sight.

"This was not through cowardice, as you think, but through a wisdom which you ought to approve, if you cannot admire it. Had we been in days of peace, we know that with a little more pressure of the witnesses, many priests would have been compromised; for Mrs. Surratt's house was their common rendezvous; it is more than probable that several of them might have been hung. But the Civil War was hardly over. The Confederacy, though broken down, was still living in millions of hearts; murderers and formidable elements of discord were still seen everywhere, to which the hanging or exiling of those priests would have given a new life. Riots after riots would have accompanied and followed their execution. We thought we had had enough of blood, fires, devastations and bad feelings. We were all longing for days of peace: the country was in need of them. We concluded that the best interests of humanity was to punish only those who were publicly and visibly guilty; that the verdict might receive the approbation of all, without creating any new bad feelings. Allow us also to tell you that there was nothing that good and great man feared so much as to arm the Protestants against the Catholics, and the Catholics against the Protestants."

But if any one has still any doubts of the complicity of the Jesuits in the murder of Abraham Lincoln, let him look at the very elaborate plan of escape prepared by the priests of Rome to save the lives of the assassins and the conspirators. John Surratt was in Washington the 14th of April helping Booth in the perpetration of the assassination. The priest, Charles Boucher, swears that only a few days after the murder, John Surratt was sent to him by Father Lapierre, of Montreal; that he kept him concealed in his parsonage of St. Liboire from the end of April to the end of July, then he took him back, secretly, to Father Lapierre, who kept him secreted in his own father's house, under the very shadow of the Montreal bishop's palace. He swears that Father Lapierre visited Surratt often, when secreted at St. Liboire, and that Father Boucher visited him, at least twice a week, from the end of July to September, when concealed in Father Lapierre's house in Montreal.

That same father, Charles Boucher, swears that he accompanied John Surratt in a carriage, in the company of Father Lapierre, to the steamer "Montreal", when starting for Quebec: that Father Lapierre kept Surratt under lock during the voyage from Montreal to Quebec, and that he accompanied him, disguised from the Montreal steamer to the ocean steamer, "Peruvian". The doctor of the steamer "Peruvian," L.I.A. McMillan, swears that Father Lapierre introduced him to John Surratt under the false name of McCarthy, whom he was keeping locked in his state room till she left Quebec for Europe the 15th September, 1865.

But who is that Father Lapierre who takes such a tender, paternal care of Surratt? No less than the canon of Bishop Bourget, of

Montreal. He is the confidential man of the bishop; he lives with the bishop, eats at his table, assists him with his counsel, and receives his advice in every step of life. According to the laws of Rome, the canons are to the bishop what the arms are to the body.

Now, I ask: Is it not evident that the bishops and the priests of Washington have trusted this murderer to the care of the bishops and priests of Montreal, that they might conceal, feed, and protect him for nearly six months, under the very shadow of the bishop's palace? Would they have done that if they were not his accomplices? Why did they so continually remain with him day and night, if they were not in fear that he might compromise them by an indiscreet word?

But where will those bishops and priests of Canada send John Surratt when they find it impossible to conceal him any longer from the thousands of detectives of the United States who are ransacking Canada to find out his retreat? Who can suppose that any one but the pope himself and his Jesuits will protect the murderer of Abraham Lincoln in Europe?

If you want to see him after he has crossed the ocean, go to Vitry, at the door of Rome, enrolled under the banners of the pope in the 9th company of his Zouaves, under the false name of Watson. Of course, the pope was forced to withdraw his protection over him, after the government of the United States had found him there, and he was brought back to Washington to be tried.

But on his arrival as a prisoner in the United States, his Jesuit father confessor whispered in his ear: "Fear not, you will not be condemned! Through the influence of a high Roman Catholic lady, two or three of the jurymen will be Roman Catholics, and you will be safe." Those who have read the two volumes of the trial of John Surratt know that never more evident proofs of guilt were brought against a murderer.

Those jurymen were told by their father confessors that the most holy father, the pope, Gregory VII, had solemnly and infallibly declared that "the killing of an heretic was no murder." — *Jure Canonico.*

After such teachings, how could the Roman Catholic jurymen find John Surratt guilty of murder for killing the heretic Lincoln? The jury having disagreed, no verdict could be given. The government was forced to let the murderer go unpunished.

But when the irreconcilable enemies of all the rights and liberties of men were congratulating themselves on their successful efforts to save the life of John Surratt, the God of heaven was stamping again on their faces the mark of murder, in such a way that all eyes will see it.

Some time ago, I providentially met the Rev. Mr. F.A. Conwell, at Chicago. Having known that I was in search of facts about the assassination of Abraham Lincoln, he told me he knew one of those facts which might perhaps throw some light on the subject.

"The very day of the murder," he said, "I was in the Roman Catholic village of St. Joseph, Minnesota, when, at about six o'clock in the afternoon, I was told by a Roman Catholic, who was a purveyor for a great number of priests who lived in that town, where they have a monastery, that State Secretary Seward and President Lincoln had just been killed. This was told me," he said, "in the presence of a most respectable gentleman, called Bennett, who was not less puzzled than me. As there were no railroad lines nearer than forty miles, nor telegraph offices nearer than eighty miles from that place, we could not see how such news was spread in that town.

"The next day, the 15th of April, I was at St. Cloud, a town about twelve miles distant, where there was neither railroad nor telegraph; I said to several people that I had been told in the priestly village of St. Joseph, by a Roman Catholic, that Abraham Lincoln and the Secretary Seward had been assassinated. They answered me that they had heard nothing about it. But the next Sabbath, the 16th of April, when going to the Church of St. Cloud to preach, a friend gave me a copy of a telegram sent to him on the Saturday, reporting that Abraham Lincoln and Secretary Seward had been assassinated the very day before, which was Friday, the 14th at 10 p.m.

"But how could the Roman Catholic purveyor of the priests of St. Joseph have told me the same thing, before several witnesses, just four hours before its occurrence?"

I asked that gentleman if he would be kind enough to give me the fact under oath, that I might make use of it in the report I intended to publish about the assassination of Lincoln. And he kindly granted my request.

I felt that this testimony would be much more valuable if it could be corroborated by the testimonies of Messrs. Bennett and Linneman. I immediately sent a magistrate to find out if they were still living, and if they remembered the facts of the sworn declaration of Rev. Mr. Conwell. By the good providence of God, both of these gentlemen were found living.

Mr Bennett was willing to give sworn testimony verifying Mr. Conwell's story Mr. Linneman stated that he remembers when Messrs. Conwell and Bennett came to this place (St. Joseph, Minnesota) on Friday evening before the president was killed, and he asked them if they had heard about the assassinations and they replied they had not. He told them he had heard this rumor in his store from people who came in and out. But he cannot remember from whom.

I present here to the world a fact of the greatest gravity, so well authenticated that it cannot allow even the possibility of a doubt. Three or four hours before Lincoln was murdered in Washington, the 14th of April, 1865, that murder was not only known by someone, but it was circulated and talked of in the streets and in the houses of the priestly and Romish town of St. Joseph, Minnesota. The fact is undeniable; the testimonies are unchallengeable, and there were no railroad nor any telegraph communications nearer than forty or eighty miles from St. Joseph.

Naturally every one asked: "How could such news spread? Where is the source of such a rumor?" Mr. Linneman, who is a Roman Catholic, tells us that though he heard this from many in his store, and in the streets, he does not remember the name of a single one who told him that. And when we hear this from him, we understand why he did not dare to swear upon it, and shrank from the idea of perjuring himself. For every one feels that his memory cannot be so poor as that, when he remembers so well the names of the two strangers, Messrs. Conwell and Bennett. But if the memory of Mr. Linneman is so deficient on that subject, we can help him, and tell him with mathematical accuracy.

"You got the news from your priests of St. Joseph! The conspiracy which cost the life of the martyred president was prepared by the priests of Washington, in the house of Mary Surratt, 541 H Street. The priests of St. Joseph were often visiting Washington, and boarding, probably, at Mrs. Surratt's, as the priests of Washington were visiting their brother priests at St. Joseph. Those priests of Washington were in daily communication with their co-rebel priests of St. Joseph; they were their intimate friends. There was no secret among them, as there are no secrets among priests. They are the members of the same body, the branches of the same tree. The details of the murder, as the day selected for its commission, were as well known among the priests of St. Joseph, as they were among those of Washington. The death of Lincoln was such a glorious event for those priests! That infamous Lincoln, who had dared to fight against the Confederacy of the South after the Vicar of Christ had solemnly declared that their cause was just, legitimate and holy! That bloody tyrant, that godless and infamous man, was to receive, at last, the just chastisement of his crimes, the 14th of April! What glorious news!"

How could the priests conceal such a joyful event from their bosom friend, Mr. Linneman? He was their confidential man: he was their purveyor: he was their right hand man among the faithful of St. Joseph. They thought that they could be guilty of a want of confidence in their bosom friend, if they did not tell him all about the glorious event of that great day. But, of course, they requested him not to mention their names, if he would spread the joyful news among the devoted Roman Catholic people of St. Joseph. Mr. Linneman has honorably and faithfully kept his promise never to reveal their names, and today, we have in our hand, the authentic testimonies signed by him that, though somebody, the 14th of April, told him that President Lincoln was assassinated, he does not know who told him that!

The 14th of April, 1865, the priests of Rome knew and circulated the death of Lincoln four hours before its occurrence in their Roman Catholic town of St. Joseph, Minnesota. But they could not circulate it without knowing it, and they could not know it without belonging to the band of conspirators who assassinated President Lincoln.

CHAPTER LVII

Alone on my knees, in the presence of God, on the 1st of January, 1855, I took the resolution of opposing the acts of simony and tyranny of Bishop O'Regan. I was far from understanding the logical consequences of my struggle. My only object was to force him to be honest, just and Christian towards my people who had left their country and all that was dear to them in Canada, to live in peace in Illinois, under what we then considered the holy authority of the Church of Christ. But we were absolutely unwilling to be slaves of any man in the land of liberty.

If anyone at that hour, could have shown me that this struggle would lead to a complete separation from the Church of Rome, I would have shrank from the task. My only ambition was to purify my Church.

From the beginning, however, I had a presentiment that the power of the bishops would be too much for me, and that, sooner or later, they would crush me. But my hope was that when I fell, others would take my place and fight the battles of the Lord, till a final victory would bring the Church back to the blessed days when she was the spotless spouse of the Lamb.

In the autumn of 1856, our struggle against the Bishop of Chicago had taken proportions which could not have been anticipated either by me or by the Roman Catholic hierarchy of America. The whole press of the United States and Canada, both political and religious, were discussing the causes and the probable results of the contest.

At first, the bishops were indignant at the conduct of my lord O'Regan. They had seen with pleasure, that a priest from his own diocese would probably force him to be more cautious and less scandalous in his public and private dealings with the clergy and the people. But they also hoped that I should be paralyzed by the sentence of excommunication, and that the people, frightened by those fulminations, would withdraw the support they had given me. They were assured by Spink, that I would lose my suit at Urbana, and should, when lodged in the penitentiary, become powerless to do any mischief in the Church.

But their confidence was soon changed into dismay when they saw that the people laughed at the excommunication; that I had gained my suit, and that I was triumphing on that very battlefield from which no priest, since Luther and Knox, had come out unscathed. Everywhere, the sound of alarm was heard, and I was denounced as a rebel and schismatic. The whole body of the bishops repaired to hurl their most terrible fulminations at my head. But before taking their last measure to crush me, a supreme effort was made to show us what they considered our errors. The Rev. Messrs. Brassard, curate of Longueuil, and Rev. Isaac Desaulnier, president of St. Hyacinthe College, were sent by the people and bishops of Canada to show me the scandal of my proceedings, and press me to submit to the will of the bishop by respecting the so-called sentence of excommunication.

The choice of those two priests was very clever. They were certainly the most influential that could be sent. Mr. Brassard had not only been my teacher and benefactor at the college of Nicolet. He had loved me since as his own child, and I cherished and respected him as my own father. The other, Rev I. Desaulnier, had been my classmate in the college from 1822 to 1829, and we had been united during the whole of that period, as well as since, by the bonds of the sincerest esteem and friendship. They arrived at St. Anne on November 24th, 1856.

I heard of their coming only a few minutes before their arrival; and nothing can express the joy I felt at the news. The confidence I had in their honesty and friendship, gave me, at once, the hope that they would soon see the justice and holiness of our cause, and they would bravely take our side against our aggressor. But they had very different sentiments. Sincerely believing that I was an unmanageable schismatic, who was creating an awful scandal in the Church, they had not only been forbidden by the bishops to sleep in my house, but also to have any friendly and Christian communication with me. With no hatred against me, they were filled with horror at the thought that I should be so scandalous a priest, daring to trouble the peace and destroy the unity of the Church.

On their way they had often been told that I was not the same man, and that I had become sour and gloomy, abusive, insolent, and haughty; that also I would insult them, and perhaps advise the people to turn them away from my premises. They were pleasantly disappointed, however, when they saw me running to meet them with the most sincere affection and joy. I told them that all the treasures of California brought to my house would not make me half so happy as I was made by their presence.

I at once expressed my hope that they were the messengers sent by God to bring us peace and put an end to the deplorable state of things which was the cause of their long journey. Remarking that they were covered with mud, I invited them to go to their sleeping rooms, to wash and refresh themselves.

"Sleeping rooms! sleeping rooms!!" said Mr. Desaulnier, "but our written instructions from the bishops who sent us, forbid us to sleep here on account of your excommunication."

Mr. Brassard answered, "I must tell you, my dear Mr. Desaulnier, a thing which I have kept secret till now. After reading that prohibition of sleeping here I said to the bishop that if he put such a restraint upon me, he could choose someone else to come. I requested him to let us both act according to our conscience and common sense and today they tell me that we cannot begin our mission of peace by insulting a man who gives us such a friendly and Christian reception. The people of Canada have chosen us as their deputies, because we are the most sincere friends of Chiniquy. It is by keeping that character that we will best fulfill our sacred and solemn duties. I accept, with pleasure, the sleeping room offered me."

Mr. Desaulnier rejoined: "I accept it also, for I did not come here to insult my best friend, but to save him."

These kind words of my guests added to my joy. I told them: "If you are here to obey the voice of your conscience and the dictates of your common sense, there is a glorious task before you. You will soon find that the people and priest of St. Anne have also done nothing but listen to the voice of their honest conscience, and followed the laws of common sense in their conduct towards the bishop. But," I added, "this is not the time to explain my position, but the time to wash your dusty faces and refresh yourselves. Here are your rooms, make yourselves at home."

After supper they handed me the letters addressed to me by the bishops of Montreal, London, and Toronto, to induce me to submit to my superior, and offer me the assurance of their most sincere friendship and devotedness if I would obey.

I answered: "If I have fallen into a bottomless abyss as you say, and that you will draw me out of it, not only God and men will bless you, but I will also forever bless you for your charity. The first thing, however, you have to do here, is to see if I am really fallen, with my people, into that bottomless abyss of which you speak."

"But are you not excommunicated," quickly rejoined Mr. Desaulnier, "and, not withstanding that excommunication, have you not continued to say your mass, preach, and hear the confessions of your people? Are you not then fallen into that state of irregularity and schism which separate you entirely from the Church, and to which the pope alone can restore you?"

"No, my dear Desaulnier," I answered, "I am no more excommunicated than you are. For the simple reason that an act of excommunication which is not signed and certified is unworthy of any attention. Here is the act of the so-called excommunication, which makes so much noise in the world! Examine it yourself; see if it is signed by the bishop or certified by anybody." And I handed him the document.

After they had examined it for more than half an hour without saying a word, he at last broke his silence: "If I had not seen it with my own eyes, I could never have believed that a bishop can play such a sacrilegious comedy in the face of the world. You have several times published it in the press, but I confess that your best friends, and I among the rest, did not believe you. It could not enter our minds that a bishop should be so devoid of common honesty, as to have proclaimed before the whole world that you were excommunicated. But, in the name of common sense, why is it that he has not signed his sentence of excommunication, or get it signed and countersigned by some authorized people, when it is so evident that he wanted to excommunicate you?"

"His reason is very clear," I answered; "I had threatened to bring him before the civil court if he dared to destroy my character by interdict or excommunication; and he found that the only way to save himself was not to sign that paper. The first thing I would have to do in a prosecution is prove the signature of the bishop. Where could I find a witness who would swear that this is his signature? Would you swear it yourself, my dear Desaulnier?"

"Oh! no, for surely it is not his signature, nor that of his grand vicar or secretary. But without going any further," added he, "we must confess to you that we have talked to the bishop, when passing through Chicago, asking him if he had made any public or private inquest against you, and if he had found you guilty of any crime. He was embarrassed by our questions, but we told him that it was necessary for us to know all about your public and private character, when we were coming to press you to reconcile yourself to your bishop.

"He answered that he had never made any inquest about you, though you had requested him several times to do it, for the simple reason that he was persuaded that you were one of his best priests. Your only defect, he said, was a spirit of stubbornness and want of respect and obedience to your superior, and your meddling with his dealings with his diocesans, with which you had no business. He told us also that you refused to go to Kahokia. But his face became so red, and his tongue was so strangely lisping when he said that, that I suspected it was a falsehood; and we have now, before our eyes, your documents which prove that it was more than a falsehood — it was a lie.

"He proffered another lie also, when he said that he had signed, himself, the act of excommunication, for surely this is not his handwriting. Such conduct from a bishop is very strange. If you would appeal to the pope, and go to Rome with such documents in hand against that bishop, you would have an easy victory over him. For the canons of the Church are clear and unanimous. A bishop who pronounces such grave sentences against a priest, and makes use of false signatures is himself suspended and excommunicated, *ipso facto*, for a whole year."

Mr. Brassard added: "Cannot we confess to Chiniquy that the opinion of the bishops of Canada is that Bishop O'Regan is a perfect rogue? If Chiniquy would appeal to the pope, he would soon be reinstated by a public decree of His Holiness."

Our discussion kept us up till 3:00 a.m. without coming to any satisfactory issue. We adjourned to the next day, and went to take some rest after a short prayer.

The 25th of November, at 10 a.m. we shut ourselves up in my study, and resumed the discussion of the best plans of putting an end to the existing difficulties. To show them my sincere desire of stopping those noisy and scandalous struggles without compromising the sacred principles which had guided me from the beginning of our troubles, I consented to sacrifice my position as pastor of St. Anne, provided Mr. Brassard would be installed in my place. It was decided, however, that I should remain with him, as his vicar and help, in the management of the spiritual and temporal affairs of the colony. The promise was given me that on that condition the bishop would withdraw his so-called sentence, give back to the

French Canadians of Chicago the church he had taken away from them, put a French-speaking priest at the head of the congregation, and forgive and forget what he might consider our irregular conduct towards him, after we should have signed the following document:

TO HIS LORDSHIP O'REGAN, BISHOP OF CHICAGO.

MY LORD: — As my actions and writing in opposition to your orders have, since a few months, given some scandals, and caused some people to think that I would rather prefer to be separated from our holy Church than to submit to your authority, I hasten to express the regret I feel for such acts and writings. And to show to the world and to you, my bishop, my firm desire to live and die a Catholic, I hasten to write to your lordship that I submit to your sentence, and that I promise hereafter to exercise the holy ministry only with your permission. In consequence, I respectfully request your lordship to withdraw the censures and interdicts you have pronounced against me and those who have had any spiritual communication with me. I am, my lord, your devoted son in Christ,

C. CHINIQUY

It was 11 p.m. when I consented to sign this document, which was to be handed to the bishop and have any value, only on the above conditions. The two deputies were beside themselves with joy at the success of their mission, and at my readiness to sacrifice myself for the sake of peace. Mons. Desaulnier said: "Now we see that Chiniquy has been right with his people from the beginning, that he never meant to create a schism and to put himself at the head of a rebellious party, to defy the authority of the Church. If the bishop does not want to live in peace with the people and pastor of St. Anne after such a sacrifice, we will tell him that it is not Chiniquy, but Bishop O'Regan, who wants a schism. We will appeal to the pope. I will go with Chiniquy, and we will easily get there the removal of that bishop from the diocese of Chicago."

Mr. Brassard agreed and added that he also would accompany me to Rome to be the witness of my innocence, and the bad conduct of the bishop. He added that it would not take him a week to raise twice the amount of money in Montreal we would require to go to Rome.

After thanking them for what they had done, I asked Mr. Desaulnier if he would be brave enough to repeat before my whole people what he had just said before me and Mr. Brassard in the presence of God.

"Surely, I would be most happy to repeat before your whole people that it is impossible to find fault with you in what you have done till now. But, you know very well, I will never have such an opportunity, for it is now 11:00 at night, your people are soundly sleeping, and I must start tomorrow morning at 6:00 to take the

Chicago train at Kankakee at 8 a.m."

I answered: "All right!"

We knelt together to make a short prayer, and I led them to their rooms, wishing them refreshing sleep, after the hard work of the day. Ten minutes later I was in the village, knocking at the door of six of my most respectable parishioners, and telling them:

"Please do not lose a moment; go with your fastest horse to such and such a part of the colony; knock at every door and tell the people to be at the church at five o'clock in the morning to hear with their own ears what the deputies from Canada have to say about our past struggles with the Bishop of Chicago. Tell them to be punctual at five o'clock in their pews where the deputies will address them words which they must hear at any cost."

A little before five the next morning Mr. Desaulnier, full of surprise and anxiety, knocked at my door and said:

"Chiniquy, do you not hear the strange noise of buggies and carriages which seem to be coming from every quarter of the globe. What does it mean? Have your people become crazy to come to church at this dark hour, so long before the dawn of day?"

"What! what!" I answered, "I was sleeping so soundly that I have heard nothing yet. What do you mean by this noise of carriages and buggies around the chapel? Are you dreaming?"

"No, I am not dreaming," he answered; "not only do I hear the noise of a great many carriages, wagons, and buggies; but, though it is pretty dark, I see several hundred of them around the chapel. I hear the voices of a great multitude of men, women, and even children, putting questions to each other, and giving answers which I cannot understand. They make such a noise by their laughing and jokes! Can you tell me what this means? I have never been so puzzled in my life."

I answered him: "Do you not see that you are dreaming. Let me dress myself that I may go and see something of that strange and awful dream!"

Mr. Brassard, though a little more calm than Desaulnier, was not, himself, without some anxiety at the strange noise of that multitude of carriages, horses, and people around my house and chapel at such an hour. Knocking at my door, he said "Please, Chiniquy, explain that strange mystery. Do that people come to play us some bad trick, and punish us for our intruding in their affairs?"

"Be quiet," I answered. "My dear friends, you have nothing to fear from that good and intelligent people. Do you not remember that last night Desaulnier said that he would be honest and brave enough to repeat before my whole people what he had said before you and me, and in the presence of God. I suppose that some of the angels of heaven have heard those words, and have carried them this night to every family, inviting them to be here at the chapel, that they might hear from your own lips what you think of the grand and glorious battle they are fighting in this distant land for the principles of truth and justice, as the gospel secures them to every disciple of Christ."

"Well! well!" said Desaulnier, "there is only one Chiniquy in the world to take me in such a trap, and there is only one people under heaven to do what this people is doing here. I would never have given you that answer had I not been sure that I would never have had the opportunity to fulfill it. Who would think you would play me such a trick? But," he added, "though I know that this will terribly compromise me before certain parties, it is too late to retract, and I will fulfill my promise."

It is impossible to express my own joy and the joy of that noble people when they heard from the very lips of those deputies that, after spending a whole day and two nights in examining all that had been done by their pastor and by them in that solemn and fearful contest, they declared that they had not broken any law of God, nor of His holy Church; and had kept themselves in the very way prescribed by the canons.

Tears of joy were rolling down every cheek when they heard Mr. Desaulnier telling them, which Mr. Brassard confirmed, that the bishop had no possible right to interdict their pastor, since he had told them that he was one of his best priests; and that they had done well not to pay any attention to an act of excommunication which was a sham and sacrilegious comedy, not having been signed nor certified by any known person. Both deputies explained the document I had signed and the conditions attached to it. They continued, "If he (Bishop O'Regan) does not accept those conditions we will tell him it is not Mr. Chiniquy, but he who wants a schism, and we will go with Mr. Chiniquy to Rome to plead his cause and prove his innocence before his Holiness."

After this, we all knelt to thank and bless God; and never people went back to their homes with more cheerful hearts than the people of St. Anne on that morning of November 25, 1856.

At 6:00 a.m., Mr. Desaulnier left for Chicago, to present my conditional act of submission to the bishop, and press him, in the name of the bishops of Canada, and in the name of all the most sacred interests of the Church, to accept the sacrifice and the submission of the people of St. Anne, and to give them the peace they wanted and were purchasing at such a price. The Rev. Mr. Brassard had remained with me, waiting for a letter from the bishop to accompany me and put the last seal to our reconciliation.

The next day he received the following note from Mr. Desaulnier:

Bishopric of Chicago, Nov. 26th, 1856

The Rev. Mr. Brassard,

Monsieur, It is advisable and indispensable that you should come here, with Mr. Chiniquy, as soon as possible. In consequence, I expect you both day after tomorrow, in order to settle that matter definitely.

Respectfully yours,
ISAAC DESAULNIER

After reading that letter with Mr. Brassard, I said, "These cold words mean nothing good. I regret that you have not gone with Desaulnier to the bishop. You know the levity and weakness of his character, always bold with his words, but soft as wax at the least pressure. My fear is that the bulldog tenacity of my lord O' Regan has frightened him, and all his courage and bravados have melted away before the fierce temper of the Bishop of Chicago. But let us go. Be sure, however, my dear Mr. Brassard, that if the bishop does not accept you to remain at the head of this colony, to protect and guide it, no consideration whatever will induce me to betray my people and let them become the prey of the wolves which want to devour them."

We arrived in Chicago, the 28th, at about 10 a.m. Mr. Desaulnier was waiting for us. He was pale as a dead man. Taking him a short distance from the crowd, I asked him, "What news?"

He answered, "The news is that you and Mr. Brassard have nothing to do but to take your bags and go to Canada. The bishop is unwilling to make any arrangements with you. He wants me to be the temporary pastor of St. Anne, and he wants you, with Mr. Brassard, to go back quietly to Canada and tell the bishops to mind their own business."

"And what has become of the promise you have given me and to my people, to go with me and Mr. Brassard to Rome if the bishop refused the proposed arrangements you had fixed yourselves?"

"Tat! tat!" answered he. "The bishop does not care a straw about your going, or not going to Rome. He has put me as his grand vicar at the head of the colony of St. Anne, from which you must go in the shortest time possible."

"Now, Desaulnier," I answered, "you are a traitor, and a Judas, and if you want to have the pay of Judas, I advise you to go to St. Anne. There you will receive what you deserve. The beauty and importance of that great colony have tempted you and you have sold me to the bishop in order to become a grand vicar and eat the fruits of the vine I have planted there. But, you will soon see your mistake. If you have any pity for yourself, I advise you never to put your feet into that place any more."

Desaulnier answered, "The bishop will not make any arrangements with you unless you retract publicly what you have written against him on account of his taking possession of the church of the French Canadians of Chicago, and you must publish, in the press that he was right and honest in what he did in that circumstance."

"My dear Mr. Brassard," I said, "can I make such a declaration conscientiously and honorably?"

That venerable man answered me. "You cannot consent to do such a thing."

"Desaulnier," I said, "do you hear? Mr. Brassard and your conscience, if you have any, tell you the same thing. If you take sides against me with a man whom you have yourself declared yesterday to be a sacrilegious thief, you are not better than he is. Go and work with him. As for me, I'm going back to St. Anne."

"What will you do there," answered Mr. Desaulnier, "when the bishop has forbidden you to remain?"

"What will I do?" I answered. "I will teach those true disciples of Jesus Christ to despise and shun the tyrants and the traitors. Go, traitor! and finish your Judas work! Adieu!"

I then threw myself into the arms of Mr. Brassard who was almost speechless, suffocated in his sobs and tears. I pressed him to my heart and said! "Adieu! my dear Mr. Brassard. Go back to Canada and tell my friends how the cowardice and ambition of that traitor has ruined the hope we had of putting an end to this deplorable state of affairs. I go back among my brethren of St. Anne with more determination than ever to protect them against the tyranny and impiety of our despotic rulers. It will be more easy than ever to show them that the Son of God has not redeemed us on the cross that we might be slaves of those heartless traders in souls. I will more earnestly than ever teach my people to shun the modern gospel of the bishops in order to follow the old Gospel of Jesus Christ as the only hope and life of our poor fallen humanity."

Mr. Brassard wanted to say something, but his voice was suffocated by his sobs. The only words he could utter when pressing me to his heart were, "Adieu, dear friend, adieu!"

CHAPTER LVIII

It was evident that the betrayal of Mr. Desaulnier would be followed by new efforts on the part of the bishop to crush us. Mr.

Brassard wrote me from Canada in December, "All the bishops are preparing to hurl their thunders against you and your people on account of your heroic resistance to the tyranny of the Bishop of Chicago. I have told them the truth, but they don't want to know it. My lord Bourget told me positively that you must be forced at any cost to yield to the authority of your bishop, and he has threatened to excommunicate me if I tell the people what I know of the shameful conduct of Desaulnier. If I were alone I would not mind this excommunication and would speak the truth but such a sentence against me would kill my poor old mother. I hope you will not find fault with me if I remain absolutely mute. I pray you to consider this letter confidential. You know very well the trouble you would put me into by its publication."

The French Canadians of Chicago saw at once that their bishop, strengthened by the support of Desaulnier would be more than ever determined to crush them. They thought that the best way to force him to do them justice was to publish a manifesto of their grievances against him and make a public appeal to all the bishops of the United States and even to the pope.

On the 22nd of January, 1857, *The Chicago Tribune* was requested by them to publish the following document:

At a public meeting of the French and Canadian Catholics of Chicago held in the hall of Mr. Bodicar on the 22nd January, 1857, Mr. Rofinot being called to preside and Mr. Franchere, acting as a secretary, the following addresses and resolutions being read have been unanimously approved:

"Editors of the *Tribune*, — Will you allow a thousand voices from the dead to speak to the public through your valuable paper? Everybody in Chicago knows that a few years ago, there was a flourishing congregation of French people coming from France and Canada in this city. They had their priest, their church, their religious meeting. All that is now dispersed and destroyed.

"The present Bishop of Chicago has breathed his deadly breath upon us. Instead of coming to us as a father, he came as a savage enemy; instead of helping us as a friend, he has put us down as a revengeful foe. He has done the very contrary to which was commanded him by the Gospel. Instead of guiding us with the cross of the meek Jesus, he has ruled over us with an iron rod.

"Every Sunday the warm-hearted and generous Irish go to his church to hear the voice of his priest in his English language. The intelligent Germans have their pastors to address them in their mother tongue. The French people are the only ones now who have no priest and no church. And is it from lack of zeal and liberality? Ah! no, we take the whole city of Chicago as a witness that there was not in Chicago a better looking little church than the French Canadian church called St. Louis. But, alas! we have been turned out of it by our very bishop. We owe to ourselves and to our children to raise from the tomb, where Bishop O'Regan has buried us, a voice to tell the truth.

"As soon as Bishop O'Regan came to Chicago, he was told that the French priest was too popular, that his church was attended not only by his French Canadian people, but that many Irish and Germans were going daily to him for their religious duties. It was whispered in the ears of his Rt. Reverence that, on account of this, many dollars and cents were going to the French priest which would be better stored in his Rt. Reverence's purse.

"Till that time the bishop was not, in appearance, taking much trouble about us. But as soon as he saw that there were dollars and cents at stake, we had the honor to occupy his thoughts day and night."

There follows a detailed account of Bishop O'Regan's perfidious maneuverings that robbed the French congregation of both their French priest and their beautiful church and parsonage. The letter concludes with the following resolutions:

"Resolved, 1st. That the Right Rev. O'Regan, Bishop of Chicago, has entirely lost the confidence of the French and Canadian population of Chicago since he has taken away from us our church.

"Resolved, 2nd. That the Right Rev. O'Regan has published a base slander against the French and Canadian population of Chicago, when he said he took our church from our hands on the pretense that we could not pay for it.

"Resolved, 3rd. That the Right Rev. O'Regan, having said to our deputies, who went to inquire from him by what right he was taking our church from us to give to another congregation: 'I have the right to do what I like with your church, and your church properties; I can sell them and put the money in my pocket, and go where I please with it,' has assumed a power too tyrannical to be obeyed by a Christian and a free people.

"Resolved, 4th. That the nature of the different suits which the Right Rev. O'Regan has had before the civil courts of this state, and which he has almost invariably lost, have proved to the whole people of Illinois that he is quite unworthy of the position he holds in the Catholic Church.

"Resolved, 5th. That the Right Rev. O'Regan is here publicly accused of being guilty of simony for having extorted one hundred dollars from a priest to give him permission to officiate and administer the sacraments among us.

"Resolved, 6th. That the Right Rev. O'Regan, in forbidding the Irish and German Catholics to communicate with the French Catholic Church, and allowing the French and Canadians to communicate with the Irish and German churches, has acted with a view to deprive the French church of religious fees and other donations, which acts we consider unjust and against the spirit of the Church, and more resembling a mercantile transaction than a Christian work.

"Resolved, 7th. That the French and Canadian people of Illinois have seen with feelings of grief and surprise that the Rev. Mr. Desaulnier has made himself the humble valet of the merciless and shameless persecutor of his countrymen.

"Resolved, 8th. That the Rev. Mr. Chiniquy, pastor of St. Anne, deserves the gratitude of every Catholic of Illinois, for having put a stop to the rapacious tyranny of the Bishop of Chicago.

"Resolved, 9th. That the French Catholics of Chicago are determined to give all support in their power to the Rev. Mr. Chiniquy, in his struggle against the Bishop of Chicago.

"Resolved, 10th. That a printed copy of these resolutions be sent to every bishop and archbishop of the United States and Canada, that they may see the necessity of giving to the Church of Illinois a bishop more worthy of that high position.

"Resolved, 11th. That a copy of these resolutions be sent to His Holiness Pius IX, that he may be incited to make inquiries about the humiliated position of the Church in Illinois, since the present bishop is among us.

"Resolved, 12th. That the independent and liberty-loving press of the United States be requested to publish the above address and resolutions all over the country.

"P.F. ROFINOT, President
"DAVID FRANCERE, Secretary"

That cry of more than two thousand Roman Catholics of Chicago, which was reproduced by almost the whole press of Illinois and the United States, fell as a thunderbolt upon the head of my lord O'Regan and Desaulnier. Many bishops' letters were published denouncing me and my people as infamous schismatics, whose pride and obstinacy were troubling the peace of the Church.

But the most bitter of all was a letter from my lord Bourget, Bishop of Montreal, who thought the best and only way to force the people to desert me was by forever destroying my honor. But he had the misfortune to fall into the pit he had dug for me in 1851.

The miserable girl who had made accusations against me then was dead, but he had still in hand the lying accusations obtained from her against me. Having probably destroyed her sworn recantation written by the Jesuit Father Schneider, he was unaware of the three sworn copies of her recantation I had kept. He thought he could safely publish that I was a degraded man, who had been driven from Canada by him, after being convicted of some enormous crime, and interdicted.

This declaration was brought before the public, for the first time, by him, with an hypocritical air of compassion and mercy for me, which added much to the deadly effect he expected to produce. Here, in part, are his own words, addressed to the people of

Bourbonnais, and through them, to the whole world: "I must tell you that on the 27th of September, 1851, I withdrew all his powers, and interdicted him, for reasons which I gave him in my letter addressed to him; a letter which he has probably kept. Let him publish that letter if he finds that I have persecuted him unjustly."

I immediately replied to him by sending him, through the press, the recantation of the girl, accompanied by the letter he had written prior to my leaving Canada which contained the following statement:

"I can not but thank you for your labors among us, and I wish you in return the most abundant blessings from heaven. You shall ever be in my remembrance and in my heart, and I hope that Divine Providence will permit me, at a future time, to testify all the gratitude I owe you."

I then reminded him of our parting conversation when I requested a tangible token of his esteem: "You answered that you would be happy to give me one, and you said: 'What do you wish?'"

"I wish," I said, "to have a chalice from your hands to offer the holy sacrifice of the mass the rest of my life."

You answered: "I will do that with pleasure;" and you gave an order to one of your priests to bring you a chalice that you might give it to me. But that priest had not the key of the box containing the sacred vases; that key was in the hands of another priest, who was absent for a few hours.

I had not the time to wait; the hour of the departure of the trains had come. I told you: "Please, my lord, send that chalice to the Rev. Mr. Brassard, of Longueuil, who will forward it to me in Chicago." And the next day one of your secretaries went to the Rev. Mr. Brassard, gave him the chalice you had promised me, which is still in my hands. And the Rev. Mr. Brassard is there still living, to be the witness of what I say, and to bring that fact to your memory if you have forgotten it.

Well, my lord, I do believe that a bishop will never give a chalice to a priest to say mass, when he knows that that priest is interdicted. And the best proof that you know very well that I was not interdicted by your rash and unjust sentence, is that you gave me that chalice as a token of your esteem, and of my honesty, etc.

Ten thousand copies of this exposure of the depravity of the bishop were published in Montreal. I asked the whole people of Canada to go to the Rev. Mr. Schneider and to the Rev. Mr. Brassard to know the truth, and many went. The bishop remained confounded. It was proved that he had committed against me a most outrageous act of tyranny and perfidy; and that I was perfectly innocent and honest, and that he knew it.

A few days after the publication of that letter in Canada, Mr. Brassard wrote me: "Your last letter has completely unmasked our poor bishop, and revealed to the world his malice, injustice and hypocrisy. He felt so confounded by it, that he has been three days without being able to eat or drink anything, and three nights without sleeping. Everyone says that the chastisement you have given him is a terrible one, when it is in the face of the whole world; but he deserved it."

When I received that last friendly letter from Mr. Brassard on the 1st of April, 1857, I was far from suspecting that on the 15th of the same month, I should read in the press of Canada, the following lines from him:

St. Roch De L'Achigan, Le 9 Avril, 1857

Messieurs: — I request you to insert the following lines in your journal. As some people suspect that I am favoring the schism of Mr. Chiniquy, I think it is my duty to say that I have never encouraged him by my words or writings in that schism. I must say that, last November, when I went to St. Anne, accompanied by Mr. Desaulnier, Superior of St. Hyacinthe College, my only object was to persuade that old friend to leave the bad ways in which he was walking. And in Chicago I pressed him to put himself in a canonical way.

I, more than anyone else, deplore the fall of a man whom, I confess, I loved much, but for the sake of whom I will not sacrifice the sacred ties of Catholic unity. I hope that all the Canadians who were attached to Mr. Chiniquy when he was united to the Church, will withdraw from him in horror of his schism. For before anything else, we must be truly and faithfully Catholic.

However, we have a duty to perform towards the man who has fulfilled such a holy mission in our midst, by establishing the society of temperance. It is to call back, with our prayers, that stray sheep who has left the true Pastor's fold.

I request all journals to reproduce this declaration.

Truly yours,
MOSES BRASSARD, Pastor

I felt that there was not a line of sentiment of Mr. Brassard in that letter. I smelt Bishop Bourget's hand, from the beginning to the end. I thought, however that it was my duty to address him. The letter I wrote is too lengthy to reproduce. In essence it was an appeal to his conscience, integrity and honesty as one friend to another.

The effect of that letter upon Mr. Brassard was still more powerful than I had expected. It forced him to blush at his own cowardice, and to ask my pardon for the unjust sentence he had passed upon me to obey the bishop. Here are parts of his letter to me:

St. Roch, 29 May, 1857

MON CHERE CHINIQUY, — I am more than ever convinced that you have never been legally interdicted, since Bishop Bourget told me that Bishop O'Regan had interdicted you privately, in his private room. Ligouri says that it is a nullity, and that it can have no effect. I beg your pardon for what I wrote against you. I have been forced to do it. Because I had not yet sufficiently condemned you, and that my name, which you were citing in your writings, was giving you too much power, and a too clear condemnation of Bishop O'Regan, the Bishop of Montreal, abusing his authority over me, forced me to sign that document against you. I would not do it today if it were to be done again. Keep silence on what I tell you in this letter. It is all confidential. You understand it.

Your devoted friend,
L.M. BRASSARD

No priest in Canada had more deserved the reputation of honor than Mr. Brassard. Not one ever stood so high in my esteem. His sudden and unexpected fall filled my heart with an unspeakable sadness. It snapped the last thread which held me to the Church of Rome. Till then, it was my firm conviction that there were many honest, upright priests in that Church, and Mr. Brassard was, to me, the very personification of honesty. How can I describe the shock I felt when I saw him there, in the mud, a monument of the unspeakable corruption of my Church! The perfidious Delilah had seduced and destroyed this modern Samson, enchained, as a trembling slave, at the feet of the new implacable Moloch: "The authority of the bishop." He had not only lost the fear of God and the respect he owed to himself by publicly declaring that I was guilty, when he knew that I was innocent, but he had so completely lost every sentiment of honesty, that he wanted me to keep secret his declaration of my innocence at the very moment he was inviting my whole country, through the press, to abhor and condemn me as a criminal!

I read again and again the strange letter. Every word of it was destroying the last illusions which had concealed from my mind the absolute and incurable perversity of the Church of Rome. I had no hard feelings against this last friend whom she had poisoned with the wine of her prostitutions. I felt only a profound compassion for him. I pitied and forgave him from the bottom of my heart. But every word of his letter sounded in my ears as the warning voice of the angel sent to save Lot from the doomed city of Sodom: "Escape for thy life. Look not behind thee; neither stay thou in all the plain. Escape to the mountain lest thou be consumed." (Gen. 19:17)

CHAPTER LIX

I had not forgotten the advice given me by Archbishop Kenrick, of St. Louis, April 9th, 1856, to address my complaints to the pope himself. But the terrible difficulties and trials which had constantly followed each other, had made it impossible. The betrayal of Desaulnier and the defection of Brassard, however, had so strangely complicated my position, that I felt the only way to escape the wreck which threatened myself and my colony, and to save the holy cause God had entrusted to me, was to strike such a blow to our haughty persecutor that he could not survive it. I determined to send to the pope all the public accusations which had been legally proved and published against the bishop, with copy of the numerous and infamous suits which he had almost invariably lost before the civil courts, and the sentences of the judges who had condemned him. This took me nearly two months of the hardest labors of my life. I had gathered all those documents, which covered more than two hundred pages and mailed them to Pope Pius IX, accompanied by only the following words: "Holy Father, for the sake of your precious lambs which are slaughtered and devoured in this vast diocese by a ravening wolf, Bishop O'Regan, and in the name of our Saviour Jesus Christ, I implore your holiness to see if what is contained in these documents is correct or not. If everything is found correct, for the sake of the blood shed on Calvary, to save our immortal souls, please take away the unworthy bishop whose daily scandals cannot longer be tolerated by a Christian people."

To prevent the pope's servants from throwing my letter with those documents into their waste baskets, I sent a copy of them all to Napoleon III, Emperor of France, respectfully requesting him to see, through his ambassador at Washington, and his consul at Chicago, whether these papers contained the truth or not. I told him how his countrymen were trampled under the feet of Bishop O'Regan, and how they were ruined and spoiled to the benefit of the Irish people; how the churches built by the money of the French were openly stolen, and transferred to the emigrants from Ireland.

Napoleon had just sent an army to punish the Emperor of China on account of some injustice done to a Frenchman. I told him "the injustice done to that Frenchman in the Chinese Empire is nothing to what is done here every day, not against one, but hundreds of your majesty's countrymen. A word from the Emperor of France to His Holiness will do here what your armies have done in China: force the unjust and merciless oppressor of the French of Illinois to do them justice."

I ended my letter by saying: "My grandfather, though born in Spain, married a French lady, and became, by choice, a French citizen. He became a captain in the French navy, and for gallant service, was awarded lands in Canada, which by the fate of war fell into the hands of Great Britain. Upon retiring from the service of France he settled upon his estates in Canada, where my father and myself were born. I am thus a British subject by birth, an American citizen by adoption, but French still in blood and Roman Catholic in religion. I, therefore, on the part of a noble French people, humbly ask your majesty to intercede with His Holiness, Pope Pius IX, to have these outrages righted."

The success of this bold step was more prompt and complete than I had expected. The emperor was, then, all powerful at Rome. He had not only brought the pope from Civita Vecchia to Rome, after taking that city from the hands of the Italian Republicans, a few years before, but he was still the very guardian and protector of the pope.

A few months later, when in Chicago, the Grand Vicar Dunn showed me a letter from Bishop O'Regan, who had been ordered to go to Rome and give an account of his administration, in which he had said: "One of the strangest things which has occurred to me in Rome, is that the influence of the Emperor Napoleon is against me here. I cannot understand what right he has to meddle in the affairs of my diocese."

I had learned since, that it was really through the advice of Napoleon that Cardinal Bidini, previously sent to the United States to inquire about the scandal, gave his opinion in our favor. The cardinal consulted the bishops of the United States, who unanimously denounced O'Regan as unfit. He was immediately ordered to Rome, where the pope unceremoniously transferred him from Chicago to a diocese extinct more than 1,200 years ago, called "Dora." This was as good as a bishopric in the moon. He consoled himself by taking the hundreds of thousands of dollars he had stolen to Ireland where he established a bank and died in 1865.

On the 11th of March, 1858, at about ten o'clock p.m., I was not a little pleased to hear the voice of my devoted friend, Rev. M. Dunn, grand vicar of Chicago, asking my hospitality for the night. His first words were: "My visit here must be absolutely incognito. In ordering me to come and see you, the Bishop of Dubuque, who is just named administrator of Chicago, advised me to come as secretly as possible." He then said: "Your triumph at Rome is perfect. You have gained the greatest victory a priest ever won over his unjust bishop.

"Our good administrator has been advised to put an end, at once, to all the troubles of your colony, by treating you as a good and faithful priest. I come here, not only to congratulate you on your victory, but also to thank you, in my name, and in the name of the Church, for having saved our diocese from such a plague; for Bishop O'Regan was a real plague. A few more years of such administration would have destroyed our holy religion in Illinois.

"However, as you handled the poor bishop pretty roughly, it is suspected at a distance, that you and your people are more Protestant than Catholic. We know better; that the act of excommunication was a shameful and sacrilegious comedy. But in many distant places that excommunication was accepted as valid and you are considered by many as a real schismatic. Bishop Smith asks you to give him a written act of submission which he will publish to show the world that you are still a good Roman Catholic priest."

I thanked the grand vicar for his kind words and good news and I asked him to help me to thank God for guiding me through all these terrible difficulties. We both knelt and repeated the sublime words of gratitude and joy of the old prophet: "Bless the Lord, Oh! my soul, and all that is within me, bless His holy name, . . . " (Ps. 103) I then took a piece of paper, and with joy and gratitude to God, slowly prepared to write.

But as I was considering what form I should give to that document, a sudden, strange thought struck my mind. I said to myself: "Is not this a providential opportunity to silence those mysterious voices which are troubling me almost every hour, that, in the Church of Rome we do not follow the Word of God but the lying traditions of men?" I then wrote in my own name, and the name of my people:

"My lord Bishop Smith, Bishop of Dubuque and administrator of the diocese of Chicago: — We want to live and die in the holy Catholic, apostolic and Roman Church, out of which there is no salvation, and to prove this to your lordship, we promise to obey the authority of the Church according to the word and commandments of God as we find them expressed in the gospel of Christ."

                                                    "C. CHINIQUY"

I handed this writing to Mr. Dunn, and said: "What do you think of this act of submission?"

He quickly read it, and answered, "It is just what we want from you."

"All right," I rejoined. "But I fear the bishop will not accept it.

Do you not see that I have put a condition to our submission? I say that we will submit ourselves to the bishop's authority, but only according to the Word of God and Gospel of Christ."

"Is not that good?" he replied.

"Yes, my dear Mr. Dunn, this is good, very good indeed," I answered, "but my fear is that it is too good for the bishop and the pope."

"What do you mean?" he asked.

"I mean that though this act of submission is very good, I fear lest the pope and the bishop reject it."

"Please explain yourself more clearly," answered the grand vicar. "I do not understand the reason for such a fear."

"My dear Mr. Dunn," I continued, "I must confess to you a bleeding wound which is in my soul for many years. It has never been healed by any of the remedies I have applied to it. You know well that there is not a living priest who has studied the Holy Scriptures and the Holy Fathers with more attention and earnestness these last few years than I have. It was not only to strengthen my own faith, but also the faith of our people, and to be able to fight the battles of our Church against her enemies, that I spent so many hours of my days and nights in those studies. But, though I am confounded and ashamed to confess it, the more I have studied and compared the Holy Scriptures and the Holy Fathers with the teachings of our Church, the more my faith has been shaken, and the more I have been tempted to think, in spite of myself, that our Church has, long ago, given up the Word of God and the Holy Fathers, in order to walk in the muddy and crooked ways of human and false traditions. Strange and mysterious voices haunt me day and night, saying: 'Do you not see that in your Church of Rome, you do not follow the Word of God, but only the lying traditions of men?' What is more strange and painful is, that the more I pray to God to silence these voices, the louder they are repeated. It is to put an end to those awful temptations that I have written this conditional submission. I want to prove to myself that I will obey the Word of God and the gospel of Christ in our Church, and I shall be happy all the rest of my life, if the bishops accept this submission. But I fear it will be rejected."

Mr. Dunn promptly replied, "Your are mistaken, my dear Mr. Chiniquy. I am sure that our bishop will accept this document as canonical, and sufficient to show your orthodoxy to the world."

"If it be so," I replied, "I will be a most happy man."

It was agreed that on the 25th of March I would go with him to Dubuque, to present my act of submission to the administrator of the diocese, after the people had signed it. Accordingly, at seven p.m. on that day, we both took the train at Chicago for Dubuque, where we arrived next morning. At eleven a.m. I went to the palace of the bishop, who received me with marks of the utmost cordiality and affection. I presented him our written act of submission with a trembling hand, fearing he would reject it. He read it twice, and throwing his arms around me, he pressed me to his heart.

I felt his tears of joy mixed with mine, rolling down my cheeks, as he said: "How happy I am to see that submission! How happy the pope and all the bishops of the United States will be to hear of it, for I will not conceal it from you; we feared that both you and your people would separate from the Church, by refusing to submit to her authority." I answered that I was not less happy to see the end of those painful difficulties, and I promised him that, with the help of God, our holy Church would not have a more faithful priest than myself.

At the dinner hour he gave me the place of honor on his right at his well prepared, though frugal table. I was happy to see that there was no wine nor beer to tempt the weak. Before the dinner was over, the bishop said to Mr. Dunn: "You will accompany Mr. Chiniquy to St. Anne next Sabbath to announce to the people in my name the restoration of peace. No doubt it will be joyful news to the colony of Father Chiniquy. After so many years of hard fighting, the pastor and the people of St. Anne will enjoy the days of peace and rest which are now secured to them."

Then addressing me, the bishop said: "The only condition of that peace is that you will spend fifteen days in retreat and meditation in one of the religious houses you will choose. After so much noise and controversies, it will do you good to pass those days in meditation and prayer, in one of our beautiful and peaceful solitudes."

I answered him: "I consider it as a crowning act of kindness to offer me those few days of calm and meditation after the terrible storms of those last three years. If your lordship has no objection, I will go to the beautiful solitude where M. Saurin has built the celebrated Monastery, College, and University of St. Joseph, Indiana. I hope that nothing will prevent my being there next Monday, after going next Sabbath with Grand Vicar Dunn to proclaim the restoration of the blessed peace to my people of St. Anne."

"You cannot make a better choice," answered the bishop.

"But, my lord," I rejoined, "I hope your lordship will have no objection to give me a written assurance of the perfect restoration of that long-sought peace. There are people who will not believe me when I tell them how quickly and nobly your lordship has put an end to all those deplorable difficulties. I want to show them that I stand today in the same relation as before these unfortunate strifes."

"Certainly," said the bishop, "you are in need of such a document. I will write it at once."

But he had not yet written two lines, when Mr. Dunn looked at his watch and said: "We have not a minute to lose, if we want to be in time for the Chicago train."

I then said: "Please, my lord, address me that important document to Chicago, where I will get it at the post office on my way to the University of St. Joseph next Monday." The bishop having consented, I hastily took leave of him, with Mr. Dunn, after having received his benediction.

While returning to St. Anne the next day, we stopped at Bourbonnais to see the Grand Vicar Mailloux, one of the priests who had been sent by the bishops of Canada to help my lord O'Regan to crush me. We found him as he was going to his dining room to take his dinner. He was visibly humiliated by the complete defeat of Bishop O'Regan at Rome.

After Mr. Dunn had told him that he was sent to proclaim peace to the people of St. Anne, he coldly asked the written proof of that strange news. Mr. Dunn answered him: "Do you think, sir, that I would be mean enough to tell you a lie?"

"I do not say that you are telling me a lie," replied Mr. Malloux, "I believe what you say. But, I want to know the condition of that unexpected peace. Has Mr. Chiniquy made his submission to the Church?"

"Yes, sir," I replied, "here is a copy of my act of submission."

He read it, and coldly said: "This is not an act of submission to the Church, but only to the authority of the gospel, which is a very different thing. This document can be presented by a Protestant; but it cannot be offered by a Catholic priest to his bishop. I cannot understand how our bishop did not see that at once."

Mr. Dunn answered him: "My dear Grand Vicar Mailloux, my hope was that you would rejoice with us at the news of the peace. I am sorry to see that I was mistaken. However, I must tell you that if you want to fight, you will have nobody to fight against; for Father Chiniquy was yesterday accepted as a regular priest of our holy Church by the administrator. This ought to satisfy you."

I listened to the unpleasant conversation of those two grand vicars without saying a word. But I was again troubled by those mysterious voices in my mind: "Do you not see that in the Church of Rome, you do not follow the Word of God, but only the lying traditions of men?"

I felt much relieved to come to St. Anne where the people had gathered on the public square to receive us and rend the air with their cries of joy at the happy news of peace.

The next day, 27th of March, was Palm Sunday, one of the grand festivities of the Church of Rome; there was an immense concourse of people, attracted not only by the religious solemnity of the feast; but also by the desire to see and hear the deputy sent by their bishop to proclaim peace. He did it in a most elegant English address, which I translated into French. He presented me with a blessed palm, and I offered him another loaded with beautiful flowers as a public sign of the concord which was restored between my colony and the authorities of the Church.

That my Christian readers may understand my blindness, and the mercies of God towards me, I must confess here, to my shame, that I was glad to have made my peace with those sinful men, which was not peace with my God. But, that great God had looked down upon me in mercy. He was soon to break that peace with the great apostate Church, which is poisoning the world with the wine of her enchantments, that I might walk in the light of the Gospel and possess that peace and joy which passeth all understanding.

CHAPTER LX

Bishop Smith fulfilled his promise of a testimonial letter. It was filled with kind expressions of esteem towards my people and myself. I had never had a document in which my private and public character were so kindly appreciated. My gratitude to the bishop was boundless. At once I addressed a short letter to thank him and request him to pray for me during the happy days of retreat at the Monastery of St. Joseph.

The venerable Grand Vicar Saurin, and his assistant Rev. M. Granger received me in the monastery with the most sincere kindness. I found in them both the very best types of priests of Rome. Grand Vicar Saurin is justly considered one of the highest intellects Rome has ever given to the United States. There is not, perhaps, a man who has done so much for the advancement of that Church in this country as that highly gifted priest. My veneration for him increased every time I conversed with him. The only things which pained me were:

1. When some of his inferior monks came to speak to him, they had to kneel and prostrate themselves as to a god, till he told them

to rise.

2. Though he promised to the numerous Protestant parents who entrusted their boys and girls to his care for their education, never to interfere with their religion, he was, nevertheless, incessantly proselytizing them. Several of his Protestant pupils were received in the Church of Rome, and renounced the religion of their fathers, in my presence, on the eve of Easter of the year.

While, as a priest, I rejoiced in the numerous conquests of my Church over her enemies, in all her colleges and nunneries, I objected to the breach of promise, connected with those conversions. I, however, then thought, as I think today, that a Protestant who takes his children to a Roman Catholic priest or a nun for their education, had no religion. It was absurd to promise to respect the religion of a man who has none. How can we respect that which does not exist?

I had never before realized how good it was to be alone with Christ and tell Him all I had done, said, and taught. Those few days of rest and meditation in the Gospel were more precious to me since God had directed me to put the Gospel as the fundamental stone of my faith in the act of submission I had just given to my bishop. My Church had never been so dear to me as since she had accepted that conditional submission. My soul was rejoicing in those thoughts when on the 5th of April (Monday after Easter) Grand Vicar Saurin handed me a letter from Mr. Dunn telling me that a formidable new storm, brought by the Jesuits, was about to break on me.

The next morning, Mr. Saurin handed me another letter from the Bishop of Dubuque, and with a sympathy which I will never forget, he said: "I am sorry to see that you are not at the end of your troubles, as you expected. Bishop Smith orders you back to Dubuque with words which are far from being friendly." But, strange to say, this bad news, left me perfectly calm and cheerful on that day. In my dear Gospel, which had been my daily bread, the last eight days, I had found the helmet for my head, the breastplate and the shield to protect me, and the unconquerable sword with which to fight. From every page, I heard my Saviour's voice: "Fear not, I am with thee." (Isaiah 43:5)

When on my way back to Dubuque, I stopped at Chicago to know from my faithful friend, Mr. Dunn, the cause of the new storm. He said: "You remember how Grand Vicar Mailloux was displeased with the conditional submission you had given to the bishop. As soon as we had left him, he sent the young priest who is with him to the Jesuits of Chicago. The Jesuits agreed. They immediately sent to Dubuque, and said to the bishop: 'Do you not see that Chiniquy is a disguised Protestant; and has not submitted himself to your authority, but to the authority of his Bible alone? Do you not fear that the whole body of the bishops and the pope himself will condemn you for having fallen into the trap?' Our administrator, though a good man is like soft wax and can be manipulated. The Jesuits, who want to rule the priests and the Church with an iron rod, and who are aiming to change the pope and the bishops into the most heartless tyrants, have advised the administrator to force you to give an unconditional act of submission. You were evidently too correct the other day, your act of submission was too good for the bishops and the pope. What will you do?"

I replied: "I do not know, but be sure of this, I will do what our great and merciful God will tell me."

"Very well," he answered; "may God help you!" Not long after, Mr. Dunn was excommunicated by his bishop.

In Dubuque I went immediately to the bishop's palace. I found him in the company of a Jesuit and I felt myself as a poor helpless ship between two threatening icebergs.

"Your lordship wants to see me again?" I said.

"Yes, sir, I want to see you again," he answered.

"What do you want from me, my lord?" I replied.

"Have you the testimonial letter I addressed to you at Chicago last week?"

"Yes, my lord, I have it with me."

"Will you please show it to me?" he replied.

"With pleasure — here it is," and I handed him the precious document.

As soon as he had assured himself that it was the letter in question, he ran to the stove and threw it into the fire. I ran to save that document which was more valuable and precious to me than all the gold of California, but it was too late. It was in ashes. I turned to the bishop and said: "How can you take from me a document which is my property and destroy it without my permission?"

He answered me with an impudence that cannot be expressed on paper: "I am your superior, and have no account to give you."

I replied: "Yes, my lord, you are my superior indeed! You are a great bishop in our Church, and I am nothing but a poor miserable priest. But there is an Almighty God in heaven, who is as much above you as He is above me. That great God has granted me rights which I will never give up to please any man. In the presence of that God I protest against your iniquity."

"Have you come here to lecture me?" replied the bishop.

"No, my lord, I did not come to lecture you; I come at your

command, but was it to insult me?"

"I ordered you to come because you deceived me the last time," he answered. "You gave me an act of submission which you knew very well is not an act of submission. I accepted it then, but I was mistaken; I reject it today."

I answered: "How can you say that I deceived you? The document I presented you is written in good, plain English. It is there on your table; I see it. You read it twice and understood it well. If you were deceived by its contents you deceived yourself. You are, then, a self-deceiver, and you cannot accuse me of having deceived you."

He then took the document, read it slowly; and when at the words, "we submit ourselves to your authority, according to the Word of God as we find it in the Gospel of Christ," he stopped and said: "What do you mean by this?"

I answered, "I mean what you see there. I mean that neither I nor my people will ever submit ourselves to anybody, except according to the eternal laws of truth, justice, and holiness of God, as we find them expressed in the Bible."

He angrily answered, "Such language on your part is sheer Protestantism. I cannot accept such a conditional submission from any priest."

Again I heard the mysterious voice: "Do you not see that in your Church of Rome you do not follow the Word of God, but the lying traditions of men?"

Thanks be to God, I did not silence the voice in that solemn hour. In ardent, silent prayer, I said: "Oh my God! speak, speak again to Thy poor servant, and grant me the grace to follow Thy holy Word!" I then said to the bishop: "You distress me by rejecting this act of submission, and asking another. Please explain the nature of the new one you require from me and my people."

More subdued and polite, the bishop said: "I hope, Mr. Chiniquy, that, as a good priest, you do not want to rebel against your bishop, and that you will give me the act of submission I ask. Take away 'Word of God,' 'Gospel of Christ,' and 'Bible' from your present document, and I will be satisfied."

"But, my lord, with my people I have put these words because we want to obey only the bishops who follow the Word of God. We want to submit only to the Church which respects and follows the Gospel of Christ."

Irritated, he quickly answered: "Take away from your act of submission 'Word of God,' and 'Gospel of Christ,' and 'Bible!' or I will punish you as a rebel."

"My lord," I replied, "those expressions are there to show us and to the whole world that the Word of God, the Gospel of Christ, and the Bible are the fundamental stones of our holy Church. If we reject those precious stones, on what foundations will our Church and our faith rest?"

He answered angrily: "Mr. Chiniquy, I am your superior, I do not want to argue with you. You are my inferior; your business is to obey me. Give me at once an act of submission, in which you will simply say that you and your people will submit yourselves to my authority, and promise to do anything I bid you."

I calmly answered: "What you ask me is not an act of submission, it is an act of adoration. I do absolutely refuse to give it."

"If it be so, sir," he answered, "you can no longer be a Roman Catholic priest."

I raised my hands to heaven, and cried with a loud voice: "May God Almighty be forever blessed."

I took my hat, and went to my hotel. I locked the door and fell on my knees, to consider in the presence of God what I had just done. There the awful, undeniable truth stared me in the face. My Church could not be the Church of Christ! That sad truth had not been revealed to me by any Protestant, nor any other enemy of the Church. It had been told by one of her most learned and devoted bishops! My Church was the deadly, the irreconcilable enemy of the Word of God, as I had so often suspected!

I was not allowed to remain a single day longer in that Church without positively and publicly giving up the Gospel of Christ! It was evident to me that the Gospel was only a blind, a mockery to conceal her iniquities, tyrannies, superstitions, and idolatries. The only use of the Gospel in my Church was to throw dust in the eyes of the priests and people! It had no authority. The only rule and guide was the will, the passions, and the dictates of sinful men!

There on my knees alone with God I knew that the voice which had so often troubled and shaken my faith was the voice of my merciful God. It was the voice of my dear Saviour who was bringing me out of the ways of perdition in which I had been walking. And I had tried so often to silence that voice!

"My God! my God!" I cried, "The Church of Rome is not Thy church. To obey the voice of my conscience, which is Thine, I gave it up. When I had the choice, I could not give up Thy Holy Word. I have given up Rome! But, oh Lord, where is Thy Church? Oh! speak!! where must I go to be saved?"

For more than one hour I cried to God in vain; no answer came. To add to that distress, the thought flashed across my mind that by giving up the Church of Rome, I had given up the Church of my dear father and mother, of my brother, my friends, and my country — in fact, all that was near and dear to me! I did not regret the sacrifice, but I felt as if I could not survive it. With tears, I cried to God for more strength and faith but all in vain.

Then I felt that an implacable war was to be declared against me. The pope, the bishops, and priests would attack and destroy my character, my name and my honor, in their press, from their pulpit, and in their confessionals. I tried to think of someone who would come to my help. Every one of the millions of Roman Catholics were bound to curse me. My best friends — my own people — even my own brothers were bound to look upon me with horror as an apostate, a vile outcast! Could I hope for help or protection from Protestants? No! for my priestly life had been spent in writing and preaching against them.

How could I go again into that world where there was no room for me. Life suddenly became to me an unbearable burden. Instant death seemed to me the greatest blessing in that awful hour! I took my knife to cut my throat. But my merciful God, who wanted only to show me my own helplessness, stopped my hand and the knife fell to the floor.

At first, I thought that death would be a great relief, but then, I said to myself, "If I die, where will I go? Oh, my dear Saviour," I cried, "come to my help!"

In that very instant I remembered that I had my dear New Testament with me. With a trembling hand and a praying heart I opened the book at random — but, no! not I, my God Himself opened it for me. My eyes fell on these words: "YE ARE BOUGHT WITH A PRICE. BE NOT YE THE SERVANTS OF MEN." (I Cor. 7:23)

Those words came to my mind, more as light than articulated sound. They suddenly gave me the knowledge of the great mystery of a perfect salvation through Christ alone. They at once brought a great and delightful calm to my soul. I said to myself: "Jesus has bought me," I said again to myself; "then He has saved me! and if so, I am saved, perfectly saved, forever saved! Jesus is my God; the works of God are perfect. My salvation must, then, be a perfect salvation. But how has He saved me? What price has He paid for my poor guilty soul?"

The answer came as quickly as lightning: "He bought you with His blood shed on the cross! He saved you by dying on Calvary!"

I then said to myself again: "If Jesus has perfectly saved me by shedding His blood on the cross, I am not saved, as I have thought and preached till now, by my penances, my prayers to Mary and the saints, my confessions and indulgences, not even by the flames of purgatory!"

In that instant, all things which, as a Roman Catholic, I had to believe to be saved — the chaplets, indulgences, scapularies, auricular confession, invocation of the Virgin, holy water, masses, purgatory, etc., vanished from my mind like a huge tower, when struck at the foundation, and crumbles to the ground. Jesus alone remained in my mind as the Saviour of my soul!

Oh! what a joy I felt at this simple, but sublime truth! But it was the will of God that this joy should be short. It suddenly went away with the beautiful light which had caused it and my poor soul was again wrapped in the most awful darkness. However profound that darkness was, a still darker object presented itself before my mind. It was as a very high mountain, but not composed of sand or stones, it was the mountain of my sins. I saw them all standing before me. Then in horror I saw it moving towards me as if, with a mighty hand, to crush me. I tried to escape, but in vain. I felt tied to the floor, and the next moment it had rolled over me. I felt crushed under its weight, as heavy as granite. I could scarcely breathe! My only hope was to cry to God for help.

With a loud voice, heard by many in the hotel, I cried: "O my God! have mercy upon me! My sins are destroying me! I am lost, save me!" But it seemed God could not hear me. The mountain prevented my cries from reaching Him, and hid my tears. I suddenly thought that God would have nothing to do with such a sinner, but to open the gates of hell to throw me into that burning furnace prepared for his enemies which I had so richly deserved!

I was mistaken. After eight or ten minutes of unspeakable agony, the rays of a new and beautiful light began to pierce through the dark cloud which hung over me. In that light, I clearly saw my Saviour, bent under the weight of His heavy cross. His face was covered with blood, the crown of thorns was on His head, and the nails in His hands. He was looking to me with an expression of compassion, of love, which no tongue can describe. Coming to me, He said: "I have heard thy cries, I have seen thy tears, I have given Myself for thee. My blood and My bruised body have paid thy debts; wilt thou give Me thy heart? Wilt thou take My Word for the only lamp of thy feet, and the only light of thy path? I bring thee eternal life as a gift."

I answered: "Dear Jesus, how sweet are Thy words to my soul! Speak, oh! speak again! Yes, beloved Saviour, I want to love Thee; but dost Thou not see that mountain which is crushing me? Oh! remove it! Take away my sins!"

I had not done speaking when His mighty hand touched the mountain, and it rolled into the deep and disappeared. At the same time I felt as if a shower of the blood of the Lamb were falling upon me to purify my soul. And suddenly, my humble room was transformed into a real paradise. The angels of God could not be more happy than I was in that most mysterious and blessed hour of my life.

With an unspeakable joy, I said to my Saviour: "Dear Jesus, the gift of God! Thou hast brought me the pardon of my sins as a gift. Thou hast brought me eternal life as a gift! Thou hast redeemed and saved me, beloved Saviour; I know, I feel it. But this is not enough. I do not want to be saved alone. Save my people also. Save my whole country! I feel rich and happy in that gift; grant me to show its beauty and preciousness to my people that they may rejoice in its possession."

This sudden revelation of salvation as a gift had so completely transformed me that I felt quite a new man. The unutterable distress of my soul had been changed into an unspeakable joy. My fears were replaced by a courage and a strength such as I had never experienced. The popes with their bishops and priests and millions of abject slaves might now attack me. I felt that I was a match for them all.

My great ambition was to go back and tell my people what the Lord had done for my soul. I washed my tears away, paid my bill, and took the train to go back to my dear countrymen. That same hour they were very anxious and excited, for they had just received a telegram from the Bishop of Dubuque telling them: "Turn away your priest for he has refused to give me an unconditional act of submission." They had gathered in great numbers to hear the reading of that strange message. But they unanimously said: "If Mr. Chiniquy has refused to give an unconditional act of submission he has done right. We will stand by him to the end." However, I knew nothing of that admirable resolution. I arrived at St. Anne on the Sabbath day at the hour of the morning service. There was an immense crowd at the door of the chapel. They rushed to me and said: "You are just coming from the bishop; what good news have you to bring us?"

I answered: "No news here, my good friends. Come to the chapel and I will tell you what the Lord has done for my soul."

When they had filled the large building I told them: "Our Saviour, the day before His death, said to His disciples: 'I will be a scandal to you, this night.' ("All ye shall be offended because of Me this night." Matt. 26:31, Mark 14:27)

"I must tell you the same thing. I will be, today, I fear, the cause of a great scandal to every one of you. But as the scandal which Christ gave to His disciples has saved the world, I hope that, by the great mercy of God, the scandal I will give you will save you. I was your pastor till yesterday! But I have no more that honor today, for I have broken the ties by which I was bound as a slave at the feet of the bishops and of the pope."

This sentence was scarcely finished, when a universal cry of surprise and sadness filled the church: "Oh! what does that mean!" exclaimed the congregation.

"My dear countrymen," I added, "I have not come to tell you to follow me! I did not die to save your immortal souls; I have not shed my blood to buy you a place in heaven; but Christ has done it. Then follow Christ and Him alone! Now, I must tell you why I have broken the unbearable yoke of men, to follow Christ. You remember that, on the 21st of March last, you signed, with me, an act of submission to the authority of the bishop of the Church of Rome, with the conditional clause that we would obey him only in matters which were according to the teachings of the Word of God as found in the Gospel of Christ.

"It was our hope that our Church would accept such a submission. And your joy was great when you heard that Bishop Smith had accepted the submission. But that acceptance was revoked. Yesterday, in the presence of God, Bishop Smith rejected with the utmost contempt the act of submission we had given him, and which he had accepted only two weeks ago, because the Word of God was mentioned in it! When I respectfully requested him to tell me the nature of the new act of submission he wanted from us, he ordered me to take away from it 'the Word of God, the Gospel of Christ, and the Bible' if we wanted to be accepted as good Catholics! We had thought, till then, that the sacred Word of God and the holy Gospel of Christ were the fundamental and precious stones of the Church of Rome. We loved her on that account; we wanted to remain in her bosom, even when we were forced to fight as honest men against that tyrant, O'Regan.

"But, yesterday, I have learned from the very lips of a bishop of Rome that we were a band of simpletons in believing those things. I have learned that the Church of Rome has nothing to do with the Word of God, except to trample it under their feet, and to forbid us to name it even in the solemn act of submission we had given.

"When I requested the bishop to give me the precise form of submission he wanted from us, he answered: 'Give me an act of submission, without any condition, and promise that you will do anything I bid you.'

"I replied: 'This is not an act of submission, it is an act of adoration! I will never give it to you!'

"'If so,' said he, 'you can no longer be a Roman Catholic priest.'

"I raised my hands to heaven, and with a loud and cheerful

voice, I said: 'May God Almighty be forever blessed!'"

I then told them something of my desolation, when alone in my room; of the granite mountain, of my tears, and of my despair. I told them also how my bleeding, dying, crucified Saviour had brought me forgiveness of my sins; how He had given me eternal salvation, as a gift, and how rich, happy, and strong I felt in that gift. I then spoke to them about their own souls.

In substance, I said: "I respect you too much to impose myself upon your honest consciences, or to dictate what you ought to do on this most solemn occasion. I feel that the hour has come for me to make a great sacrifice; I must leave you! but, I will not go away before you tell me to do so. You will yourselves break the ties so dear which have united us.

"Please pay attention to these, my parting words: If you think it is better to follow the pope than Christ; better to trust in the works of your hands, in your own merits, than in the blood of the Lamb, shed on the cross, to be saved; if you think it is better to follow the traditions of men than the Gospel; and if you believe that it is better to have a priest of Rome who will keep you tied as slaves to the feet of the bishops and who will preach to you the ordinances of men, rather than have me preach to you nothing but the pure Word of God, tell me by standing up, and I will go!"

The chapel was filled with sobs; tears were flowing from every eye, but not one moved to tell me to leave them! I was puzzled. I had hoped that many, enlightened by the copies of the New Testament that I had given them, tired of the tyranny of the bishops, and disgusted with the superstitions of Rome, would be glad to break the yoke with me, to follow Christ. But, I was afraid that most would not dare to break their allegiance to the Church and publicly give up her authority.

After a few minutes of silence, during which I mixed my tears and my sobs with those of my people, I was filled with astonishment. I saw a great and mysterious change in their countenances and their manners. They were speaking to me with the tears in their eyes, and their manly faces beaming with joy. Their sobs told me that they were filled with new light and new strength, ready to make the most heroic sacrifices, to follow Christ and Him alone. Those brave, honest and happy faces were telling me more eloquently than speech: "We believe in the gift, we want to be rich, happy, free, and saved in the gift: we do not want anything else: remain among us and teach us to love both the gift and the Giver!"

With inexpressible hope and joy, I told them: "My dear countrymen! The Mighty God, who gave me His saving light yesterday, can grant you the same today. He can save a thousand souls as well as one. I see in your noble and Christian faces that you do not want any more to be slaves of men. You want to be the free children of God, intelligent followers of the Gospel! The light is shining, and you like it. The gift of God has been given to you! Let all those who think it is better to follow Jesus Christ than the pope, better to follow the Word of God than the traditions of men; let all those of you who want me to remain and preach to you only the Word of God as we find it in the Gospel of Christ, tell me by rising up.

Without a single exception that multitude arose! More than a thousand of my countrymen had forever broken their fetters. They had crossed the Red Sea and exchanged the servitude of Egypt for the blessings of the Promised Land!

CHAPTER LXI

How shall I express the surprise and joy I felt after the service. Alone in my humble study I considered, in the presence of God, what His mighty hand had just wrought. The people who saw Lazarus to come forth from the grave were no more amazed than I was when more than a thousand of my countrymen so suddenly came out from the grave of degrading slavery in which they were born and brought up.

My joy, however, suddenly changed when I considered the unworthy instrument which God had chosen to do that work. I felt this was only the beginning of the most remarkable religious reform ever to occur on this continent. I was dismayed that I would meet the terrible difficulties which Luther, Calvin and Knox had met. Those giants had many times been almost discouraged. What would become of me, seeing that I was so deficient in knowledge, wisdom and experience!

Many times during the night I said to my God in tears: "Why hast Thou not chosen a more worthy instrument?" I would have shrank before the task had not God said to me in His Word: "For ye see your calling, brethren, how that not many wise men after the flesh, not many mighty, not many noble, are called: but God hath chosen the foolish things of the world to confound the wise; and God hath chosen the weak things of the world to confound the things which are mighty, and base things of the world, and things which are despised, hath God chosen, yea, the things which are not, to bring to naught the things that are, that no flesh should glory in His presence." (I Cor.1:26-29)

These words calmed my fears and gave me new courage. Next morning, I said to myself: "Did not God alone do the great things of yesterday: Why should I not rely upon Him for the things which remain to be done? I am weak but He is mighty. I am unwise, but He is the God of light and wisdom; I am sinful, but He is the God of holiness; He wants the world to know that He is the worker."

The new battle my dear countrymen and I had to fight against Rome in those stormy but blessed days would make the most interesting book. See the surprise and desolation of the wife and children when the father returned from that service and said: "My dear wife and children, I have, forever, left the Church of Rome, and hope that you will do the same. The ignominious chains by which we were tied, as the slaves of the bishops and of the pope, are broken. Christ Jesus alone will reign over us now. His Holy Word alone will rule and guide us. Salvation is a gift; I am happy in its possession."

In another house, the husband had not been able to come to church, but the wife and children had. It was now the wife who announced to her husband that she had, forever, renounced the usurped authority of the bishops and the pope: and that it was her firm resolution to obey no other master than Christ, and accept no other religion than the one taught in the Gospel.

There were in many places, confusion, tears, angry words and bitter discussions. But the God of truth, light and salvation was there. The storms were soon calmed, the tears dried, and peace restored.

That week the Gospel had achieved one of the most glorious victories over its implacable enemy, the pope. Out of 500 families which were around me in St. Anne, 405 had not only accepted the Gospel of Christ as their only authority, but had publicly given up the name of Roman Catholics to call themselves Christian Catholics.

Most admirable was the strong determination to read for themselves the Divine Gospel which had made them free from the bondage of man. Half of the people had never been taught to read. Every house, as well as our chapel was soon turned into a schoolhouse. Our school boys and girls were the teachers, and the fathers and mothers, the pupils. In a short time, all except those who refused to leave Rome began to read for themselves the Holy Word of God.

But the victory over the pope was not yet complete. The usurped authority of the bishops had been destroyed, and the people had determined to accept none but the authority of Christ. Yet many errors and superstitions remained in their minds, as a mist after the rising of the sun, to prevent them from seeing clearly the saving light of the Gospel. It was my duty to root out these noxious weeds. But I knew the formidable difficulties the reformers of the fifteenth century had met, the deplorable divisions which had spread among them, and the scandals which had so seriously retarded and compromised the reformation.

I cried to God for wisdom and strength. We, like all Roman Catholics, were much given to the worship of images and statues. On the walls of our chapel hung fourteen beautiful pictures called "The Way of the Cross," representing the passion of Jesus. Each was surmounted with a cross. One of our favorite devotional exercises was to kneel, three or four times a week, before them, prostrate ourselves and say with a loud voice: "Oh! holy cross, we adore thee." We used to address our most fervent prayers to them, as if they could hear us, asking them to change our hearts and purify our souls!

We also had a beautiful statue, or rather idol, of the Virgin Mary, as a child learning to read at the feet of her mother, St. Anne. It was a masterpiece of art, sent to me by some rich friends from Montreal not long after I had left to form the colony of St. Anne in 1852. We had frequently addressed our most fervent prayers to those statues, but after the blessed pentecost on which we had broken the yoke of the pope, I never entered my church without blushing at the sight of those idols on the altar.

I would have given much to have the pictures, crosses and images removed. But I was afraid of harming some of my people who were yet too weak in their religious view to bear it. I was just then reading how Knox and Calvin had made bonfires of all those relics of old paganism, and I wished I could do the same; but I felt like Jacob, who could not follow the rapid march of his brother, Esau. "The children are tender and the flocks and herds with young are with me. If men should overdrive them one day, all the flock will die." (Gen 43:13)

Our merciful God saw my perplexity and taught me how to get rid of those idols without harming the weak.

One Sabbath I preached on the second commandment: "Thou shalt not make to thyself any graven image . . . "(Exod. 20:4) I remained in the chapel to pray after the people had left. I looked up to the group of statues on the altar, and said to them: "My good ladies, you must come down from that high position: God Almighty alone is worshiped here now: if you could walk out of this place I would politely invite you to do it. But you are nothing but mute, deaf, blind and motionless idols; you have eyes, but you cannot see; ears, but you cannot hear; feet, but you cannot walk. What will I do with you now? Your reign has come to an end."

I suddenly remembered that when I had put these statues on their high pedestal I had tied them with a slender, strong silk cord to prevent them from falling. I said to myself: "If I were to cut that string the idols would surely fall the first time the floor shook." Their fall and destruction would then scandalize no one. I took my knife and scaled the altar, cut the string, and said: "Now, my good ladies, take care of yourselves, especially when the chapel is shaken by the wind, or the coming in of the people."

I never witnessed a more hearty laugh than at the beginning of the services the next Sabbath. When the people fell on their knees to pray, the two idols, deprived of their silk support, after a couple of jerks which, in former days, we might have taken for a friendly greeting, fell down with a loud crash, and broke into fragments. Old and young, strong and weak, and even babes in the faith, after laughing to their hearts' content at the sad end of their idols, said to each other: "How foolish and blind were we to trust these idols to protect us when they cannot take care of themselves!" The last vestige of idol worship disappeared with the dust and broken fragments of those poor helpless statues. The very next day, the people themselves destroyed all the images before which they had so often abjectly prostrated themselves.

It had been my plan from the beginning to let the people draw their own conclusions as much as possible from their own study of the Holy Scriptures. I guided their steps in a way that they understood that we were both led by the almighty and merciful arm of God.

After prayerfully searching the Scriptures, the great majority had found that Purgatory was a diabolical invention to enrich the priests of Rome at the expense of their poor blind slaves. But quite a number were not altogether free from this. I did not know how to destroy that error without injuring some of the weak children of the Gospel.

All Souls Day (1st Nov.) had come, when we used to take up collections to have prayers and masses said for the souls in purgatory. I said to them from the pulpit: "Since we have left the Church of Rome for the Church of Christ, we have spent many pleasant hours together in reading and meditating upon the Gospel. You know it contains not a single word about purgatory. We have learned that only the blood of the Lamb, shed on the Cross, can purify our guilty souls from sin. I know, however, that a few of you have retained something of the views taught to you in the Church of Rome concerning purgatory. I do not want to trouble you by useless discussions on the subject, or by refusing the money you want to give for the souls of your dear departed parents and friends. The only thing I want to do is this: You used to have a small box passed to you to receive that money. Today, instead of one box, two boxes will be passed, one white, the other black. Those who, like myself, do not believe in purgatory, will put their donations in the white box, and the money will be given to the poor widows and orphans of the parish, to help them to get food and clothing for winter. Those of you who still believe in purgatory will put their money into the black box for the benefit of the dead. The only favor I ask is that you tell me how to convey the donations to the departed. I tell you frankly that the money you give to the priests never goes to the benefit of the souls of purgatory. The priests everywhere keep the money for their own."

My remarks were followed by a general smile. Thirty-five dollars were put in the white box for the orphans and widows, and not a cent fell into the box for the souls of purgatory. From that day, by the great mercy of God, our dear converts were perfectly rid of that ridiculous and sacrilegious belief.

To deal with all the errors and idolatries of Rome we had two public meetings every week in which everyone had the liberty to question me and discuss the various subjects announced at the last meeting. The doctrines of auricular confession, prayers in foreign language, the mass, holy water and indulgences, were calmly examined, discussed, and thrown overboard one after the other in a very short time. The good done in those public discussions was incalculable. Our dear converts not only learned the great truths of Christianity, but they learned also how to teach them to their relations, friends and neighbors.

Many came long distances to see that strange religious movement which was making so much noise all over the country. Few of them went back without some rays of the saving light which the Sun of Righteousness was so abundantly pouring upon me and my dear brethren of St. Anne.

Three months after our exit from the land of bondage we were six thousand French Canadians marching towards the Promised Land.

At night I would silently pace the streets of our town and hear from almost every house, sounds of reading the Holy Scriptures or the melodies of our delightful French hymns! How many times I united my feeble voice with that old prophet, in the rapture of my joy: "Bless the Lord, O my soul: and all that is within me, bless His holy name." (Ps. 103:1)

But gold cannot be purified without fire. On the 27th of July I received through a friend, a copy of a letter written by the Roman Catholic Bishop of Illinois (Duggan) to several of his co-bishops: "The schism of the apostate, Chiniquy, is spreading with incredible and irresistible velocity. I am told that he has ten thousand followers. Though I hope that this number is an exaggeration, it shows that the evil is great; and that we must not lose any time in trying to open the eyes of the deluded people he is leading to perdition.

I intend to visit the very citadel of that deplorable schism next Tuesday the 3rd of August. As I speak French almost as well as English, I will address the deluded people of St. Anne in their own language. My intention is to unmask Chiniquy and show what kind of a man he is. Then I will show the people the folly of believing that they can read and interpret the Scriptures by their own private judgment. After which I will easily show them that out of the Church of Rome there is no salvation. Pray to the blessed Virgin Mary that she may help me reclaim that poor deceived people."

Having read that letter to the people on the first Sabbath of August, I said: "We know a man only after he has been tried. So we know the faith of a Christian only after it has been through the fire of tribulations. I thank God that next Tuesday will be the day chosen by Him to show the world that you are worthy of being in the front rank of the great army Jesus Christ is gathering to fight His implacable enemy, the pope, on this continent. Let every one of you come and hear what the bishop has to say. Not only those who are in good health must come, but even the sick must be brought to hear and judge for themselves.

"If the bishop fullfils his promise to show you that I am a depraved and wicked man, you must turn me out. You must give up or burn your Bibles, at his bidding, if he proves that you have neither the right to read, nor the intelligence to understand them. If he shows you that, out of the Church of Rome, there is no salvation, you must, without an hour's delay, return to that Church and submit yourselves to the pope's bishops. But if he fails (as he will surely do) you know what you have to do. Next Tuesday will be a most glorious day for us all. A great and decisive battle will be fought here, such as this continent has never witnessed, between the great principles of Christian truth and liberty, and the lies and tyranny of the pope.

"I have only one word more to say: From this moment to the solemn hour of the conflict, let us humbly, but fervently ask our great God, through His beloved and eternal Son, to look down upon us in His mercy, enlighten and strengthen us, that we may be true to Him, to ourselves, and to His Gospel. Then the angels of heaven will unite with all the elect of God on earth to bless you for the great and glorious victory you will win."

Never had the sun shone more brightly on our beautiful hill than on the 3rd of August, 1858. The hearts had never felt so happy, and the faces had never been so perfectly the mirrors of joyful minds, as on that day, among the multitudes which began to gather from every corner of the colony, a little after twelve o'clock, noon.

Seeing that our chapel, though very large, would not contain half the audience, we raised a large platform ten feet high in the middle of the public square in front of the chapel. We covered it with carpets and put a sofa and a good number of chairs for the bishop and his priests, and one for myself, and a large table for the different references books I wanted to have at hand to answer the bishop.

At about two o'clock his carriage arrived, followed by several others filled with priests. He was dressed in his white surplice, and his official "bonnet carré" on his head to more surely command the respect and awe of the multitude.

I had requested the people to keep silence and show him all the respect and courtesy due a gentleman.

As soon as his carriage was near the chapel, I gave a signal and up went the American flag to the top of a mast to warn the ambassador of the pope that he was not treading the land of the holy inquisition and slavery, but the land of freedom and liberty. The bishop understood it. For raising his head to see that splendid flag of stripes and stars waving to the breeze, he became pale as death. And his uneasiness did not abate when the thousands around him rent the air with the cry: "Hurrah for the flag of the free and the brave!"

The bishop and his priests thought this was the signal I had given to slaughter them for they had been told several times that I and my people were so depraved and wicked that their lives were in great danger among us. Several priests who had not much relish for the crown of martyrdom jumped from their carriages and ran away, to the great amusement of the crowd. Seeing the extreme terror on the face of the bishop, I ran to tell him that there was not the least danger, and assured him of the pleasure we had to see him in our midst.

I offered my hand to help him down from his carriage, but he refused it. After some minutes of trembling and hesitation, he whispered a few words in the ear of his Grand Vicar Mailloux, who was well known by my people.

Rising slowly, the vicar said with a loud voice: "My dear French Canadian countrymen, here is your holy bishop. Kneel down, and he will give you his benediction." But to the great dismay of the poor grand vicar, this well laid opening for the battle failed entirely. Not a single one of that immense multitude cared for the benediction. Nobody knelt.

Thinking that he had not spoken loud enough, he raised his voice and cried: "My dear fellow countrymen: This is your holy bishop. He comes to visit you. Kneel down, and he will give you his benediction."

But nobody knelt. And worse, a voice from the crowd answered: "Do you not know, sir, that here we no longer bend the knee before any man? It is only before God we kneel."

The whole people cried "Amen!" to that noble answer. I could not refrain a tear of joy. This first effort of the ambassador of the pope to entrap my people had failed. But though I thanked God, I knew the battle was far from over. I implored Him to bide with us, to be our wisdom and our strength to the end. Seeing the bishop's countenance as distressed as before, I offered him my hand again but he refused it the second time with supreme disdain, but accepted the invitation I gave him to come to the platform.

Half way up the stairs he turned, and seeing me following him, he put forth his hand to stop me and said: "I do not want you on this platform; go down and let my priests alone accompany me."

I answered him: "It may be that you do not want me there, but I want to be at your side to answer you. Remember that you are not on your own ground here, but on mine!"

He then, silently and slowly, walked up. When on the platform, I offered him a good arm chair, which he refused, and sat on one of his own choice, with his priests around him. I then addressed him as follows: "My lord, the people and pastor of St. Anne are exceedingly pleased to see you in their midst. We promise to listen attentively to what you have to say, on condition that we have the privilege of answering you."

He answered angrily: "I do not want you to say a word here."

Then stepping to the front, he began his address in French, with a trembling voice. But it was a miserable failure from beginning to end. In vain did he try to prove that out of the Church of Rome there is no salvation. He failed still more miserably to prove that the people have neither the right to read the Scriptures, nor the intelligence to understand them. He said such ridiculous things on that point that the people went into fits of laughter. Some said: "This is not true. You do not know what you are talking about. The Bible says the very contrary."

But I stopped them by reminding them of the promise they had made not to interrupt him.

A little before closing his address, he turned to me and said: "You are a wicked, rebel priest against your holy Church. Go from here into a monastery to do penance for your sins. You say that you have never been excommunicated in a legal way! Well, you will not say that any longer, for I excommunicate you now before this whole people."

I interrupted him and said: "You forget that you have no right to excommunicate a man who has publicly left your Church long ago."

He seemed to realize that he had made a fool of himself in uttering such a sentence, and stopped speaking for a moment. Then, recalling his lost courage, he took a new and impressive manner. He told the people how their friends, their relatives, their very dear mothers and fathers in Canada were weeping over their apostasy. He spoke with great earnestness of the desolation of all those who loved them, at the news of their defection from their holy mother Church. Then he asked with great emphasis and earnestness: "My dear friends, please tell me what will be your guide in the ways of God after you have left the holy Church of your fathers, the Church of your country; who will lead you in the ways of God?"

The answer was a most complete and solemn silence. Was that silence the result of a profound impression, or was it the silence preceding the storm? I could not say. But I must confess that, though I had not lost confidence in God, I was not without anxiety. I could have easily confounded the bishop in a few words; but it was much better to let the rebuke come from the people.

The bishop, hoping that the silence was proof that he had touched their hearts, exclaimed a second time with still more power and earnestness: "My dear French Canadian friends: I ask you, in the name of Jesus Christ, your Saviour and mine, in the name of your desolated mothers, fathers, and friends who are weeping along the banks of your beautiful St. Lawrence River — I ask it in the name of your beloved Canada! Answer me! Now that you refuse to obey the holy Church of Rome, who will guide you in the ways of salvation?"

Another solemn silence followed but not for long. When I had invited the people to come and hear the bishop, I requested them to bring their Bibles. Suddenly an old farmer, raising his Bible over his head with both hands, said: "This Bible is all we want to guide us in the ways of God. We do not want anything but the pure Word of God to teach us what we must do to be saved. As for you, sir, you had better go away and never come here any more."

And more than five thousand voices said "Amen!" to that simple, sublime answer. The whole crowd filled the air with cries: "The Bible! the Holy Bible, the holy Word of God is our only guide in the ways of eternal life! Go away, sir, and never come again!"

The battle was over. The bishop had lost.

Suffocated by his sobs, he sat or rather fell into the armchair, and I feared at first lest he should faint. When I saw that he was recovering enough to hear what I had to say, I stepped to the front of the platform. But I had scarcely said two words when I felt as if the claws of a tiger were on my shoulders. I turned and found that it was the clenched fingers of the bishop, who was shaking me while he was saying with a furious voice, "No! no! not a word from you."

As I was about to show him that I had a right to refute what he had said, my eyes fell on a scene which baffles all description. Only those who have seen the raging waves of the sea suddenly raised by the hurricane can have an idea of it. The people had seen the violent hand of the bishop raised against me; they had heard his insolent and furious words forbidding me to say a single word in answer. A universal cry of indignation was heard: "The infamous wretch! Down with him! He wants to enslave us again! He denies us the right of free speech! He refuses to hear what our pastor has to reply! Down with him!"

At the same time many rushed to scale the platform, and others began to tear it down. That whole multitude, absolutely blinded by their uncontrollable rage, were as a drunken man who does not know what he does. I had *read* of such things, but I hope I never see it again. I rushed to the head of the stairs, and with great difficulty repulsed those who were trying to lay their hands on the bishop. In vain I raised my voice to calm them, and make them realize the crime they wanted to commit. No voice could be heard in the midst of such confusion. It was very providential that we had built the scaffold with strong materials.

Happily, we had in our midst a very intelligent young man called Bechard, who was held in great respect. I called him to the platform and requested him, in the name of God, to appease the blind fury of that multitude. Strangely his presence and a sign from his hand acted like magic.

"Let us hear what Bechard has to say," whispered every one to his neighbor, and there was a sudden, profound calm. In a few appropriate and eloquent words, that young gentleman showed the people that, far from being angry, they ought to be glad at the exhibition of the tyranny and cowardice of the bishop. Had he not confessed the weakness of his address when he refused to hear the answer? Had he not confessed that he was the vilest and the most impudent of tyrants to deny them the sacred right of speech and reply? Had he not proved, before God and man, that they had done well to reject, forever, the authority of the Bishop of Rome? Had he not given them unanswerable proof that that authority meant the most unbounded tyranny and ignominious moral degradation of his blind slaves?

Seeing that they were anxious to hear me, I then told them: "Instead of being angry, you ought to bless God for what you have heard and seen from the Bishop of Chicago. He has not given us a single argument to show that we were wrong when we gave up the words of the pope to follow the words of Christ. Was he not right when he told you that there was no need, on my part, to answer him? Do you not all agree that there was nothing to refute in his address? Has not our merciful God brought that bishop into your midst today to show you what I have often told you, that there was nothing manly, nothing honest, or true in him? Have you heard from his lips a single word which could have come from the lips of Christ? A word which could have come from that great God who so loved His people that He sent His eternal Son to save them? Was there a single sentence in all you have heard which would remind you that salvation through Christ was a gift? — that eternal life was a *free* gift? Have you heard anything from him to make you regret that you are no longer his obedient and abject slaves?"

"No! no!" they replied.

"Then, instead of being angry with that man, you ought to thank him and let him go in peace," I added.

"Yes! Yes!" replied the people, "but on condition that he shall never come again."

Then Mons. Bechard stepped to the front, raised his hat, and cried with his powerful voice, "People of St Anne! you have just gained the most glorious victory which has ever been won by a people against their tyrants. Hurrah for St. Anne, the grave of the tyranny of the bishops of Rome in America!"

That whole multitude, filled with joy, rent the air with the cry: "Hurrah for St. Anne, the grave of the tyranny of the bishops of Rome in America!"

I then turned towards the poor bishop and his priests, whose distress and fear were beyond description: "You see that the people forgive you; but I advise you not to repeat that insult here. Please take their advice; go away as quickly as possible. I will go with you to your carriage, through the crowd, and I pledge myself that you will be safe, provided you do not insult them again."

Opening their ranks, the crowd made a passage, through which

I led the bishop and his priests to their carriages. This was done in the most profound silence, only a few women whispering to the prelate as he was hurrying by: "Away with you, and never come here again. Hence forward we follow nothing but Christ."

Crushed by waves of humiliation, that bishop, whose beginning had been so brilliant, after his shameful defeat at St. Anne on the 3rd of August, 1858, was soon to end his broken career in the lunatic asylum of St. Louis, where he is still confined today.

CHAPTER LXII

On the 3rd of August, 1858, on the hill of St. Anne, Illinois, the marvelous power of the Gospel had pulverized the power of Rome and put to flight the haughty representative of the pope. The banners of Christian liberty were raised on the very spot marked by the bishop as the future citadel of popery in the United States. Such work was so much above my capacity, that I felt more its witness than its instrument. The only sentiments I felt were unspeakable joy, and gratitude to God. But the greater the favors from heaven, the greater the responsibilities.

The news of that sudden reformation spread like lightning over America and Europe. An incredible number of letters from Episcopalians, Methodists, Congregationalists, Baptists and Presbyterians, of every rank and color, kindly pressed me for details. Feeling too young and inexpert in the ways of God to give a correct appreciation of the Lord's doings among us, I generally answered them: "Please come and see with your own eyes the marvelous things our merciful God is doing in the midst of us, and you will help us to bless Him."

In less than six months more than one hundred venerable ministers of Christ and prominent Christian laymen of different denominations visited us.

I am happy to say that those eminent Christians, without any exception, after having spent from one to twenty days with us declared that it was the most remarkable and solid evangelical reformation among Roman Catholics they had ever seen. The Christians of Chicago, Baltimore, Washington, Philadelphia, New York, Boston, etc., expressed desire to hear from me of the doings of the Lord among us. I addressed them in their principal churches and was received with such kindness and interest, for which I shall never be able sufficiently to thank God.

After many serious and prayerful considerations, we decided to connect ourselves with that branch of the vine most nearly identical with the French Protestants, which gave so many martyrs to the Church of Christ. Accordingly, it was our privilege to be admitted to the Presbyterian Church of the United States. The Presbytery of Chicago had the courtesy to adjourn their meeting from that city to our humble town, on the 15th of April, 1860. I presented them with nearly two thousand converts including myself, who were received into full communion with the Church of Christ.

This solemn action was soon followed by the establishment of missions and congregations in Chicago, Aurora, Kankakee, Middleport, Watseka, Momence, Sterling, Manteno, etc., where the light of the Gospel had been received by large numbers of our French Canadian emigrants when I had previously visited them.

Precious souls wrenched from the iron grasp of popery now totaled about six thousand five hundred. It was much beyond my hopes, and it would be difficult to express the joy it gave me. But my joy was not without a mixture of anxiety. It was impossible for me alone to distribute the bread of life to such multitudes scattered over several hundred miles. I determined, with the help of God, to raise a college where the children of our converts would be prepared to preach the Gospel. Thirty-two of our young men offered themselves and I began teaching them the preparatory course of study for their future evangelical work.

Scotland chose 1860 to celebrate the tercentenary anniversary of her Reformation and the management committee invited me to address their general meetings in Edinburgh. After the close of that great council I was invited during the next six months to lecture in Great Britain, France, and Switzerland, and to raise funds necessary for our college. More than 15,000 dollars were handed me for our college by the disciples of Christ.

In 1874 I was again invited to Great Britain to make the congratulatory address of the English people to the Emperor of Germany and Bismark, for their noble resistance to the encroachments of popery. I addressed the meetings in Exeter Hall under the presidency of Lord John Russell, on the 27th of January, 1874. The next day several Gospel ministers pressed me to publish my twenty-five years' experience of auricular confession as an antidote to the criminal and too successful efforts of Dr. Pusey, who wanted to restore that infamous practice among the Protestants of England.

After much hesitation and many prayers, I wrote the book entitled: "The Priest, the Woman, and the Confessional," which God has blessed to the conversion of many.

I spent the next six months in lecturing on Romanism in the

principal cities of England, Scotland and Ireland.

On my return, pressed by the Canadian Church to leave my colony of Illinois for a time to preach in Canada, I went to Montreal, where, in the short space of four years, we had the unspeakable joy to see seven thousand French Canadian Roman Catholics and emigrants from France publicly renouncing the errors of the popery to follow the Gospel of Christ.

In 1878, exhausted by the previous years of incessant labors, I was advised by my physicians to breathe the bracing air of the Pacific Ocean. I crossed the Rocky Mountains and spent two months lecturing in San Francisco, Portland, Oregon, and in the Washington Territory, where I found a great many of my French countrymen, many of whom received the light of the Gospel with joy.

After this I preached in the Sandwich Islands, crossed the Pacific to the Antipodes, and lectured two years in Australia, Tasmania, and New Zealand. It would require a large volume to tell the great mercies of God towards me during that long, perilous, but interesting voyage. During those two years I gave 610 public lectures and came back to my colony of St. Anne with such perfectly restored health that I could say with the Psalmist: "Bless the Lord, O my soul." "Thy youth is renewed like the eagle's." (Ps. 103:1,5)

But the reader has the right to know something of the dangers through which it has pleased God to make me pass.

Rome is the same today as she was when she burned John Huss and Wishart, and when she caused 70,000 Protestants to be slaughtered in France, and 100,000 to be exterminated in Piedmont in Italy.

On the 31st of December, 1869 I forced the Rt. Rev. Bishop Foley of Chicago to swear before the civil court at Kankakee that the following sentence was an exact translation of the doctrine of the Church of Rome as taught today in all the Roman Catholic seminaries, colleges, and universities, through the "Summa Theologica" of Thomas Aquinas (vol. iv. p. 90): "Though heretics must not be tolerated because they deserve it, we must bear with them till, by a second admonition, they be brought back to the faith of the Church. But those who, after a second admonition, remain obstinate to their errors, must not only be excommunicated, but they must be delivered to the secular power to be exterminated."

Because of this law of the Church of Rome, which is today in full force, not less than thirty public attempts have been made to kill me since my conversion.

The first time I visited Quebec, in the spring of 1859, fifty men were sent by the Bishop of Quebec (Baillargeon) to force me to swear that I would never preach the Bible, or kill me if I refused.

At 4 a.m., sticks were raised above my head, a dagger stuck in my breast, and the cries of the furious mob were ringing in my ears: "Infamous apostate! Now you are in our hands. You are a dead man if you do not swear that you will never preach your accursed Bible."

Never had I seen such furious men around me. Their eyes were more like tigers than of men. I expected every moment to receive the deadly blow, and I asked my Saviour to come and receive my soul. But the would-be murderers cried again: "Infamous renegade! Swear that you will never preach any more your accursed Bible, or you are a dead man!"

I raised my eyes and hands towards heaven and said: "Oh! my God! hear and bless the last words of Thy poor servant: I solemnly swear that so long as my tongue can speak, I will preach Thy Word, as I find it in the Holy Bible!" Then opening my vest said: "Now! Strike!"

But my God was there to protect me: they did not strike. I went through their ranks into the street where I found someone to drive me to Mr. Hall, the mayor of the city and said: "I just escaped, almost miraculously, from the hands of men sworn to kill me if I preach again the Gospel of Christ. I am, however, determined to preach again today at noon even if I have to die in the attempt." I put myself under the protection of the British flag.

Soon more than 1,000 British soldiers were around me with fixed bayonets. They formed themselves into two lines along the streets through which the mayor took me in his own sleigh to the lecture room. I then delivered my address on "The Bible," to at least 10,000 people. After this, I had the joy of distributing between five and six hundred Bibles to the hungry multitude.

I have been stoned twenty times. On the 10th of July, 1873, the Rev. P. Goodfellow, standing by me when going out of his church, was struck several times by stones which missed me. His head was so badly cut that he fell on the ground bathed in blood. I took him up in my arms, though wounded and bleeding myself. We would surely have been slaughtered there, had not a noble Scotchman opened the door of his house, at the peril of his own life, to give us shelter against the assassins of the pope.

The mob, furious that we had escaped, broke the windows and besieged the house from 10 a.m. till 3 the next morning. Many times they threatened to set fire to the house. They were prevented only from fear of burning the whole town including their own dwellings. Several times they put long ladders against the walls hoping to reach the upper rooms, and find and kill their victim. All this was done under the eyes of five or six priests.

At Montreal in the winter of 1870, coming out of Cote Street Church where I had preached, accompanied by Principal MacVicar, we received a volley of stones which would have seriously, if not fatally, injured the doctor had he not been protected by a thick fur cap and overcoat.

After a lecture given at Paramenta, near Sidney, Australia, I was again attacked with stones by the Roman Catholics. One struck my left leg with such force that I thought it was broken, and I was lame for several days. In New South Wales, Australia, I was beaten with whips and sticks which left marks upon my shoulders.

At Marsham, in the same province, on the 1st of April, 1879, the Romanists took possession of the church where I was speaking, rushed towards me with daggers and pistols, crying: "Kill him! Kill him!" In the tumult, I providentially escaped through a secret door. To escape death I had to crawl on hands and knees a pretty long distance in a ditch filled with mud.

In the same city, as I was waiting for the train, a well-dressed lady came near and spat in my face. I was blinded, my face covered with filth. She immediately fled, but was soon brought back by my secretary and a policeman, who said: "Here is the miserable woman who has just insulted you. What shall we do with her?" I was then almost done cleaning my face. I answered: "Let her go home in peace. She has not done it of her own accord; she was sent by her confessor. She thinks she has done a good action. When they spat in our Saviour's face, He did not punish those who insulted Him. We must follow His example." And she was set at liberty, to the great regret of the crowd.

In 1879, while lecturing in Melbourne, Australia, I received a letter from Tasmania, signed by twelve ministers of the Gospel, saying: "We are much in need of you here for though the Protestants are in the majority, the administration of the country is almost entirely in the hands of Roman Catholics, who rule us with an iron rod. We wish to have you among us, though we do not dare to invite you to come. The Roman Catholics have sworn to kill you, and we fear that they will fulfill their promises. But, though we do not dare ask you to come, we assure you that there is a great work for you here, and that we will stand by you with our people. If you fall, you will not fall alone."

I answered: "We are soldiers of Christ, and must be willing to die for Him, as He did for us. I will go."

On the 24th of June, as I was delivering my first lecture in

Hobart Town, the Roman Catholics, with the approval of their bishop, broke the door of the hall and rushed towards me crying, "Kill him! kill him!" The mob was only a few feet from me, brandishing their daggers and pistols, when the Protestants threw themselves between us and a furious hand-to-hand fight occurred, during which many were wounded. The soldiers of the pope were overpowered but the governor had to put the city under martial law for four days and call the whole militia to save my life from the assassins.

In a dark night, as I was leaving the steamer on the Ottawa River, Canada, twice the bullets of the murderers whistled at no more than two or three inches from my ears.

The 17th of June, 1884, after I had preached in Quebec on the text: "What would I do to have eternal life," a mob of more than 1,500 Roman Catholics, led by two priests, broke the windows of the church and attacked me with stones. More than one hundred stones struck me, and I would surely have been killed there but for two heavy overcoats, which I put one over my head, and the other around my shoulders. Numbers of policemen and other friends who came to my rescue were wounded. My life was saved only by an organization of a thousand young men, who, under the name of Protestant Guard, wrenched me from the hands of the would-be murderers.

When the bishops and priests saw that it was so difficult to put me out of the way with stones, sticks, and daggers, they determined to destroy my character. Thirty-two times my name has been called before the civil and criminal courts of Kankakee, Joliet, Chicago, Urbana, and Montreal. I have been accused by Grand Vicar Mailloux of having killed a man and thrown his body into a river to conceal my crime.

I have been accused of setting fire to the church of Bourbonnais. Seventy-two false witnesses were brought by the priests to support this last accusation. But, thanks be to God, at every time the very lips of the perjured witnesses gave proof that they were swearing falsely, at the instigation of their father confessors. My innocence was proven by the very men who had been paid to destroy me. In this last suit Father Brunet was found guilty of inventing the accusations and supported them by false witnesses. He was condemned to pay 2,500 dollars or go to jail for fourteen years.

He chose jail having the promise from his Roman Catholic friends that they would break the doors of his prison and let him go free to some remote place. He was incarcerated at Kankakee, but on a dark and stormy night, six months later, he was rescued and fled to Montreal 900 miles away. There he made the Roman

Catholics believe that the blessed Virgin Mary, dressed in a beautiful white robe had come in person to open the gates of the prison.

I do not mention these facts to create bad feelings against the poor blind slaves of the pope. It is only to show that the Church of Rome today is absolutely the same as when she reddened Europe with the blood of the martyrs. My motive in speaking of those murderous attacks is to induce the readers to help me to bless God, who has so mercifully saved me from the hands of the enemy. With Paul, I could often say: "We are troubled on every side, yet not distressed; we are perplexed, but not in despair; persecuted, but not forsaken; cast down, but not destroyed; always bearing about in the body the dying of the Lord Jesus, that the life also of Jesus might be made manifest in our body." (II Cor. 4:8-10)

Those constant persecutions, far from hindering the onward march of the evangelical movement to which I have consecrated my life, seem to have given it a new impulse. I will never forget the day, after the terrible night when more than a thousand Roman Catholics had come and severely wounded me with stones, more than one hundred of my countrymen asked me to enroll their names under the banner of the Gospel, and publicly sent their recantation of the errors of Rome to the bishop.

Today, the Gospel of Christ is advancing with irresistible power among the French Canadians from the Atlantic to the Pacific Oceans. Among those converts we count now twenty-five priests and more than fifty young zealous ministers who had been born in the Church of Rome.

In hundreds of places the Church of Rome has lost her prestige and the priests are looked upon with indifference, if not contempt, even by those who have not yet accepted the light.

A very remarkable religious movement has also been lately inaugurated among the Irish Roman Catholics, under the leadership of Revs. McNamarra, O'Connor, and Quinn, which promises to keep pace with, if not exceed the progress of the Gospel among the French.

Today, more than ever, we hear the good Master's voice: "Lift up your eyes and look on the fields, for they are white already to harvest." (John 4:35)

WIN CATHOLICS TO CHRIST

Before Catholics can be born again, they must first understand that they are lost...

This book quotes 37 main Catholic doctrines from the 1994 Catechism, then compares each one with the Bible. Catholics quickly see that their religion teaches a false gospel that will never get them to heaven.

Lovingly written by an ex-Catholic, it clearly explains the gospel and invites Catholics to trust Christ alone for their salvation.

Whether you use it as a reference tool for yourself, or give it to Catholics to read, this is a powerful witnessing tool.

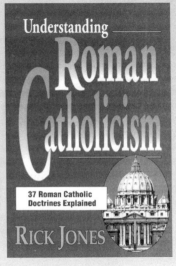

Understanding Roman Catholicism

37 Roman Catholic Doctrines Explained

RICK JONES

222 pages, paperback

"20 Catholics have been saved in the last two weeks as a result of this book."

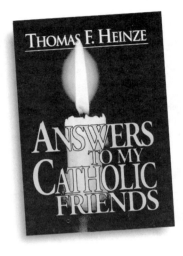

ANSWERS TO MY CATHOLIC FRIENDS

BY THOMAS F. HEINZE

A great little book to give Catholics!

As an evangelical missionary in Italy, Thomas Heinze found that Roman Catholics have certain questions about Protestants, and about the Bible. The ecumenical movement in their own church has made it more important than ever for them to obtain answers to these questions.

Written lovingly to Roman Catholics, this book uses Scriptures to explain major differences between Catholic and Protestant beliefs. So Catholics won't think this is Protestant theology from an "unapproved" Bible, Heinze uses their own New American Bible. Readers quickly see that the Catholic church cannot save, only faith alone in Jesus can.

With a loving, soul-winning message and invitation to trust Christ alone, it's a great book to give Catholics. It's inexpensive, too! *62 pages, paperback*

ISBN: 0-937958-52-2
Published by Chick Publications